WHERE THREE WORLDS MET

WHERE THREE WORLDS MET

SICILY IN THE EARLY MEDIEVAL MEDITERRANEAN

SARAH DAVIS-SECORD

CORNELL UNIVERSITY PRESS
Ithaca and London

First published 2017 by Cornell University Press
First paperback printing 2020

Library of Congress Cataloging-in-Publication Data

Names: Davis-Secord, Sarah C., author.
Title: Where three worlds met : Sicily in the early medieval Mediterranean / Sarah Davis-Secord.
Description: Ithaca : Cornell University Press, 2017. | Includes bibliographical references and index.
Identifiers: LCCN 2016048269 (print) | LCCN 2016048732 (ebook) | ISBN 9781501704642 (cloth : alk. paper) | ISBN 9781501712586 (epub / mobi) | ISBN 9781501712593 (pdf)
Subjects: LCSH: Sicily (Italy)—History—To 1500. | Mediterranean Region—History—476–1517. | Christianity and other religions—Islam. | Islam—Relations—Christianity.
Classification: LCC DG867.2 .D38 2017 (print) | LCC DG867.2 (ebook) | DDC 945.8 / 02—dc23
LC record available at https: / / lccn.loc.gov / 2016048269

ISBN 978-1-5017-5216-2 (paperback)

"Could any soil
Be more agreeable to me, or any
Where I would rather moor these tired ships,
Than Sicily?"

—Virgil, *The Aeneid*, trans. Robert Fitzgerald, bk. 5, ll. 38b–41a

Contents

Maps and Illustrations

Maps

Illustrations

Acknowledgments

Like the many travelers whose voyages form the basis for this book, I have been on a long and sometimes perilous journey while bringing this work to completion. This is the type of trip that cannot be undertaken alone, and along the way I have benefited from the help, advice, support, and friendship of countless individuals and institutions.

While it began at the University of Notre Dame, this work matured during my time at the University of Texas at Arlington and the University of New Mexico. My many friends and colleagues at those institutions have been of significant assistance to me in my travels. Among others, I particularly thank Justine Andrews, Cathleen Cahill, Christine Caldwell Ames, Paul Cobb, Caroline Goodson, Tim Graham, Penny Ingram, Marie Kelleher, Courtney Luckhardt, Tom Noble, Michael A. Ryan, Andrew Sandoval-Strausz, Alan Stahl, Julia Schneider, John Van Engen, and Robin Vose. I could do nothing without the cheerful assistance of the administrative staff of the UNM History Department—Yolanda Martinez, Barbara Wafer, Dana Ellison, and Hazel Mendoza-Jayme. My parents, Terry and Catherine Davis, and my parents-in-law, Bill and Linda Secord, have encouraged, prodded, loved, and supported me throughout. My parents taught me that I could do anything I wanted with my life, gave me opportunities that they themselves had not had, and have always taken an interest in my work—all of which I appreciate more than words can express.

My editors at Cornell University Press, both Peter Potter and Mahinder Kingra, have been unfailingly helpful and insightful readers of this work. Bethany Wasik and the rest of the team at Cornell University Press have been wonderful to work with and quick with responses to my many questions. I thank Romney David Smith for the beautiful maps. The two outside readers for the press, Clifford Backman and Karla Mallette, provided helpful observations and suggestions that significantly improved the book. All of its shortcomings remain my own responsibility.

I have also profited from being a member of several dynamic and productive intellectual communities, notably the medievalists of the University of

Notre Dame, the History Department and the Institute for Medieval Studies at the University of New Mexico, and the broad spectrum of Mediterranean scholars involved in the Mediterranean Studies NEH Summer Institute and the Mediterranean Seminar. Funding for my research has come from the Medieval Academy of America, the National Endowment for the Humanities, the University of Notre Dame, the University of Texas at Arlington, and the University of New Mexico. I could not have done this work without access to great libraries: I have relied upon the collections at the University of Notre Dame's Hesburgh Library (in particular the Medieval Institute library and its librarian, Dr. Julia Schneider), Princeton University's Firestone Library, and the University of Chicago's Regenstein Library, as well as the interlibrary loan department at the University of New Mexico. Likewise, I have utilized the Cambridge Digital Library of Geniza texts by Cambridge University Library and the transcriptions of Geniza documents by the Princeton Geniza Project. I thank Hereford Cathedral (particularly its librarian Rosemary Firman and the library and archives assistant James North), the British Library, the University of Oxford's Bodleian Libraries, and the University of Cambridge's Fitzwilliam Museum for permission to reproduce the images included herein.

A special version of thanks is due to Olivia Remie Constable. Remie died before the book reached its final form, but it has been shaped in countless ways both by her presence in my life and by her absence. I can only hope that she would have been proud of this small contribution to the study of the medieval Mediterranean world that she loved so much and did so much to advance.

My greatest thanks are due to the two people who travel with me not only in scholarship but also in life, my husband, Jon, and my daughter, Sage. Jon is due double thanks, as he has not only loved and supported me throughout the process of writing and rewriting this book (at times virtually solo parenting while I wrote, despite his own pressing deadlines) but also read nearly every word of it and saved me from countless instances of my own convoluted thought processes and sentence structures. Even more importantly, he is wonderful—as a partner, a scholar, and a father to our amazing daughter. There is no one else with whom I would want to sail the seas of life, love, and the study of the Middle Ages.

Abbreviations

AASS	*Acta Sanctorum*
BAS Arabic	*Biblioteca arabo-sicula, ossia raccolta di testi Arabici che toccano la geografia, la storia, le biografie e la bibliografia della Sicilia, testi arabici*. Edited by Michele Amari. Leipzig: F. A. Brockhaus, 1857–1887. 2nd revised ed. by Umberto Rizzitano. 2 vols. Palermo: Accademia Nazaionale di Scienze Lettere e Arti, 1988.
BAS Ital.	*Biblioteca arabo-sicula, ossia raccolta di testi Arabici che toccano la geografia, la storia, le biografie e la bibliografia della Sicilia, versione italiana*. Edited by Michele Amari. 2 vols. Turin: E. Loescher, 1880–1889. 2nd revised ed. by Umberto Rizzitano et al. 3 vols. Palermo: Accademia Nazaionale di Scienze Lettere e Arti, 1997–1998.
Ben-Sasson	Ben-Sasson, Menahem. *The Jews of Sicily 825–1068: Documents and Sources*. Jerusalem: Ben-Zvi Institute, 1991.
BGA	*Bibliotheca Geographorum Arabicorum*. 8 vols. Edited by M. J. de Goeje. Leiden: E. J. Brill, 1870–1894.
BHG	*Bibliotheca Hagiographica Graeca*. 3rd ed. Edited by François Halkin. 3 vols. Subsidia Hagiographica 8a. Brussels: Société des Bollandistes, 1957. Reprinted 1986.
BHL	*Bibliotheca Hagiographica Latina*. Edited by Société des Bollandistes. Subsidia Hagiographica 6. Brussels: Société des Bollandistes, 1898–1901.
EI^2	*Encyclopædia of Islam*. 2nd ed. Edited by P. J. Bearman, Th. Bianquis, C. E. Bosworth, E. van Donzel, W. P. Heinrichs et al. 12 vols. Leiden: E. J. Brill, 1960–2005.
LP	*Liber Pontificalis*. Edited by L. Duchesne. Paris: E. de Boccard, 1955–1957.
Medit. Soc.	Goitein, S. D. *A Mediterranean Society: The Jewish Communities of the Arab World as Portrayed in the Documents of the Cairo Geniza*. 6 vols. Berkeley: University of California Press, 1967–1993.

MGH	*Monumenta Germaniae Historica*
ODB	*The Oxford Dictionary of Byzantium*. Edited by Alexander P. Kazhdan et al. 3 vols. New York: Oxford University Press, 1991.
PG	*Patrologia Graeca*
PL	*Patrologia Latina*
Simonsohn	Simonsohn, Shlomo. *The Jews in Sicily*. Vol. 1, *383–1300*. Leiden: E. J. Brill, 1997.
al-Wansharīsī	al-Wansharīsī, Aḥmad ibn Yaḥyā. *al-Miʿyār al-mʿurib wa-al-jāmiʿ al-maghrib ʿan fatāwā ahl Ifrīqiyah wa-al-Andalus wa-al-Maghrib*. Edited by Muḥammad Hajjī. 13 vols. Rabat: Wizārat al-Awqāf wa al-Shu'ūn al-Islāmīyah lil-Mamlakah al-Maghribīyah, 1981–1983.

Timeline

535	Conquest of Sicily from the Goths by Byzantine general Belisarius
650s–810s	Muslim raids on Sicily from Egypt and North Africa
800–909	Aghlabid *Emīrate* of Ifrīqiya, capital at Qayrawān
827–902	Aghlabid conquest of Sicily
	831 Palermo conquered
	878 Syracuse conquered
	902 Taormina conquered
909	Fatimid Caliphate proclaimed in North Africa
947	Ascension of Hasan ibn Ali al-Kalbī, first governor in what would become a hereditary line of Sicilian *emīrs*
969–973	Fatimid capital moved to Cairo
	Zīrids (973–1148) appointed as Fatimids' governors in Ifrīqiya
960s–1030s	Byzantine naval assaults on Muslim Sicily
	1038 Norman mercenaries participated in one such attack
1040–1053	al-Samsam b. Yusuf, last Kalbid governor of Sicily, claimed title of *emīr*, but internal divisions and Byzantine attacks prevented his true power
	Sicily breaks up into multiple petty states
1050s	Political disorder and famine in Zīrid North Africa due to invasions by the Bedouin Banū Hilāl, drought, and famine
1057	Zīrid capital of Qayrawān abandoned in favor of al-Mahdiyya
1059	Reggio Calabria conquered by the Norman brothers Robert Guiscard and Roger de Hauteville
1061–1091	Norman conquest of Sicily
	1061 Messina conquered
	1072 Palermo conquered
	1091 Noto conquered
1081	Battle of Dyrrhachium (Durazzo)
1085	Death of Robert Guiscard

1101	Death of Count Roger I
1130	Kingdom of Sicily proclaimed by Roger II (1095–1154)
1135–1148	Roger II's conquests in North Africa 1135 Djerba conquered 1146 Tripoli conquered 1148 al-Mahdiyya, Sfax, Sūsa, and Kerkennah Islands conquered
1147–1149	Roger II's raids into Byzantine territory in Greece
1158–1160	Almohad reconquest of the "Norman Kingdom of Africa"
1166–1189	Reign of King William II, "the Good"
1194	Death of Tancred, last Norman King of Sicily Hohenstaufen family inherits rule of Sicily, through Constance of Sicily and her husband Henry VI, Holy Roman emperor
1194–1250	Frederick II, king of Sicily (from 1198) and Holy Roman emperor (from 1220)

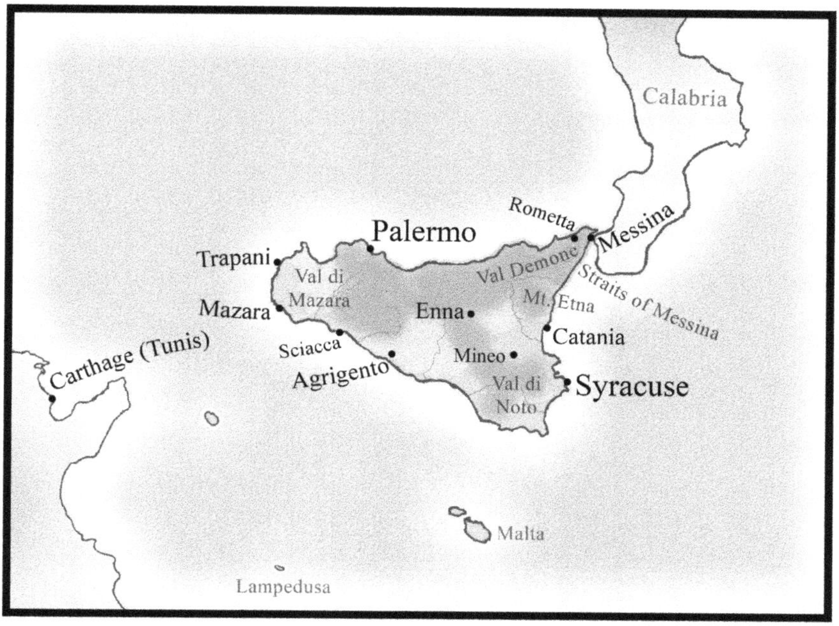
Calabria
Rometta
Messina
Palermo
Trapani
Val di Mazara
Val Demone
Straits of Messina
Mazara
Mt. Etna
Enna
Catania
Carthage (Tunis)
Sciacca
Mineo
Agrigento
Val di Noto
Syracuse
Malta
Lampedusa

Map 1. Sicily

WHERE THREE WORLDS MET

Introduction

On April 19, 2015, a ship carrying more than 700 refugees who were seeking asylum in Europe capsized off the coast of Libya. Of the passengers on board, only twenty-eight were rescued by the coast guards and made their way alive to the small Sicilian island of Lampedusa.[1] This, the deadliest known Mediterranean shipwreck in history, represents only one of many such voyages in recent years.[2] In 2015 alone, more than a million refugees arrived in Europe by sea—more than 150,000 of whom attempted to enter Europe via Sicily and southern Italy—and nearly four thousand of them died en route, according to the UNHCR.[3] This trend does not appear to be abating. As of January 2016, more than 5,000 such would-be migrants had made similar journeys into Italy, representing an increase of nearly

1. Patrick Kingsley, Alessandra Bonomolo, and Stephanie Kirchgaessner, "700 Migrants Feared Dead in Mediterranean Shipwreck," *Guardian*, April 19, 2015, https://www.theguardian.com/world/2015/apr/19/700-migrants-feared-dead-mediterranean-shipwreck-worst-yet.

2. The UNHCR tallies the arrivals by sea in the Mediterranean region and maps their routes. See the interactive map at http://data.unhcr.org/mediterranean/regional.php. A map focused more closely on Italy is found at http://data.unhcr.org/mediterranean/country.php?id=105.

3. "UNHCR Update #5 Italy—Sea Arrivals (January 2016)," last modified Feb. 26, 2016, p. 1, https://data.unhcr.org/mediterranean/download.php?id=755. For an academic analysis of migration to and from Sicily in the modern period, see Maria Sorbello, "Multiculturalism in the Mediterranean Basin: An Overview of Recent Immigration to Sicily," in *Sicily and the Mediterranean: Migration, Exchange, Reinvention*, ed. Claudia Karagoz and Giovanna Summerfield (New York: Palgrave Macmillan, 2015), 179–194.

fifty percent from the previous January.[4] Many of these refugees, fleeing the devastations of war, genocide, and extreme poverty in Africa and the Middle East, trace a path from northern Africa into southern Europe via Sicily and southern Italy—and, as the route through the Balkans closes, many observers suspect that the number of people seeking to cross into Sicily will continue to increase.[5] The sea voyage from North Africa to Sicily, though short in distance, is dangerous.[6] Those who do safely arrive on the island then find themselves in fortified detention centers and embroiled in a lengthy legal process.[7]

As much as the plight of these asylum seekers is a particularly modern problem, it highlights an enduring aspect of Sicily's history: its close proximity to both North Africa and Europe, which makes such migration appear to be easy. This geographical location has allowed the island to participate, to some degree, in the political, cultural, and economic orbits of both regions and to serve at times as a bridge between them. The movement of populations to and through Sicily is, indeed, not a new phenomenon. Recent DNA analysis has revealed that the modern population of Sicilians features significant genetic heterogeneity due to millennia of conquests and migrations: their gene pool contains links to Greeks, Tunisian Berbers and other North African populations, Normans, and, to a lesser extent, Arabs.[8] For all of its recorded history,

---

4. "UNHCR Update #5 Italy—Sea Arrivals (January 2016)." These numbers increase by the day, as boats continue to arrive on Sicily's shores or capsize before arrival. The International Organization for Migration provides up-to-date tracking of migrants and deaths at http://migration.iom.int/europe/.

5. Jim Yardley, "After Europe and Turkey Strike a Deal, Fears Grow That Migrants Will Turn to Italy," *New York Times*, April 14, 2016, http://www.nytimes.com/2016/04/15/world/europe/after-europe-and-turkey-strike-a-deal-fears-grow-that-migrants-will-turn-to-italy.html?_r=0.

6. The Strait of Sicily, or Sicilian Channel, which separates the island from modern Tunisia, is only ninety nautical miles wide but features countervailing wind patterns and water currents that often prove disastrous for ships navigating those waters. John H. Pryor, "Winds, Waves, and Rocks: The Routes and the Perils along Them," in *Maritime Aspects of Migration*, ed. K. Friedland (Cologne: Böhlau, 1989), 71–85, esp. 77–78.

7. Memphis Barker, "What Happens to African Migrants Once They Land in Italy During the Summer?" *Independent*, August 22, 2014, http://www.independent.co.uk/news/world/africa/what-happens-to-african-migrants-once-they-land-in-italy-during-the-summer-9681473.html. There have been some attempts to resettle some migrants in Sicilian towns experiencing declining populations. See Barbie Latza Nadeau, "Refugees Head to Sicily in 'Biblical Exodus,'" *Daily Beast*, April 24, 2014, http://www.thedailybeast.com/articles/2014/04/24/refugees-head-to-sicily-in-biblical-exodus.html. On the other hand, more recent reports out of Sicily have concerned the problems of finding shelter as well as the violent backlash that many migrants are experiencing there. See for example, Steve Scherer, "Italy Struggles to House Migrants in Third Year of Mass Arrivals," *Reuters*, April 29, 2016, http://www.reuters.com/article/us-europe-migrants-italy-shelters-idUSKCN0XQ1HY.

8. Cornelia Di Gaetano et al., "Differential Greek and Northern African Migrations to Sicily Are Supported by Genetic Evidence from the Y Chromosome," *European Journal of Human Genetics* 17 (2009): 91–99; and Cristian Capelli et al., "Moors and Saracens in Europe: Estimating the Medieval North African Male Legacy in Southern Europe," *European Journal of Human Genetics* 17 (2009): 848–852.

in fact, Sicily has featured an ethnically and linguistically mixed population as a result of such large-scale migrations, successive conquests, and the resulting processes of acculturation, religious conversion, settlement, and linguistic change. Phoenicians, Greeks, Vandals, Goths, Romans, Arabs, Berbers, Franks, and Normans—including many types of Christians, Muslims, and Jews—have all lived on the island in large numbers, sometimes simultaneously, and each of these groups has left its mark on the island's physical and cultural history.

How the current wave of refugees from Africa and the Middle East will shape the island's future remains to be seen, but their presence in Sicily highlights another aspect of its history beyond its syncretism: Sicily's simultaneous geographical location at the center of the Mediterranean basin and conceptual location on a series of boundaries between different—often rival and even hostile—political, cultural, and religious societies. Today, that conceptual boundary might be described as dividing the continents of Europe and Africa—or, by some, as the border between the Western world and the Islamic world—but throughout history the division has been imagined in a variety of different ways.[9] Under the early Roman Empire, Sicily was the frontier of imperial control and, later, the center of its maritime hegemony. During the Middle Ages, it was (or was imagined to be) located on or near the conceptual borders between vast religiopolitical "civilizations" (such as Islam and Christianity or Latin Christendom and Greek Christendom), as well as, at times, between dynastic rivals (for example, between the Abbasid and Fatimid Caliphates). As the location of those boundaries, the nature of what they were supposed to divide and how, and their degree of permeability shifted and changed throughout this period, so too did the role and position of Sicily within the premodern Mediterranean system. So, we might ask, where *was* Sicily during these centuries? Was it at an edge—say, of Europe, or of Islam, or of Byzantium—or at the center of an interconnected cross-cultural system? Did it divide Christianity, both of the Greek and Latin varieties, from Islam, of both Sunni and Shiite communities, or unite them in a web of economic and cultural connections that made the island, in fact, a center of the Mediterranean system rather than a periphery?

The basic outline of Sicily's long history only confirms the confusion. Politically, the island has had a variety of identities throughout its history: as a

9. Of course, many scholars have written of these boundary regions as zones of unity and interaction rather than division. As Linda Darling points out: "The frontier divides one society from another, while the borderland is where they overlap and blend." Darling, "The Mediterranean as a Borderland," *Review of Middle East Studies* 46, no. 1 (2012): 55. For more on this historiographical debate, see discussion below in this chapter.

part of the associated ancient Greek colonies known as Magna Graeca, the Latin Roman Empire, Greek Christian Byzantium, the Aghlabid province of the Sunni Abbasid Caliphate, the Shiite Fatimid Caliphate, the Latin Christian Norman kingdom, the French House of Anjou, the expansive Mediterranean Kingdom of Aragon, and, from the mid-nineteenth century, the modern nation-state of Italy. Each of these highly varied political-cultural units controlled, for some length of time, this island that was itself very rarely a base for independent political rule. Culturally, too, Sicily has historically been diverse, due in large part to these successive conquests and the subsequent changes in religion and culture. During the centuries considered in this book—from the sixth-century incorporation of the island into the Byzantine Empire, through the period of Muslim rule (827–1061), until the end of Norman rule there in the late twelfth century—Sicily moved, broadly speaking, from the Latin Christian world into the Greek Christian one, then into the Islamicate civilization, and then back into Latin Christendom.[10] But the reality of the situation, as with most cases, was much more complex. Neither the "Christian world" nor the "Muslim world" was a monolithic entity that operated uniformly during the Middle Ages. In fact, Sicily was often, at one and the same time, part of various Muslim worlds, both Sunni and Shiite, and various Christian societies, both Greek and Latin. Thus the meaning of Sicily in its capacity as a border zone was constantly in a state of change. So, should we consider the island as the center of a large-scale Mediterranean system or as an area on the edge of one or the other of these three major religious-political-cultural regions? Was it simply geographically advantageous as a trading hub or stopping point along longer paths of sea travel, conquered by various polities because they desired the economic potential it offered?[11] I argue that only by

10. See Marshall Hodgson, *The Venture of Islam*, 3 vols. (Chicago: University of Chicago Press, 1974), for the first use of the term "Islamicate" to describe the broadly multicultural world under Muslim political control. This designation, a parallel to "Latinate," is intended to describe the wide premodern region that participated in the culture of Islam, or was strongly influenced by it, without implying that everyone within that region was necessarily Muslim. I use "Islamicate world" interchangeably with "the Muslim world" and "dār al-Islām," which translates as "the House of Islam" and refers to territories under Muslim political control. The theoretical counterpart of the dār al-Islām was the dār al-ḥarb, or the "House of War"—the areas of the world not under Islamic political control. As we will see, however, the boundaries between the Muslim and non-Muslim worlds were very porous and not always militarized. For more on the legal debate about the dār al-Islām versus the dār al-ḥarb, see chapter 5.

11. Cf. the question asked by Peregrine Horden in his plenary lecture, "Poseidon's Oar: Horizons of the Medieval Mediterranean" at the Forty-Eighth International Congress on Medieval Studies, May 10, 2013, about "where" our particular historical regions were located, both conceptually and culturally. He urged medievalists to probe the "horizons" or boundaries of their regions of study, ultimately suggesting that "the Mediterranean" as a conceptual space could extend far beyond the shores of the sea itself. This mirrors a contemporary trend among scholars of the premodern Medi-

investigating these questions, can we view the island—and its variety of connections to other regions—as representative of the fundamental shifts and changes that took place in the larger Mediterranean system during the Middle Ages.

In this book, I examine these connections—patterns of travel and communication between Sicily and elsewhere—in order to understand the island's role(s) within the broader Mediterranean system of the sixth through twelfth centuries.[12] Travel between Sicily and other regions in the Mediterranean basin has, in fact, been formative for the island's population, culture, economy, and politics. Many acts of travel to and from medieval Sicily also involved crossing one (or more) of the theoretical boundaries on which it lay, just as today's migrants seek to cross national boundaries that also entail economic, cultural, and religious differences. These patterns of travel and communication bring spaces (and people) closer together, even across perceived boundaries, and create linkages between disparate societies. This methodology also allows us to view the island across time and conquests, instead of keeping our study within politically defined historical periods. Thus we can understand the history not only of the island but also of the Mediterranean system itself—how it changed over time and how transitions, from one historical period to another, took place within that system. Tracing the movements of travelers—pilgrims and traders, diplomats and delegations, popes and potentates, raiding parties and conquering armies—to and from the island, both within each period of rule and

---

terranean to find "the Mediterranean" as far afield (geographically) as England and Russia. Despite its current popularity, this trend has a long pedigree as well, since the "grandfather" of Mediterranean studies, Fernand Braudel, himself described a Mediterranean that extended far into the hinterlands. Fernand Braudel, *The Mediterranean and the Mediterranean World in the Age of Philip II*, 2 vols. (New York: Harper and Row, 1972).

12. For one analysis of the difference between travel and communications, see Michael McCormick, "Byzantium on the Move: Imagining a Communications History," in *Travel in the Byzantine World: Papers from the Thirty-Fourth Spring Symposium of Byzantine Studies, Birmingham, April 2000*, ed. Ruth Macrides (Aldershot: Ashgate Variorum, 2002), 3–29. He classifies travel as the movement of people and communications as the movement of everything else, from items to ideas (4–6). On the other hand, see Marco Mostert, "New Approaches to Medieval Communication?," in *New Approaches to Medieval Communication*, ed. Marco Mostert (Turnhout: Brepols, 1999), 15–37. Mostert defines communication as an exchange of information that is essential for the very existence of human society (18). Sophia Menache claims that communication "may be defined as a symbolic behavior that occurs between two or more participating individuals. It has the characteristics of being a transactional process; it is affective, purposive, goal-directed behavior that can have instrumental or consummatory ends." Menache, "Introduction: The 'Pre-History' of Communication," in *Communication in the Jewish Diaspora: The Pre-modern World*, ed. Sophia Menache (Leiden: E. J. Brill, 1996), 2. In this book, I use communication more in the later sense—as the transactional process that can either cause or result from the movements of people and things. These transactions can link together both individuals and, in part, the societies from which they come—whether or not that was the original intent of the traveler.

across the transitions from one to another, allows us to reconstruct networks of travel, exchange, conflict, and communication that formed both the island's conceptual place and its functional roles within overlapping Mediterranean systems. The focus of this study, then, is not only the island itself but also the people and products that traveled to and from the island and thus linked it with other places—and often with several locations at once. I do not simply ask questions about who ruled the island at what time, but rather how it worked within larger structures of Mediterranean communications, what its rulers chose to do with the island, and how it functioned at the boundaries of the Greek, Latin, and Muslim worlds. Travelers, the items and ideas they brought with them, the connections to places both far and near that their trips entailed, and the patterns of economic, cultural, and political dependence that thence developed all constitute the lens through which we can view much larger networks of interaction and exchange within the Mediterranean Sea region of the early and central Middle Ages.

Sicily as a Borderland

As we will see, the nature and meaning of the Sicilian borderland meant different things to different travelers, rulers, and communication partners over time. In addition, the creation or repositioning of a political or religious boundary line did not necessarily or immediately mean the cessation or realignment of communications and travel across the border: thus we will see both the ambiguity of the border itself and the multiplicity of the types of people who crossed those borders. At the same time, we must not expect that simply because a certain pattern of travel, exchange, or transmission obtained at a given time, it must necessarily have also done so in earlier or later periods. Nor should we imagine that, even when connections did persist across periods of major transformation and political change, those networks meant the same thing or functioned for the same reasons as they had done earlier. In fact, as the patterns of communication and travel shifted, so did their meanings and, thus, the conceptual utility of these connections for locating Sicily within wider systems. Much of this book, then, will explore the porous nature of boundary lines, the fluidity of movement across perceived borders, and the causes behind either break or continuity in the patterns of such border crossing during periods of political and social change.

Therefore, it is worthwhile to briefly consider the definition and scholarly understandings of medieval borderlands. As popular as it is, the very idea of borders or frontiers can be a troublesome concept when applied to the premodern period. But borderlands have been of great interest to scholars in recent decades, leading to a surplus of scholarship on the topic and some attempts to synthesize historical approaches and to develop a coherent definition of the concept. While contemporary maps, even those representing the past, tend to draw dark lines between political or civilization-level units (such as "Christendom" and "Islam"), the medieval on-the-ground reality was often far messier and more complex, leading also to heterogeneity in the usage of these terms by modern scholars: some consider frontiers as linear boundaries of political demarcation, others as nonlinear divisions between cultures or barriers between different religions, etc.[13] Still others use the concept of the frontier to discuss the development of supposedly unique institutions in borderlands areas, positing the existence of a particular type of "frontier society" in regions where various peoples or cultures met and interacted—either violently or more peacefully.[14] Other sets of scholars have discussed borderlands more in terms of zones than as lines or societies, especially as zones of interaction between various groups and peoples.[15]

In some senses, then, a borderland can be both a place of separation and a space for interaction: a location where several states, cultures, or civilizations meet each other, oftentimes both sharing cultural elements or diplomatic relationships and vying for resources or political or religious supremacy. These regions thus tend to be characterized by diversity—of both population and legal and administrative practices—and interaction, often violent, between various populations. Indeed, medieval border zones were often spaces in which diverse populations and competing rulers struggled to shift the dividing line between them, as each attempted to expand the area under their domain or influence. Even when this competition did not manifest itself in open warfare, medieval borderlands were typically contested spaces that presented opportunities for military or cultural advancement. At the same time, as many historians

---

13. See, for example, the introduction to the essays found in Robert Bartlett and Angus MacKay, eds., *Medieval Frontier Societies* (Oxford: Clarendon Press, 1989), iv-vii.

14. Many medievalists now avoid positing the existence of unique "frontier societies" in border regions, preferring to contextualize their particular region in comparison with a broader society or a political center. Nora Berend, "Medievalists and the Notion of the Frontier," *The Medieval History Journal* 2 (1999): 55–72. Indeed, I do not argue either for or against the uniqueness of any type of "frontier society" or culture in Sicily, but rather for the uniqueness of the relationships of communication that developed between Sicily as the borderland and other regional sites of power, as well as of the ways in which they changed over time. Thus, I tend to privilege use of the term "borderland" over that of "frontier," even if medieval polities themselves sometimes viewed the island as a far edge of their society or as a site of potential military expansion as in a classic definition of the frontier. When I do use the term "frontier," I try to restrict it to that meaning.

15. Berend, "Medievalists," 55ff. See also many of the essays in David Abulafia and Nora Berend, eds., *Medieval Frontiers: Concepts and Practices* (Aldershot: Ashgate, 2002).

of medieval cross-cultural relations have shown, violence and more peaceful coexistence were not mutually exclusive.[16] Thus, for example, Sicily could, at one and the same time, be a site for Christian-Muslim trade, conflict, and diplomacy. And, indeed, the contested nature of the border zone often was the very reason for its importance, both in terms of cross-cultural relations and for the interests of the larger civilizations on whose edges it lay: each side wanted to hold or gain access to it and all that it offered.

From the sixth through the twelfth centuries, then, Sicily functioned in a number of different ways at the border of each of the three major civilizations that overlapped on or near the island; the definition of Sicily as a borderland thus differed for each of its communication partners and from era to era. And yet, by looking across these three periods of rule, spanning roughly seven centuries, we can identify a number of common themes relating to the nature of the island as a medieval borderland. To begin with, Sicily served as a borderland because it was geographically distant from its political capital, though in some periods that distance was greater than at other times (and, during the Norman period, the island itself became the center of political power). Because of this distance, the matter of communication and travel became one of paramount importance, both for the development of connections between regions and for the culture and economy of the borderland itself. Geographical distance between center and periphery established a twofold pattern of communication: it meant that a mechanism for communication was both necessary and often lengthy, risky, or difficult. In order for a remote capital to maintain administrative control over a province, ships must be able to regularly sail back and forth, bringing new governors, administrative edicts, and messengers. At the same time, because this type of travel could be time-consuming, costly, challenging, or dangerous, Sicily slipped out of the direct control of its political center on several occasions—either completely or partially—and at other times someone tried but failed to use the island as a base for setting up rival independent rule. Likewise, the island's successive conquests resulted from the inability of a political center to maintain its hold over the island (either because of distance or diminished resources). So, to some degree, the nature of the connections with which the island was involved depended both upon the necessity of a communications network and the difficulty of such communication; long and dangerous journeys create communication patterns that differ from communications maintained with closer locations.

16. See for example the now-classic argument in David Nirenberg, *Communities of Violence* (Princeton, NJ: Princeton University Press, 1996).

While much of the travel and communication that occurred along these routes took place between the political center and the province, political rulers by no means held a monopoly on communication with the island. The necessity for a robust system of communications between the borderland and its center thus created patterns of travel that helped the island to develop cultural and economic connections more widely. As a result, cultural and economic commodities, as well as people and ideas, traveled back and forth between the center and the province, but also between the island and other prominent locations within the region, especially as new centers of power arose. In fact, because the distance between the borderland and its center could at times be quite far, the primary economic and cultural contacts for the people of the borderland might be ones much closer at hand—but belonging to a different state, culture, religious civilization, or language group. This pattern of intercultural communications is in fact characteristic of the Mediterranean system as a whole, but especially so for its islands and for borderland provinces that were geographically distant from their ruling capitals.

Because of its shifting conceptual location along the borders of multiple societies, the island also came to perform an important mediating role in relations between these larger political or cultural units. At times, this meant that the borderland was the front line of military aggression, warfare, rebellion, and conquest. At other times (and sometimes simultaneously), it could be a site of diplomacy, trade, and the transfer of ideas and cultural or artistic elements. The borderland region could thus be a site of fruitful cultural or economic exchange as well as a vital site for the mediation of political relationships between larger polities, alongside or alternating with violent conflict. This factor, in turn, made the borderland, as an area of intense cross-cultural contact, a necessary and desirable location for all of the cultures that met and interacted there. Sicily, like other Mediterranean borderland regions, assumed a primary importance in political and cultural relations between the different polities that shared that border, although the meaning and significance of this role differed over time.

Because the borderland region was so important as a mediator between the cultures that it was supposed to divide, it could be an attractive area for military and political expansion. So, while the island's distant political capital might desire to maintain direct control over it, this would often prove difficult, either because of distance and diminished resources or because of distractions closer to the capital, and so the region fell to numerous successive conquests. Therefore, in addition to being a space of interaction and contestation, a borderland is also a place that experienced many changes in political leadership and regular violence. Conquest, rebellion, raids, and other types of violent interaction are fundamental aspects of life at a mutually desirable borderland location and, as such, form a basic part of our discussion of the island's history and place in systems of communication. While other medieval borderlands might be pulled back and forth between only two polities, Sicily, by virtue of its central location in the Mediterranean, could be (and was) repeatedly conquered by a long list of different societies—in large part because each determined that ruling the island was in their greatest interest.

Altogether, then, the role of a borderland is contingent upon the patterns of communication with which it was involved. Travel thus forms a central aspect of both internal and external relations between the borderland and other regions, both near and far. Travel between the border and its administrative center and communication between the region and other spaces of cultural, political, or economic importance created webs of connection that defined the borderland and its role within larger systems. It is the resilience, even after successive conquests by rival powers, of the networks of communication within which it was located that made Sicily such a unique and important space in the Mediterranean region. It was precisely because communication patterns, once established, could be used and exploited by successive rulers of the island for their own purposes that Sicily took on the particular roles that it played in various periods across the Middle Ages. Therefore, Sicily's place in the Mediterranean—at once on the periphery of competing empires and at the very center of communication networks between them—comes into sharp focus only when we examine in detail what patterns of travel and communication the island was engaged in, how they were established and maintained, and how they shifted, remained, or were transformed after political conquest.

More broadly, movement and communication across political, cultural, or geographical boundaries are central aspects of Mediterranean studies as a whole. Indeed, one of the most common ways of debating the Mediterranean Sea in previous historiography has been to ask whether the region, as a whole, was a site of unity or division. This can be traced back to two of the progenitors of Mediterranean history, Henri Pirenne and Fernand Braudel. Pirenne imagined an early medieval Mediterranean divided by religious-political warfare and a consequent break in the cross-Mediterranean trade that had defined the ancient Roman Mediterranean.[17] On the other hand, Braudel sought to define the region by means of its shared geographical and cultural characteristics and the similarities in environmental factors that created a coherent unit

17. Henri Pirenne, *Mohammed and Charlemagne* (London: G. Allen & Unwin, 1939).

over the long span of years, despite political or cultural divisions.[18] This debate essentially asks whether the medieval Mediterranean was one place or many, and how useful it might be to consider it as one place for the purposes of study. However, as Peregrine Horden and Nicholas Purcell have pointed out more recently, modern historians should not assume that the premodern Mediterranean was necessarily one or the other—always either interconnected as a unitary system or necessarily fragmented into subregions. Rather, we must investigate the various reasons for either connectivity or division at various times in history in order to make clear the variety of ways in which the Mediterranean did or did not operate as a coherent unit or a series of subunits.[19] This book does just that, by focusing on one location across many centuries and through multiple changes in religion, culture, economy, and political rule, and by asking how the goods and people who traveled to and from the island thus linked it conceptually with other spaces in the Mediterranean region.

In particular, the study of travel and travelers illuminates the intricate networks of communication and contact that defined Sicily's place—its "horizons"—within the premodern Mediterranean: evidence of a traveler arriving on the island is indicative both of a preexisting connection that could be exploited and of a desire to foster such connections, for a variety of potential reasons.[20] At some points we will see communications patterns established in one period of rule that persisted into a new era, occasionally at the same time in which other types of communication experienced rupture. Between the sixth and twelfth centuries, then, Sicily's patterns of connection to other regions of the Mediterranean were transformed by complex combinations of political, cultural, and economic need—that is, how the island functioned within larger Mediterranean communications networks hinged on what it was being used for vis-à-vis both its larger political-cultural world and the societies on its borders, rather than on geography, tradition, or standard assumptions about continuity or discontinuity in the wake of political conquest. The answer to where Sicily was located during these six centuries thus depended on who was asking the question and why.

---

18. Braudel, *The Mediterranean.*

19. Peregrine Horden and Nicholas Purcell, *The Corrupting Sea: A Study of Mediterranean History* (Oxford: Blackwell, 2000).

20. In this manner, I have relied heavily on the methodological models provided by Michael McCormick, *Origins of the European Economy: Communications and Commerce, A.D. 300–900* (Cambridge: Cambridge University Press, 2001); and Olivia Remie Constable, *Trade and Traders in Muslim Spain: The Commercial Realignment of the Iberian Peninsula, 900–1500* (Cambridge: Cambridge University Press, 1994).

Sicily's Place in History

To be sure, Sicily's population has been in contact with peoples from various regions of the Mediterranean for millennia; external communications are indeed key to understanding the island's place in history. Sicily's earliest inhabitants are estimated to have arrived there in the first stages of human migration from Africa (around 30,000 BCE), as evidenced by Paleolithic and Neanderthal tools uncovered at archaeological sites on the island.[21] Starting around 10,000 BCE, the archaeological evidence on Sicily increases and suggests that the population of the island remained one of hunters and gatherers long after the peoples of the Near East and northern Europe had begun a settled agricultural life indicative of the Neolithic economy.[22] Prehistoric Sicilians slowly adopted agriculture, functional pottery, and life in villages around the sixth millennium BCE—cultural characteristics that had been common in the rest of the Mediterranean much earlier.[23] Trade with nearby islands also developed around this time, first in obsidian from the island of Lipari and then, around the fourth millennium, in pottery, wool, and textiles traded between Sicily and Malta.[24] Around 1400 BCE the early Greek peoples of the Aegean migrated to Sicily, southern Italy, and other regions of the western Mediterranean, drawing Sicily into the Mycenaean world, in which it remained until the eleventh century BCE. At that time, the Mycenaean empire collapsed and Sicily's external involvement was limited to contact with mainland Italy.

Later, Greek settlement led to Sicily's becoming one of the key players in some of the most important historical events in the ancient world. The second phase of Greek colonization of Sicily and southern Italy began in the eighth century BCE; together, these two regions formed the larger territory known as Magna Graeca. In Sicily, Greek settlers began to establish population centers in the south and east of the island from the 730s BCE. Many of these cities were closely linked to the economy and culture of the Hellenistic eastern Mediterranean.[25] The Greeks introduced cities, coins, and extensive agricultural cultivation to the eastern half of the island, while at the same time Phoenicians from northern Africa were establishing trading emporia

---

21. R. Ross Holloway, *The Archaeology of Ancient Sicily* (London: Routledge, 1991), 1–2.

22. Ibid., 2–7.

23. Ibid., 7–13. Holloway theorizes that this slow development is the product of an underpopulated island without the high population pressures that would have induced early humans to build houses and begin growing their food.

24. Ibid., 13–20.

25. For more on the Greeks in Sicily and their networks in the Mediterranean, see Irad Malkin, *A Small Greek World: Networks in the Ancient Mediterranean* (Oxford: Oxford University Press, 2011), esp. 97–118.

at several locations on the western half of the island.[26] By the sixth century BCE, the Greeks and the Carthaginians—overlords of the Phoenician trading cities—had come into conflict on the island, leading to the consolidation of small empires under Greek tyrants, with Syracuse as the most powerful city. Hellenistic culture spread throughout the island as the Greeks dominated the Phoenician settlements. Then, in the fourth century BCE, Sicily was brought into the large-scale conflicts of the Greek city-states due to its importance as a source of grain and as an important trading partner of Corinth. The island served as a major battleground during the Peloponnesian Wars and then later in the wars between Carthage and the Greeks.

Subsequently, the island came to play a significant role in the wars of Rome. Sicily was located at a midpoint between Carthage and Rome—close enough for each to threaten the security of the other and agriculturally rich enough to be desirable for conquest by both sides. Sicily thus also became the focus of fighting during the Punic Wars between Rome and Carthage. It was captured by Rome in the middle of the third century BCE and became the first overseas Roman province in 241 BCE. Sicily received its first *praetor* (magistrate) in 227 BCE, and its provincial administration developed as a model for other overseas provinces, while Rome's interest in the island expanded from security against Carthage to exploitation of its agricultural resources.[27] Under Roman rule, the island was quite prosperous and served as a vital source of grain for Rome and its army, through the imposition of the grain tithe that would later develop into a fixed tax called the *annona*. After the Roman conquest of Egypt in 30 BCE, that territory surpassed the island's grain cultivation, and Sicily became only a secondary source of food supplies for Rome.[28] The landscape of Roman Sicily—like other locations in the Roman Mediterranean—featured large estates called *latifundia*, which were worked by slaves, and the island exported wine, timber, wool, and sulphur, in addition to grain. These agricultural estates were complemented by cities where wealthy landowners lived (the primary Roman cities being Syracuse, Catania,

26. Holloway, *Archaeology*, 10–11.

27. Ibid., 109ff. See also John Serrati, "Garrisons and Grain: Sicily between the Punic Wars," in *Sicily from Aeneas to Augustus: New Approaches in Archaeology and History*, ed. Christopher Smith and John Serrati (Edinburgh: Edinburgh University Press, 2000), 115–133. Serrati writes that "the Roman concept of a *provincia* developed in tandem with government structures on Sicily" (122). Thus Sicily played a significant role in the development of the Roman provincial system and Rome's expansion throughout the Mediterranean.

28. Serrati theorizes that the grain tithe was adopted by the Romans in 227 BCE from the practice of the Carthaginians of exacting a grain tithe on their subjects in the west of Sicily, and from that of the king of Syracuse, Hieron, who taxed in grain his subjects in the east. Serrati, "Garrisons and Grain," 122–126.

and Palermo) and where the Latin language and culture predominated. This Roman social and economic structure on Sicily persisted into the fourth and fifth centuries CE, even after the empire's capital moved from Rome to Constantinople in 330. When North Africa was controlled by the Vandals in the fifth century, Sicily may have regained its importance as a breadbasket for the empire, but it, too, was drawn into the struggle between Rome and the Germanic "barbarians."

Sicily was one of many Mediterranean spaces contested between these new Germanic powers and the Roman Empire. Captured in turn by Vandals and Ostrogoths in the second half of the fifth century CE, Sicily was then recovered for the Roman Empire in 535–536 by Emperor Justinian's General Belisarius during the so-called Gothic wars. The major written source concerning late antique Sicily, the register of letters of Pope Gregory I, shows a sixth-century Sicily that was significantly different from the ancient Roman island dominated by *latifundia*.[29] Property was by then held in smaller plots by smaller landowners, and the land was worked by free, rent-paying peasants.[30] Byzantine Sicily's cities were administrative and ecclesiastical in function and served as fortified refuges for the surrounding population during times of Muslim invasion, as we will see in chapter 2. There were also many rural villages on Sicily, which increased in prominence as the late antique West, more broadly, saw a decline in the number of urban centers and important market towns.

During the centuries of Byzantine rule, Sicily again became the focus of contests between competing Mediterranean powers, as the site of struggles between the Greek empire and the Germanic kings of the West. From 547–551 CE Gothic invasions again threatened Constantinople's major western possessions, and these were followed by the Lombard invasions that would eventually detach all of the northern and central Italian territories from the Byzantine Empire. The Exarchate of Ravenna fell to the Lombards in 751, although Byzantium retained a few small footholds in southern Italy and Sicily, which itself never fell into Lombard hands. Despite these significant losses, Byzantine administration was maintained on the island until the Muslim conquest of the ninth century, which began in 827 and was completed by 902. However, Sicily began to operate within the orbit of the Islamicate world long before the official conquest by Muslim rulers from North Africa. Communication

29. Gregory the Great, *Registrum espitularum libri*, ed. Dag Norberg, *Corpus Christianorum Series Latina*, vols. 140 and 140A (Turnhout: Brepols, 1982). Translation in John R. C. Martyn, trans., *Letters of Gregory the Great*, 3 vols. (Toronto: PIMS, 2004). For more on the use of Gregory's letters as a source of the history of Byzantine Sicily, see Martyn, *Letters of Gregory the Great*, vol. 1, 24–29; and Andre Guillou, "La Sicile Byzantine: État de recherches," *Byzantinische Forschungen* 5 (1977): 95–145.

30. "Sicily," *ODB*, 3: 1891.

patterns began to link the Greek Christian–ruled island with the Muslim regions of North Africa and Egypt even as early as the seventh century CE. Muslim raids on Sicily are noted in chronicles from as early as around the year 652. Between 703 and 827 semiregular attacks on Sicily's shores were conducted by troops from North Africa, who captured both booty and slaves. In the early ninth century, however, these attacks changed from economic raids to invasions of conquest, culminating in the complete takeover of Sicily by Muslim forces between 827 and 902.

Ruling Sicily from the early ninth through the mid-eleventh centuries, Muslims created there a society and government about which many questions remain due to a scarcity of sources.[31] Governors of Sicily, with their capital at Palermo, were appointed by the Aghlabid *emīrs* in Qayrawān until the Fatimid regime took over North Africa and Sicily in the tenth century. Over time, the island's population came to be dominated by Arabic-speaking Muslims, made up of Berber and Arab immigrants from Africa along with some converts (presumably, since little is known for sure about conversion patterns) from among the Greek population. Nonetheless, small Greek Christian communities continued to live in eastern regions of the island, and many survived there until the Norman invasion in the eleventh century. The island as a whole appears to have developed social, economic, and cultural patterns consistent with the rest of the dār al-Islām (the "House of Islam," or the Muslim world). One eyewitness description of late-tenth-century Sicily depicted the island as having mosques, Islamic schools, and other hallmarks of Muslim society, suggesting that under Muslim rule Sicily's culture, government, and economy came to resemble those of North Africa, its closest partner in relationships of travel and exchange.

By the eleventh century, Sicily was ruled by a semi-independent dynasty of Muslim governors called the Kalbids, whose independence arose during the period of the Fatimid caliphate. Based in Cairo, the Fatimids were either incapable of or uninterested in maintaining a strong control over the island and their other western Mediterranean possessions. By the 1050s, Kalbid power had itself fractured, and the island was ruled by multiple local and competing *emīrs*. At the same time, Constantinople revived its semiregular efforts to reconquer the island. It was in this context that the Latin Christian Norman invaders, working first as mercenaries for the Byzantines and later for themselves, wrested control of the island from the Muslims between 1060/1061 and 1091.

31. Two new narrative histories of the period have been published on the basis of what evidence does remain. Leonard C. Chiarelli, *A History of Muslim Sicily* (Venera, Malta: Midsea Books, 2011); and Alex Metcalfe, *The Muslims of Medieval Italy* (Edinburgh: Edinburgh University Press, 2009).

Transformed from an independent county to a kingdom united with southern Italy in 1130, Sicily was ruled by Norman kings until a new ruling family, the Hohenstaufens, came to power in 1194. Norman leaders introduced Latin language and Latin Christian institutions to the island, which nonetheless retained a sizeable Muslim population.[32] Sicily under the Normans became more closely oriented to western Europe, although the rulers maintained contacts with the Islamic world and kept many Muslim courtiers, artists, and scholars at their court in Palermo. Connections with the Islamicate world persisted despite the change in political and religious leadership on the island, but these connections were maintained, shifted, and managed by the Normans in order to advance their unique interests. The Hohenstaufen rulers both maintained many of the Norman kings' traditions and transformed them, drawing Sicily nearer to Latin Europe through their simultaneous kingship of Germany.

The rule of the Hohenstaufens in the Kingdom of the Two Sicilies lasted only until the death of King Frederick II (also Holy Roman emperor from 1220) in 1250, after which time Sicily fell successively under the control of French and then Aragonese external rule.[33] Upon his death, competition between Frederick's sons (both legitimate and illegitimate), and the desire of the papacy to replace the rule of this family in the south with that of someone more malleable to papal will, prompted Charles of Anjou, brother of the French king Louis IX, to invade Sicily and southern Italy and to claim them as his own. Charles was proclaimed king of Sicily in 1265, but it was not until 1268 that he was finally able to defeat the final Hohenstaufen heir. Angevin rule in Sicily was not to last long. In a 1282 uprising known as the Sicilian Vespers, the Angevins were overthrown, and Sicily came into the hands of Peter III of Aragon.[34] Charles of Anjou abandoned the island and continued his rule from a base at Naples, in a polity known as the Angevin Kingdom of Naples. Despite Angevin attempts to restore their rule over the island, the Aragonese Kingdom of Sicily remained independent until 1409, when it was formally incorporated into the Crown of Aragon. After changing hands several more times in the early modern period, Sicily was politically united to mainland Italy in 1860–1861.[35]

---

32. For more on the island's Muslim population, see Alex Metcalfe, *Muslims and Christians in Norman Sicily: Arabic-Speakers and the End of Islam* (New York: Routledge, 2002).

33. David Abulafia, *The Western Mediterranean Kingdoms, 1200–1500: The Struggle for Dominion* (New York: Longman, 1997); and Abulafia, *A Mediterranean Emporium: The Catalan Kingdom of Majorca* (Cambridge: Cambridge University Press, 1994).

34. Steven Runciman, *The Sicilian Vespers: A History of the Mediterranean World in the Later Thirteenth Century* (Cambridge: Cambridge University Press, 1958).

35. Lucy Riall, *Sicily and the Unification of Italy: Liberal Policy and Local Power, 1859–1866* (Oxford: Clarendon Press, 1998).

Sicily's Geographical Place in the Mediterranean

How historians have viewed Sicily's history and its role within broader systems of exchange and communication has, in many ways, been shaped by the island's geographical location. It is, indeed, commonplace for scholars to note that the island is located at the dividing point between the eastern and western basins of the Mediterranean Sea, and at the midpoint between its northern and southern shores. As a result, it is often claimed that Sicily's location at the center of the sea made it a "nexus" of east-west communications, a "stepping-stone" or a "crossroads" of the Mediterranean, a "hub" of regional systems, or a "bridge" between northern and southern shores of the Mediterranean basin. Such general characterizations place Sicily unchangingly at the center of communication networks in the western or central Mediterranean region and often privilege the island as an important player in Mediterranean-wide economic, cultural, and political developments—all simply because of where it is located. However, this book argues that we must carefully examine the precise, and shifting, historical conditions of Sicily's connectivity in order to understand the actual role(s) that the island played in various networks at different times.[36] Geography itself did not determine what roles the island played within wider systems, and it should not determine how historians write about them.[37] Nonetheless, geographical considerations can serve as an important foundation for understanding how the ease or difficulty of travel to and from Sicily could impact the island's networks and connections.

Sicily is the largest Mediterranean island, covering nearly 10,000 square miles.[38] The island's terrain varies from fertile plains to rolling hills and rocky mountains, with its highest point on Mount Etna, Europe's tallest active volcano, at an altitude of around 11,000 feet. While we often speak of the island as sitting centrally in the Mediterranean, in geographical terms Sicily is bounded by the Mediterranean on the west and south, the Ionian Sea on the east, and the Tyrrhenian Sea on the north. The island is roughly triangular—a fact often noted in medieval texts—and surrounded by a number of smaller volcanic

---

36. For the concept of "connectivity" in the study of the Mediterranean, see Horden and Purcell, *Corrupting Sea*.

37. See, for example, the (admittedly dated) claim that "the history of Sicily is, first of all, a study in geographical determinism, but the many regimes on that island tell too of what a changing thing even geography is. . . . A barometer of Mediterranean power, Sicily was always easy to conquer and hard to rule. And that, like geography, becomes a theme of Sicilian history." Raymond Grew, "Review of *A History of Sicily* 3 vols., M. I. Finley and Denis Mack Smith," *American Historical Review* 75 (1969): 537–539.

38. Compare to the next largest Mediterranean islands: Sardinia, which comprises just over 9,000 square miles, and Cyprus, covering 3,500 square miles.

islands, lying both singly and in clusters. Sicily is within a short boat ride from several other major landmasses of the Mediterranean basin: it is separated from mainland Italy by the Strait of Messina, which, although only two and a half miles wide, is notoriously difficult to navigate.[39] Within close range (fifty nautical miles) is Malta, separated from Sicily by waters known as the Malta Channel. Sicily is also near to the modern African country of Tunisia (roughly contiguous with the medieval Islamic province of Ifrīqiya, as it will be referred to in this book, alternately with North Africa), about ninety miles across the Sicilian Channel, or the Strait of Sicily. This proximity, to both Italy and North Africa, provided the opportunity for Sicily to be linked to both the Muslim territories of the Mediterranean's southern shores and to Christian Europe. However, the extent and meanings of such linkages were determined by the need and interest of the island's rulers and communications partners, not by this convenient geographical placement.

Because of the historiographical importance of Sicily's agricultural production, its environment, landscape, and fertility have also been perceived as key to the island's role in larger economic systems. Sicily's climate features cool, rainy winters and hot, dry summers.[40] The south of the island is particularly arid, blown by the sirocco winds from Africa. The island's interior is dry, requiring irrigation, but also features rich and fertile soil, suitable for grain cultivation.[41] Sicily's grain yield in the premodern period is widely held to have been high in comparison with other regions.[42] Its primary wheat crop during antiquity and the Middle Ages was hard durum wheat (*triticum durum*), a grain with a high gluten content and thus the ability to withstand long periods of storage and shipment.[43] Due to these agricultural needs, water was a vital part of the Sicilian landscape—a fact often noted in the accounts of medieval travelers to the island. Sicily has a number of rivers and streams, including the Simeto River (near Catania), Belice River (in the region of Māzara), Platani River (close to Agrigento), and Tellaro River, in the Syracuse region—several of

39. The Strait of Messina has long been associated with the mythological Scylla and Charybdis. See John H. Pryor, *Geography, Technology and War: Studies in the Maritime History of the Mediterranean, 649–1571* (Cambridge: Cambridge University Press, 1988), 92.

40. Ellen Churchill Semple, *The Geography of the Mediterranean Region: Its Relation to Ancient History* (New York: Ams, 1931), 85–92. For seasonal climate variations in the Mediterranean region, see also Pryor, *Geography*, 12–20.

41. David G. Basile, "Agricultural Sicily," *Economic Geography* 17 (1941): 109–120.

42. See for example Cicero's claim that Sicily's grain yield was eight to one. Catherine Delano Smith, *Western Mediterranean Europe: A Historical Geography of Italy, Spain and Southern France since the Neolithic* (London: Academic Press, 1979), 196.

43. Naum Jasny, *The Wheats of Classical Antiquity* (Baltimore: Johns Hopkins Press, 1944), esp. 23–24, 91. See also Andrew M. Watson, *Agricultural Innovation in the Early Islamic World: The Diffusion of Crops and Farming Techniques, 700–1100* (Cambridge: Cambridge University Press, 1983), 20–23.

FIGURE 1. Ponte d'Ammiraglio, built in the early twelfth century by the Norman official George of Antioch (d. 1151 or 1152). This bridge once spanned the Oreto River, which has now been diverted. Photo by author.

which are currently much drier than they were during the Middle Ages. The twelfth-century geographer al-Idrīsī and other visitors to the island also noted the many mills, streams, and irrigation systems that watered the gardens and orchards on the island. The once-wide Oreto River (see figure 1), running through Palermo, powered mills and watered gardens and orchards along its banks, according to the tenth-century observer Ibn Ḥawqal. Hot springs also dotted the island's landscape, and the twelfth-century visitor Ibn Jubayr mentioned that they were used in some places as public baths.

Covered in hills and mountains, two-thirds of the island rises to an elevation of one thousand feet or higher, and the soil is rocky and prone to erosion in most of the northern and eastern parts of the island.[44] The island's mountains have also played a significant role in its history, slowing attempts at conquest and allowing for pockets of resistance against invaders. Mountaintop fortresses and walled cities—like those at Termini and Cefalù, which were described by medieval visitors—aided in the island's defense. Some of these fortified cities were built during the period of Muslim dominion, and some during or after the Norman conquest.[45] The primary mountains of Sicily are an extension of the Apennine range that runs through the mainland of Italy. Sicily's

44. For terracing in general, see Delano Smith, *Western Mediterranean Europe*, 183–185.

45. See for example al-Idrīsī's twelfth-century account of the small coastal town of Caronia, where he noted the presence of an old fortress with a newly built citadel. Abū ʿAbd Allāh Muḥammad al-Idrīsī, *Opus Geographicum sive "Liber ad eorum delectationem qui terras peragrare studeant,"* ed. Enrico Cerulli and Francesco Gabrieli et al., 2nd ed. (Naples/Rome: Istituto Universitario Orientale di Napoli/Istituto Italiano per il Medio ed Estremo Oriente, 1970–1984), fasc. 5, 593–594.

highest range is called the Nebrodi Mountains, which reach from the toe of Italy westward toward the tip of North Africa along the northern length of the island. Much of the rest of Sicily is generally mountainous as well, with most of the island lying above one thousand feet. Mount Etna was a very active volcano throughout the Middle Ages and continues to be so today, producing fertile soil on its slopes and spectacular eruptions that have provoked comment from the island's many visitors.

Ports form another vital aspect of Sicily's geographical environment and the island's participation in seaborne travel.[46] The island's most active medieval port cities were Trapani on the western tip, Syracuse with its two natural harbors in the southeast, and Palermo and Messina on the northwest and northeast respectively. Other Sicilian ports included Catania and Marsala, and during the Muslim period we see ships docking near Māzara (modern Mazara del Vallo, referred to as Māzara in Latin sources), Girgenti (Agrigento), and al-Shāqqa (Sciacca) on Sicily's southern coast. These port cities, much more than inland towns and community centers, will be the focus of this book, since they were the points of connection between the island and other regions.

Because travel is the lens through which this book views Sicily, it is also important to understand the sea routes by which ships arrived at the island's ports. There is some dispute among scholars of the medieval Mediterranean about whether medieval sea-lanes were predetermined routes based on tradition, port availability, and weather patterns, or whether travel routes could vary with circumstances and conditions. John Pryor argues that medieval winds and weather conditions, in combination with the limitations of medieval naval technology, determined not only the routes that were most favored by commercial vessels but also the locations of the most important battles between the Christian and Muslim powers.[47] His conclusion was that the coastal journey along the north shore of the Mediterranean was greatly preferred to either a shorter passage across open waters or a journey along the southern shore of the sea, which had fewer natural safe harbors.[48] Taking advantage of islands and harbors, this northern route is supposed to have been preferred at all times, regardless of the religious or political affiliation of the ship's captain. Therefore, this *route des îles* depended, for greatest advantage, on control of

46. For a discussion of Mediterranean port types and their physical circumstances, see Delano Smith, *Western Mediterranean Europe*, 359ff.

47. See his statement that "certain aspects of the physical geography of the Mediterranean Sea, when considered in relation to the capabilities of the maritime technology of the time, exercised a profound effect on the course of conflict and competition between Islam and Christendom over a very long period of time." Pryor, *Geography*, xiv.

48. For more on the relative safety of the northern over the southern shore of the Mediterranean, see ibid., 21–24.

certain islands, of which the Balearics were most important in the western Mediterranean, Crete in the eastern basin of the sea, and Sicily in the center.[49] If Pryor's theory of trunk routes is correct, control of Sicily helped to determine the course of the "struggle" between Islam and Christianity in the Mediterranean.

To be sure, Sicily does lie on a crossing point within the east-west lanes of Mediterranean sea travel. Based on sea currents, wind patterns, and the limitations of medieval naval technology, this most-effective course through the Mediterranean followed a counterclockwise direction. According to Pryor, these trunk routes went from Alexandria to the Levantine coast, from there to Cyprus, Rhodes, and then to Crete before advancing north along the western coast of the Greek archipelago, across to Apulia in southern Italy, and then on to Calabria before touching on the eastern part of Sicily. At Sicily, Pryor notes, the trunk routes split, giving captains the choice of sailing north through the Strait of Messina and following the coastline of southern Europe all the way to the Strait of Gibraltar or heading south through the Sicilian Channel before traveling west to Sardinia and then either north to southern France or west to the Balearics via open water.[50] Eastward journeys originating in the western Mediterranean were easier to take due to the counterclockwise direction of the prevailing current patterns, but Pryor emphasizes that the island-to-island route along the northern shore of the Mediterranean was still much preferred. Such a route would have privileged both the Christian-held regions of the northern Mediterranean shores (and therefore Christian ships) and Sicily in particular as the largest of the islands in the chain and the one in the center of the entire sea, connecting the eastern and western basins of the sea.[51] This circumstance might suggest that whoever held Sicily could control the entire Mediterranean, but it more often happened that whichever power controlled the wider central Mediterranean region thus could and wanted to control Sicily.

In contrast to this geographical and climatological perspective, Horden and Purcell emphasized the importance of other factors that influenced connectivity within the Mediterranean outside of the standard trunk routes.[52] They pointed out that not only were the southern shores more often sailed than Pryor allows, but that the northern route was not uniformly preferred.[53] The

49. Ibid., 91–94.

50. Ibid., 7 and 87–101.

51. Sicily could also serve as a stopover for both southern and northern journeys. Ibid., 24.

52. Horden and Purcell, *Corrupting Sea*, 135ff.

53. Ibid., 139–140. See also Abraham L. Udovitch, "Time, the Sea, and Society: Duration of Commercial Voyages on the Southern Shores of the Mediterranean during the High Middle Ages," in

evidence in the following chapters shows that, in fact, Sicily's greatest connectivity was determined by political and economic associations rather than weather, currents, technology, or other influences that purportedly shaped the long-distance Mediterranean sea-lanes. So, too, did the island's most-used ports change—Messina was not, for example, always the most common port we see in the evidence and appears more prominently in the Norman-era sources than in earlier texts.

The primary routes of sea travel found in this study are those between Sicily and North Africa (Ifrīqiya), Egypt, and the eastern Mediterranean. Some westward sea travel between Sicily and Spain (al-Andalus) took place, certainly, but the relative amount of that travel seems to have been far lower than movement between the central and eastern Mediterranean zones. Many of the trips recorded from the period of our study thus contradict the expectations of Pryor's trunk route theory. The direct westward passage from Egypt, in fact, is found to have been quite common in Geniza letters that discuss the economic connections between Egypt, Ifrīqiya, and Sicily.[54] Vessels navigated the African coastline from Alexandria to Tripoli, at which point, Ruthi Gertwagen maintains, they could either head northwest to Sicily's southern shore by way of Malta or continue along the coastal route to al-Mahdiyya. Abraham Udovitch has utilized the Geniza records to collect data on the lengths of journeys along the southern Mediterranean shores, finding great variation in the times that it took to sail these paths. An average of three or four weeks was needed to pass from Alexandria to North Africa or Sicily, and only slightly less for trips proceeding from west to east.[55] The course of these voyages from Alexandria followed closely along the seashore until halfway to Tripoli, at which point ships moved farther out to sea. In addition to these long-distance routes, there were also a great number of shorter journeys that appear, from the evidence presented below, to have formed a significant part of Sicily's communication connections and that suggest greater possibilities for winter voyages than a

---

La navigazione mediterranea nell'alto Medioevo (Spoleto: Presso la sede del Centro, 1978), 503–546; and T. Lewicki, "Les voies maritimes de la Méditerranée dans le haut Moyen Âge d'après les sources arabes," in *La navigazione mediterranea nell'alto Medioevo* (Spoleto: Presso la sede del Centro, 1978), 447–453.

54. Ruthi Gertwagen, "Geniza Letters: Maritime Difficulties along the Alexandria-Palermo Route," in *Communication in the Jewish Diaspora: The Pre-modern World*, ed. Sophia Menache (Leiden: E. J. Brill, 1996), 73–91. See also the variety of routes taken by Geniza merchants as discussed in Jessica L. Goldberg, *Trade and Institutions in the Medieval Mediterranean: The Geniza Merchants and Their Business World* (Cambridge: Cambridge University Press, 2012), esp. 261–276 passim.

55. See his statement that "sailings from West to East, which could exploit the favorable prevailing northwesterly winds, travelled, perhaps surprisingly, only at a slightly more rapid rate than the journeys going in the opposite direction. This fact, too, corroborates our view, that while the wind was paramount in determining the duration of any sea voyage, even its impact was moderated and attenuated by practices and attitudes which were land based." Udovitch, "Time, the Sea, and Society," 514.

strict belief in the impassability of the Mediterranean by medieval ships in the winter would imply.[56]

Travel by land was, of course, never an option for the entire trip to or from an island, but it too played a role in Sicily's connections with other places in the Mediterranean world. During the Byzantine and Norman periods, for example, many travelers arrived on the island after an overland trip through Italy or made their way to Rome after docking at the island's ports (often first via Naples and then on to the land route). During the period of Muslim rule, many Geniza letters refer to bundles of goods that were transported by caravan across northern Africa and then shipped to Sicily from various Ifrīqiyan ports (the primary ones being Sūsa, Sfax, and al-Mahdiyya). In addition, not every long-distance trip across the Mediterranean necessarily stopped in Sicily, suggesting again that forces outside of geography determined the uses to which the island was put at various times. The operation of overland routes within northern Africa—connecting the central Mediterranean basin with either the western Mediterranean region (i.e., the Maghrib and Spain) or the eastern, via Egypt—in combination with the possibility of year-round sea voyages between North Africa and Sicily, meant that Muslim-ruled Sicily could maintain networks of exchange and communication with a wide swath of the Islamicate world as mediated by primarily overland routes—many of which would therefore not be described in the sources as travel to or from Sicily.

The island does not appear timelessly as the nexus of Mediterranean sealanes or at the crossroads of a wider system, and the communications and connections between Sicily and elsewhere depended upon economic, political, and religio-cultural factors much more than geographic ones. That is, the conceptual place of Sicily at a given moment in time was not determined by its location along shipping lanes or its geographical proximity to both northern and

56. In just one example, one of our twelfth-century travelers, Ibn Jubayr, noted that the path from Trapani, a major port in western Sicily, to North Africa was known to be navigable in all seasons. See also the findings of Horden and Purcell that year-round seafaring appears to have been more common in Mediterranean history than previously believed. "Potentially all-round connectivity was matched by potentially year-round enterprise." Horden and Purcell, *Corrupting Sea*, 143. Contrast this, however, with the conclusion by Abraham Udovitch concerning sea voyages in the southern Mediterranean that "the sailing season was scrupulously observed. Maritime commerce was firmly restricted to the months between April and late September. . . . I have not found a single example of a *commercial* voyage between Alexandria and North Africa in the eleventh century outside the normal months of the sailing season." Udovitch, "Time, the Sea, and Society," 532. This does not necessarily mean that Ibn Jubayr was uninformed, however. It is possible that the very short trip between western Sicily and North Africa was possible during winter precisely because it was so brief. His own journey to Sicily took him from Acre in October to Sicily in November, quite late in the season to be on the water.

southern shores of the Mediterranean, but by the purposes to which the island was put by its leaders and the connections they maintained to larger political-cultural units in the region. The Latin, Greek, and Muslim worlds exerted varying levels of "gravitational pull" that moved the island either nearer to or farther from their centers of power; at times the forces of attraction from different directions acted simultaneously to keep Sicily in tension between the three worlds. At other times, the island was drawn from one orbit into another. Such an analysis illuminates not only the particular linkages with which Sicily maintained contact with Constantinople, Rome, or Qayrawān, for example, but also the ways in which the three major political-religious civilizations of the medieval Mediterranean region interacted on and around Sicily, as a microcosm of more sweeping shifts and patterns within the Mediterranean system as a whole.

Sources

Not simply geography, then, but more complex combinations of need, opportunity, and interest determined when and to where Sicily was connected across the sixth to twelfth centuries. In order to understand these larger forces that worked to place Sicily either within or in relationship with the Greek, Latin, and Muslim worlds, we will examine, in the following chapters, the types of travelers—and thus the types of connections—that linked Sicily with other locations in the medieval Mediterranean at various times, and the ways in which those networks of travel and exchange shifted due to broader forces. The main categories of travelers include those on military, political, and diplomatic journeys (envoys, warriors, and officials), those traveling for intellectual or religious purposes (such as pilgrims, scholars, and geographers), and those on economic trips (merchants and the goods they shipped). I have found these travelers in a wide variety of texts from many locations throughout the Mediterranean: saints' lives, merchants' letters, Islamic legal decisions, chronicles, and others, in Greek, Latin, Judeo-Arabic, and Arabic. Each of these tidbits taken individually does not tell a complete story, but, accumulated and compared across periods of political change, they reveal patterns in which new links arose prior to military conquest, and old connections persisted despite political change.

One of the challenges of studying Sicily's medieval past with any specificity is the paucity of extant sources preserved on the island itself. Chronicles, chancery records, mercantile contracts, and biographical data are generally missing from Sicily in the Byzantine and Islamic periods, and although such sources begin to survive from the Norman period, there are far fewer than historians would wish for. Therefore, most of the texts used in this book originated outside of the island and sometimes only provide the briefest of glimpses of the island's shores. Essentially, then, I have accumulated anecdotes about people and goods that entered or left the island, with which I trace patterns and their transformations over time. This methodology allows me to view networks of communication from a variety of angles and across many centuries, but it also has its limitations. Firstly, there is little consistency over time in the types, genres, and languages of the sources available, making it difficult to compare them directly. While, for example, Latin papal letters and Greek saints' lives can provide a wealth of information about Byzantine Sicily, these sources disappear from view during the period of Muslim rule on Sicily when Arabic biographical dictionaries and *fatwās* (Islamic legal decisions) and Judeo-Arabic merchants' letters appear more prominently. Such changes in the source base over time necessitate a flexible approach to the kinds of data that can be gathered and the uses to which the material can be put.

A second hazard is that individual references may represent exceptions rather than the rule. There is, in fact, no way to know for sure whether a single act of travel simply tells us about one person or indeed represents masses of other travelers who do not appear in the sources. However, I have followed Michael McCormick in presuming that, for each act of travel we do see in a text, we must infer that a ship was available to transport that individual, that certain ports were open to welcome that and other ships, and that those ships followed routes of travel that were to some degree regularized—and that, therefore, other travelers must have made the same voyage during the same period, although they may have done so for various other reasons than our traveler.[57] Amassing as many data points as possible, even if they arise from different types of sources, also helps protect against the accusation that our anecdotes may be isolated cases.

Thirdly, many of these sources are themselves suspect, either for dealing with events that are clearly supernatural (such as miracle accounts) or for having been written with an obvious agenda or chronological distance (such as the Arabic chronicles and biographical dictionaries, which, though they typically contain materials copied from earlier texts, generally date from the thirteenth to fourteenth centuries). Throughout this book, I make it clear when my sources have such limitations. However, I take what could be termed a "maximalist" position on these texts and their utility. Even when they contain information that is clearly spurious or probably manufactured, I believe they

57. See also McCormick's defense against the question of whether isolated references should be viewed as the norm or the exception. McCormick, *Origins*, 3ff.

can teach us something about the attitudes and expectations of the text's author and audience. In other words, they depict acts of travel that must reflect a pattern of communication that either existed or was desired, remembered, or manufactured for particular reasons. Thus, for example, although I do not allege that a miracle-working saint did in actual fact take a magical journey from a Sicilian bathhouse to one in Constantinople in a single day, the description of such a journey by a hagiographer informs us of the desirability of an easy trip between the two locales. Therefore, I have endeavored to use all of the sources that are available and to try to learn from them whatever they have to tell me about the construction, memory, and desire for connection between Sicily and other places between the sixth and twelfth centuries.

Organization

Because each of the periods under consideration offers the historian radically different levels and types of extant source material, we cannot ask the exact same questions of each historical period. Instead, I have accumulated a series of stories about travelers in order to identify patterns within each of the periods of rule and across the transitions between them. This process is akin to assembling a puzzle with many of the pieces missing. The picture that emerges is not always complete, but I believe it is recognizable. In such a situation, it is important not to infer that the communications networks found in one period must have existed in others—we cannot presume that the blank spaces in our puzzle from one historical period look like the image we can see from another era. Indeed, the chapters that follow carefully set out what can and what cannot be known on the basis of the existing sources and thus how the nature of the sources shapes our understanding of Sicily within its Mediterranean context over time.

Chapter 1 begins with the Byzantine period of rule on Sicily (sixth to ninth centuries) and examines the web of connections linking the island to the Greek Christian world of the eastern Mediterranean and, simultaneously, to the Latin Christian world of Rome and the Franks. Travel along the Sicily–Constantinople route was most common in the early Byzantine period, but strong connections with Greek southern Italy, Frankish Aachen, and Latin Rome made the island a useful tool for Constantinople in its diplomatic and military relationships with the western regions. Indeed, this chapter shows that Sicily could and often did function as an extension of the political authority of Constantinople into Italy, which was both useful and necessary as part of the larger program of the empire at the time.

In chapter 2, treating the same centuries as the first chapter, we will see that Sicily began to be more connected to the Islamic world during the centuries prior to the Muslim conquest in the ninth century. Covering the period of transition to Muslim rule, this chapter shows that Sicily began to "drift" closer to Muslim northern Africa already in the seventh century. This growing relationship was established through a series of both military and diplomatic connections that brought Muslims into contact not only with Greek Christians in Sicily but also, due to the relationship between the island and Latin Christendom as seen in chapter 1, with Latin Christians. In some ways, then, we see Byzantine Sicily acting as a meeting ground in the central Mediterranean for Muslims, Greek Christians, and Latin Christians.

Chapter 3 covers the years of Muslim dominion (ninth to mid-eleventh centuries), when the island's ports were most regularly in communication with those of North Africa and Egypt. The largest body of evidence for these connections comes from merchant letters from the Cairo Geniza, which detail trade and migration. Through these data, we see Sicily deeply integrated into the regional trade networks that connected the Muslim-controlled power centers of the central Mediterranean. At the same time, geographical treatises in Arabic, representing the conceptual placement of Sicily within the wider Muslim world, place Sicily at the edge. As central as the island clearly was to economic communications in the central Mediterranean, there is reason to believe that, as a part of the wider dār al-Islām, Sicily was much more peripheral. Marginality does not necessarily mean that the island was somehow less important or valuable to the larger civilization of which it was a part; indeed, we will see that Sicily played very significant roles in the systems of the Muslim Mediterranean.

Chapter 4 considers the period of transition from Muslim to Latin Christian rule (mid-eleventh to twelfth centuries) to ask how the Christian conquest of Sicily affected the patterns of economic exchange established during the preceding centuries. Despite the military and political break, and the creation of a new border between Islam and Christianity, travelers from the Muslim world continued to sail to Christian Sicily and thus to cross the newly drawn border between territories that had been closely linked for centuries. Continuity, at least in some patterns of communication, marked the first century of Norman administration on the island.

Chapter 5, on the other hand, shows the discontinuities behind the apparent continuities in the Norman period of Sicily during the twelfth century. Here I examine the Muslim population of the island, as viewed from both inside and outside of Sicily, and Muslim reactions to living for the first time on the "wrong" side of the new boundary between religiopolitical cultures. While

Norman Sicily appears in many respects as a story of continuity—of maintained economic links with North Africa and the persistence of Muslim population on the island—it is also the case that these enduring connections to the Islamic world and the newly revived ones to the Greek world were manipulated by the Normans for novel reasons. They sought to bring their island fully into the center of the Mediterranean Sea and to use these connections to promote an image of themselves as powerful rulers in the "Mediterranean" style (as they perceived it). At the same time, the island's Muslim inhabitants were increasingly cut off from their coreligionists in the wider Muslim world, demonstrating the disjunction between the Norman self-presentation and the reality of life for the island's minority Muslim population.

Study of the Mediterranean and its societies, while not new, is of especially heightened interest right now among scholars of the premodern world.[58] This fact is due, in part, to the desire of a contemporary globalized world to look beyond political divisions and to examine the borderlands, the places of mixing and interaction, that help us to understand the cross-cultural relationships that matter to us today. Because the medieval Mediterranean region was inherently multicultural—a space where Christians, Muslims, and Jews from many different sects, communities, and polities interacted in a wide variety of ways, both peaceful and not—it is a vital region for asking and answering questions of concern to both medieval and contemporary people. Mediterraneanists, for example, have the opportunity to answer questions about how medieval peoples solved the problems of interreligious interaction, conflict over political and social boundaries, and the role of economic concerns in sociocultural and political relationships. This book seeks to contribute to these discussions by examining how one island was integrated into all of those systems both in turn and at once, how it formed a border between spaces of Muslim and Christian dominion, and also, at times, a zone of interaction between them, and how it served a variety of roles along these borders, depending on the needs and interests of its rulers and the communications networks in which the island was involved.

58. Many works of scholarship have been published that attempt to understand the Mediterranean region across huge spans of time. See David Abulafia, *The Great Sea: A Human History of the Mediterranean* (Oxford: Oxford University Press, 2011); and Cyprian Broodbank, *The Making of the Middle Sea: A History of the Mediterranean from the Beginning to the Emergence of the Classical World* (Oxford: Oxford University Press, 2013).

Chapter 1

Sicily between Constantinople and Rome

> Gregory then set sail from the city of Constantinople, and he reached the city of Rome on the twenty first day of the month of June, and there he worshipped the tombs of the holy and most praiseworthy Apostles, and visited every holy place in the city. . . . They [Gregory, his father, and ecclesiastical leaders] went on to a ship and left Rome of the sixteenth of the month of August, and reached Sicily on the tenth of September, landing in the city of Palermo. And the bishop of the city of Palermo welcomed them with great honour, surrounded by his clergy and all the citizens and all the monks and nuns.
>
> Leontios, *Vita S. Gregorii Agrigentini*[1]

Pilgrims, messengers, administrators, warriors, saints, and immigrants: Sicily's shores welcomed a wide variety of travelers during the period of Greek dominion. Between Emperor Justinian's reconquest of the island from the "barbarian" Ostrogoths in 535 CE and the Muslim invasion beginning in 827 CE, the imperial capital at Constantinople was the primary location that sent official travelers—governors, military forces, and envoys bearing news—to the island and received them in reply. It was also the destination of many traveling Sicilian saints and scholars, since the Greek city was the cultural as well as political capital of the Byzantine Empire. But Constantinople was by no means the only location that was closely linked with Sicily through patterns of travel and communication: many individuals, groups, and the goods and institutions they brought with them also arrived in Sicily from other locations of religious, cultural, and political significance throughout

1. Leontios, Presbyter of Rome, *Vita S. Gregorii Agrigentini*, *BHG* 707; *PG* 98, 550–715. This quote is taken from c. 38 and c. 47. English translation by John R. C. Martyn, *A Translation of Abbot Leontios' Life of Saint Gregory, Bishop of Agrigento* (Lewiston, NY: Edwin Mellen Press, 2004), 167, 177.

the Mediterranean (especially Rome and Jerusalem), thus tying Sicily into larger networks of culture, power, and communication in the early medieval Mediterranean region.[2]

The ports of Byzantine Sicily, indeed, bustled with ships sailing to and from Constantinople, Rome, Egypt, and North Africa. Muslims, Jews, Latins, and Greeks arrived on the island, at some times for peaceful purposes and at other times for war. The patterns of this travel demonstrate two of the fundamental aspects of the position and role of Sicily within the early medieval Mediterranean: Byzantine Sicily was both a center of political and cultural activity within the region and a shifting, unstable frontier between the three major civilizations of the Mediterranean basin. In these ways, the communication networks in which Greek Sicily was involved reflected many of the larger changes taking place within the early medieval Mediterranean. These were centuries in which Muslims, Latin Christians, Greek Christians, and, to an extent that is hard to quantify in this period, Jews interacted, fought, and shared common cultures, even as political and cultural boundaries in the region were beginning to harden.

Indeed, Sicily's geopolitical significance took on new meaning during the later centuries of the Byzantine period, as Muslim naval activity in the area intensified and Byzantium struggled to maintain its borders. Sicily under Byzantine rule operated both as the far western frontier of the empire (especially after the loss of Greek territory in mainland Italy to the Lombards, emphasized by the 751 fall of the Exarchate of Ravenna) and as a center of official communication between Constantinople and the western Mediterranean—particularly, Latin Rome and the emergent powers of Muslim North Africa and Frankish Europe. As the western bulwark of Byzantine power, Sicily was often the focus of intense military and political activity during these centuries. Constantinople was determined to maintain its hold over the island despite the difficulty of such a project when so many forces, both in the western Mediterranean and at home in Asia Minor, worked contrary to this agenda. Diplomatically, too, the Greeks often used the island as a site of political discussions, a source of envoys, or a resting place for messengers traveling from Constantinople to the European mainland. At the same time, Byzantine-controlled Sicily never fully pulled away from the orbit of Rome—the island featured both papal estates and numerous Latin Christian churches—and thus could act as a sort of meeting ground between the two Christian civili-

2. For Byzantine patterns of travel in general, see the essays in Macrides, *Travel in the Byzantine World*.

zations, which were growing increasingly apart in both administrative and cultural senses, especially after the mid-eighth century (see map 2). After the loss of North Africa to the Muslims in the seventh and eighth centuries, Sicily's importance to Constantinople was further magnified, even as the imperial government struggled to maintain its hold over this distant island in the face of growing Muslim military and naval dominance in the region. Thus, across the centuries from 535 to 827, the island operated both as a type of physical boundary—although an unstable and incomplete one—dividing the three civilizations of the early medieval Mediterranean and as a locus of cross-cultural communication between them. With ships, goods, information, and people moving between the Greek, Latin, and Muslim worlds via Sicily, the island was the site of overlap and conversation among the three civilizations, just as much as—or even more than—it marked a line of separation between them.

Several categories of travel and communication help to illuminate the system that developed in the central Mediterranean during these centuries. The first, and most prevalent, type of travel to and from Sicily during the Byzantine period was that conducted for political, military, or diplomatic reasons. The abundance of governmental travel in the extant sources is partly a result of the preservation of certain types of texts relating to the Byzantine centuries and partly due to the interests of those sources. Latin papal letters and

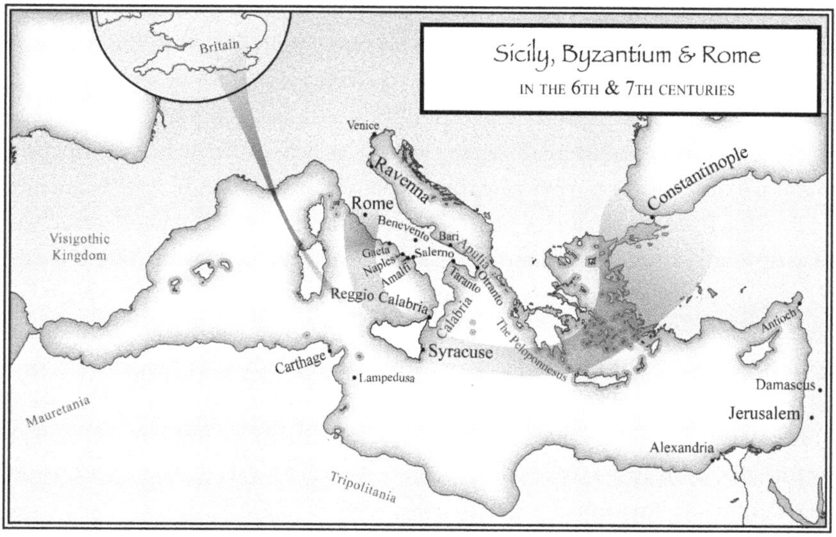

MAP 2. Sicily, Byzantium, and Rome in the sixth and seventh centuries

Latin and Greek chronicles reveal diplomatic and military travelers tasked with maintaining or restoring order in the empire's territories in Italy, negotiating with the popes in Rome, or, as we will see further in chapter 2, settling peace treaties with Muslim North Africa.

A second kind of traveler in the Byzantine Mediterranean world was those people who took to sea in the course of their religious careers, spiritual pilgrimages, and intellectual pursuits. A number of such travelers went to or through Sicily on their journeys to Rome, Jerusalem, or Constantinople, while others were born and raised on the island and traveled toward the intellectual and religious capital at Constantinople in order to advance their careers. Greek hagiographies from Sicily and southern Italy record the lives and deeds of Greek saints from the region, as well as their travels throughout the Mediterranean world. These hagiographical sources are particularly numerous for the ninth and tenth centuries, and they therefore provide instructive anecdotes about individual interactions between Greek monks and Muslim invaders to Sicily, such as monks who sailed on Muslim ships as captives or those who defended their lands against the Muslim raiders by miraculous means. Early medieval Latin pilgrimage accounts, papal letters, and papal biographies also inform us about travelers to Sicily from Europe.

A third type of travel was that which connected Sicily to broader economic networks within the Mediterranean system. Virtually none of the extant sources from this period directly pertain to commerce or the shipments of the grain *annona*.[3] Because this type of activity is so rarely represented in the surviving source material from the Byzantine era, definitive conclusions are impossible to establish. Interest in Sicily's contribution to the early medieval Mediterranean economy is persistent, however, particularly because of its historical status as a major source of grain for the Roman Empire. Nonetheless, as Michael McCormick has argued, it is possible to assume that shipments of merchandise hovered just below the surface of the travel for which we do have records: that is, for every sea voyage of a saint, official, or pilgrim, we might presume that an entire shipload of unrecorded mercantile products made the voyage as well. The bulk of the travel that we can trace may not have been explicitly economic, but it may imply economic exchange that would have taken place along similar routes and on the very same ships. Still, Sicily's economy in the Byzantine period is impossible to fully understand, and we are left with more questions than answers.

---

3. For an overview of the surviving sources, see McCormick, *Origins*.

Political, Diplomatic, and Military Connections to Constantinople

After Sicily was politically united to Constantinople in the sixth century—as part of Justinian's efforts to regain the lost glory of Rome by means of conquest in the western Mediterranean—it initially held the status of a *provincia* and was governed by a *praetor*, a civil provincial official in charge of local security, finances, and judicial affairs.[4] However, in the late seventh century, the island was designated a *theme*—a major military and territorial unit of the empire—after which time it was ruled by a *stratēgos*, a military general also responsible for financial and judicial administration.[5] Status as a *theme* raised the importance of Sicily within the empire, and particularly within its western regions.[6] At some point in the eighth century, Constantinople also took direct control of the ecclesiastical administration of Sicily, transferring it from the jurisdiction of Rome to that of the patriarch of Constantinople. Sicily's status as both a military and an ecclesiastical province necessitated a high level of communication between the island and the empire's distant capital. Given that most of the imperial holdings in the West would fall away over the course of the seventh and eighth centuries, maintaining control of Sicily was of high importance to Constantinople, even when that proved to be difficult, and therefore the patterns of communication between the two locations emphasize the island's significance in the empire.

Constantinople was an imperial capital that lay at a considerable distance from Sicily—roughly 1,300 nautical miles, depending upon the route taken—meaning that communication between the two places was a serious undertaking that

4. Rome sent the first *praetor* to Sicily in 227 BCE. On Sicily during the years before and after this development, see Serrati, "Garrisons and Grain," 115–133.

5. Byzantine provincial administration was based on the Roman model of *provincia* but was altered and enhanced throughout the centuries of rule from Constantinople. The system of *themes* was created to group Byzantine territories into large units that were ruled by a joint military and civil administration. See Salvatore Borsari, "L'amministrazione del tema di Sicilia," *Rivista storica italiana* 66 (1954): 131–158; Guillou, "La Sicile Byzantine," 98; and John F. Haldon, "Economy and Administration: How Did the Empire Work?," in *The Cambridge Companion to the Age of Justinian*, ed. Michael Maas (Cambridge: Cambridge University Press, 2005), 28–59.

6. On the integration of Byzantine Italy within the Byzantine Empire writ large, see Michael McCormick, "The Imperial Edge: Italo-Byzantine Identity, Movement and Integration, A.D. 650–950," in *Studies on the Internal Diaspora of the Byzantine Empire*, ed. Hélène Ahrweiler and Angeliki Laiou (Washington, DC: Dumbarton Oaks, 1998), 17–52. McCormick ponders whether there was consistency or transformation over time in regard to imperial appointments in Sicily and southern Italy versus local recruitment of civil and ecclesiastical administrators (see esp. 38–40). I do not have data complete enough to hazard an answer to that question.

necessitated a long and potentially dangerous journey by sea.[7] Nonetheless, the emperors at Constantinople regularly dispatched administrative officials and military forces to the island—even, sometimes, when the capital was under siege. This type of political communication between Sicily, as the province, and Constantinople, as its imperial capital, took place for a wide variety of reasons—from military actions and the suppression of rebellions to administrative updates, the transmission of important news, and personnel replacements.[8] Armies, naval fleets, governors, and administrators arrived on the island at various times to enforce the political order, restore central rule, or attempt to conquer or recover the island. Sometimes, directed by leaders from the capital, Sicilian governors or military troops were enlisted in movements against other regions—for example, Rome or Byzantine territories in Italy. At other times, Sicily itself was the target of military attacks or forceful attempts at restoring order after attempted rebellions. Through all of these acts of travel and communication, it is evident that Sicily played a key role in the western agenda of the Byzantine Empire. Without the ability to quantify the communications that linked the province and the capital, it is nonetheless possible to clearly see the vital role that Sicily played in the Byzantine conception of its empire and its role in the Mediterranean world system.

Between the sixth and ninth centuries CE, Sicily remained dependent on its political capital for governors, military leaders, and administrators, despite several attempts at revolt against Constantinopolitan authority. Local officials were appointed from Constantinople and often returned there when their service ended. Moreover, whenever a Byzantine Sicilian governor attempted to gain political independence, Constantinople was quick to quash the rebellion.

---

7. Given the variability of routes and winds, the distances and durations of premodern sea voyages are difficult to estimate. Jonathan Conant has estimated the length of sixth-century journeys from Constantinople to North Africa by way of Sicily as between 1,200 and 1,400 nautical miles, with journeys lasting between one and three months. The trip between North Africa and Sicily is itself only ninety nautical miles. See Jonathan P. Conant, *Staying Roman: Conquest and Identity in Africa and the Mediterranean, 439–700* (Cambridge: Cambridge University Press, 2012), 214–216, esp. table 4.3. The speed of sea travel could vary considerably, as Michael McCormick has demonstrated for the early medieval period. He points out, for example, that the ship on which Pope Martin I was taken captive (on which event see chapter 2) took seventy-eight days to sail from Messina to Constantinople, at an average speed of only one knot—far lower than the expected capability of contemporary ships; this average is thrown off by our ignorance of how long the layovers were at various ports along the way. See McCormick, *Origins*, 481ff. The locus classicus for medieval Mediterranean sea routes as they intersected with weather patterns and technology is Pryor, *Geography, Technology and War*, esp. his map, figure 2, on p. 14.

8. For an overview of the challenges of Constantinople's communication with its provinces throughout the existence of the Byzantine Empire, see Anna Avramea, "Land and Sea Communications, Fourth-Fifteenth Centuries," in *The Economic History of Byzantium*, ed. Angeliki E. Laiou (Washington, DC: Dumbarton Oaks, 2002), 57–90.

At the same time, Constantinople depended on Sicily and its governors both to maintain the conceptual boundaries between Byzantine and non-Byzantine territories and to push against those supposed borders, as well as to enforce Constantinople's will in the western Mediterranean. The balance of power between Greek Christian, Latin Christian, and North African Muslim polities in the central Mediterranean was maintained or upset, in large part, by means of communications in and through Sicily.

The very fact that Constantinople appointed, monitored, and replaced Sicily's governors necessitated the establishment of a fluid communications system between Constantinople and Syracuse. Administrative travel and the movements of Greek officials to the island and back created the sea route between Sicily and the eastern Mediterranean, a route which was then utilized for broader communications between province and capital. That Constantinople closely watched over the island's affairs is quite clear. For example, the letters of Gregory the Great (ca. 540–604, pope from 590), many of which refer to the administration, agriculture, and churches of Sicily, mention several times that a *praetor* had been replaced by Constantinople for his poor performance or misdeeds. During Gregory's pontificate, in fact, Sicily was ruled by four different *praetors*: Justin (590–592), who was replaced by Libertinus (593–598), then Leontius (598–600), and Alexander (600–?). In order for Constantinople to know about poor leadership in Sicily, there had to have been relatively regular communication between the two locales providing regular updates on provincial administration. Ships, messengers, overseers, and replacement officials—both seen in the sources and surmised from other evidence—must have arrived regularly at Sicily's ports and been dispatched from there on the voyage to Constantinople; this traffic was likely even more regular than our sources can reveal. Regular but unremarkable communications between province and center—tax collection, appointment of lower-ranking officials, and the sending of regular administrative news—necessitated frequent travel to and from Sicily's ports, but those acts might not have been deemed worthy of inclusion in the written records that survive.[9] And yet, the arrival and dispatch of news about the events in Sicily or Constantinople demonstrate that a significant pattern of communication existed between the two places.

---

9. For more on western Mediterranean ports in the context of the larger Byzantine Empire, see Philip De Souza, "Western Mediterranean Ports in the Roman Empire, First Century B.C. to Sixth Century A.D.," *Journal of Mediterranean Studies* 10 (2000): 229–254; Vera von Falkenhausen, "Reseaux routiers et ports dans l'Italie meridionale byzantine (Vie–XIe s.)," in *Hē Kathēmerinē zōē sto Vyzantio: tomes kai synecheies stēn Hellēnistikē kai Rōmaikē paradosē: praktika tou 1. diethnous symposiou, 15–17 Septemvriou 1988*, ed. C. G. Angelidē (Athens: Kentro Vyzantinōn Ereunōn / E.I.E., 1989), 709–731; and Elisabeth Malamut, *Les îles de l'Empire byzantin: VIIIe–XIIe siècles* (Paris: Universite de Paris, 1988).

Once established, these lines of regular ship traffic and communication could then be used for other purposes, such as mercantile, spiritual, and other types of journeys.

One of the most politically significant acts of travel between Constantinople and Sicily was the transfer of the imperial capital from Constantinople to Syracuse in 663 by Emperor Constans II (630–668, emperor from 641). His journey from Constantinople to the island was not taken via the direct sea route but was mediated through both Byzantine and Latin territories in mainland Italy, in reverse of many important diplomatic or military journeys between East and West that included a stop in Sicily: most often, we see political travelers from Constantinople stopping in Sicily before then traveling north into Italy. This move of the imperial administration to Sicily took place after Constans unsuccessfully attempted to defend Byzantine Italy from the Lombard invaders and then visited Rome.[10] He abandoned the military endeavor in Italy, retreated to Sicily, and set up his imperial residence in the provincial capital of Syracuse. During his time in Sicily, Constans fortified the island's navy and defensive structure and reformed the imperial mint at Syracuse.[11] His administrative and military concerns were thus clearly focused on Sicily itself, both as an important province within the empire and as an outpost of Byzantine power in the Mediterranean.

While the island served as the seat of the entire imperial government, Sicily's importance within the Byzantine Empire reached a high point, but this was an isolated episode of such imperial attention. Constans's imperial rule from Syracuse was cut short by his assassination in 668 CE and a subsequent attempted rebellion.[12] The emperor was murdered in the baths of Daphne in Syracuse by one of his servants, named Andrew son of Troilos, after which an Armenian named Mizizos was proclaimed emperor in Syracuse. Imperial agents quickly arrived from Constantinople, executed the rebel, and restored order to the island. The chronicler Theophanes attributed Constans's murder

10. For a Latin account of Constans's twelve-day visit to Rome and subsequent travel to Naples, whence he went to Syracuse via Reggio, see the *Life* of Pope Vitalian (657–672), *LP* I.LXXVIII, c. 135–136. This source also claims that Constans was an oppressive and unpopular ruler in Sicily, levying outrageous taxes and stealing from churches. See also John F. Haldon, *Byzantium in the Seventh Century: The Transformation of a Culture*, rev. ed. (Cambridge: Cambridge University Press, 1997), 59–63.

11. On Constans's time in Sicily and his naval reforms: Salvatore Cosentino, "Constans II and the Byzantine Navy," *Byzantinische Zeitschrift* 100, no. 2 (2008): 577–603; Pasquale Corsi, "Costante II e Siracusa," *Archivio storico siracusano*, 1985, 157–167; and Constantin Zuckerman, "Learning from the Enemy and More: Studies in 'Dark Centuries' Byzantium," *Millennium: Jahrbuch zu Kultur und Geschichte des ersten Jahrtausends n.Chr. / Yearbook on the Culture and History of the First Millennium C.E.* 2 (2005): 79–135.

12. Theophanes the Confessor, *Chronographia*, ed. Carl De Boor (Leipzig: B. G. Teubner, 1883), A.M. 6160.

to his unpopularity in Constantinople due to his rough handling of his opponents in the theological debate over the nature of Christ; he had several adversaries, including his brother Theodore, the Roman pontiff Martin (whom he had exiled), and the prominent spiritual leader Maximus the Confessor, but it is not clear who exactly was behind the emperor's death. On the other hand, the Latin life of Pope Vitalian in the *Liber Pontificalis* claims that Constans's death resulted from his tyrannical rule over the Sicilian population, suggesting that local governance rather than imperial politics was to blame for the failure of this experiment in having a western capital for the empire.[13]

Also unclear is Constans's motivation for abandoning the historical capital of Constantinople in favor of a distant island in the West. A complex combination of political and military needs may have prompted Constans's temporary westward move of the imperial court: that is, this may have been an attempt to reconfigure the empire with its capital closer to the "heart" of the Mediterranean (and closer to Rome) in response to contemporary events. The mid-seventh century saw the beginning of large-scale Muslim invasions of Byzantine territory, and Constans's activities in Sicily had the (temporary) effect of strengthening the island's resistance to the Muslim onslaught. Very early in his reign—prior to the relocation to Syracuse—Constans had had to contend with the loss of Alexandria (abandoned by the Byzantine garrison in 642) and Arab movement west into Byzantine North Africa. Constans's empire also faced Muslim assaults in Anatolia and Armenia and the first Muslim naval strikes into the Mediterranean. He responded to the attacks of Arab ships on eastern Mediterranean islands by initiating diplomatic contact with Muʿāwiya ibn Abī Sufyān (governor of Syria from 640, caliph, 660/661–680), but warfare within the Mediterranean continued.

Constans's transfer to the western capital, therefore, may have been part of an effort to fortify the position of Sicily in the Mediterranean against the Muslim naval threat, shoring up Constantinople's western provincial outpost and thus, by extension, protecting Constantinople itself.[14] It is also possible that the move may have been intended to shift the center of the empire westward, away from the increasingly aggressive Muslim state, based in nearby

---

13. *Life* of Pope Vitalian (657–672), *LP* I.LXXVIII, c. 135–136. The execution of the rebel—and the dispatch of his head to Constantinople—is found in the *Life* of Pope Adeodatus II (672–676), *LP* I.LXXVIII, c. 137. For the Muslim raid on Sicily that followed this rebellion, see chapter 2.

14. J. B. Bury saw in Constans's residence at Syracuse a fully developed policy to shore up the western defenses of the empire in order to protect not only the island of Sicily but also the entire western arm of Byzantium. John B. Bury, "The Naval Policy of the Roman Empire in Relation to the Western Provinces from the 7th to the 9th Century," in *Scritti per il centenario della nascita di Michele Amari* (Palermo: Societá siciliana per la storia patria, 1910), 21–34.

Damascus.[15] However, Constans's son, Constantine IV, continued to fulfill some functions of the imperial government from Constantinople while his father was in Syracuse; Constantinople was not completely abandoned, and indeed the imperial administration returned there after Constans's murder. Whatever the specific motivation—whether for defense or for offense—it is clear that seventh-century Sicily was considered vital to the safety of the Byzantine government and useful as a possible bulwark against Muslim advances. Nonetheless, as will be seen in the following chapter, Sicily during this period began to experience the first of a century-long series of semi-regular raids on its southern shores by Muslim forces from North Africa, bringing the island slowly into the orbit of the dār al-Islām even as Greek emperors struggled to maintain the island's position within the Byzantine Empire.

Constans's move may also have been a political decision to protect himself from enemies in Constantinople. Sicily was often utilized as a site of exile for political enemies of the imperial family, and a type of self-exile may have been one of the motives for the transfer by the emperor, who had made plenty of enemies with his policies on matters of theological doctrine. Sicily's status as a *theme* provided Constans with a location that was at once far from the center of action in Constantinople and administratively important enough to serve as the capital of the empire. Moreover, Syracuse and Constantinople needed to have already had a regular and dependable flow of communications between them in order for the Sicilian capital to have served, even briefly, as a viable seat of rule for the empire as a whole. The preexistence of this communications system shows that the Byzantines had been sending governors and officials and messengers to the island regularly—in fact, much more regularly than the extant sources demonstrate—and that Constans knew he could rule adequately from there. This already-established route of communications facilitated the transfer of the central government to such a (relatively) remote edge of the empire and allowed for the flow of information from the periphery necessary for governance of the center. At the same time, the location of the imperial government in Sicily would not and could not have taken place if the island had not been considered an integral part of the imperial agenda in relation to the western Mediterranean powers.

15. George Ostrogorsky saw in this move a combination of personal motivation—escaping from a Constantinople where Constans had lost support—and an attempt to incorporate the western Mediterranean more deeply into the empire. George Ostrogorsky, *History of the Byzantine State*, trans. Joan Hussey, rev. ed. (New Brunswick, NJ: Rutgers University Press, 1969), esp. 121–123.

The choice of a borderland region as a temporary imperial capital also speaks to the importance of the western frontier zone in seventh-century Byzantium. While much of the historical scholarship has focused on the Syrian frontier with Islam and the Balkan frontier with the Slavs, the western frontier with Islam was also clearly considered vital for protecting Byzantine interests. This was an empire focused on its *limes*—its boundaries with the Latin world, the Greek territories in southern Italy that were breaking away, the Bulgars and other groups on the Balkan frontier, and the Muslim world on the Syrian frontier and, indeed, in the central Mediterranean region.[16] Constans's decision may have been one intended to shore up the frontier in one region, by means of his imperial presence; if so, his choice to strengthen an island in the Mediterranean, rather than the Syrian or Balkan frontier, may reflect his perspective on the importance of this particular border zone within the empire as a whole.

Although the presence of the imperial administration and court in Sicily was brief, Constantinople continued to send officials, messengers, and administrators to Sicily on a regular basis. Many official visits to Sicily from Constantinople were occasioned by violent incidents and rebellions on the island, much like the one following Constans II's assassination. For example, Theophanes the Confessor (d. 818) notes in his *Chronographia* that in 718 Emperor Leo III (r. 717–741) dispatched to Sicily a man named Paul, whom he appointed to be the *stratēgos* (general) for the island.[17] Paul traveled with a group of imperial guards charged with regaining control over the island after Sergius, the previous governor, had rebelled against Constantinople and declared a rival emperor in Syracuse. This Sicilian rebellion took place during a massive Muslim siege of Constantinople (717–718), but the emperor was nonetheless willing and able to dispatch officers to quell it and thus maintain control over the

16. The study of the Syrian frontier is extensive. See, for example, on warfare in that region, John F. Haldon and Hugh Kennedy, "The Arab-Byzantine Frontier in the Eighth and Ninth Centuries: Military Organisation and Society in the Borderlands," *Zbornik radova Vizantološkog instituta* 19 (1980): 79–116, repr. in Hugh Kennedy, *The Byzantine and Early Islamic Near East* (Aldershot: Variorum, 2006), VIII; Michael Bonner, "Some Observations concerning the Early Development of Jihad on the Arab-Byzantine Frontier," *Studia Islamica* 75 (1992): 5–31, repr. in *Arab-Byzantine Relations in Early Islamic Times*, ed. Michael Bonner, 401–427 (Aldershot: Ashgate, 2004); and Michael Bonner, *Aristocratic Violence and Holy War: Studies in the Jihad and the Arab-Byzantine Frontier* (New Haven, CT: American Oriental Society, 1996). For the impact of this warfare on the economy and settlement patterns in the area, see Michael Decker, "Frontier Settlement and Economy in the Byzantine East," *Dumbarton Oaks Papers* 61 (2007): 217–267. For the Balkan frontier of Byzantium, see, among others, Paul Stephenson, *Byzantium's Balkan Frontier: A Political Study of the Northern Balkans, 900–1204* (Cambridge: Cambridge University Press, 2000).

17. Theophanes, *Chronographia* A.M. 6210, I.398.6–20.

government of Sicily.[18] He clearly considered it to be in the empire's best interest to deploy the resources necessary to do so, even in the face of threats to the imperial capital, a conclusion suggesting that the loss of the western frontier would also threaten the center of Byzantium.

The final outcome of this story, and its analysis by Theophanes, shows that the maintenance of order in and control of Sicily was of central importance for the entirety of Byzantium's western possessions. The rebel Sergius fled to the Lombards in Calabria, leaving behind his puppet emperor Basil (renamed Tiberius), whom the imperial appointee Paul beheaded alongside the rebellious generals. Those heads were sent back to Constantinople while Paul remained on the island to enforce order. According to Theophanes, "As a result, great order prevailed in the western parts . . . all the western parts were pacified."[19] Pacifying Sicily was thus equated with bringing order to all of Byzantium's western holdings.

Sergius's rebellion was not the only such uprising on the part of the Sicilian Greek leaders. Sicily's significant distance from Constantinople, and its position at the edge of the empire, meant that, despite imperial efforts to control the island, it was in a prime location for those wishing to break free from Byzantine central authority. Likewise, the relative independence from Constantinople of the southern Italian Greek cities may have provided a model for the aspirations of Sicilian governors hoping for greater local power. In 780/781, for example, the Sicilian ruler Elpidios rebelled against imperial authority after having been in office only a few months. In response, the empress Irene (regent, 780–797, regnant, 797–802) commanded a *spatharios* (a member of the imperial guard) named Theophilos to sail to Sicily and arrest Elpidios, but the Sicilians refused to hand the latter over.[20] The following year, Irene sent to Sicily an entire fleet, led by an official named Theodore, to put down the revolt; the Byzantine forces at last triumphed over the rebels.[21]

The latter rebellion took place during a period of peace between Byzantine Sicily and Muslim North Africa—a pause in the semiregular raids on Sic-

18. For more on this attack and the turmoil in Byzantium during the reign of Leo III the Isaurian (717–741), see Warren T. Treadgold, *A History of the Byzantine State and Society* (Palo Alto, CA: Stanford University Press, 1997), 346–356. There is significant historiographical debate on whether it was also Emperor Leo III who transferred ecclesiastical control of Sicily (and other western provinces) from Rome to the patriarch of Constantinople, in an attempt to bolster Constantinople's control over these western regions, or whether this transfer had taken place prior to his time. For the debate and bibliography, see Haldon, *Byzantium in the Seventh Century*, 90, n. 132; and Vivien Prigent, "Les empereurs isauriens et la confiscation des patrimoines pontificaux d'Italie du sud," *Mélanges de l'École Française de Rome, Moyen Âge* 116, no. 2 (2004): 557–594.

19. Theophanes, *Chronographia* A.M. 6210, I.398.6–20.

20. Ibid. A.M. 6273, I.454.28–30.

21. Ibid. A.M. 6274, I.454.26–9.

ily's southern shores that will be detailed in chapter 2. This peace between Syracuse and Qayrawān was one of several treaties that halted the regular raiding parties from Egypt and Ifrīqiya that had been attacking the island for around a century by that point.[22] The initial aim of these raids does not appear to have been the conquest of the island, but rather the collection of booty and slaves. Nonetheless, Greek Sicily was facing regular security threats that prompted Constantinople to increase its grip on the island. The late eighth century was a time when Constantinople tried to preserve Sicily as a Byzantine stronghold in the Mediterranean, perhaps fearing that the island's loss would spell the end of Byzantine power in the western Mediterranean. At the time, Byzantium maintained only loose control over other formerly Greek lands in Italy, having lost direct influence in the majority of southern Italy. Even the Exarchate of Ravenna had been drifting away from Greek control and functioned independently in many arenas; it would fall to the Lombards in 751, leaving Sicily as the last holdout of direct Byzantine power in the West. Despite Irene's successful defense of Sicily against internal rebellion, less than fifty years later the island would fall under Muslim control, and Constantinople would never again wield great influence in the western Mediterranean.[23] The imperial government could not know this future, however, and the continued efforts (even until the eleventh century) to reclaim the island demonstrate Sicily's centrality in the Byzantine agenda.

That said, not all of the acts of travel between Constantinople and Syracuse indicate the island's importance to the empire; in fact, some imply nearly the opposite. At several points during the eighth century's political tumult, for example, Sicily served as a place of exile for political rebels whom the Byzantine ruler wanted to keep far away from the political center of Constantinople. Theophanes's *Chronographia* mentions several cases of political exiles who were sent to Sicily so that they could not continue to cause trouble in the imperial capital. Despite the island's history as a site of repeated rebellions, Sicily presented itself to some emperors as an expedient spot for marginalizing political troublemakers. In these cases, the distance between the two locations was key to the effectiveness of the political move.

22. The dating of the earliest Muslim attacks on Sicily is uncertain. See chapter 2 for a discussion of the raids and the diplomatic efforts between Sicily and Qayrawān after the initiation of these raids.

23. Byzantine rulers attempted to regain control of Sicily a number of times during the ensuing centuries, but none of those attempts was successful. For details, see chapter 3. Byzantium also maintained a level of influence over some regions of southern Italy, but direct rule in Italy was on the decline. For more on southern Italy in the ninth and tenth centuries, see Barbara M. Kreutz, *Before the Normans: Southern Italy in the Ninth and Tenth Centuries* (Philadelphia: University of Pennsylvania Press, 1996); and Vera von Falkenhausen, "Between Two Empires: Byzantine Italy in the Reign of Basil II," in *Byzantium in the Year 1000*, ed. Paul Magdalino (Leiden: E. J. Brill, 2003), 135–159.

In 789/790 both Emperor Constantine VI (780–797) and his mother, Empress Irene, banished their political rivals to Sicily.[24] Constantine VI likewise sent rebels to exile on this and other islands in the year 792/793.[25] Distance and relative inaccessibility were vital for keeping an exiled person far from the center of political power. However, because Constantinople maintained regular communications with Syracuse, it was possible for the rulers to remain aware of the activities of their exiles. It is important to note that Sicily was not the only location chosen for receiving political deportees, as there were many islands closer to Asia Minor that routinely served as places of exile, such as the Princes Islands in the Sea of Marmara and Aegean islands such as Patmos. In some cases, Sicily may have been preferred because a particular governor of Sicily was deemed to be trustworthy in safeguarding against rebel activities. In any event, the island was both geographically far from the capital and conceptually near to it—near enough that the imperial government could keep a close watch on its rivals' actions, by means of established networks of communication. Thus, it seems, Sicily could be considered both close to and far from Constantinople, depending on the political need.

While geographically distant from Constantinople, the island was directly adjacent to Greek-claimed territories in southern Italy. Proximity to these Greek regions of southern Italy was thus another advantage Sicily had in its political utility for Constantinople. During its years under Byzantine rule, Sicily often functioned as a link between Constantinople and the Byzantine territories in mainland Italy, both as a transit point for messengers and as a base for enforcing order in Italy, particularly when the mainland Greek cities were more successful in their efforts to establish their independence from imperial rule. Greek imperial officers often sailed to Sicily and stayed there briefly before taking the land or sea route to Greek lands in Italy.

One example of Constantinople's use of Sicilian government officials against Byzantine territories in Italy occurred around the year 709. Felix, archbishop of Ravenna (r. 705–723), attempted to liberate his city from Byzantine rule, and so Emperor Justinian II (669–711, r. 685–695 and 705–711) sent the governor of Sicily, Theodorus, to take hold of Felix and the rebels. Theodorus and the Greek fleet sailed from Sicily to Ravenna to carry out the order. He arrested and shackled the rebels aboard a ship, alongside the riches they had purportedly stolen, and sent them to Constantinople.[26] Felix was exiled to Pontus until around 712,

---

24. Theophanes, *Chronographia* A.M. 6282, I.464.25–465.5.

25. Ibid. A.M. 6285, I.469.11–15.

26. The *Life* of Pope Constantine (708–715), *LP* I.XC, c. 170. See also Bishop of Ravenna Agnellus, *Liber pontificalis ecclesia Ravennatis*, ed. Claudia Nauerth, 2 vols., Fontes Christiani (Freiburg: Herder, 1996).

when the next emperor, Philippicus, restored him to the church in Ravenna and had him sent back there with an escort, again by way of Sicily.[27] Sicily does not necessarily lie on the most obvious route between Ravenna and Constantinople, and, notably, other trips between the two cities did not always involve Sicily. Therefore, on these trips there must have been compelling but unstated reasons for the entourage to stop on the island. It is not clear from the text if Sicilian officials were involved in this return trip or why Sicily was the chosen route between Constantinople and Ravenna. Nonetheless, this anecdote allows us to see Sicily and its officials as key factors in Constantinople's attempts to maintain power in southern Italy, even when geography was not the determining reason for using Sicily as a way station along the journey.

The *Royal Frankish Annals* contain a reference to similar activity in the year 788. It is recorded that Emperor Constantine VI ordered the governor Theodorus to destroy the city of Benevento in revenge for the emperor not having received Charlemagne's daughter as his wife.[28] The Byzantine forces traveled from Sicily to Calabria, where they met the Frankish-allied Beneventan troops in battle but were defeated. Thus we again see a Sicilian governor tasked with carrying out imperial edicts on the mainland. While its placement close to mainland Italy certainly made the island useful geographically, the presumed ability of the island's officials to raise appropriate armies and attack the mainland, along with the trust the emperor placed in those distant representatives to carry out such campaigns, demonstrates the island's conceptual utility to the Byzantine Empire. Sicily was not simply a distant province at the periphery of the empire but was at times an integral extension of the central authority of Constantinople.

In general, then, early medieval Sicily's communications with Constantinople show the island in a number of important roles: a site of political rebellion and exile, an agent of imperial authority within Italy, and a stronghold of Byzantine power along the vulnerable three-way border at the far western edge of the empire. Sicily and its governors acted in the West as an extension of Constantinople, relying on a steady stream of officials, news, messengers, and troops between the capital and the island. The island also functioned as a specific site of imperial authority when it was the temporary capital of the empire under Constans II, and even though this was a brief and isolated instance, it demonstrates the multiple ways in which Sicily was deemed central to the goals and safety of the Byzantine Empire as a whole. As the bulwark of Byzantine

---

27. Agnellus, *Liber pontificalis ecclesia Ravennatis*, c. 145.

28. *Annales regni Francorum, inde ab a. 741. usque ad a. 829*, ed. F. Kurze, *MGH, Scriptores rerum Germanicarum in usum scholarum*, vol. 6 (Hannover, 1895). The year 788 contains this note: "Interea Constantinus imperator propter negatam sibi regis filiam iratus Theodorum patricium Siciliae praefectum cum aliis ducibus suis fines Beneventanorum vastare iussit."

power in the central Mediterranean, Sicily both protected the empire's western edge and represented imperial authority in the region. And, in the case of revolt against Constantinople, the island could serve as a base for rival power and as a stepping-stone to the center of the empire: if rebels were to gain power on the island, they might be able to use the established relationship between Syracuse and Constantinople to assert their claim to authority over all of Byzantium. Even when the emperors were distracted by business closer to home, the imperial authorities strenuously worked to maintain their hold over Sicily. By keeping control of this island borderland, the Byzantines were able to use Sicily in the enforcement of their will in Italy as well as in diplomatic relationships with sites of power in the Latin world, Rome, and the Frankish court (represented by Aachen) and, after the mid-seventh century, with the new centers of Muslim power in North Africa.

Political, Diplomatic, and Military Connections to Latin Christendom

While Sicily functioned as an important Byzantine borderland in the western Mediterranean and maintained close communications with Constantinople, ties between Sicily and Rome and the Latin world also remained strong. Having been a Roman province for several centuries, the island featured a population with many Latin speakers and numerous Latin churches. Due also to the persistence of communication networks between Rome and Sicily, the island was never fully detached from the Latin West in terms of culture, religion, and, to some degree, politics. Simply because the island shifted from Roman to Germanic and then to Greek administration does not mean that cultural or social connections between the island and Rome were severed. The endurance of these links is partly due to the continued presence of a Latin population and the maintenance of papal estates on the island, and many Sicilians remained adherents of the Latin Church. Simultaneous connections to Rome and to Constantinople allowed the island to function, in some ways, as part of both the Latin and Greek worlds and therefore as a vital point of connection between them. Thus, in addition to functioning as a link between Constantinople and the Byzantine-claimed territories in mainland Italy—both as a transit point for messengers and as a base for enforcing order in Italy—Sicily could serve as a mediator in communications between Constantinople and Rome.[29]

---

29. For more on the chaotic political scene of early medieval southern Italy, see among others: Kreutz, *Before the Normans*; Vera von Falkenhausen, *La dominazione bizantina nell'Italia meridionale dal*

Indeed, Sicily functioned as an important node in the networks of communication that existed between emperors in Constantinople and popes, kings, and emperors in the West. In terms of papal-imperial business and diplomacy, Sicily appears to have been a regular stop on the route between Constantinople and Rome, although it was not the only path for information or messengers between the two places.[30] Official and political business between Rome and Constantinople was conducted often by way of Sicily and, it appears, less often via an overland route. Many early medieval travelers between Constantinople and Italy made Sicily a way station on their travels, even if their business did not directly involve the island. For example, in 653 Pope Martin I (649–655) was arrested in Rome and taken by ship to Constantinople. The journey, which lasted from the middle of June until mid-September, followed a route through Sicily as well as many other Mediterranean ports.[31] In this case, even though the affair had nothing to do with Sicily, a Sicilian Byzantine official was involved in the delegation sent to Ravenna. A similar journey took place in 709, when Pope Constantine (708–715) answered a summons by the Byzantine emperor Justinian II to appear at Constantinople. The papal party, as detailed in the pope's *vita* in the *Liber Pontificalis*, journeyed to the Byzantine capital by way of Sicily, although their return trip did not follow the same route, and they skipped Sicily on that second leg.[32] Evidently, therefore, various itineraries were available for travelers between mainland Italy and the Byzantine capital during the early eighth century. Sicily was, however, an obvious choice of route when the pope and his entourage were traveling on the orders of the

---

IX all'XI secolo (Bari: Ecumenica Editrice, 1978); and Vera von Falkenhausen, "A Provincial Aristocracy: The Byzantine Provinces in Southern Italy (9th–11th Century)," in *The Byzantine Aristocracy, IX to XIII Centuries*, ed. M. Angold, BAR International Series 221 (Oxford: B.A.R., 1984), 211–235. The equally complex religious situation in the region is addressed by Valerie Ramseyer, *The Transformation of a Religious Landscape: Medieval Southern Italy, 850–1150* (Ithaca, NY: Cornell University Press, 2006).

30. For the background of papal-imperial relations more broadly at this time, see Judith Herrin, "Constantinople, Rome, and the Franks in the Seventh and Eighth Centuries," in *Margins and Metropolis: Authority across the Byzantine Empire* (Princeton, NJ: Princeton University Press, 2013), 220–238.

31. This journey is reconstructed from both the *Life* of Pope Martin (649–655), *LP* I.LXXVI and Martin's letters, collected in *Narrationes de exilo sancti Martini* (*BHL* 5592), which is edited and translated by Bronwen Neil in *Seventh Century Popes and Martyrs: The Political Hagiography of Anastasius Bibliothecarius* (Turnhout: Brepols, 2006). In the second letter of Martin to Theodore in Neil's translation (172–221, esp. c. 9, pp. 180–183), Martin claims that his prison-boat ("navis, id est carcer meus," line 15) departed from Rome on June 17 and arrived in Messina on July 1. Michael McCormick has pieced together the various sources to reconstruct the entire route and duration of the trip. McCormick, *Origins*, 483–488.

32. "Pontifex cum suis Siciliam perrexit, ubi Theodorus patricius et stratigos, langore detentus, occurrens pontifici magna cum veneratione salutans atque suscipiens, medellam adeptus est celerem." *Life* of Pope Constantine, *LP* I.XC, c. 172. For more on this pope's journey in its entirety, see Alessandro Taddei, "Some Topographical Remarks on Pope Constantine's Journey to Constantinople (AD 710–711)," *Eurasian Studies* 11 (2013): 53–78.

Byzantine emperor or through the political agency of Sicilian officials—even when they did not have any particular business to transact on the island. This fact may have been due to a larger number of Constantinople-bound ships sailing from Sicilian ports than from other ports in Italy. Likewise, Sicily's importance as a transit point for papal-imperial business may have resulted from the involvement of Greek Sicilian officials as representatives of the imperial government. In either case, officials frequently chose routes involving Sicily over other routes to Constantinople; that is, Sicily often found itself at the nexus of Byzantine-Latin relationships even when a stopover there was not necessitated by the involvement of Sicilian personnel.

There is also evidence that, during the seventh through ninth centuries, Roman Church officials traveled to Sicily on administrative business that did not involve transactions with Greeks. Representatives of the Latin Church at Rome traveled to the island to govern the Latin churches there and the agricultural lands in papal estates. The papal patrimony in Sicily was concentrated in the cities of Syracuse and Palermo, and some Sicilian lands were also held by the churches of Milan, Ravenna, and other mainland Italian cities.[33] Latin sources show that early medieval popes frequently traveled to Sicily, either personally or via their officials, on routine affairs of land and church administration. Papal visits to Sicily are recorded from the sixth century and continued at least through the eighth century. One of the earliest papal visitors, Pope Vigilius (537–555), arrived on the island very soon after Justinian's reconquest of Sicily from the Goths: he traveled from Rome to the Sicilian city of Catania, where he appointed priests and deacons.[34] He then sailed to Constantinople in order to negotiate with the emperor Justinian I (r. 527–565) and empress Theodora (500–548) about a dispute over ecclesiastical leadership. Later, after an illness, Vigilius died in Syracuse, whence his body was taken to Rome for burial.[35] Vigilius obviously deemed the island useful both as a stopover en route to the eastern Mediterranean and as a significant place within the wider Latin Church. Other popes and their officials, throughout the sixth through ninth

33. Papal lands throughout the Mediterranean world are discussed by Thomas F. X. Noble, *The Republic of St. Peter: The Birth of the Papal State, 680–825* (Philadelphia: University of Pennsylvania Press, 1984), 10–11 passim. Many of the letters of Gregory the Great deal with matters of administration of these papal estates and Latin Christian churches on the island; in fact, he wrote more letters to the administrators of the patrimony in Sicily (seventy-four) than to those of all other papal patrimonies combined. For an introduction to the papal patrimony in Sicily and a list of Gregory's letters to its administrators, see Martyn, *Letters of Gregory the Great*, vol. 1, 91ff. For two of the most regular correspondents who held the position of administrator of the patrimony, Peter the Subdeacon and Maximian, see Martyn, *Letters of Gregory the Great*, vol. 1, 98–99.

34. *Life* of Pope Vigilius (537–555), *LP* I.LXI, c. 105.

35. Ibid., c. 108, l.11–12.

centuries, likewise traveled to Sicily regularly, demonstrating the island's integral position in the Mediterranean system and its role as a node of Rome-Constantinople communications.

This integration of Greek-ruled Sicily with the church in Rome is most evident in the corpus of letters written by Gregory the Great (pope from 590 to 604). Pope Gregory maintained continuous contact with Sicily and left a series of letters concerning the island that serves as the most important source of information about Sicily in the sixth century. For example, one of Gregory's earliest extant letters, written in 590, was sent to all of the island's bishops, and in it he appointed Peter as his subdeacon on the island, in charge of administering the Sicilian patrimony on the pope's behalf.[36] Throughout his letters, Gregory shows himself to have been deeply concerned with the political, ecclesiastical, and economic affairs of the island. Also the personal owner of extensive lands and the founder of several monasteries in Sicily, Gregory remained, throughout his papacy, in regular contact with his agents and with the Roman clergy on the island.[37] He intervened often in the affairs of the Sicilian churches, appointed and corresponded with local bishops, founded monasteries and convents on Sicily, and kept a watchful eye on the Greek *praetors* who ruled the island on behalf of Constantinople.[38] For example, he wrote a letter in 590 to Justin, the *praetor* of Sicily, in which he noted that he would be closely observing Justin's administration of the island.[39]

The connection between Greek Sicily and the church at Rome continued throughout the seventh and eighth centuries, even at the highest level of church authority.[40] In fact, several popes from those years were born and educated on the island, some from the Latin population and some from the Greek.[41] Pope Agatho (r. 678–681) was originally from Sicily (*natione Sicula*), although very little is known of his life there; he seems not to have maintained a particularly

36. Gregory the Great (Gregorius Magnus), *Registrum epistularum libri*, Epis. 1.1.

37. For a study of the people who transmitted Gregory's letters to the island, see John R. C. Martyn, *Pope Gregory's Letter-Bearers: A Study of the Men and Women Who Carried Letters for Pope Gregory the Great* (Newcastle: Cambridge Scholars Publishing, 2012).

38. For a discussion of Gregory's several letters that address issues concerning the island's Jewish population—virtually the only source to mention this community during the Byzantine period—see Schlomo Simonsohn, *Between Scylla and Charybdis: The Jews in Sicily* (Leiden: E. J. Brill, 2011), 12–14.

39. This letter also briefly discusses the business of the grain allowance from Sicily to Rome. Gregorius Magnus, *Registrum epistularum libri*, Epis. 1.2.

40. On the foundation of Greek monasteries in Rome in these centuries, and the possible origins of their founders, see McCormick, "The Imperial Edge," 31–32, and n. 29.

41. For one perspective on the broader religiopolitical significance of these Sicilian-born popes, see Thomas F. X. Noble, "Greek Popes: Yes or No, and Did It Matter?," in *Western Perspectives on the Mediterranean: Cultural Transfer in Late Antiquity and the Early Middle Ages, 400–800 AD*, ed. Andreas Fischer and I. N. Wood (London: Bloomsbury, 2014), 77–86.

close relationship with the island.[42] Likewise born in Sicily was Pope Leo II the Younger (682–683), who was renowned for his knowledge of both Greek and Latin; his biographer asserts that he translated into Latin the acts of the Third Council of Constantinople (680–681), which condemned Monothelitism.[43] Another seventh-century pope, Conon (686–687), was born in Greece but was raised and educated in Sicily before he traveled to Rome and took leadership of the Latin Church.[44] Also raised and educated in Sicily was Pope Sergius I (687–701), whose father, Tiberius, was of Syrian origin, having migrated to Palermo (called at the time Panormus; see figure 2) from Antioch.[45] Likewise, Pope Stephen III (768–772) was born in Sicily and moved as a youth to Rome, where he became a cleric and a monk in St. Chrysogonus's monastery before ascending to the papacy.[46] Despite having been transferred to Greek political control, Sicily was, to some significant degree, still considered part of the Latin Church, such that the island could be the source of so many popes during these centuries. The island may have served as a convenient source of Greek-educated candidates during a period in which Constantinople continued to try—increasingly unsuccessfully—to appoint and approve the election of the popes. Sicily, with its connections to both churches, may have been an easy place for emperors to find candidates for the papacy with enough familiarity with the two traditions to serve the interests of both institutions.

Some of the relations between Byzantium and the leaders of western Europe, as directed through Sicily, were more hostile. For example, the *vita* of Pope John VI (r. 701–705) records that the Byzantine exarch of Italy, Theophilactus (r. 701 / 702–709), traveled from Sicily to Rome for unknown reasons and encountered there a violent reception.[47] In Rome he was met by the local military troops ("militia totius Italiae"), who attempted to kill him. The pope sheltered the Byzantine official, thus demonstrating his commitment to maintaining an amiable relationship with the Byzantine emperor, even if the local popula-

42. *Life* of Pope Agatho (678–681), *LP* I.LXXXI, c. 140, line 1. Agatho's most notable act was to send a delegation from Rome to Constantinople for the Sixth Ecumenical Council, a.k.a. the Third Council of Constantinople (680–681), which settled the matter of Monothelitism and healed relations between Rome and Constantinople, albeit temporarily. His biographer mentions nothing about the route by which these envoys traveled, so we have no idea if they stopped in Sicily along the way.

43. *Life* of Pope Leo II, "the Younger," (682–683), *LP* I.LXXXII.

44. *Life* of Pope Conon (686–687), *LP* I.LXXXV, c. 157. We are also told that Conon appointed an unpopular and divisive figure, one Constantine, a deacon from Syracuse, as the administrator of the patrimony in Sicily and dealt with other business related to the patrimony.

45. *Life* of Pope Sergius I (687–701), *LP* I.LXXXVI, c. 158, l.1–2. Tiberius and his family may have migrated to Sicily when Antioch fell to Muslim conquerors in 638 CE.

46. *Life* of Pope Stephen III (768–772), *LP* I.XCVI, c. 262.

47. *Life* of Pope John VI (701–705), *LP* I.LXXXVII, c. 165.

FIGURE 2. Floor mosaics from the ancient city Panormus (later, Palermo). The city was originally founded by Phoenicians in the eighth century BCE but was later a Roman and then a Greek city. Photo by author.

tion was less welcoming to the Greek envoy. A more detailed account of hostile relations between Rome and Constantinople being negotiated via Sicily concerns a confrontation that took place in 732, during the first iconoclastic period. Pope Gregory III (731–741) sent a representative named George to the Byzantine capital with a condemnation of Emperor Leo's position on iconoclasm. George failed in his mission the first time he traveled from Rome to Constantinople, so he was sent a second time. This second attempt to deliver the pope's message was disrupted by George's yearlong detention in Sicily, and the letter never made it to Constantinople.[48] Later, the pope tried again to send the Byzantine emperor a condemnation of iconoclasm, this time with Constantine the *defensor*. On his way to Constantinople, he passed through Sicily where he and his party were arrested and imprisoned by Sergius, the *stratēgos* of Sicily, who was acting on the emperor's orders.[49] Sergius confiscated the letter and held Constantine captive for nearly a year. In this extended episode, the Sicilian Byzantine official obstructed the ability of Rome to

48. *Life* of Pope Gregory III (731–741), *LP* I.XCII, c. 191.
49. Ibid., c. 193.

communicate with Constantinople its displeasure on the divisive issue of iconoclasm. Sicily, as a regular stopping point on Rome-to-Constantinople journeys, was well situated to act as a regional representative of the emperor and his policies, as well as an intermediary in the relationship between pope and emperor—whether that enhanced or limited the actual communication between the two parties.

Like these popes, the Frankish ruler Charlemagne also used Sicily as a locus of political leverage with the Byzantine Empire. In this, he appears to have been following the established pathways of East-West communication by way of Sicily. One potential point of tension between Charlemagne and Constantinople was the political and military opportunity the island presented to western rulers: one could invade Sicily to claim it as his own and thus gain a foothold in a Byzantine territory with strong connections to Constantinople. This suggestion is not found in Latin sources, however, but only in Greek ones: for the year 800/801, Theophanes recorded that Charlemagne had planned a naval attack on Byzantine Sicily in order to conquer the island for his new empire. The chronicle stated that the Frankish emperor then abandoned this plan and decided instead to seek the hand of Empress Irene as his wife and thus sent ambassadors to Constantinople on that mission.[50] Even if this story was fabricated by the Greeks in their response to Charlemagne's claim to be the Roman emperor, it demonstrates that they recognized the possibility that Sicily could potentially be used as a stepping-stone between West and East. Another example of Sicily as a locus of political conflict between eastern and western claimants to the Roman imperial title concerns a Byzantine official from Sicily who defected to the court of Charlemagne in the year 800, for an unknown reason. He stayed in Charlemagne's service for ten years before requesting that he be sent back to Sicily.[51] The story of this official may reflect the competition between East and West over claims to authority. Both of these examples, however tenuous, suggest that Sicily served, to some western political leaders, as a nearby representative of the Byzantine Empire and thus as a mediator of both diplomacy and potential aggression. Charlemagne's supposed choice between conquering the island and marrying the empress suggests that the island could, in fact, be as much of a key to uniting the two empires as could a marriage alliance.

---

50. Theophanes, *Chronographia* A.M. 6293 I.475.11–15. This plan of Charlemagne's is not attested in western sources, either because it was an invention by the Greeks or because the western chroniclers did not find it important enough to record abandoned military plans.

51. *Annales regni Francorum*, 811: "et cum eis Leo quidam spatharius, natione Siculus . . . ante annos X Romae ad imperatorum, cum ibi esset, de Sicilia profugit et redire volens patriam remittitur."

Sometimes the Rome-to-Constantinople route through Sicily is only implied in the extant sources by notifications about the transmission of news. Several early sources relate that western leaders received important messages from Constantinople by means of ambassadors sent to Rome by Greek Sicilian officials, but we learn nothing else about the trips to and from Sicily. For example, in 713 a messenger arrived in Sicily from Constantinople and announced that Anastasius II (713–715) had deposed Philippicus (711–713) and replaced him as emperor; this news then traveled from Sicily to Rome.[52] Another similar incident is found in the brief notice that in 799 Michael, the governor of Sicily, sent a representative named Daniel to the court of Charlemagne, although the business he was charged with conducting between Charlemagne and Sicily's governor is unknown.[53] He may have been carrying news or orders on behalf of Sicily or, like many of the other messengers found in the sources, on behalf of Constantinople via Sicily's Byzantine officials. It is likely that other such travel between the two courts occurred but was not documented, as the arrival of a Sicilian envoy to Charlemagne's court was not recorded as an incident out of the ordinary. Most travel by messengers is only implied in our sources, through the record of the news that was transmitted or by a report that envoys appeared as passengers on ships on which other travelers were sailing. For example, there is a brief reference in a saint's life to both imperial and papal envoys sailing on the same ship from Constantinople to Sicily as the holy man, but we learn nothing of the missions on which these messengers traveled.[54] The travels of these particular envoys are not known from other sources, and it is likely that many other such journeys took place but were not recorded in surviving texts.

Two letters dated November 813, written by Pope Leo III (795–816) to Charlemagne, also provide evidence that news traveled from Constantinople to both Rome and the Frankish imperial court via Sicily. In the first, Leo mentions a letter sent to him on Charlemagne's behalf by the Sicilian *stratēgos*, Gregory, in response to one that the pope had delivered. The pope's letter conveys that the Byzantine emperor Michael (Michael I Rangabe, r. 811–813) had entered a monastery and had been replaced on the imperial throne. Leo explains to Charlemagne in the letter that he had learned the news from a papal representative

52. *Life* of Pope Constantine (708–715), *LP* I.XC, 226.3–5.

53. *Annales regni Francorum*, 799.

54. The British saint Willibald sailed on the same vessel as the messengers of both Emperor Leo III, "the Isaurian," (717–741) and Pope Gregory II (715–731) on his return journey from the Holy Land. "Et post duos annos, navigaverunt inde cum nuntiis pape et Cesaris in insulam Siciliam, ad urbem Siracusam." *Hodoeporicon S. Willibaldi*, in *Itinera Hierosolymitana et descriptiones Terrae Sanctae bellis sacris anteriora*, vol. 1, ed. Titus Tobler and Augustus Molinier (Osnabruck: Zeller, 1966, c. 30, p. 272. For more on this holy man's travels, see discussion below in this chapter.

who had traveled from Rome to Gregory's court in Sicily.[55] The second letter from Leo continues the discussion of the events in Constantinople, bringing news about the ascension of Leo V, "the Armenian," (r. 813–820) to the imperial throne.[56] These two pieces of correspondence indicate that at times both Rome and the emperor's court relied on Sicilian officials for news from Constantinople and that Sicilian envoys were accustomed to taking such news to Europe. The movement of information via Sicily also suggests that travel both between Constantinople and Sicily and between Sicily and Rome was routine: Sicily stayed regularly connected to both the Greek and Latin Christian worlds, simultaneously sending messengers to and receiving them from multiple places.

On the other hand, some accounts of communications between Constantinople and Rome highlight the fact that Sicily was not the only route by which information or envoys traveled between Constantinople and the West. In 797, the emissary Theoctistos, sent by Nicetas, the *stratēgos* of Sicily, arrived at Aachen with a letter for Charlemagne from an emperor (Constantine VI, r. 780–797) who had in the meantime been deposed in Constantinople (by his mother, Empress Irene, r. 797–802).[57] That vital piece of information had already reached Aachen by another route before the Sicilian messenger arrived, making the deposed emperor's message obsolete before it even arrived at Aachen. This anecdote shows that the overland route was sometimes faster than the sea route through Sicily.[58] This, then, suggests that Sicily acted as a significant node in the communication linkage between Rome, the Frankish court, and Constantinople not simply for its geographical expedience but for other reasons as well. Indeed, if messages could reach Rome or Aachen more quickly by routes not involving Sicily, then the utilization of the island as a stopover in other instances must have been related to other factors, such as the perceived reliability of particular Sicilian officials or the ease of finding passage to the island's ports from the eastern Mediterranean. The use of Sicily as a transit point reflected official needs and communication patterns, not simply the necessity to transmit information in the fastest way possible, meaning that in certain instances Sicily could serve as a proxy for imperial authority within the western Mediterranean and a point of connection between East and West. At the edge of the empire, Sicily was also a useful mediator of the relationships between Byzantium and the societies at its borders.

55. Leonis III, *Papae Epistolae X*, ed. Ernst Dümmler, Karl Hampe, *MGH*, *Epistolae Karolini aevi*, vol. 5 (Hanover, 1898–1899), 97.34–42 and 99.13–14.

56. Ibid., 99–100.

57. *Annales regni Francorum*, 797. See also McCormick, *Origins*, 886–887.

58. McCormick suggests the contrary: that, during the eighth century, the route through Sicily was the primary one used for travel between Rome and Constantinople. McCormick, *Origins*, 501–508.

Intellectual and Religious Connections to the Eastern Mediterranean

While the travel routes, ports, and shipping connections between Syracuse and Constantinople may have been initially developed for administrative and diplomatic purposes, intellectual or spiritual pursuits also motivated significant levels of travel between Sicily and the Greek world, as well as with the eastern Mediterranean more broadly. In fact, the most prevalent Greek textual sources for Sicily are saints' lives (Greek, sing. *bios*, pl. *bioi*; Latin, sing. *vita*, pl. *vitae*) that describe the lives, miracles, and careers of southern Italian and Sicilian monastics, many of whom traveled widely.[59] These saints' biographies and miracle accounts reveal, alongside details of the vibrancy of Greek monastic culture and the Muslim military attacks in the region, a high degree of connectivity between Sicily and the religious centers of Constantinople, Jerusalem, and Rome in particular and between the eastern and western Christian worlds more generally.[60] Education, the advancement of a career (either ecclesiastical or governmental), and spiritual pursuits spurred Greek saints to travel to and from the island; from the mid-seventh century, these motivations combined with that of fleeing the Muslim raids on Sicily. During the

59. For an introduction to and further bibliography on these saints' lives, see G. da Costa-Louillet, "Saints de Sicile e d'Italie Méridionale aux VIIIe, IXe et Xe siècles," *Byzantion* 29/30 (1959/1960): 89–173; Stephanos Efthymiadis, "Les saints d'Italie méridionale (IXe–XIIe s.) et leur rôle dans la société locale," in *Byzantine Religious Culture: Studies in Honor of Alice-Mary Talbot*, ed. E. Fisher, S. Papaioannou, and D. Sullivan (Leiden: E. J. Brill, 2011), 347–372; Mario Re, "Italo-Greek Hagiography," in *The Ashgate Research Companion to Byzantine Hagiography*, ed. Stephanos Efthymiadis, vol. 1 (Farnham: Ashgate, 2011), 227–258; and Eleni Tounta, "Saints, Rulers and Communities in Southern Italy: The Vitae of the Italo-Greek Saints (Tenth to Eleventh Centuries) and Their Audiences," *Journal of Medieval History* 42, no. 4 (2016): 429–455. Also of great assistance in the study of early Byzantine saints is the Dumbarton Oaks Hagiography Database, available at http://www.doaks.org/research/byzantine/resources/hagiography-database.

60. On Byzantine Christian religious culture in Sicily in general, see Salvatore Borsari, *Il monachesimo bizantino nella Sicilia e nell'Italia Meridionale pre-normanne* (Naples, 1963); Paolo Collura, "Il monachesimo prenormanno in Sicilia," *Archivio Storico Siciliano*, 4th ser., 8 (1982): 29–45; and Vera von Falkenhausen, "Chiesa greca e chiesa latina in Sicilia prima della conquista araba," *Archivio storico siracusano* 5 (1978–1985): 137–155; and Paul Oldfield, *Sanctity and Pilgrimage in Medieval Southern Italy, 1000–1200* (Cambridge: Cambridge University Press, 2014), 21–50. On the pilgrimages of southern Italian Greek saints, see Gennaro Luongo, "Itinerari dei santi italo-greci," in *Pellegrinaggi e itinerari dei santi nel Mezzogiorno medievale*, ed. Giovanni Vitolo, Europa mediterranea-Quaderni 14 (Naples: Liguori, 1999), 39–56; and Mario Re, "From Greek Southern Italy to Jerusalem: Monks, Saints and Pilgrims," in *Routes of Faith in the Medieval Mediterranean: History, Monuments, People, Pilgrimage Perspectives. Proceedings of the International Symposium (Thessalonike, 7–10 November 2007)*, ed. Evangelia Hadjitryphonos (Thessaloniki, 2008), 171–176. For the movement of Byzantine saints in the medieval world in general, see Elisabeth Malamut, *Sur la route des saints byzantins* (Paris: CNRS, 1993); and Catia Galatariotou, "Travel and Perception in Byzantium," *Dumbarton Oaks Papers* 47 (1993): 221–241. For pilgrimages to contemporary Greek saints' tombs in general, see Alice-Mary Talbot, "Pilgrimage to Healing Shrines: The Evidence of Miracle Accounts," *Dumbarton Oaks Papers* 56 (2002): 153–173.

period of Muslim attacks on the island—starting from the mid-seventh century—references to movements away from Sicily increased in number, possibly reflecting larger trends among the general population of the island in the wake of these violent incursions.[61] Often, these biographies show the saints taking advantage of this forced exile in order to travel more widely in the Mediterranean—either on pilgrimage or by way of furthering their religious education or careers in Rome or Constantinople. Thus many of the recorded voyages with a religious inspiration or goal were also motivated by the need to find a safer location to live and work. At the same time, Sicily featured a thriving Greek monastic culture and had several shrines of important early Christian martyrs, such as SS. Agatha and Lucy. Many pilgrims, both Greek and Latin, who traveled to Sicily as part of their longer journeys throughout the Christian Mediterranean visited these shrines en route to Jerusalem.

Many of these saintly Greek Sicilians traveled widely, crisscrossing the Mediterranean, north and south and east and west. Some individuals journeyed between southern Italy and northern Africa and from Rome to Constantinople and Jerusalem, all within one trip or over a lifetime.[62] For instance, the *Life* of St. Gregory of Agrigento (ca. 559–630) depicts him as traveling for many years between Sicily, Roman North Africa, Tripoli, Antioch, Constantinople, Rome, and Jerusalem.[63] On his first voyage, he departed from Agrigento (in south central Sicily) on a ship for Carthage, whence he sailed with some Roman monks to Tripoli in the Levant.[64] He made pilgrimage to Jerusalem, received monastic training there, and then returned to Sicily on a Palermitan ship that had docked at Tripoli; with him were three Roman monks who stopped over in Sicily en route back to Rome. Gregory then departed again for the eastern Mediterranean, where he eventually met and talked with the emperor in Constantinople.[65] From there he traveled to Rome and thence to Sicily via Palermo, as we saw in this chapter's epigraph, where he worked

61. On the depictions of interreligious violence and the contemporary Christian fears that these texts reveal, see Jonathan P. Conant, "Anxieties of Violence: Christians and Muslims in Conflict in Aghlabid North Africa and the Central Mediterranean," *al-Masāq* 27 (2015): 7–23.

62. For Byzantine pilgrimages to Jerusalem in general, see Alice-Mary Talbot, "Byzantine Pilgrimages to the Holy Land from the Eighth to the Fifteenth Century," in *The Sabaite Heritage in the Orthodox Church from the Fifth Century to the Present*, ed. Joseph Patrich (Leuven: Peeters, 2001), 97–110. For Italo-Greek pilgrimages to Jerusalem in particular, see Re, "From Greek Southern Italy to Jerusalem."

63. There are conflicting opinions about the dating of Gregory's life, and here I follow that of Martyn; see Martyn, *A Translation*, 115–117.

64. The voyage to Carthage is related twice: in Leontios, *Vita S. Gregorii Agrigentini*, c. 7–8, the hagiographer claims that it took three days to sail and, in c. 25, he states that it was ten days.

65. His journey between Carthage and Tripoli in the Levant lasted twenty days, according to *Vita S. Gregorii Agrigentini* (c. 11). From Tripoli to Sicily he sailed for fifteen days (c. 19). His meeting with the emperor is in c. 37, and the voyage from Constantinople to Rome is in c. 38.

miracles before going back to Agrigento.[66] There he was brought up on false charges of sexual impropriety, was tried and imprisoned in Rome, worked miracles, was released after two years in prison, and then was invested as bishop of the Sicilian church at Agrigento—but not before traveling a second time to Constantinople.[67] Both the pope in Rome and the emperor in Constantinople are depicted in this source as being deeply invested in the ecclesiastical affairs of Sicily, and this saint is closely connected to the highest levels of government and church in both cities; in addition, he makes pilgrimages, studies, and learns the monastic life in various places throughout the Christian Mediterranean world, both Greek and Latin. Such a high level of religious connectivity between Sicily and both Rome and Constantinople, as well as between the important ports and cities of the eastern Mediterranean (namely Antioch and Tripoli), was due, in part, to the availability of ships sailing to and from Sicilian ports: ships that embarked on administrative or economic business could also provide passage for pilgrims and intellectuals. The ship on which Gregory and his companions sailed from Tripoli back to the island, for instance, was identified as a ship from Palermo that was in Tripoli on business.[68] Likewise, his travels were made possible by the fact that the Sicilian Church maintained strong ties to both the Roman and Constantinopolitan churches.[69] In the late antique period, Sicily's church and administration were closely linked to both, just as they were still closely connected to each other: in this *bios* we see the pope and emperor corresponding directly by letter and envoy, and each taking an interest in ecclesiastical elections in Sicily. The narrative of Gregory's travels demonstrates just how easily Sicily of the sixth and early seventh centuries could communicate with both the late Roman world and that of the Byzantine eastern Mediterranean.

Despite his many travels, Gregory of Agrigento was committed to a career on the island, but many of the Italo-Greek saints became famous for their activities elsewhere after early lives in Sicily. At some time in the early ninth century, for example, Methodios I (d. 847), a Sicilian by birth who later became the patriarch of Constantinople (843–847), traveled to the imperial capital from his home in Sicily in order to seek a career in administration but instead entered

---

66. In c. 47 it is stated that the sea voyage from Rome to Palermo lasted twenty-six days, but we are not told about the ports they may have stopped at along the way.

67. The departure from Rome after his release from prison and his second visit to Constantinople are described in c. 82–85. In c. 89, he sails from Constantinople to Rome and thence to Agrigento.

68. *Vita S. Gregorii Agrigentini*, c. 19.

69. At some date in the early eighth century, Constantinople took jurisdiction of the Sicilian churches away from Rome. For the debate on dating this event, see Haldon, *Byzantium in the Seventh Century*, p. 90, n. 132.

the Church and rose to the position of patriarch.[70] Athanasios of Methone (d. late ninth century) was also born in Sicily, in the eastern coastal city of Catania, but his family moved to the Peloponnese in Greece when he was young due to the Muslim raids on the island; he later became bishop of the Peloponnesian city of Methone.[71] Many similar saints' lives and careers demonstrate that the monastic world of southern Italy and Sicily was a dynamic one, especially in the ninth and tenth centuries, and was closely connected to both the Greek Church based at Constantinople and the Latin one at Rome. Not only did numerous *bioi* record the deeds of saints whose works and miracles attained significance within the broader culture of Greek Christianity, but also each of those biographies mentions monasteries full of other Greek religious who also lived, worked, and prayed in Sicily and who may, themselves, have also traveled far and wide but whose lives and travels went unrecorded. In chapter 2, many of these hagiographical texts will be used to discuss patterns of flight and migration from the island during the period of Muslim raids.

One of the most dramatic hagiographical stories of travel back and forth between Sicily and Constantinople is fantastical but effectively represents both the geographical distance and the close relationship that existed between the province of Sicily and the capital at Constantinople. The story of a demon-possessed man named Heliodorus is featured in the *Life* of Leo of Catania, who lived during the last quarter of the seventh century; he was born in Ravenna but ascended to the episcopacy of Catania.[72] The villain in the story is a native of Sicily and the son of an elite Christian woman named Barbara. The hagiographer tells us that Heliodorus learned magic on the island from

---

70. *Vita Methodii*, *BHG* 1278; *AASS* v. 23, June XIV, 439–447; *PG* 100, 1243–1262. He also spent time in Rome like many of the saints discussed. Ibid., *PG* 100, 1248.

71. There is no extant *bios* for Athanasios of Methone, so we must rely on the funeral oration for him by Peter of Argos, *Epitaphios*, *BHG* 196; *PG* 104, 1365–1380, in *Novae patrum bibliothecae*, vol. 9, ed. and trans. Giuseppe Cozza-Luzi and Angelo Mai (Rome: Consilium propag. christ. nomini, 1888), pt. 3, 31–51. On the identity and writings of Peter of Argos, see A. Vasiliev, "The 'Life' of St. Peter of Argos and Its Historical Significance," *Traditio* 5 (1947): 163–191.

72. There are several versions of the biography of Leo of Catania (*BHG* 981–981e). The longest and most detailed is *Vita Leonis Ep. Cataniae*, *BHG* 981b, *AASS* v. 6, February XX, 226–229. Critical edition and English translation in *The Greek Life of St. Leo Bishop of Catania (BHG 981b)*, ed. A. G. Alexakis, trans. S. Wessel (Brussels: Société des Bollandistes, 2011). For more on the various versions and their editions, see Alexakis, *Greek Life*, 9–37. The edition of a briefer version of Leo's *Life* (*BHG* 981) is found in A. Acconcia Longo, "La vita di s. Leone vescovo di Catania e gli incantesimi del mago Eliodoro," *Rivista di studi bizantini e neoellenici* 26 (1989): 3–98. The various versions of his biography date his life to either the late seventh or mid-eighth century. There is, naturally, much doubt about the historicity of Leo of Catania, and Alexakis asserts that he is certainly fictitious; see Alexakis, *Greek Life*, 79–85. For our purposes, all that matters is how travel between Sicily and Constantinople is depicted—not whether these trips really happened (as they most surely did not).

a Jewish magician and proceeded to make a pact with Satan.[73] According to the *bios*, Heliodorus, inspired by the devil, wrought terror not only in Catania but also across the whole island (πάσης ὁμοῦ τῆς Σικελῶν νῆσου).[74] He caused women to expose themselves in public (by creating a magical river that forced them to lift their dresses); he disrupted commerce with his magic (by making stones appear as gold), which consequently caused a famine; and he incited the lust of all the young women in the area.[75] The eparch Loukios sent a letter to the emperors in Constantinople about the problem of this evildoer, and they in response sent an official named Herakleides to Sicily with a sixty-day deadline to get there and back with Heliodorus in custody. This two-month time frame for the round-trip journey between Constantinople and Sicily may give an estimate of the average expected length of such a voyage at that time, or, as the story's events suggest, it may have seemed too brief of a window in which to operate.[76] The hagiographer tells us that Herakleides departed immediately (apparently having no trouble finding a ship leaving for Sicily right away) and did in fact arrive in thirty days. Contrary to plan, however, when Herakleides arrived in Sicily, he too fell under the spell of the demoniac: the imperial messenger was enticed to disregard his sixty-day deadline when Heliodorus promised him a magical one-day trip back to Constantinople.[77] The offer of this shortened voyage was obviously too enticing to pass up—indicating either that the time frame was considered too brief or that the seaborne trip was dangerous enough to be feared and avoided when possible.

Thus Heliodorus presented himself as willing to go to Constantinople to face punishment—even offering to transport himself and the official there with his magic—but, upon arrival, he used his magical powers to extinguish all the fires in the city, which then caused a widespread famine. Threatened with capital punishment, he escaped back to Sicily—again via magic.[78] A second time, Herakleides was sent to Sicily to retrieve the magician, and again they returned to Constantinople in a single day: the first magical journey took place via the water in bathhouses (entering one in Catania and exiting another in

73. *Vita Leonis Ep. Cataniae*, c. 10–12. For more on anti-Judaism in the Italo-Greek saints' lives, see Re, "Italo-Greek Hagiography," 238–239.

74. *Vita Leonis Ep. Cataniae*, c. 13, ll. 9–12.

75. Ibid., c. 13–15.

76. Note that we do not know the season in which this anecdote was supposed to have taken place; presumably, it was safely within the sailing season so that there would have been no need to overwinter in Sicily. This implies, of course, that it was expected that a trip between Constantinople and Sicily and back could all take place within one sailing season, even if sixty days was considered a bit hurried.

77. *Vita Leonis Ep. Cataniae*, c. 19–20.

78. Ibid., c. 22.

Constantinople), and the second by sailing in an enchanted boat, which disappeared after disembarking both the passengers and their supplies.[79] Both times, Heliodorus used similar spells in order to escape back to Catania when threatened with capital punishment in Constantinople. His final demise came at the hands of the saintly bishop of Catania, Leo, who called upon God's power and dragged the man into a furnace that burned him up, Bishop Leo himself walking out unscathed.[80] When news of Leo's success in vanquishing the magician reached Constantinople, the emperors sent him a letter inviting him to visit the capital city, where he worked several miracles before returning home to Sicily; after he died, he was buried there and worked at least one postmortem miracle.[81]

This tale of magical trips from Sicily to Constantinople and back highlights both the physical distance and the conceptual nearness of the capital to the province in the Byzantine mentality. The island produced both the demon-possessed magician and the saint who foiled his evildoing, but Constantinople was the constant reference for dealing with the problem. The hagiographer emphasizes the emperors' rapid response and their deep concern for events in Sicily, and he even includes the full text of the letter sent to them from the Sicilian official. He also describes at some length the means and pathways of these amazing journeys—even detailing the ports the characters passed on their magical ship to Constantinople and the manner in which they docked there. And while the gullible imperial messenger serves as a literary counterpoint to the saintly Leo, his actions also demonstrate the length of the round-trip journey between Constantinople and Sicily and the appeal of a truncated voyage. The sixty-day deadline imposed by the imperial administration may have appeared to the official to be too short of a window for the successful completion of his task, or he may have succumbed to the magic because of the potential dangers of the voyage. In either case, the promise of the magical one-day journey was enough to draw Herakleides under the magician's spell.

The expectation of regular and relatively common communication between Constantinople and Syracuse was vital for the story's resolution, even though a Sicilian bishop was its hero and a Sicilian its villain. Throughout the story, the emperors were kept aware of the events unfolding in the western province as they were happening, and the Sicilians, likewise, were alert to events in Constantinople. This indicates that messengers were understood to have regularly sailed between the two locations, sending and bringing news; other-

79. Ibid., c. 21 and c. 25.

80. Ibid., c. 34.

81. Ibid., c. 35. For his burial and this miracle, see c. 37–38.

wise, this particular element of the tale would not have been believable to the audience. At the same time, the length of time allotted for the trip and the allure of a one-day journey demonstrate that communications between the island and the imperial capital were considered difficult and potentially dangerous, even while necessary. In one episode at Constantinople, Herakleides's wife spits in the face of the magician who was responsible for her husband's travel to such a faraway place twice, as though it was commonly understood that taking two such trips was both remarkable and undesirable, though whether due to danger or because of extended time away from home is unclear.[82] Nonetheless, this story as a whole demonstrates that swift and regular communication between Sicily and Constantinople was to be expected, although perhaps not enjoyed.

As incredible as the trips of Herakleides and the magician may be, the stories about these journeys reflect the assumption that ships sailing between Sicily and the eastern Mediterranean were widely available. In fact, saints from elsewhere in the Greek world regularly took advantage of the travel routes that arrived on Sicily's shores, arriving there during their travels around the Mediterranean world, on pilgrimages, or with the intention to live at one of the many monasteries on the island. For example, the saint Gregory of Dekapolis (797–842) was born in southern Asia Minor, became a monk, and, in about the year 830, began to travel throughout the East and West, visiting Sicily among many other areas.[83] He stayed for some time at Syracuse and performed miracles there—demonstrating the island's significance within the wider world of Greek religious culture as one location in the life of a wandering miracle worker. Like several of the other Byzantine saints who traveled around the Mediterranean, Gregory also encountered dangers and difficulties at sea due to Muslim ships and suspected Muslim pirates. Indeed, his *bios* states that Greek sailors at first refused to transport him to Sicily as he had wished because they feared the Muslim naval activity in the area. As will be seen in chapter 2, Muslim seafaring near Sicily increased in the mid-ninth century due to the initiation of the conquest of Sicily in 827. Gregory's eagerness to travel to Sicily may have been a reflection of his holy desire to place himself into a contested area on the frontier of Greek Christendom in order

82. "'Look,' she said, 'at what a scum and an abomination who forced my husband to travel the island of Sicily for the second time.'" ('Βλέπετε,' φησίν, 'οἷον κάθαρμα καὶ βδέλυμα τὸν ἐμὸν σύνευνον ἐποίησεν τὴν τῶν Σικελῶν νῆσον ἐκ δευτέρου καταλαβεῖν'.) c. 26, ll. 10–12.

83. He traveled to Ephesus, Thessaloniki, Rome, Syracuse, Otranto, and then back to Thessaloniki before going to Constantinople and Mount Olympus. Ignatius the Deacon, *Vita Gregorii Decapolitae, BHG* 711, in *La vie de saint Grégoire le Décapolite et les Slaves macédoniens au IXe siècle*, ed. Francis Dvornik (Paris: Champion, 1926). See also Cyril Mango, "On Re-reading the Life of St. Gregory the Decapolite," *Byzantina* 13 (1985): 633–646; and McCormick, *Origins*, 198–203.

to strengthen its position against the forces of Islam. Or, perhaps, Gregory simply wanted to participate in the thriving monastic culture of Sicily and southern Italy, a desire reflected in the many saints' biographies from the period. In either case, Gregory's journey demonstrates that Christian ships continued to sail from the eastern Mediterranean to Sicily during times of naval warfare and Muslim invasion, even if at times there was resistance or delay because of the potential dangers of such a voyage.

One such saint who encountered numerous dangers at sea was Elias the Younger of Enna (823–903), whose departure from the island was not a voluntary one.[84] The life of Elias coincided with the commencement of the Aghlabid effort to conquer Sicily outright, after many years of raids for booty and slaves. His family, nobility from Enna, a hilltop town in the south central part of the island, had initially fled to a castle called Santa Maria in Calabria, southern Italy, in order to escape the attacking Muslims, who were said to have come from Carthage.[85] Despite this search for a safe location, as a child, Elias was caught up in the Muslim raids and was captured twice by Muslims from North Africa: the *bios* describes "Saracens" rushing up and overpowering him.[86] He was saved by a Byzantine fleet the first time but sold into slavery in North Africa after the second capture.[87] He escaped from his owners and then traveled widely throughout the Mediterranean world: first to Jerusalem and then to other cities in the Holy Land, Antioch, several cities in Greece, Alexandria, Carthage, Rome, and other locations of significance (but not, in fact, Constantinople).[88] Eventually, Elias returned to Sicily—by then mostly Muslim-controlled—in order to visit his mother before traveling to southern Italy and thence on pilgrimage to Rome.[89] Elias encountered quite a few Muslims in the course of his journeys, conversed with and converted some of them, and worked miracles such as prophesying the outcomes of battles between the Muslims and the Byzantines—for example, the Muslim conquest

84. *Vita Eliae Iunioris*, *BHG* 580; *AASS* v. 37, August XVII, 479–509. Edition and Italian translation in Giuseppe Rossi Taibbi, *Vita di sant'Elia il Giovane* (Palermo: Istituto Siciliano di Studi Bizantini e Neoellenici, 1962). Elias is discussed by McCormick in *Origins*, esp. 244–254, as one example of a Christian sold into slavery in the Muslim world. For further examples of Christians sold into slavery in the Muslim world, see his table 9.2 on p. 249.

85. *Vita Eliae Iunioris*, c. 3, esp. ll. 55–58.

86. "Ὡς οὖν ἐξῆλθον καὶ προέβησαν ἱκανόν, ἐξαίφνης αὐτοῖς ἐπιδραμόντες Σαρακηνοὶ πάντας αὐτοὺς ἐχειρώσαντο." Ibid., c. 6, ll. 108–110.

87. *Vita Eliae Iunioris*, c. 6ff.

88. For his escape from slavery and subsequent travels, see *Vita Eliae Iunioris*, c. 17ff. See the map in Malamut, *Sur la route des saints byzantins*, 257. En route back to Sicily, Elias engaged in conversation with Muslim co-passengers and converted them. See *Vita Eliae Iunioris*, c. 23–24.

89. *Vita Eliae Iunioris*, c. 25–29.

of Taormina in 902.[90] News of his holy life reached Constantinople, and he received an invitation to the capital from Emperor Leo VI (886–912). He set off but died en route, at Thessaloniki, so although his spiritual life and work were known in Constantinople, and although he traveled throughout much of the eastern Mediterranean, he never actually made it there. This life of holy wandering and pilgrimage also intersected closely with the broader trends at work in the Mediterranean region of the ninth and early tenth centuries: the Muslim conquest of Sicily had, during his lifetime, both begun and come nearly to completion; he was captured as a slave by Muslims but was saved by Byzantine warships in the region who were attempting to defend the island against Muslim aggression; and he traveled to the traditional Christian holy sites in both the eastern and western Mediterranean worlds, in the midst of the large-scale changes taking place in the balance of power between Latins, Greeks, and Muslims. This was a Mediterranean world experiencing upheaval, violence, and conquest, but also one that offered broad connectivity and opportunities for extensive travel between Greek Christian, Latin Christian, and Muslim regions.

Intellectual and Religious Connections with the Latin World

Within these transformations, Rome retained and even gained significance as a site of spiritual and cultural power. Like Gregory of Agrigento and Elias of Enna, many other Sicilian Greek saints made pilgrimages or ecclesiastical business trips to Rome and thus contributed to the linkage of the Greek and Latin Christian worlds via Sicily. Many of the *bioi* of these ninth- and tenth-century Italo-Greek saints also illustrate the ways that travel to Rome could be combined with flight from the Muslim attacks on Sicily, often with a stopover in southern Italy.[91] Leo-Luke of Corleone (ca. 815–915), for example, was born in the Sicilian town of Corleone (an inland town a short distance south of Palermo) sometime in the early ninth century and entered the famous monastery of St. Philip of Agira, on the western edge of Mount Etna (in the province of

90. For the conversion of Muslims, see *Vita Eliae Iunioris*, c. 23–25; for the miracles and prophesies, see c. 31–65; for the fall of Taormina, see c. 49.

91. For more on how these *bioi* might indicate demographic changes—the de-Hellenization or re-Hellenization of the island and southern Italy—see, among others, Judith Herrin, "The Process of Hellenization," in *Margins and Metropolis*, 33–57, esp. 38–42. For historiography on this question, see Ibid., nn. 25–31. See also chapter 2 for more on demographic changes at this time.

Enna).[92] When that city began to suffer from the Muslim raids, Leo-Luke and many other monks moved northward to Calabria. Prior to settling into a monastery there, however, he visited the pilgrimage shrines of Rome. The *Life* of Joseph the Hymnographer (d. ca. 886) likewise depicts the saint's flight from Sicily to the eastern Mediterranean because of Muslim raids, ecclesiastical career in Constantinople, and sea voyage from there to Rome as an emissary.[93] En route, Joseph was captured by Muslim pirates and taken hostage on Crete but was ransomed and returned to Constantinople (for more, see chapter 2), so it is unclear if his intended route would have taken him through Sicily before he went on to Rome. Nonetheless, his biography demonstrates the close connections between the island and the two centers of rival Christian power, Rome and Constantinople.

Another such saint who traveled widely in the Mediterranean world was the southern Italian St. Elias Spelaiotes (864–960). He was born on the Italian mainland, in Reggio Calabria, but moved to Sicily to live as an ascetic.[94] By the time of this voluntary migration to Sicily (in reverse of the common pattern of flight from the island), a large portion of the island was under Muslim political control. Nonetheless, this Elias chose the life of a Greek hermit in this political and religious borderland, perhaps as a spiritual exercise in self-denial or perhaps as an attempt to represent Greek Christianity in a contested space. Whatever his motivation, his experiment did not last long, as Elias left the island after a close friend died at the hands of Muslim raiders.[95] After this self-exile from Sicily, he traveled frequently back and forth across the wider Mediterranean world, spending time in monastic retreats on Patras, in Calabria, and near Rome. His spiritual career and wanderings, like the other Elias's, thus incorporated both the Greek world of the eastern Mediterranean and the Latin region near Rome, as well as Greek southern Italy and an increasingly Muslim-controlled Sicily. Also like many other saints', his life and travels demonstrate that movement across the shifting Mediterranean boundaries between Christian and Muslim territories continued—even during times of rising Muslim power in the region and despite the dangers associated with traveling to

92. The *vita* of Leo-Luke of Corleone only exists in a later Latin translation, *Vita Leonis Lucae Corilionensis Abbatis*, *BHL* 4842; *AASS* March I, 97–102. Latin edition and Italian translation in Maria Stelladoro, *La Vita di San Leone Luca di Corleone* (Grottaferrata: Badia Greca di Grottaferrata, 1995). For eleventh- and twelfth-century Sicilian and southern Italian Greek saints who made pilgrimages to Rome, see Re, "Italo-Greek Hagiography," 242–243.

93. Theophanes the Monk, *Vita Iosephi hymnographi*, *BHG* 944–947b; *AASS* v. 10, April III, 266–276, in *Monumenta graeca et latina ad historiam Photii patriarchae pertinentia*, ed. A. Papadopoulos-Kerameus (St. Petersburg, 1901), 2: 1–14.

94. *Vita S. Eliae Spelaeotae*, *BHG* 581; *AASS* v. 43, September III, 843–888.

95. Ibid., 850–851.

or living in an area of interreligious warfare—and that those boundary lines did not always appear as a barrier to those who wished to cross them.

Such movements between Sicily and Rome did not immediately end when Sicily fell into Muslim hands. Several Sicilian monks whose lives date from the tenth and early eleventh centuries are also depicted as living on the island prior to flight from it and serve as testimony to the continued presence of a Greek Christian population on the island under Muslim rule. For example, the monk Christopher (fl. late tenth century), along with his sons Makarios (d. ca. 1000) and Sabas (d. ca. 990), fled Sicily because of Muslim violence but then continued traveling for other purposes.[96] They were originally from Collesano (a short distance east of Palermo) and, as a family, entered the monastery of St. Philip of Agira. They and many of their companions moved to southern Italy after Muslim raiders wrought destruction in Sicily.[97] When this family of monastics moved to Merkourion, in northern Calabria, the brothers Sabas and Makarios founded a church and monastery dedicated to St. Michael, while Christopher made a pilgrimage to Rome before returning to southern Italy. Sabas himself later traveled to Rome, where he died, although his attempt to make a pilgrimage to Jerusalem was thwarted by interreligious violence there.[98] Likewise, Vitalis of Castronuovo (d. ca. 994) traveled regularly between Sicily and southern Italy, spending time in Rome and Bari among other locations.[99] By this time, Sicily was essentially completely controlled by Muslim rulers, and the saint experienced violent encounters with Muslim attackers: Vitalis was on the verge of being killed while defending his monastery, and when his attacker was struck by lightning, he was healed by the saint and then promised to do no further harm to Christians.[100] The interactions between these saints and their Muslim aggressors could thus be both violent and miraculously peaceful at the same time. In spite of the monks' miraculous powers, the Muslim incursions into the island were, for many Greek Sicilians, cause for migration to southern Italy, whence many took the

96. Orestes, Patriarch of Jerusalem, *Lives* of Saints Christopher and Makarios, *BHG* 312, and *Life* of Saint Sabas of Collesano, *BHG* 1611, in *Historia et laudes SS. Sabae et Macarii iuniorum e Sicilia auctore Oreste Patriarcha Hierosolymitano*, ed. Giuseppe Cozza-Luzi (Rome: Typis Vaticanis, 1893). Many other monks from the extended family and monastic network of Christopher, Sabas, and Makarios also fled to southern Italy; see among others, Salvatore Borsari, *Il monachesimo bizantino*.

97. For example, the life of St. Luke of Demenna (d. 993), which exists only in a Latin translation, *Vita S. Lucae abbatis*, *BHL* 4978; *AASS* October VI, 337–341.

98. St. Sabas had to settle for a spiritual visit to the Holy Land. For this spiritual journey, see Orestes, *Historia*, c. XLIII, 59–61. For other Byzantine monks who did make the pilgrimage to Jerusalem, see Talbot, "Byzantine Pilgrimages to the Holy Land."

99. This biography also only exists in a later Latin translation. *Vita S. Vitalis Abbatis*, *BHL* 8697; *AASS* March II, 26–34.

100. *Vita S. Vitalis Abbatis*, *AASS* March II, 31.

opportunity to make pilgrimage to Rome. Thus these religious visits to Rome were closely connected to travel for the purpose of resettling farther away from danger and again demonstrate the multifaceted motivations behind some of the journeys taken during this time. Again, we see that Sicily could be a locus of connection to the Roman Latin world—especially for purposes of pilgrimage, but also, as above, for the transfer of information, officials, and envoys—for many individuals coming from the Byzantine Empire to both Latin Rome and Greek southern Italy.

In reverse of these voyages from Greek Sicily and southern Italy toward Rome, religious journeys also led many people from Latin Christendom to visit Sicily. Latin Christian pilgrims journeying between East and West occasionally stopped there en route to the Holy Land, taking the opportunity to visit the martyrs' shrines maintained on the island. Christian pilgrims from western Europe traveling to Jerusalem had several routes available to them, so Sicily was not a necessary stopping point on the journey but was often a convenient one. Later, during the period of Muslim control over the island, the island became less convenient for Latin travelers and was thus less often visited by them. Nonetheless, several examples of early European Christian pilgrimage accounts include references to time spent in Sicily, its shrines, and its natural sights. One such traveler is the late-seventh-century Arculf, whose trip likely took place sometime before 688. He was a bishop from Gaul who passed through Sicily on one leg of his trip to the Holy Land.[101] His visit to the island, as described in Adamnan's account of his journey, was especially memorable because of the salt he tasted from one of the island's mountains, which he compared to that of the Dead Sea.[102] The other major detail recorded for this leg of his trip was the rumbling of the volcano Mount Vulganus, which is on an island twelve miles from the northeastern shore of Sicily.[103] Such accounts of the volcanic activity on and near Sicily remained a regular feature of travelers' accounts throughout the medieval period.

Willibald, an eighth-century traveler from Britain, also passed through the island on his way to the Holy Land. While there, he, like Arculf before him, witnessed some of Sicily's legendary sights, including volcanic activity. Huneberc of Heidenheim's account of St. Willibald's travels (in the *Hodoeporicon*)

---

101. The pilgrimage account does not reveal details of his journey to or from the Holy Land, but two references to Arculf's experiences in Sicily demonstrate that at least one leg of his trip passed through the island. Adamnan, *De locis sanctis*, ed. Denis Meehan (Dublin: Dublin Institute for Advanced Studies, 1958).

102. Adamnan, the author of the travel account, reported that Arculf had tasted a very salty salt that originated from a mountain in Sicily: "Aliter vero sal in quodam Siculo monte haberi solet." Adamnan, *De locis sanctis*, II.17.3–5.

103. Ibid., III.6.1–3.

describes the saint and his companions traveling overland from Britain to Rome and then on to Terracina and Gaeta, whence they sailed to Naples.[104] At Naples they caught an Egyptian ship to Reggio Calabria, and after two days in Reggio the party sailed to the eastern Sicilian city of Catania.[105] There, they visited the shrine of the virgin martyr Agatha and caught sight of the famous volcano Mount Etna. The party stayed in Catania for three weeks before they traveled by ship to Syracuse, then departed for the East via a stopover in the Peloponnese. The return journey, several years later, passed through Constantinople, where they stayed for two years. After departing Constantinople, the group appears to have sailed straight to Syracuse, for no intermediary stops are recorded for the return trip as they were for the first half of Willibald's journey. On this return leg of his travels, Willibald was accompanied by messengers of both Emperor Leo III and Pope Gregory II, demonstrating the overlap in itineraries of papal and imperial envoys with other types of travelers, including pilgrims and, possibly, merchants.[106] This ship, with its variety of passengers, sailed directly to Syracuse and then went on to Catania again before visiting an erupting volcano on a small island north of Messina on the way back to Naples.

Although Arculf and Willibald passed through Sicily, other early travel accounts reveal that there were a number of popular alternate pilgrimage routes across the Mediterranean that did not include Sicily. Bernard, a Frankish monk, traveled around the year 870 from Rome to Alexandria via Bari and Taranto, in Apulia, bypassing Sicily altogether.[107] He chose this route despite the fact that Bari and Taranto were at the time in Muslim hands (as were parts of Sicily) and that this route involved much more overland travel than the path through Sicily would have demanded. The Frankish party sailed from Taranto to Alexandria on Muslim ships, alongside captive Christian slaves from southern

---

104. Huneberc of Heidenheim, *Hodoeporicon S. Willibaldi,* in *Itinera Hierosolymitana et descriptiones Terrae Sanctae bellis sacris anteriora*, vol. 1, ed. Titus Tobler and Augustus Molinier (Osnabruck: Zeller, 1966), 241–281. The sections concerning Willibald's trip toward the Holy Land via Sicily are c. X–XII, 255–260. Cf. *Itinerarium S. Willibaldi*, in *Itinera Hierosolymitana*, vol. 1, c. V, 287–288.

105. "Navim illi de Egypto invenerunt, et illic intro ascendentes navigaverunt in terram Calabriae ad urbem, que dicitur Regia. Et ibi manentes duos dies, levaverunt se et venerunt in insulam Siciliam quod est in urbem Catanensem, ubi requiescit corpus sancte Agathe virginis." *Hodoeporicon S. Willibaldi*, c. X, 256.

106. "Et post duos annos, navigaverunt inde cum nuntiis pape et Cesaris in insulam Siciliam, ad urbem Siracusam." The return trip through Sicily is recorded in *Hodoeporicon S. Willibaldi*, c. XXX, 272–273. Cf. *Itinerarium S. Willibaldi*, in *Itinera Hierosolymitana*, vol. 1, c. XIV, 293–294.

107. Halevi places the journey between the spring and autumn of 867. See Leor Halevi, "Bernard, Explorer of the Muslim Lake: A Pilgrimage from Rome to Jerusalem, 867," *Medieval Encounters* 4 (1998): 24–50. Edition found in *Itinerarium Bernardi Monachi Franci*, ed. Tobler and Molinier, *Itinera Hierosolymitana*, 307–320.

Italy who were being sent to various ports within the Islamic world.[108] The different itinerary may reflect changes in shipping patterns that were already beginning to take shape, or it may simply reflect the individual choices made by these different parties of pilgrims.

In general, we see that some western Christian pilgrims used Sicilian ports on their voyages to or from the Holy Land, while others did not pass through Sicily on their trips. The picture gathered from these data is that of an island that maintained close connections with both of the major Christian civilizations in the Mediterranean and, increasingly, with the Muslim world of North Africa and the eastern Mediterranean. Sicily was the primary spot at which the civilizations met and, in some ways, overlapped, creating not simply a geographical center point, but a political and social nexus between the Greek and Latin worlds—one that would increasingly involve the third major Mediterranean civilization, that of Islam.

Economic Connections to the Wider Mediterranean World

One last aspect of early medieval Sicily's participation in broader Mediterranean systems of travel and communication must be mentioned, even though details are scarce: that of commercial travel and economic exchange. In addition to being a political province of Byzantium and in contact with the Latin world—the site of political maneuverings at the local, papal, and imperial levels—and one closely connected to both Rome and the eastern Mediterranean in terms of spiritual affairs, Sicily was also economically integrated into larger Mediterranean networks of exchange—linked primarily with Constantinople but also, possibly, with southern Italy, Latin Europe, and Muslim North Africa. Unfortunately, the extent of these linkages is hard to discern due to the lack of economic source material from the early Middle Ages. In fact, the entire economy of Sicily during both the Byzantine and Islamic periods is poorly understood due to a dearth of relevant source material, particularly in comparison with the much richer data available for the years of Sicily's history

108. *Itinerarium Bernardi Monachi Franci*, c. IV–V, 310–311. Bernard claimed that there were six ships, on which 9,000 Christian prisoners were held: two ships sailed for North Africa (which port city is unknown) with 3,000 Christians; two left for Tripoli with 3,000 Christians on board; and two ships were bound for Alexandria with the final 3,000 prisoners. The unreliability of medieval numerical reckoning does not prohibit us from understanding the basic truth that considerable travel, simultaneously by willing and unwilling Christian passengers, was taking place between the northern and southern shores of the Mediterranean Sea in the ninth century.

that are covered by the Cairo Geniza evidence, which allows some glimpse into economic connections from the eleventh century and beyond.[109] The Byzantine period in particular remains poorly elucidated because of the nature of the extant sources for those years. Most of the textual sources from this early period do not directly concern economic matters, although they do demonstrate the high level of shipping in and around Sicily that might have also included economic activity—such as trade, piracy, or shipments of the grain tax to Constantinople. In addition, each of the ships on which imperial messengers, pilgrims, or other travelers sailed may have also contained loads of unrecorded commercial goods or grain.[110]

Indeed, it is the question of grain shipments that has occupied most of the academic discussion about medieval Sicily's economy and its economic connections within the Mediterranean. Scholars have debated the importance of Sicily for the grain supply of late antique Constantinople, particularly in

---

109. Beginning in the tenth century, the Cairo Geniza letters contain a wealth of information about Jewish trade in the central Mediterranean, much of which concerned Sicily. This information will be discussed in chapter 3.

110. Maritime archaeology near Sicily could help flesh out our picture of trade to and from Sicily in the early Middle Ages, but I have found no reports of early Byzantine wrecks near Sicily that contain evidence of grain or other commercial shipments. For instance, the Pantano Longarini wreck has no remaining cargo, and the "Church Wreck" off Marzamemi (both of which were excavated from the shores near Syracuse) carried the architectural elements for building a Byzantine basilica. Sarah Marie Kampbell, "The Pantano Longarini Shipwreck: A Reanalysis" (MA thesis, Texas A&M University, 2007); Gerhard Kapitän, "The Church Wreck off Marzamemi," *Archaeology* 22, no. 2 (1969): 122–133; and Peter Throckmorton and Gerhard Kapitän, "An Ancient Shipwreck at Pantano Longarini," *Archaeology* 21, no. 3 (1968): 182–187. The Cefalù wreck (mid-sixth century, northern shore of the island) has been plundered too seriously for a definitive conclusion, but the evidence suggests that it was a military rather than a commercial ship—possibly one of the warships sent by Constantinople to recover the island from the Goths in 535. Gianfranco Purpura, "Il relitto bizantino di Cefalù," *Sicilia Archeologica* 51 (1983): 93–105. Seventh-century Byzantine shipwrecks such as the one found at Yassi Ada, off the coast of Asia Minor, demonstrate that Greek ships containing commercial cargoes were certainly sailing the eastern Mediterranean at this time, and the cargo of this wreck consisted of roughly 900 amphorae filled with low-quality wine or olive oil. For more on Yassi Ada, see George F. Bass and Frederick H. van Doornick Jr., *Yassi Ada: A Seventh-Century Byzantine Shipwreck* (College Station: Texas A&M University Press, 1982); and Deborah N. Carlson, Justin Leidwanger, and Sarah M. Kampbell, *Maritime Studies in the Wake of the Byzantine Shipwreck at Yassiada, Turkey* (College Station: Texas A&M University Press, 2015). On the other hand, a number of wrecks from the late Roman Empire demonstrate clearly that foodstuffs and other products had been shipped between North Africa and Italy via Sicily during that time, likely as part of the *annona*. See, for example, David Gibbins, "A Roman Shipwreck of c. AD 200 at Plemmirio, Sicily: Evidence for North African Amphora Production during the Severan Period," *World Archaeology* 32 (2001): 311–334; and Jeffrey G. Royal and Sebastiano Tusa, "The Levanzo I Wreck, Sicily: A 4th-century AD Merchantman in the Service of the Annona?," *International Journal of Nautical Archaeology* 41, no. 1 (2012): 26–55. For shipwreck evidence that the *annona* shipments ended between 600 and 625 CE, see Sean Kingsley, "Mapping Trade by Shipwrecks," in *Byzantine Trade, 4th–12th Centuries: The Archaeology of Local, Regional and International Exchange, Papers of the Thirty-Eighth Spring Symposium of Byzantine Studies, St John's College, University of Oxford, March 2004*, ed. Marlia Mundell Mango (Farnham: Ashgate, 2008), 31–36.

regard to the impact of the island's loss to the Muslim conquest. The question for most scholars has been whether the Muslim takeover of Byzantine lands in the western Mediterranean dealt an unrecoverable blow to the food supply and economy of Byzantium or whether perhaps Constantinople had already found alternate supplies of grain prior to that event.[111] Roman and Byzantine sources in general do not commonly refer to merchants or trade. The fact that these grain shipments from Sicily would have been primarily managed by the government, as part of the annual grain tax (*annona*) rather than as private commerce, probably explains why individual merchants do not play a very large role in the textual sources on Byzantine Sicily. In addition, the types of texts extant from the Byzantine period of Sicily's history—mostly chronicles and saints' lives—were particularly unconcerned with mercantile activities, failing to record evidence of economic matters even when they could have done so.[112] For example, Leo of Catania's *bios*, for all its interest in travel by water, mentions nothing about food sources arriving at or departing from Sicily by sea. Such a limited source base means that we cannot recreate a full picture of the economic connections in which Byzantine Sicily was involved. The few texts that do mention Sicily's contribution to the *annona*—such as a few letters from Gregory the Great written in the 590s or the *vita* of Pope John V (685–686)—do so only cursorily and cannot allow for the reconstruction of quantities or the degree to which Sicily's economy depended upon grain cultivation.[113]

111. John Teall argues that, by the seventh century, Sicily's major grain exports had shifted to Rome rather than Constantinople, and that it was the loss of Egypt that most affected the food supplies of Constantinople. He concedes the possibility of continuing shipments of grain from Syracuse to Constantinople, although he believes that these would have been private and sporadic rather than officially sponsored and regular. Increasingly, the central lands of the Byzantine Empire depended for their grain on the lands to their north—through Black Sea ports—as well as Syria and, most importantly, the capital's own Anatolian hinterland. Therefore, Sicily, while traditionally an important granary for the Roman Empire, was, by the time of the Arab conquest of the island, shipping its produce to nearby locations, such as mainland Italy. Teall thus finds that the loss of Sicily and North Africa to the Arabs was no major blow to the Byzantine Empire and that it was "treated with almost a curious indifference" in regard to food supplies. John L. Teall, "The Grain Supply of the Byzantine Empire, 330–1025," *Dumbarton Oaks Papers* 13 (1959): 87–139. This suggests that, while Sicily has traditionally been viewed as a primary granary for the Roman Empire, both in the West and the East, the island's agricultural importance during the Byzantine centuries may in fact have been much smaller than many scholars presume. One of the primary points that I want to make across this book is that, indeed, we must not presume that because connections existed during one period, they necessarily did so in previous or succeeding periods.

112. Michael McCormick discusses this issue in the introduction to his *Origins*, esp. 12–19.

113. Gregory the Great's letters contain several references to grain from Sicily being important in Rome, and he directly managed the grain cultivated on the papal estates on the island. See, among other letters, Gregorius Magnus, *Registrum epistularum libri*, Epis. 1.2 (590), 1.70 (591), 9.31 (598), 9.107 (599), and 9.116 (599). In letter 1.70, for example, we see Gregory himself allotting fifty pounds of gold for the purchase of new grain to be stored in Sicily and then shipped to Rome at a later date. The biography of Pope John V claims that the emperor issued an exemption for the grain tax on many of

One hagiographical source that may allude to grain shipments is the *Life* of St. Gregory of Agrigento (ca. 559–630), who was said to have sailed from Sicily to Carthage, whence he and three other monks boarded a ship to the Levant. After visiting Jerusalem, they took passage on a ship that had been in the port of Tripoli on some kind of business, and thence returned to Palermo.[114]

While Sicily's local economy and its precise role within the larger Byzantine economy is difficult to recreate, some things are known about the island's agricultural production in the late antique and Byzantine periods. During the late Roman period, in the fourth and fifth centuries, Sicily maintained a typically Roman society and economy. Important urban centers dotted the island (in particular Syracuse, Palermo, and Catania); agricultural land was organized in large *latifundia*; and Latin language and culture predominated. However, by the end of the Byzantine period, the island's social structure, culture, and population had changed significantly. Under Greek rule, the island featured many rural villages and very few large urban centers or important market towns, with most of the land being used for the cultivation of grains such as wheat—whether for local use or long-distance trade is unknown.[115] Wealthy urban dwellers, who in earlier centuries might have participated in the cross-Mediterranean trade in luxury goods, were now diminished in number, in parallel with larger patterns of social and economic change within the West at this time. With this decrease in urbanization and, consequently, in the number of urban markets on the island, Byzantine Sicily's economy grew more dependent on agricultural output. First Rome and later Constantinople relied on the grain from Sicily for their food supply—but the degree of this dependence cannot be quantified. When North Africa was lost to the Vandals in the fifth century, Sicily became one of the most important sources of grain for the city of Rome, and it continued to export wheat during the Byzantine period, although the quantity and overall importance of this export are unknown.

The importance of Sicily's grain cultivation to ancient Rome has led many historians to assume that its role as a food supplier continued throughout the

---

the lands of the papal patrimony in Sicily and Calabria, which, he asserts, the papacy had been unable to pay regularly. *Life* of Pope John V (685–686), *LP* LXXXIV.

114. Leontios, *Vita S. Gregorii Agrigentini*, 579–582, c. 19. See also Harry Magoulias, "The Lives of the Saints as Sources of Data for the History of Commerce in the Byzantine Empire in the VIth and VIIth Cent.," *Kleronomia* 3 (1971): 313. Magoulias suggests that this was a grain shipment from Sicily to the eastern Mediterranean, but the text is not as sure; in fact, the hagiographer admits that he did not know what kind of business the Palermitan ship was engaged in.

115. "Sicily," *ODB*, 3: 1891; Guillou, "La Sicile Byzantine."

Middle Ages.[116] Following this assumption, the question of when the island's grain supply lost its vitality—thereby relegating the island to an economic backwater within Italy and within Europe as a whole—has become a central concern for many economic historians of the Middle Ages.[117] Implicit in this discussion is the idea that Sicily had been an economic hub in the Roman and late antique periods, only to fall behind at some date as the merchants of mainland Italy and Spain took the lead in Mediterranean-wide systems of trade and exchange. As we shall see in chapters 3 and 4, it is only during the tenth and eleventh centuries, when commercial documents and letters appear in the source record, that the question of Sicily's centrality to Mediterranean food supplies can be raised. This does not mean, however, that Byzantine Sicily did not play a role in late antique and early medieval commercial affairs or food supplies: it only means that very little movement of agricultural or other commercial products to and from Sicily can be found in the sources for the centuries of Byzantine rule in Sicily. The fact that the extant sources were not concerned with trade does not prohibit us from imagining that commerce continued unrecorded, perhaps indeed taking place on some of the very ships on which our recorded travelers sailed.

Regardless of the quantitative changes that may have taken place in Sicily's grain production, contributions to the *annona*, or participation in commercial trade, it is clear that Sicily retained an important place in Constantinople's conception of its western frontier in the Mediterranean Sea between the sixth and ninth centuries. Politics, diplomacy, religious and intellectual concerns, and, perhaps to some degree, economic exchanges connected the island to the Byzantine imperial center in ways that demonstrate the dense, if unquantifiable, network of connections between Sicily and the Greek world of the east-

---

116. For more on Sicily's wheat shipments during Roman rule on the island, see Peter Garnsey, "Grain for Rome" in *Trade in the Ancient Economy*, ed. Peter Garnsey, Keith Hopkins, and C. R. Whittaker (London: Chatto and Windus, 1983), 118–130. Sicily's grain output was shipped to Rome as tributes, rents, and taxes more than as a commercial export. See Garnsey's statement that, by the second century CE, Sicily's "tax-grain was normally paid over by producers and proprietors to city-magistrates or liturgists acting under the general supervision of imperial officials" (123). By the late third and early fourth century, those shipping Sicily's grain to Rome became public employees (127–128). At the same time, imperial grain production increased, making privately traded grain less of an option. See also Keith Hopkins, "Taxes and Trade in the Roman Empire (200 B.C.–A.D. 400)," *Journal of Roman Studies* 70 (1980): 101–125.

117. The later economic relationship between northern and southern Italy is one of the primary concerns in David Abulafia's *The Two Italies* (Cambridge: Cambridge University Press, 1977), esp. 4ff. For more historiography on "what went wrong" with Sicily, see Clifford R. Backman, *The Decline and Fall of Medieval Sicily: Politics, Religion, and Economy in the Reign of Frederick III, 1296–1337* (Cambridge: Cambridge University Press, 1995).

ern Mediterranean.[118] At the same time, preexisting links with the Latin world and with southern Italy allowed the island to function both as an extension and agent of Greek power in the West and as an important juncture in long-distance travel to and from Rome, Aachen, and other sites within the West. As we will see in chapter 2, early medieval Sicily was also, from the seventh century, a significant and active borderland zone between Christian territories—both Latin and Greek—and the expanding Islamic world. At the same time as the Latin and Greek Christian worlds were overlapping in and around Sicily, Muslims—some of them sailors on ships, as we have seen already, and some of them warriors, envoys, officials, and perhaps even merchants—began to slowly draw Sicily into the orbit of the Muslim Mediterranean in ways that would continue to impact the island and its region for the rest of the Middle Ages.

118. Michael McCormick has used anecdotes about religious and other travelers to craft a picture of a lost world of economic exchange in the early medieval Mediterranean. He asserts that the very networks I have identified here are themselves indicative of economic activity. McCormick, *Origins*.

Chapter 2

Sicily between Byzantium and the Islamic World

> Afterwards, the Saracens who had sailed from Rome came to Sicily, where they occupied the aforementioned city and slaughtered many of the population who had taken refuge in fortifications or in the mountains and, taking with them lots of booty or bronze, they returned to Alexandria.
>
> *Vita* of Pope Adeodatus II[1]

During the Byzantine centuries, Greek and Latin travelers to and from Sicily were examples and, indeed, agents of the complex web of connections between the Latin and Greek Christian worlds as they overlapped on Sicily. From the seventh century onward, Sicily also began to be drawn into the Islamicate world, as represented primarily by the political center of Qayrawān and the many seaports of Aghlabid Ifrīqiya (modern Tunisia) and Egypt. Long before Sicily became a Muslim province in the ninth century, in fact, considerable travel and communication were conducted between the island and the dār al-Islām, making the island increasingly important as a zone of interaction between Muslims and Christians, both Greek and Latin. Although, as in the sixth and seventh centuries, economic movements cannot be quantitatively reconstructed from the remaining data, by the eighth century, there is clear evidence of semiregular ship travel between the shores of Sicily and Aghlabid Ifrīqiya. While most of this traffic was of a military nature—with regular raids on Sicily's southern shores starting in the seventh century of the common era—evidence also points to both diplomatic and, perhaps, even commercial transactions occurring between Sicily and Muslim

1. "Postmodum venientes Sarraceni Siciliam, obtinuerunt praedictum civitatem et multa occisione in populo qui in castris seu montanis confugerant fecerunt, et praeda nimia vel aere qui ibidem a civitate Romana navigatum fuerat secum abstollentes Alexandriam reversi sunt." *Life* of Pope Adeodatus II (r. 672–676), *LP* I.LXXVIII, c. 137, 346–347 (translation mine).

North Africa while the island remained under the administrative control of Constantinople.

The introduction of Muslim powers into the western Mediterranean thus expanded the communication networks in which Sicily participated, in effect broadening the island's place in the region rather than constricting or isolating it. New networks were opened while preexisting ones were maintained, even if altered. It is true that the relative amount of travel along each of the routes shifted and rebalanced over time, as Sicily conceptually drew closer to Muslim Africa and drifted farther from the Greek eastern Mediterranean. As the central Mediterranean Sea became populated with more and more Muslim-sailed ships, the waters around Sicily came to be linked more closely with northern Africa. At times we see ships from the Christian world encountering difficulties when sailing into hostile waters, but these voyages did not cease. The island, at the nexus of these three worlds, continued for some time to be a place of interaction and connection between Muslims and Christians, even if a preponderance of these interactions, as they appear in the sources, were hostile. Even violent interaction—and especially regularly recurring violent contact, such as that which took place during the nearly annual Muslim raids against Sicily—is a type of exchange that requires travel and the infrastructure of travel, and that connects peoples and spaces, drawing them closer together in terms of communications.

Even while communications with Muslim North Africa were increasing, Sicily remained in contact with the Greek East and with the Latin West. That is, the entry of Muslim polities into Sicilian affairs caused a relatively slow shift southward—rather than a break—of the communication networks of the island, concurrent with the persistence of many of the connections between Constantinople, Sicily, and Rome (see map 3). The traditional periodization of Sicily's history draws a firm line between the Greek Byzantine era and the Muslim period, with historians of Byzantium and the Middle East divvying up their examinations of the island. If, instead, we look across these centuries, at the transition period itself, our view of Sicily's history and role within Mediterranean systems is very different. By placing the conquest of Sicily by Muslim forces in the middle of our examination rather than at the beginning or the end, we see that Muslim North Africa's involvement with Sicily transformed the island's communication networks rather than simply replacing one set of networks with another. Viewed across the period of the conquest, from the start of Muslim involvement in Sicily in the seventh century through the ninth-century conquest and into the tenth century, as Byzantine forces continued to try to retake Muslim Sicily—and by examining a variety of sources in Greek, Arabic, and Latin—political control did not necessarily determine

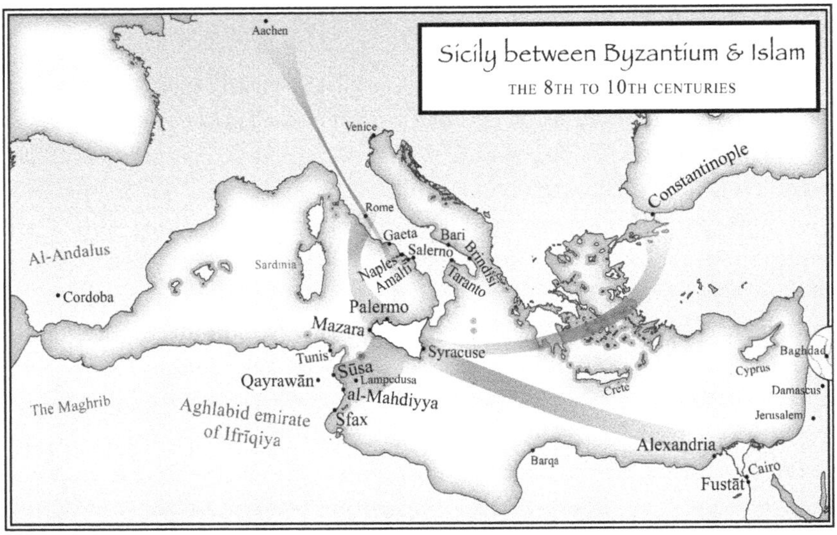

MAP 3. Sicily between Byzantium and Islam in the eighth to tenth centuries

the extent and range of the communications that defined Sicily's regional affinities and its place within those local systems. Sicily was and remained broadly interconnected within the Mediterranean system, with Muslims and Latins as well as Greek Christians, even as the shapes and meanings of these connections shifted.[2]

At the same time that military engagement was the most often recorded type of interaction between Sicily and Africa, the sources also allow glimpses of less martial communications between Greek Christians and Muslims. At times, those interactions took place because of or in the midst of battle, and at other times they could arise from diplomatic exchanges aimed at the stabilization of political and military tensions. Just as Byzantine Sicily was the site of diplomatic negotiations and the transfer of information between Greek and Latin Christian officials, so too did diplomats and envoys travel between Greek Sicily and Islamic North Africa, carrying both news and negotiations for peace.

2. It is also possible that Jewish traders were active already at this time, given that we know Jewish communities were present in Sicily from as early as the fourth century, and possibly earlier. Evidence of their commercial involvement in regional communications does not appear until the start of the Geniza evidence in roughly the tenth century. These communities and their role in Sicily's communications will be discussed in chapters 3 and 4. For an overview of Jewish settlement and life in medieval Sicily, see the introduction to Simonsohn, ix–lix; Simonsohn, *Between Scylla and Charybdis*; and Giuseppe Mandalà, "The Jews of Palermo from Late Antiquity to the Expulsion (598–1492–93)," in *A Companion to Medieval Palermo*, ed. Annliese Nef (Leiden: E. J. Brill, 2013), 437–485.

For example, the semiannual military incursions from Ifrīqiya were several times halted by truces that were officially concluded between embassies traveling between Syracuse and Qayrawān. Likewise, economic connections between the two may also have developed at this time. Because direct evidence for trade between Sicily and Ifrīqiya at this time is scarce, we can only assume the existence of economic connections that might be implied in the source record. Ships sailing back and forth within the Sicilian Strait between Ifrīqiyan ports and those of Sicily could have easily made the trip without meriting record in textual sources, and there are some suggestions that Sicily's economic conditions were attracting the attention of Qayrawān. The Arabic chronicles, although written much later than the events they describe, detail the raids on Sicily carried out from Ifrīqiya and list all of the items gathered from the island, which suggests that the Aghlabid *emīrate* was taking an increasingly economic interest in the island of Sicily. Even if these lists of valuable items reflect a nostalgic image of a lost island of wealth, they demonstrate that the memory of Sicily's conquest was tied closely to the perceived value of the products to be gained there. While the collection of war spoils was a regular part of this type of military strike, and a common way to reward soldiers for their service, it is the prolonged interest paid to the details of this booty by the later chroniclers that merits our attention. On the other hand, the products mentioned were exclusively high-value items—bejeweled icons and human slaves, for example—rather than more mundane trade items such as grain or textiles, which may also have proved attractive. At any rate, the Arabic chroniclers' focus on these spoils indicates that they associated the conquest (and, therefore, also the loss) of Sicily with the annexation of an opulent and prosperous society.

The precise reasons that in the ninth century these regular raids for the collection of booty turned into an outright conquest of Sicily are not perfectly clear. The sustained interest that North African Muslims had taken in Sicily for many years suggests that the conquest was not simply the result of a sudden revival of *jihād* ideology or a desire to expand Islamic rule into Italy. Likewise, the conquest of Sicily should not be understood as part of the same process that brought North Africa and Iberia into the Islamic world, although those conquests do provide a background for this one. The conquest of Sicily was a major undertaking that occurred more than a century after the conclusion of the initial period of Muslim expansion into the Mediterranean region, and it arose from unique impulses relating to the nature of the Byzantine-Muslim frontier in the central Mediterranean. As with the later Norman Latin takeover of Sicily, outright military conquest followed many years of involvement in the island's affairs. Sicily had been slowly entering the orbit of North Africa for several centuries prior to the ninth-century takeover. Then, as the boundary line between Byzantine and Muslim territory in the Mediterranean became more porous, the balance of power tipped far enough in Muslim favor that the outright military conquest of Sicily appeared to be advantageous for the Aghlabid administration of Ifrīqiya.

Indeed, it is the permeability of the Sicilian borderland itself that created the shift in relative power between Muslim and Christian authorities in the region. Much work has been done on the relationship between the Byzantines and the Muslims along the eastern frontier between Anatolia and Syria, and on the importance of that border zone for the health and wholeness of the Byzantine Empire.[3] Far less has been written about the western frontier, partly because the Muslim-Greek battles that took place in Syria and the eastern Mediterranean were closer to the heartlands of both civilizations, and partly because that region produced the preponderance of sources about the Muslim-Christian conflict.[4] But Sicily operated within the Byzantine Empire of the sixth through tenth centuries as an equally important frontier for Constantinople: one that both connected and separated the Greek world from the Latin Christian world and, as we will see here, one that did likewise with the Muslim world. Sicily was not simply a point on the dividing line between polities or religiopolitical civilizations; it also connected cultures in a zone of contact and conflict. The paradigm for discussing the relationships between Byzantines and Muslims has also tended to be that of conflict—both rhetorical and militarized. But some more recent work has also located shared traditions and a high degree of continuity between the Roman past and both the Christian and Islamic Middle Ages.[5] Likewise, the three cultures that overlapped in the border region of Sicily and southern Italy indeed did so with violence and war, but also with shared reliance on the Roman tradition and through diplomacy, trade, and interpersonal interactions in the midst of warfare.

During the centuries of Byzantine control, Sicily was a region where fluidity of communications made it possible for Greeks, Muslims, and Latins to contest their control over a coveted locale while also maintaining the diplo-

3. For one example among many, see Bonner, *Aristocratic Violence and Holy War*. Bonner has also studied the geographical definitions of "frontiers" in medieval Arabic texts, which focus on the Syrian border with Byzantium. Bonner, "The Naming of the Frontier: Awāṣim, Thughūr, and the Arab Geographers," *Bulletin of the School of Oriental and African Studies* 57, no. 1 (1994): 17–24.

4. See, for example, several historiographical and review essays on *jihād* and interactions along the frontiers of Islam, which, while valuable, focus exclusively on the Syrian border regions: Robert Haug, "Frontiers and the State in Early Islamic History: Jihād between Caliphs and Volunteers," *History Compass* 9/8 (2011): 634–643; and Arietta Papaconstantinou, "Confrontation, Interaction, and the Formation of the Early Islamic *Oikoumene*," *Revue des études byzantines* 63, no. 1 (2005): 167–181.

5. One notable example of such work, revealing a shared Roman inheritance in relation to interreligious violence, is Thomas Sizgorich, *Violence and Belief in Late Antiquity: Militant Devotion in Christianity and Islam* (Philadelphia: University of Pennsylvania Press, 2009).

matic and economic ties that were important to all of the parties involved. That is, this boundary zone between the Latin, Greek, and Muslim worlds was a disputed area, but one where various parties could meet, rather than a solid line of demarcation between Christians and Muslims. Sicily was often considered—by both Constantinople and local powers in Italy—an extension of Constantinople's authority and, at the same time, was an important venue for managing relationships between local Muslim powers and the Greek Byzantine world. These multifaceted relationships along the Sicilian borderland will here be viewed by means of military, political, diplomatic, and economic communications between Byzantine Sicily and Muslim North Africa, along with the consequent population transfers that wrought demographic changes in the region, which would themselves also help shape future communication networks on and around the island.

Political, Diplomatic, and Military Connections to the Muslim World

The vast majority of Muslim travelers who went to Sicily during the period of Byzantine dominion did so as members of the raiding parties that regularly arrived on the southern shores of the island and then soon returned to North Africa, like the ones in the quote that began this chapter. These military raids, conducted by both Egyptian and North African forces against southern Sicily's towns and ports, began soon after the consolidation of Muslim power in the North African province of Ifrīqiya in the seventh century, although specific dating for the first of these attacks is unclear. This long succession of military strikes on the island appears not to have been initially aimed at outright conquest of territory but rather at the collection of treasures and triumph. The Muslim conquest of Sicily, which began in 827 but was not fully completed until 902, followed nearly a century and a half of such raids. Early medieval sources in Latin, Greek, and Arabic alike contain many references to the recurrent attacks on the island by Muslim commanders and the efforts of Byzantium to defend the island, even though the details they provide—such as the dates and leadership of particular raids—are often conflicting. Most of these references appear in much later sources—which may be reproducing information from earlier texts—and thus cannot be trusted unconditionally. Without external verification, many of the earliest raids cannot be conclusively dated. Despite these debated specifics, comparison of sources in all three languages bears out a general picture of active engagement between Muslims and Christians in Sicily in the early centuries of the medieval period.

The history of Muslim involvement in and around Sicily rightly begins with the Islamic conquest of Egypt and North Africa. Military expeditions to Sicily from Muslim-held territories appear to have begun after Byzantine North Africa fell under Muslim control. The earliest raids into Africa began very soon after the Prophet's death: as early as 639 CE, an army under the commander ʿAmr b. al-ʿĀṣ set out from Palestine to Egypt and began the assault upon the Byzantine garrisons there. By 640/641 the fortress of Babylon had surrendered to the Arabs, as did Alexandria, the Byzantine capital of Egypt, in 641/642. Then, from their new base at Miṣr (Fusṭāṭ, or Old Cairo), Arab forces pushed westward during the first half of the seventh century and gained the submission—by force and by pact—of the Byzantine provinces of the Exarchate of Africa, and the Berber tribes and kingdoms of the Sahara.[6] ʿAmr b. al-ʿĀṣ led the first movements eastward from Egypt and conquered Tripoli. The succeeding raids into the Maghrib are attributed to Muʿāwiya b. Ḥudayj and ʿUqba b. Nāfīʿ, who established a permanent military base at Qayrawān in 670 from which to attack Carthage, the seat of the Byzantine exarch. By 698 Carthage had definitively fallen to the Muslim armies, and the Byzantine imperial government abandoned its hold on North Africa. The former territory of Byzantine Africa was then transformed into a new Arab province named Ifrīqiya, and Greek Sicily represented the last remaining holdout of Byzantine power in the central Mediterranean region (especially important after the fall of the Exarchate of Ravenna to the Lombards in 751). Even though still under Byzantine rule, Sicily was then drawn into the communications network of the rapidly expanding dār al-Islām—as represented locally by the provincial governments of Egypt and Ifrīqiya and more distantly by the caliphal power in Damascus (until 750) or Baghdad (after 750)—and was simultaneously elevated in political significance as the final holdout of Byzantine authority in the region.

By 705, the new province of Ifrīqiya was sufficiently pacified and organized for Mūsā b. Nuṣayr, al-Nuʿmān's successor as governor, to begin conquests beyond the western boundaries of the Byzantine Empire into the former Ro-

6. For more on the Muslim conquests of North Africa, see Michael Brett, "The Islamization of Egypt and North Africa" (lecture, Nehemia Levtzion Center for Islamic Studies, Hebrew University of Jerusalem, January 12, 2005); Brett, "The Spread of Islam in Egypt and Northern Africa," in *Northern Africa: Islam and Modernization*, ed. Michael Brett (London: Frank Cass, 1973), 1–12; Walter Kaegi, *Byzantium and the Early Islamic Conquests* (Cambridge: Cambridge University Press, 1992); Kaegi, *Muslim Expansion and Byzantine Collapse in North Africa* (Cambridge: Cambridge University Press, 2010); and Denys Pringle, *The Defence of Byzantine Africa from Justinian to the Arab Conquest: An Account of the Military History and Archaeology of the African Provinces in the Sixth and Seventh Century* (Oxford: British Archaeological Reports, 1981). For Roman North Africa in the period immediately preceding the Muslim invasions, see Conant, *Staying Roman*.

man province of Mauritania, and from there into Visigothic Spain. This last phase of Maghriban and Iberian conquests was relatively rapid, with Muslim forces entering Spain in 711 and establishing rule over the majority of the peninsula within a decade. The momentum of the conquests across North Africa and into Iberia did not at the same time extend into the Mediterranean itself, however. It was only after the establishment of stable provincial governments in North Africa (especially that of the Aghlabid *emīrate*, 800–909) that Muslims were able to take full advantage of their Mediterranean seaports in order to extend Muslim power into the sea itself: Crete came under Muslim control in 824, and Sicily's conquest began in earnest in 827. Prior to the ninth-century conquest period, Muslim raiding parties from North Africa made regular visits to Sicily's shores. It was these regular trips to Sicily, both for collection of booty and, eventually, on diplomatic missions, that began the process of bringing Greek Sicily into the orbit of the Muslim world, long before the island became an official part of the dār al-Islām.

During the seventh and eighth centuries, indeed, frequent raids were carried out against Sicily from the North African mainland, linking Greek Sicily and Muslim Ifrīqiya in a cycle of communications that were at the same time military, diplomatic, and social in nature. These attacks seem to have been aimed primarily at the collection of booty—slaves, coins, and ecclesiastical treasures are all mentioned in the sources, and it is possible that they also collected agricultural produce or other commercial goods that were not recorded—but may also have been early attempts to survey the possibility for future conquest to bring the island under Muslim dominium; some later Arabic chronicles portray the early raids in that manner. Both Greek and Arabic sources generally agree that these raids were annual or semiannual and terrorized the Greek Christian population, but that they did not result in any long-term territorial acquisition by Muslim leaders. The many Greek saints' lives written in Sicily and southern Italy contain tales of "Saracen" invaders stealing both goods and people, and convey the terror that these raids inspired in the general population and monastic communities alike. While the Arabic chronicles describe these raids as part of a long history of Muslim control over Sicily—and therefore emphasize the growth of ever-closer ties between Sicily and North Africa—the Greek *bioi* record individual episodes of raids and rapid return to Africa (and they serve as a background for the lives and miracles of their saintly subjects). These hagiographical sources also record masses of the Sicilian population moving northward or hiding in the hills to escape the attacks and then returning to their homes after the invaders had left. For some historians, these population movements have implied significant demographic changes on the island, but, because the *bioi* show populations returning to their homes, it is also possible to see the Greeks settling into a pattern of flight and return that suggests the development of predictable relationships with their harassers.

Precise dating of the earliest of these raids on Sicily is difficult, if not impossible, because the Arabic chronicles often contradict each other, and most were written long after the events they record (although many of them appear to have borrowed from other, much earlier texts). Nonetheless, these sources can be helpful if we use them with care: the specific details and dating of the attacks may be imprecise, but the pattern of regular North African interest in and communication with Byzantine Sicily is clear. Also obvious is that the later Arabic chroniclers—some writing after the island had already fallen under Latin Christian control—wanted to memorialize the conquest of Sicily with thorough detail and through the establishment of a tradition of connection that preceded the conquest; these conditions were clearly of very high importance in the historical memory of later medieval Muslims. Despite the uncertainty of the specifics, all of the extant sources record nearly annual raids on Sicily's southern shores beginning from the end of the seventh century and the start of the eighth century, which were halted only periodically by diplomatic peace treaties. It was around the middle of the eighth century that the Greeks of Sicily and the Ifrīqiyan Muslims intensified their relationship of warfare and diplomacy, as is seen across the textual sources. Over these centuries, the new Islamic regimes in North Africa and Egypt were becoming more and more interested in the people and products of Sicily, where the Greek populace and administration were increasingly focused on defense against these advances.

Because the Arabic sources can be problematic, another way to glean helpful information from the Arabic chronicles is to check their information against the Latin and Greek sources. In fact, the earliest strike on Sicily, roughly dated to the middle of the seventh century, was described exclusively in Latin sources and only in brief. These texts were concerned with describing the Muslim threats to Roman possessions in southern Italy and the papal estates in Sicily, unlike the Arabic chronicles that sought to establish a long history of Muslim claims to the island. Thus we must depend on Christian sources with a different agenda for the earliest information about the Muslim attacks, but, even so, these Latin and Greek sources often conflict with each other in regard to precise dating. The important point for our discussion, however, is not the question of whether a raid took place in one year or a different year, but the fact that we can trace a general pattern of increased Muslim involvement in the area from the mid-seventh to the early ninth centuries. The memory of these Muslim raids in each type of text can serve important roles in our understanding of Muslim-Christian interaction as it was perceived and presented, independent of our trust in specific dates and details. Both the Latin and Greek sources confirm the trend of intensifying Muslim naval activity near Sicily and southern Italy, and the escalating threat that they posed to Greek power in the area.

A case in point is the Latin textual evidence for the inception of the Muslim threat against Sicily. The first of the raids is dated to 652 by some historians, while other scholars have dismissed this date as too early for Muslims to have exercised significant naval power.[7] The supposed 652 raid is only recorded in the *Life* of Pope Martin I (649–655) in the *Liber Pontificalis*, which relates the story of Olympius, the exarch (viceroy) of Italy (649–652). This text tells us that Olympius, after he failed in an assassination attempt against the pope, gathered an army to do battle against Muslims in Sicily. These Muslim forces, the text asserts, had gained a foothold in Sicily already at this early date.[8] This seems unlikely, as there is no external evidence to support such a claim—nor indeed to confirm that a Byzantine exarch invaded the island.[9] The *vita* contains no other details about this supposed raid, its target, the exact port of origin, or the length of the Muslims' stay on the island. While there is no corroborating evidence to suggest that Muslim armies had in fact made progress in conquering any part of Sicily at such an early date, this anecdote at the very least reflects the growing awareness in Greek and Roman Italy of the Muslim advances in the central Mediterranean.

This account of the Muslim onslaught and Greek response is not trusted by all scholars because of the lack of independent verification of either the Muslim or Greek ventures into Sicily at this early date. The idea that Muslims had taken any portion of Sicilian territory as early as 652 seems doubtful—as

---

7. See Andreas N. Stratos, "The Exarch Olympius and the Supposed Arab Invasion of Sicily in A.D. 652," *Jahrbuch des österreichischen Byzantinistik* 25 (1976): 63–73. However, the Muslim armies in Egypt had access to the fleet of the Byzantines, which they seem to have been given control of as early as the 640s. See Michael Brett, "The Arab Conquest and the Rise of Islam in North Africa," in *The Cambridge History of Africa*, vol. 2, ed. J. D. Fage (Cambridge: Cambridge University Press, 1978), 490–555, for the detail of the Coptic duke Sanutius's handover of Egypt's ships to ʿAmr ibn al-ʿĀṣ. This suggests that the Muslim forces in North Africa possessed at least some naval capabilities with which they could have attacked Sicily, either for booty or for potential territorial expansion. In either event, for our purposes, the significant points are that there were Muslim raids against Sicily taking place in the centuries before the conquest period of the ninth century and that these raids brought Sicily into close connection with North Africa from a relatively early date.

8. "Qui facta pace cum sancta dei ecclesia, colligens exercitum profectus est Siciliam adversus gentem Saracenorum, qui ibidem inhabitabant." *LP* I.LXXVI, c. 133.

9. And, indeed, the other sources for Martin's life and exile make no mention of Olympius's supposed march against the Muslims in Sicily. See for example the second letter of Martin to Theodore, in *Narrationes de exilo sancti Martini* (*BHL* 5592), ed. and trans. in Neil, *Seventh Century Popes and Martyrs*, 172–221.

Muslim forces were still pushing west across North Africa and had not as of yet conquered the Greek capital at Carthage—but this does not mean that they could not have launched a naval raid in the region, simply that it is unlikely. Nor is there evidence that, if Muslim forces were indeed active in Sicily, they were interested in anything more than prisoners and booty. Such an analysis does not discount the possibility that the exarch had heard news of Muslim aggression in the central Mediterranean and preemptively moved to defend Greek control over the island, as an important site of Byzantine power in the region. Even if the year 652 is too early a date for the first Muslim raid against Byzantine Sicily, however, most sources agree that, by the late seventh century, naval advances by Muslim forces into the central Mediterranean were regular events.

One Arabic chronicle that purports to describe the earliest attacks on Sicily, the *Kitāb al-Futūḥ* (of disputed authorship), was likely written in the second half of the twelfth century.[10] In the account given in the *Kitāb al-Futūḥ*, three hundred ships were sent to the island for this early raid. The size of this fleet is likely an exaggeration but, even so, reflects the high value placed on the island, at least in the historical memory of the Arabic chronicler. This source also mentions that the North Africans had written in advance to the Sicilian leader, informing him of their intentions to attack the island. Such a detail suggests either that there may have been preexisting diplomatic relations between Syracuse and Qayrawān or that such a relationship could be imagined to have existed at this time. On the other hand, this note may reflect the chronicler's knowledge of later developments in the communication between the Aghlabids and the Byzantine government of Sicily, who subsequently established a long relationship of diplomacy.

Another, even later Arabic chronicle that records the initiation of Muslim interest in Sicily is that attributed to al-Nuwayrī (1279–1333). He claimed that the first Muslim incursion into Sicily took place in the year 653/654 and that it was led by ʿAbd Allāh ibn Qays under the authority of Muʿāwiya b. Ḥudayj, the commander of Ifrīqiya.[11] ʿAbd Allāh was victorious, returning with prisoners and treasure, including icons made of gold, silver, and jewels ("aṣnām

---

10. For more on this text, purportedly by Ibn Aʿtham al-Kūfi, see Claudio Lo Jacono, "La prima incursione musulmana in Sicilia secondo il *Kitāb al-Futūḥ* di Ibn Aʿtham al-Kūfi," in *Studi arabo-islamici in onore di Roberto Rubinacci nel suo settantesimo cumpleanno*, ed. Clelia Sarnelli Cerqua (Naples: Istituto universitario orientale, 1985), 347–363.

11. ʿAbd Allāh ibn Qays is referred to as "Awwal man ghazā jazīrat Ṣiqilliya fī al-Islām." al-Nuwayrī, *Nihāyat al-arab*, *BAS* Arabic, 425; *BAS* Ital., 2: 531. See also Ibn al-Athīr, *al-Kāmil fī al-tārīkh*, for the year AH 31, where a battle between Muslims and the Byzantine emperor is recorded (*BAS* Arabic, 215; *BAS* Ital., 2: 296).

min dhahab wa fiḍḍa mukallala bi-al-jawāhir").[12] According to the Arabic chronicler al-Balādhurī, the author of the *Futūḥ al-buldān* (ninth century CE), it was Muʿāwiya b. Ḥudayj himself, rather than his general ʿAbd Allāh ibn Qays, who led this first raid into Sicily. According to this account, ʿAbd Allāh ibn Qays also made a later assault on Sicily that garnered prisoners and elaborately decorated idols, which he then sent to the caliph Muʿāwiya in Damascus (r. 661–680 CE).[13]

Yet another chronicle contains even more conflicting evidence for this earliest raid into Sicily. Ibn ʿIdhārī (thirteenth-fourteenth centuries CE), in his *Kitāb al-bayān al-mughrib*, described the 653/654 raid as having been led by Muʿāwiya ibn Ḥudayj—a story similar to the account in the chronicle of al-Balādhurī. Ibn ʿIdhārī claimed that two hundred Muslim ships sailed to Sicily, captured prisoners and loot, and then sailed back to an unspecified port of origin. Most likely this raid would have been directed from Egypt, the base for Muslim advances in the mid-seventh century and the site of the most active formerly Byzantine port under Muslim control.[14] Although these details are conflicting and thus cause difficulty for historians wishing to trace the exact dates and origins of the raids, all of the Arabic chronicles agree on the basic story of a major raid on Sicily at an early date that yielded significant plunder and slaves. At the same time, Latin and Greek Christians in Italy seem to have been aware of Muslim advances in the region, even while they were misinformed on some of the details. Even if the contradictory evidence about the attack's leadership, port of origin, size of fleet, dates, and goals leads us to question the idea that there were Muslim raids on Sicily as early as the 650s, it is at least clear that some contemporary Christian writers and later Arabic chroniclers wished to make the case that the Muslim interest in the island had begun as soon as a Muslim base had been established in Byzantine Africa.

After the raids were initiated, possibly in the 650s, the next Muslim assault on Sicily appears to have occurred in the late 660s—either in 667 or 668/669, depending on the source we trust. One Latin source, which provided this chapter's epigraph, the *Life* of Pope Adeodatus II in the *Liber Pontificalis*, describes a raid in 669 that originated in Alexandria (with a stopover in Rome) and was directed at the city of Syracuse.[15] This text tells us that the population of Syracuse fled to secure fortresses and into the mountains for safety but

12. al-Nuwayrī, *Nihāyat al-arab*, *BAS* Arabic, 425; *BAS* Ital., 2: 531.

13. al-Balādhuri, *Futūḥ al-buldān*, *BAS* Arabic, 161; *BAS* Ital., 2: 216.

14. Ibn ʿIdhārī, *Kitāb al-bayān al-mughrib*, *BAS* Arabic, 352–353; *BAS* Ital., 2: 455: "aghzā Muʿāwiya ibn Ḥudayj jayshān fī al-baḥr ilā Ṣiqiliya fī mi'atayn markab fa-sabū wa ghanimū wa aqāmū shahr thumma anṣarafū."

15. *Life* of Pope Adeodatus II (672–676), *LP* I.LXXVIII, c. 137, pp. 346–347.

that, nonetheless, many were slaughtered. The Muslims took plunder in the form of bronze and then returned to Alexandria.[16] This Latin text mirrors the pattern presented in Greek and Arabic sources, which depict Muslim raids resulting in Greek flight into the mountains, Muslim collection of high-value goods, and a rapid return to Africa. Ibn ʿIdhārī seems to have conflated this attack with the raid of ʿAbd Allāh ibn Qays during which he acquired the bejeweled icons mentioned above, while he noted that he borrowed his information from al-Balādhurī, who dated this assault to the year 666/667.[17] Ibn al-Athīr (1160–1233) and al-Mālikī (eleventh century CE) also reported that Rūmī ("Roman," indicating in this instance simply Christians under the jurisdiction of Byzantium, rather than their ethnic or linguistic heritage) and Berber refugees landed in Sicily after the first conquest of Carthage by Ḥassān b. al-Nuʿmān in the year 693/694 (the second, decisive conquest of Carthage happened in 698).[18] These refugees, some of whom were Byzantine Christians fleeing to the last remaining foothold of Greek power in the region, were part of a larger movement of populations occurring in the early medieval Mediterranean. The capture of the port at Carthage, both geographically close to Sicily and historically linked to the island in terms of population and administration, appears to have resulted in an escalation of attacks on the island.

Raids on Sicily by Islamic forces continued into the early eighth century, intensifying further after 705, at which date the commander Mūsā b. Nuṣayr had completed the conquest of the Maghrib.[19] The consolidation of Muslim rule in western North Africa allowed the leaders there to concentrate their resources more fully on moving northward into the Mediterranean basin, notably taking most of the Iberian peninsula over the next decade. Under the chronicle entry for the year 705 CE, the *Kitāb al-bayān al-mughrib* notes that the commander Mūsā gave ʿAyyāsh ibn Akhyāl command of the Ifrīqiyan fleet, with which he was to wage further naval warfare on the islands of the Mediterranean. ʿAyyāsh ibn Akhyāl at that point attacked and plundered Syracuse, collected loot, and returned to North Africa. Like this and earlier raids, most early eighth-century attacks do not appear to have been aimed at the conquest of the island or any of its cities, although Arabic chroniclers, writing with the

16. Ibid. "Postmodum venientes Sarraceni Siciliam, obtinuerunt praedictum civitatem et multa occisione in populo qui in castris seu montanis confugerant fecerunt, et praeda nimia vel aere qui ibidem a civitate Romana navigatum fuerat secum abstollentes Alexandriam reversi sunt."

17. Ibn ʿIdhārī, *Kitāb al-bayān al-mughrib*, *BAS* Arabic, 353; *BAS* Ital., 2: 456; al-Balādhurī, *Futūḥ al-buldān*, *BAS* Arabic 161; *BAS* Ital., 2: 216.

18. Ibn al-Athīr, *al-Kāmil fī al-tārīkh*, *BAS* Arabic, 216; *BAS* Ital., 2: 297–298; al-Mālikī, *Riyāḍ al-nufūs*, *BAS* Arabic, 176–179; *BAS* Ital., 1: 238–240.

19. Ibn ʿIdhārī, *Kitāb al-bayān al-mughrib*, *BAS* Arabic, 353–354; *BAS* Ital., 2: 456.

benefit of hindsight, usually included them in general accounts of the buildup to the conquest of Sicily. Ibn ʿIdhārī included details about several eighth-century attacks on Sicily: one in 720/721, under Muḥammad b. Aws al-Anṣāri; another in 727/728, led by Bishr ibn Ṣafwān, which the governor of Ifrīqiya launched from Qayrawān and in which many prisoners were taken ("ghazā bi-nafs Ṣiqiliya wa-aṣāba bi-ha sabīan kathīran"); one in 739/740, commanded by Ḥabīb ibn Abī ʿAbda b. ʿUqba b. Nāfiʿ al-Fihrī; and yet another in 752/753, during which ʿAbd al-Raḥmān b. Habīb is said to have raided Sicily, gained prisoners and booty, and also raided on Sardinia where he imposed the *jizya*—or poll tax paid by religious minorities within the Muslim world—thus indicating at least a temporary exercise of Muslim political rule over a central Mediterranean island.[20] This fact may represent a deeper desire for political control over the Mediterranean than can be witnessed in the majority of the chronicle evidence. Imposition of the *jizya* may also have been the intention in Sicily, but for various reasons, including revolts and political turmoil in Ifrīqiya, none of the raids was able to actually establish lasting control over any part of Sicily until 827. Nonetheless, the frequent and regular military movements against Sicily had the effect of bringing the island into closer contact and communication with Muslim North Africa and of destabilizing Byzantine power there.

If the seventh- and eighth-century raids into Sicily appear to have been directed primarily at the collection of spoils of war rather than at the enforcement of Muslim political authority, the purpose of the raids shifted at some point toward outright conquest of Sicily. In most of the sources, this is depicted as happening in the mid-eighth century. For example, al-Nuwayrī's description of the conquest of Sicily mentions raids in 720/721, 727/728, and 739/740, but he dated the attack by ʿAbd al-Raḥmān b. Ḥabīb to 747/748 instead of 752/753, demonstrating again that details and exact dates could differ significantly between chronicles. According to his account, the raid of 747/748 was militarily successful and may have even resulted in the temporary establishment of Muslim authority in some areas of Sicily. However, because of a distraction in the form of news about *fitna*, or civil disorder, in Ifrīqiya, the people of Sicily restored the island to the Rūm, down to every last fortress ("maʿāqil") and stronghold ("ḥuṣūn").[21] According to al-Nuwayrī, the raid of 747/748 was led by Ḥabīb b. Abī ʿUbayda and his son ʿAbd al-Raḥmān b. Ḥabīb, who attacked

20. Ibn ʿIdhārī, *Kitāb al-bayān al-mughrib*, *BAS* Arabic, 354; *BAS* Ital., 2: 456–457. See also Ibn al-Athīr, *al-Kāmil fī al-tārīkh*, *BAS* Arabic, 218; *BAS* Ital., 2: 300. However, Muslims never effectively ruled on Sardinia, which gained independence from the Byzantine Empire at some point in this tumultuous period of the seventh and eighth centuries.

21. al-Nuwayrī, *Nihāyat al-arab*, *BAS* Arabic, 426; *BAS* Ital., 2: 532.

Syracuse, the Byzantine provincial capital. During this battle, the citizens of Syracuse fought back strenuously but were eventually routed by the Muslim forces. In the course of his attack, al-Nuwayrī tells us, the warrior ʿAbd al-Raḥmān struck the gate of the city with his sword, and the people inside the city were so afraid that they accepted the *jizya* ("hazamahum wa ḍaraba bāb al-madīna bi-sayf fa-athara fīha fa-hābuhu al-naṣārā wa-raḍū bi-al-jizya"), which should be understood as meaning that Sicily's provincial capital had recognized Muslim political authority.

Despite this apparent submission, the Ifrīqiyan Muslims were prevented from maintaining power in Sicily by the necessity of withdrawing their forces back to Qayrawān to deal with the situation there; whatever level of political authority they may have established in Syracuse at this time was forfeited. This story, and the way in which al-Nuwayrī's chronicle presents it, suggests either that by the mid-eighth century the goal of these attacks had shifted, or that his retrospective account simply identified a pattern of regular raids building from the collection of booty toward the eventual acquisition of territory. Whatever the original aims of these raids, and however we understand the details of their transaction, it is clear that the various Arabic chronicles depict the first half of the eighth century as a period of many regular attacks on Sicily's shores; it also appears that they understood the mid-eighth century as a moment of transition in Ifrīqiya's interest in Sicily.[22]

Other Arabic chronicles also present the middle of the eighth century as a point at which Ifrīqiyan Muslims began to take possession of Sicilian territory instead of simply collecting booty or slaves and returning home. Ibn al-Athīr's *al-Kāmil fī al-tārīkh*, like the other Arabic chronicles that cover the details of these incursions, contains information about the raids against Sicily in the years 727/728, 739/740, and 752/753 (to which year he dated the restoration of all Muslim holdings to the Greeks, again possibly indicating that some territories on the island had fallen under temporary Muslim control). Ibn al-Athīr also included a unique and instructive story of an attempt on the island in 734/735 led by ʿUbayd Allāh b. al-Ḥabḥāb from Ifrīqiya. This attack is not verified by other Arabic chronicles but is noteworthy because it contains specific details about a naval battle with Byzantine Greek ships, which had been mobilized in order to defend the island from the Muslim raids. After Ibn al-Ḥabḥāb

22. Jonathan Conant has calculated that 60 percent of the documented raids in the central and western Mediterranean that have been catalogued by Michael McCormick in *Origins* for the period 798–909 were directed at Sicily and southern Italy (although not all of them can be shown to have come directly from North Africa). See Jonathan P. Conant, "Anxieties of Violence: Christians and Muslims in Conflict in Aghlabid North Africa and the Central Mediterranean," *al-Masāq* 27 (2015): 7–23, esp. p. 18 and n. 55.

sailed for Sicily, according to Ibn al-Athīr, his fleet encountered one of these Greek ships and a fierce sea battle ensued. In the course of this struggle, a squadron of Muslim ships was captured, but the Byzantines were eventually routed and the Ifrīqiyans returned to North Africa victorious.[23] While there is no Greek or Latin textual evidence for a naval battle in the region at this date, this story certainly reflects later traditions of Greek naval defense of Sicily against Muslim attacks, which continued for more than a century after the island was wrested from Byzantine control. Indeed, Constantinople continued to send fleets to attempt the reconquest of island throughout the tenth and first half of the eleventh centuries. It may also be the case that this story reflects an actual change in the nature of the relationship between Greek Sicily and Muslim Ifrīqiya in the mid-eighth century.

Within a few more decades, the relationship between Sicily and North Africa would transform again to include regular diplomatic exchanges and periods of peace alongside this tradition of recurrent warfare. The second half of the eighth century and the early part of the ninth century saw a pause in military strikes against Byzantine Sicily by Aghlabid North Africa, slowed by a series of pacts made between the two powers. These treaties may have arisen in response to the more concerted efforts made by Muslim forces to conquer Byzantine Sicily or, alternatively, as a result of the greater strength of the government of North Africa and its desire for a stabilized border with the neighboring Christian power. Rather than communicating primarily through violence, the two sides began to send and receive envoys in order to ratify these pacts, keeping Greek administrators of the island in regular contact with the government at Qayrawān and its envoys. There is also some evidence that diplomatic relations were carried on during periods of peace, cementing the idea that Greek and Muslim officials and envoys traveled across the Strait of Sicily somewhat regularly and for a variety of reasons. Thus the Sicilian border between Muslim and Christian powers operated, for a time, as a locus of diverse multicultural communications, both violent and more peaceful.

The earliest evidence for these diplomatic exchanges appears primarily in the Latin sources and often includes details of the conversations that supposedly took place between ambassadors and messengers. An early ninth-century papal letter, for instance, contains details not only of a contemporary political exchange between Islamic officials and the Byzantines in Sicily but also of two previous treaties concluded between the same parties. This letter from

23. Ibn al-Athīr, *al-Kāmil fī al-tārīkh*, *BAS* Arabic, 218; *BAS* Ital., 2: 300: "sayara ibn al-Ḥabḥāb jayshan ilā Ṣiqillya fa-laqiyahum marākib al-Rūm fa-aqattalū qattālan shadīdan wa anhazimat al-Rūm wa kānū qad asarū jamāʿat al-Muslimīn fīhim ʿAbd al-Raḥmān b. Ziyād fa-baqiya asīran ilā sana ahadā wa ʿashrīn wa mi'a."

Pope Leo III (795–816) to Emperor Charlemagne, dated November 11, 813, purports to provide details and conversations concerning three early pacts between Sicilian Byzantine governors and representatives of the Aghlabid *emīrs* who traveled to Sicily to formalize the settlements.[24] According to Leo's letter, the Sicilian governor Gregory in 813 received Muslim envoys from *Emīr* Abū al-ᶜAbbās ᶜAbd Allāh, who wished to make a treaty with him. In his response to them, he referred to the earlier contracts that had been sealed between their government and previous Sicilian leaders, including one dated to 728 and one formalized with his predecessor Constantine in 804 that had been meant to last for ten years.[25]

Despite this peace overture and the history of treaties between the two sides, this offer of a truce was met with suspicion. The earlier pacts had clearly not ceased the raids on the island; indeed, the naval battle recorded by Ibn al-Athīr for the year 734/735 may have been the act that violated the treaty of 728. Leo's letter to Charles then goes on to describe the exchange that supposedly took place between the Greek governor and the Muslim ambassadors. The governor asked why the Muslims now wished to sign another accord, given that they had violated both of those earlier treaties. The envoys explained that the order for the diplomatic mission came from the caliph al-ᶜAmīn himself, the young son of Harūn al-Rashīd (d. 809), who was seeking to restore order and stability within his empire; in fact, he was killed that same year.[26] This answer seemed to satisfy the Greek official, as the two sides then signed a new ten-year treaty and exchanged prisoners.

---

24. Leonis III, *Papae Epistolae X*, *MGH*, Epis. 5, 97–99.

25. For more general work on diplomacy between Byzantium and Muslim powers, see Catherine Holmes, "Treaties between Byzantium and the Islamic World," in *War and Peace in Ancient and Medieval History*, ed. Philip de Souza and John France (Cambridge: Cambridge University Press, 2008), 141–157; and Hugh Kennedy, "Byzantine-Arab Diplomacy in the Near East from the Islamic Conquests to the Mid-Eleventh Century," in *Byzantine Diplomacy: Papers from the Twenty-Fourth Spring Symposium of Byzantine Studies, Cambridge, March 1990*, ed. Jonathan Shepard and Simon Franklin (Aldershot: Variorum, 1992), 133–143.

26. This exchange is interesting enough to warrant quoting at length: "Dicebat enim ad praedictos missos Sarracenorum: 'Quale nobiscum pactum facere vultis? cum ecce iam anni sunt octuaginta quinque, quod pactum nobiscum fecistis, et firmum non fuit. Immo et Constantius patricius, qui ante me praefuit, in decem annos vobiscum pactum firmavit usque ad futurm octavam indictionem; sed neque ipsum pactum firmum tenuistis. Nunc autem quale vobis pactum faciamus, nobis incognitum est.' Ad haec respondebant ipsi Sarracenorum missi, dicentes: 'Pater istius amiralmuminin, qui nunc apud nos regnare videtur, defunctus est, et iste relictus est parvulus. Et qui fuit servus, factus est liber; et qui liber fuit, effectus est dominus; et nullum se regem habere putabant. Sed ecce nunc, postquam omnia, quae pater suus habuit, sibi subiecit, vult firma stabilitate hoc, quod petimus, pactum servare. De Spanis autem non spondimus; quia sunt sub dicione regni nostri. Sed in quantum valemus eos superare, sicut vos, ita et nos contra illos in mare dimicare promittimus; etsi soli nos non valemus. Nos a parte nostra, et vos a vestra, a christianorum finibus eos abiciamus.'" Leonis III, *Papae Epistolae X*, *MGH*, *Epis.* 5, 98.1–14.

Pope Leo claimed to have received word of this diplomatic exchange from a messenger of the papal court who was in Sicily at the time of the agreement. No details are provided in the letter about the mission on which this papal envoy had traveled to the Greek capital at Syracuse. It appears to have been the case that such visits were a routine enough occurrence not to merit further explanation. The important factor here is that we see Greek Sicily in concurrent relationships with the pope in Rome and with the Muslim *emīr* from North Africa; messengers and envoys traveled between Syracuse, Rome, and Qayrawān with news, reports, and offers of peace. We see, too, that the papal court at Rome could serve as an intermediary for news between Sicily and the Frankish court—Pope Leo appears to have been a regular informant for Charlemagne about affairs in the central Mediterranean. This example, of simultaneous communications across several conceptual borders, further emphasizes the trilateral networks of connection in which the island was involved—and likely reflects a deeper tradition of Sicily serving as the meeting place for the three sides, Latin, Greek, and Muslim.

Other examples of news that traveled from North Africa to Rome (and thence to Aachen) via Greek Sicily confirm this pattern. Pope Leo's letters contain other reports of information that was transmitted along this route, suggesting in fact that Sicily was a regular pathway for cross-cultural communications. For instance, shortly after the conclusion of the 813 Byzantine-Aghlabid treaty—which was meant to last for a decade but was broken by violence after only a few years—the papal envoy was alerted, through the agency of yet another messenger, to the presence of seven "Moorish"—most likely meaning North African—ships ("septem navigia Maurorum") near Reggio Calabria on the Italian mainland.[27] These Muslim naval forces were reported to have despoiled an Italian village in the region and subsequently abandoned two of their ships on the shore, suggesting that the just-concluded treaty was already being breached. The envoy also informed Pope Leo of another attack by, he claimed, one hundred Ifrīqiyan ships on the island of Sardinia in June of that year, during which event the ships sank without explanation.[28] The Muslim ambassadors who reported this story then told the pope's messenger that when the survivors of this shipwreck returned to Africa and notified the families of those who had died, terrible grief and lamentation resulted ("talem luctum fecerunt, qualem nunquam ibidem fuit").[29] He then noted that this anecdote was also independently confirmed by a letter written to the Sicilian *stratēgos*

27. Ibid., 98.19–22.
28. Ibid., 98.19–36.
29. Ibid., 98.28–29.

by one of his Christian friends in Africa, indicating that normal communication continued in the Mediterranean even during a time of naval operations.[30]

This example—whether or not the details about the attack on Sardinia are precisely accurate—is significant because it again shows simultaneous communication being carried out between Sicily and Rome and between Sicily and North Africa, even about issues that concerned the North Africans more than the Christian polities in the region. Messengers regularly traveled from a variety of locations to and from the island carrying news and important communications, but also including this touching story of Muslim family grief. Greek Sicily functioned as a site for cross-cultural communication between envoys from Muslim North Africa and ones from Latin Christian Rome while they both were at the Byzantine court at Syracuse; the Latin papal court received news about emotional reactions among Muslims in Ifrīqiya through the mediation of Byzantine Sicily and transmitted that information to Charlemagne's court. Sicily appears to be the nexus of this complex set of communication that linked the Greek Christian, Latin Christian (including the Franks), and Muslim worlds.

It is noteworthy, too, that in this anecdote the Muslim ambassadors from Qayrawān reportedly had arrived in Sicily not on Muslim ships but on Venetian ones.[31] Venetian traders were active in the Mediterranean in these centuries, and the fact that they were sailing between Sicily and Qayrawān suggests that commercial traffic was maintained at this time despite the successive Muslim incursions into the region. Trade, diplomacy, warfare, and the transmission of news were all taking place at the same time, and Muslim envoys were not averse to sailing on Christian ships. In fact, these Venetian ships reportedly had destroyed two Spanish ships on the journey from North Africa to Sicily, further demonstrating the combination of trade, warfare, and diplomatic communications in the region.[32] We thus see that, in the early ninth century, the Mediterranean was being sailed by Muslims and Christians of various regions, and warfare and diplomacy could coexist alongside commercial and other types of travel through and near Sicily. The early medieval Mediterranean region around Sicily appears as a site of considerable activity and communication across regional, linguistic, and confessional boundaries.

In these reports of invasions and diplomacy between Sicily and North Africa, the Arabic and Latin sources also include implicit evidence for the communication taking place between Sicily and Constantinople at this time—in addition to the explicit evidence that was documented in the previous chap-

30. Ibid., 98.29–33.
31. Ibid., 98.35–36.
32. Ibid.

ter. The Byzantine government was obviously kept aware of the progress of Muslim advances against Sicily: the Arabic chronicles show that the imperial government regularly responded to the Muslim invasions with ships and military reinforcements sent to Sicily in order to help defend the island, indicating that the Byzantines were quickly alerted to developments in the central Mediterranean. From the seventh to the ninth centuries, indeed, Byzantine military actions against the expanding dār al-Islām took place on multiple fronts, including the Anatolian border with Syria, the walls of the city of Constantinople, and the islands of the Mediterranean Sea. Sicily and the central Mediterranean played an important role in the defense of the Byzantine Empire against the encroachment of Muslim power. Nonetheless, much of the Greek defense along this far-western frontier went undocumented in the Greek sources; this factor may explain the limited attention that Sicily's frontier with Islam has received in contemporary Byzantinist scholarship. In fact, many of the earliest Greek efforts to send military aid to Sicily appear in Latin and Arabic sources rather than Greek ones. For example, another letter sent from Pope Leo III to Charlemagne, dated August 26, 812, mentions a Byzantine fleet arriving to protect Sicily against invading Arabs.[33] The Muslims (referred to as "illa nefandissima Agarinorum gens," that is, "that most abominable people, the Hagarenes"), he wrote, had earlier that year mounted an attack on Lampedusa, a tiny island between Sicily and the Ifrīqiyan coast.[34] According to this papal letter, Lampedusa was at the time under direct Byzantine Sicilian control and was thus considered a part of Sicily. The Byzantine emperor Michael I (r. 811–813) sent a patrician and a member of the imperial guard to aid in the fight against the Muslims, and this patrician then sought assistance from the duke of Naples and the leaders of other Greek regions in Italy. The city-states of Amalfi and Gaeta contributed a number of ships, but the Neapolitan duke refused to listen to the patrician's pleas and did not aid the Greek effort, perhaps in an attempt to further distance his city from the direct control of Constantinople. The combined Christian forces assigned seven ships to scout out the Muslim vessels, thirty of which were said to have attacked and plundered Lampedusa. The Muslims—again described as a religious as well as military threat, called "nefandissimi Mauri" ("the most abominable Moors") and "Deo odibiles Mauri" ("Moors, hateful to God")—killed the members of this scouting party but were in turn slain, to the man, by the remainder of the Christian forces.[35] Even though these Muslim

33. Ibid., 96–97.

34. Ibid., 96.15–16.

35. The Latin sources thus not only record simultaneous diplomacy and violence but also indicate that, at least in the Latin world, the Muslim-Christian conflict had already begun to take on the

attacks and Greek counterattacks were not recorded in Greek sources, it is clear from the Latin evidence that Constantinople had been alerted to Muslim activity near Sicily and attempted to mount an effective defense with assistance from local cities that maintained fleets (which were important for their lucrative and growing commercial activity).

Indeed, this letter from the register of Pope Leo III is not the only source that mentions Greek naval activity near Sicily in the years before the Muslim conquest of the island. Arabic chronicles also include a number of references to the Byzantine navy using Sicily as the base for attacks on North Africa, although, again, Greek sources do not confirm this type of offensive movement in the region. For example, Ibn al-Athīr reported an assault on the North African city of Barqa in the year 681 / 682 that he claimed was carried out by Byzantine forces based in Sicily; this information is repeated in other later Arabic texts, which may have relied on Ibn al-Athīr as a source.[36] Another encounter between Byzantine and Muslim ships is related in the *Riyāḍ al-nufūs*, within the biography of the scholar Yazīd b. Muḥammad al-Jumaḥī, who is said to have died in an attack by Greek Sicilians against the vessel on which he was sailing from Ifrīqiya to Anatolia in order to wage holy war on the Byzantine frontier at al-Maṣīṣa (Mopsuestia, later known as Mamistra, located on the Byzantine frontier in southern Anatolia).[37] While this anecdote confirms the symbolic importance of the Syrian frontier for fighters of *jihād* from throughout the wider Muslim world, it also demonstrates that the central Mediterranean was a locus of conflict between Greeks and Muslims in the seventh century.

During the second half of the eighth century, as the conflict between Sicily and North Africa escalated, *ribāṭs* were built along the shores of Ifrīqiya to help defend against Christian raids and to house the frontier fighters who both defended and expanded the borders of Islam.[38] Such a buildup of North Africa's coastal defensive structure provides material evidence that Greek Sicily not only bore the brunt of Muslim attacks during these centuries but also it-

strident rhetorical tone that would characterize later interconfessional relations. The Muslims were described not only as a political or territorial enemy but also as a religious threat to Christian lands, people, and belief. Leonis III, *Papae Epistolae X, MGH*, Epis. 5, 96.25 and 29.

36. Ibn al-Athīr, *al-Kāmil fī al-tārīkh*, *BAS* Arabic, 215–216; *BAS* Ital., 2: 297. See also Ibn Khaldūn, *Kitāb al-ʿibar fī ayyām al-ʿarab wa al-ʿajam*, 14 vols. (Beirut: Dār al-Kitāb al-Lubnānī, 1983–1986), entry for AH 67 and al-Mālikī, *Riyāḍ al-nufūs*, BAS Arabic, entry for AH 69.

37. al-Mālikī, *Riyāḍ al-nufūs*, *BAS* Arabic, 179–180; *BAS* Ital., 1: 241. For more examples of scholar-warriors on the Arab-Byzantine frontier, see Bonner, *Aristocratic Violence and Holy War*.

38. Brett, "The Arab Conquest," 532. *Ribāṭs* are (often coastal) structures with both defensive and offensive purposes as well as an element of spiritual asceticism. See Antoine Borrut and Christophe Picard, "Râbata, ribât, râbita: Une institution a reconsidérer," in *Chrétiens et Musulmans en Méditerranée Médiévale (VIIIe–XIIIe s.): Échanges et contacts*, ed. Nicolas Prouteau and Philippe Sénac (Poitiers: Centre d'études supérieures de civilisation médiévale, 2003), 33–65.

self launched naval assaults against Muslim-controlled North Africa. At the very same time that Muslim and Greek ambassadors were meeting in Sicily to conclude peace treaties, therefore, both sides were not only waging defensive war but also regularly sending ships to undertake offensive raids against the other territory. The boundary between Muslim and Christian spaces was in flux, and the borderland region, thus, was the site of much activity—both contestation and communication—occurring both along and across the frontiers.

Despite these, and possibly other, unrecorded, efforts by the Byzantine navy to protect imperial territory in the central Mediterranean and to go on the offensive against Aghlabid Ifrīqiya, they were ultimately unable to mount an effective defense of the island. Muslim forces established a foothold in Sicily during the early ninth century and had subdued all of the towns of the island by the early tenth century. During the nearly seventy-five years that it took for the Aghlabid forces to gain control over the entirety of Sicily, Byzantine troops arrived to meet the Muslims in battle only a few times. Local affairs in Constantinople, combined with the growing military capabilities of the Aghlabids, made the Byzantine defense of Sicily unsuccessful. Nonetheless, Constantinople never relinquished its claim on Sicily and its southern Italian territories and would continue, up through the eleventh century, to send forces to attempt reconquest. The first Byzantine defense of the island in the ninth century followed the pattern of earlier Greek attempts to protect their western territories in the seventh and eighth centuries: they sent ships from Constantinople and sought naval support from local Italian powers. The Byzantine emperor Michael II (820–829) responded to the initial invasion of 827/828 by sending a fleet of military vessels, but the Aghlabid navy was able to blockade Syracuse and cut off supplies to the besieged city. The situation was reversed when the depleted Muslim forces attempted to leave Syracuse after the death of Asad ibn al-Furāt, the expedition's commander, at which point the combined fleets of Venice and Constantinople blocked their escape and forced the Muslim forces to burn their ships and remain on the island. These stranded troops then proceeded to begin conquering Sicilian towns and establishing Muslim rule over them.

Byzantine military aid arrived in Sicily in the years 838, 845, and 868–869, but none of the fleets sent from Constantinople was able to reverse the Muslim advances on the island, and as the Aghlabid conquest of Sicily progressed, the bulk of the island's defense was left to local Sicilian leaders and regional allies. Forces sent from Constantinople appear to have played little role in the struggle against the Aghlabid forces, with most of the resistance to Muslim advances coming from the local Sicilian population itself. Despite the inability of the

Byzantine central government to effectively defend Sicily from Muslim attacks, the complete conquest of the island took nearly seventy-five years. Resistance among the island's residents was fierce, but ultimately the Muslim forces prevailed, even though several towns had to be subdued more than once. The mountainous terrain of the island (particularly in the Val Demone, the northeastern region of the island, which held out the longest against Muslim domination; see map 1) meant that the Greek population could retreat to higher ground and form pockets of resistance to the Muslim invaders. Several cities were conquered by Muslim forces only to rise up in revolt and regain their independence, necessitating a second conquest by the Muslim troops. It was this type of local resistance, rather than robust naval defense of the island by ships from Constantinople, that caused the conquest of an island as small as Sicily to take so many years to complete.

The goals of the Aghlabid administration in transitioning from raiding to outright conquest of Sicily are not concretely discernable from the existing sources. They can partly be surmised through a comparison of the different textual sources that discuss the events of the conquest, within the broader historical context. I suggest that both economic and political forces led the Aghlabid government to decide in 827 CE to launch the attack on Sicily that was intended to bring the island under Muslim domination. The focus of the Arabic sources is on the political and diplomatic relations with the Greek Christians as the primary motivating factor that led to a decision to conquer the island. According to these later Arabic chronicles—which provide a long and dramatic account of the lead-up to the governor's dispatch of the conquering forces and the events of the conquest—the motivation behind the attack stemmed from a case of a Christian traitor from Sicily who sailed to Qayrawān in order to betray the Greeks to the Aghlabids. This common narrative, as found in the various Arabic chronicles, involves the character named Euphemius, a Byzantine Sicilian admiral who had been punished, according to most sources, for having organized a popular revolt against Constantine Souda, the *stratēgos* appointed by Emperor Michael II in 826. Other sources claim that he was being punished for an act of sexual aggression against a Greek Sicilian nun.[39] According to some accounts, Euphemius and his party defeated the Byzantine governor of Sicily and declared Euphemius the emperor of Byzan-

39. For these two different narrative descriptions of Euphemius's rebellion, see Michele Amari, *Storia dei Musulmani di Sicilia*, ed. C. A. Nallino, 2nd ed. (Catania, 1933–1939), 1: 367–381. Euphemius's story is found in Ibn al-Athīr, *al-Kāmil fī al-tārīkh*, *BAS* Arabic, rev. ed., 1: 270–271; *BAS* Ital., rev. ed., 1: 364–366; and al-Nuwayrī, *Nihāyat al-arab*, *BAS* Arabic, rev. ed., 2: 484–485; *BAS* Ital., rev. ed., 2: 113–114.

tium, from their base in Sicily. But after Greek officials defeated the rebels, the Arabic sources state, Euphemius and his family fled to Qayrawān, to the court of the Aghlabid *emīrs*, for protection and assistance in exacting revenge. The assertion, in both Arabic and Latin accounts, is that Euphemius sailed on a merchant ship to Ifrīqiya and appealed to the Aghlabid *emīr* Ziyādat Allāh (817–838) for aid in a strike against Sicily. In both versions of this story, Euphemius promised the Aghlabid governor that he would take part in the assault on Sicily (some accounts have him asking for the governorship of the island in exchange for such help) and provide helpful information to the Aghlabids if they would supply the ships and men for the attack.

Faced with this invitation to attack Sicily with the aid of an insider, then, the Aghlabid *emīr* is said to have consulted religious scholars about the legality of breaking the truce that had been signed in 813. According to al-Mālikī's *Riyāḍ al-nufūs*, there was an extensive debate in the court at Qayrawān about the legitimacy of this attack, given the standing peace treaty between the Aghlabids and the Christians.[40] Despite the fact that earlier truces had not been kept, the Arabic chronicler's account of this decision required that the Aghlabid *emīr* be scrupulous about maintaining the diplomatic and ethical upper hand. The dilemma of whether to attack or not during a period of diplomatic peace was resolved for the *emīr* when the chief *qāḍī* (judge) of Qayrawān, Asad ibn al-Furāt, queried a couple of Sicilian envoys about the veracity of a tip that Euphemius had given them: that there were Muslim prisoners being held on the island, in defiance of the peace treaty. These envoys, who were in Qayrawān on an unspecified mission, answered in the affirmative, thus giving the Muslims a legal basis on which to break the treaty and launch an attack on the island. With this turn of events, the moral and diplomatic high ground was claimed by the Muslims, and so the conquest of Sicily was both legitimated and, indeed, necessitated. Whatever their other interests in Sicily might have been—and these interests had clearly been growing in significance over the previous decades—this story of the Byzantine traitor Euphemius and of the Muslim prisoners being illegally held on the island provided the Muslims with the perfect excuse to break the treaty and launch an outright attack on the island.

Whether or not the story of Euphemius and the prisoners is a completely accurate representation of actual ninth-century people and events, it is helpful as a narrative for understanding the ways in which later Arabic chroniclers

40. al-Mālikī, *Riyāḍ al-nufūs*, *BAS* Arabic, rev. ed., 212–213; *BAS* Ital., 1: 304–308; al-Nuwayrī, *Nihāyat al-arab*, *BAS* Arabic, 483–484; *BAS* Ital., rev. ed., 2: 114–115.

understood the circumstances and causes of the shift from annual booty raids to direct conquest of Sicily. The story reflects both a literary tradition within the source material that justifies conquest and an understanding of the particular diplomatic, political, and military conditions in the central Mediterranean of the early ninth century. As with the narrative tradition concerning the conquest of Iberia in 711 that features a Christian traitor aiding the Muslim forces, the role of the Greek traitor Euphemius was considered essential for spurring the Muslim *emīr* into action. This was possibly because of the desire for insider information on Byzantine defenses and the interior of the island, and it was likely simply a convenient excuse to break the standing treaty. Despite the numerous military forays from Aghlabid ports to the southern shores of Sicily, most of the mountainous interior of the island would have been unfamiliar to the invading forces, and the long years needed to subdue the island attest to the difficulty presented by the terrain for armies that required reinforcement and resupplying by sea. Thus inside information could have been helpful to the invaders, but it is unclear how much Euphemius's advice and troops actually aided the course of the conquest; Euphemius drops from the narrative soon after the troops' departure for Sicily. The Arabic chronicle tradition needed the character of Euphemius to spark the conquest but not to conduct it.

At the same time, the tale of Euphemius's betrayal reflects the many ways in which Byzantine Sicily and Aghlabid North Africa had, by the ninth century, established a long tradition of close contact with each other. Not only were diplomatic relationships documented by the series of regular peace treaties, but, according to this anecdote, Greek Sicilian envoys were resident in Qayrawān at the time of Euphemius's arrival so that they could be consulted on the question of Muslim prisoners held illegally on the Greek island. While the entire story might be fabricated, what it does show us is the expectation by both author and audience that Christian envoys from Sicily could easily be present in Qayrawān, standing nearby, to be asked such questions. Likewise, Euphemius, whether or not he had played a role in any previous diplomatic talks between Syracuse and Qayrawān, is also clearly portrayed in these stories as having a preexisting familiarity with the political situation in Aghlabid North Africa, such that he could present to the Aghlabid rulers an offer of aid that he presumably knew they would find appealing. That is, the character of Euphemius made a calculated political decision to offer his treasonous aid to Muslim Ifrīqiya rather than to one of the Christian powers of the Italian mainland: Qayrawān was both geographically proximate and politically well known. By implication, he must have been certain that he would be received positively and that his offer of aid would be taken seriously, which shows some level of preestablished communications. And, lastly, Euphemius sailed on a merchant vessel to Qayrawān, indicating that regular shipments of some kind were understood to be moving between Sicily and Ifrīqiya. Unfortunately, very little external evidence exists for commercial relationships between Christian Sicily and Muslim North Africa at this time, but the presence of a merchant vessel in this narrative may indicate that their existence was taken for granted and, while not typically noted in the types of sources that remain from this period, probably quite regular.

The conquest itself, on the other hand, was recorded in great detail by the Arabic chroniclers. They recount the magnitude of the conquest with literary vividness, reflecting the importance of this undertaking for the collective memory of Muslim rule in the territories of the Mediterranean that, by the time these chronicles were written, had been conquered by Latin Christians. According to the chronicler al-Mālikī, for instance, the army gathered, with drums beating and battle flags flying, at the Ifrīqiyan port city of Sūsa (modern Sousse). With the chief *qāḍī* (judge) Asad ibn al-Furāt himself at the head of the forces, al-Mālikī wrote that they departed on June 25, 827, with one hundred ships and 10,000 men. Ibn al-Furāt had been chosen as the commander of the expedition despite the fact that he was a judge rather than a military official.[41] Another source reports, in accordance with the tale of the Greek traitor, that this fleet of Muslim ships was joined by Greek ones in support of Euphemius.[42] Al-Mālikī claimed that it took three days for the ships to sail from the port of Sūsa to Māzara, on the southwestern side of Sicily, where they disembarked and headed toward the capital city of Syracuse.[43] The provincial Greek capital had been a regular target of the raids in previous years, including the one in 747/748 that al-Nuwayrī described, discussed above. The 827 battle for the island's capital is said to have raged for a full year, during which time an epidemic struck the Muslim army and the commander Asad ibn al-Furāt died (from a disease that Ibn al-Athīr asserts was brought to Sicily on a ship that had arrived from Constantinople in order to aid the defenders). After the death of ibn al-Furāt, he was replaced as commander by Muḥammad ibn Abū al-Jawāri, who himself died at Castrogiovanni (modern Enna) and was replaced by one Zuhayr ibn Ghawth.[44]

41. al-Mālikī, *Riyāḍ al-nufūs*, *BAS* Arabic, rev. ed., 212–213; *BAS* Ital., 1: 304–308. For more on the career of Asad ibn al-Furāt, see William Granara, "Ibn Sabīl: Crossing Boundaries in the Biography of Asad," *Scripta Mediterranea* 19/20 (1998/1999): 259–267.

42. Ibn al-Athīr, *al-Kāmil fī al-tārīkh*, *BAS* Arabic, rev. ed., 1: 270–271; *BAS* Ital., rev. ed., 1: 364–366.

43. al-Mālikī, *Riyāḍ al-nufūs*, *BAS* Arabic, rev. ed., 212–213; *BAS* Ital. 1: 304–308.

44. Ibn al-Athīr, *al-Kāmil fī al-tārīkh*, *BAS* Arabic, rev. ed., 1: 270–271; *BAS* Ital., rev. ed., 1: 364–366.

Ibn al-Athīr's account of this story in his chronicle continues with the information that after the disastrous year of besieging Syracuse, without making any territorial gains but losing several commanders in a row, the Muslim army decided to abandon their assault and sail back to North Africa. At this point it appeared that the attempt to conquer Sicily for Islam would be a failure. However, a coalition of Byzantine and Venetian ships blockaded the port where the ships were docked, thus trapping the Muslim army on the island and, paradoxically, aiding the Muslim attackers. The North African army then decided to recommit to the conquest of the island, burned its entire fleet, and marched for the town of Mineo, which the attackers took after a three-day siege. In such a way did this inland town to the northwest of Syracuse become the first permanently held Muslim space on the island. The Muslim forces then moved on to Agrigento, which they were unable to capture due to the strong resistance of the town's inhabitants. The next town they did seize was the hilltop town of Castrogiovanni (Enna), which they used as a refuge when an army arrived from Constantinople to help in the island's defense. The Christian forces began then to take the upper hand and regained several of the lost cities, as would happen several times in the course of the conquest. The attackers retreated to Māzara, and the situation seemed hopeless for the Muslims until in 829 a fleet of Andalusīs and numerous ships from Ifrīqiya arrived and assisted them in the fight against the Christians.[45] By 830 the newly reinforced army was at the gates of Palermo, and by August / September 831 Sicily's future capital had surrendered.

A Muslim administration was established at the ancient city of Palermo at that time, even before the fall of the Byzantine capital at Syracuse (878).[46] This fact meant that for nearly fifty years the island was home to both Aghlabid Muslim and Byzantine Christian administrations: it was, in a very real sense, a part of both the Muslim and Greek Christian worlds at one and the same time. Palermo would serve as the island's capital throughout the Islamic period into the Latin Christian period, as established by the Normans in the eleventh century, and it has remained the island's capital ever since. When the Greek provincial capital of Syracuse was subdued in 878, the new Muslim administration of Sicily began minting its own coins in the former Byzantine mint

45. See the *fatwās* in Abū Jaʿfar al-Daʾūdī, *Kitāb al-amwāl*, ed. Riḍā Shahāda (Rabat: Markaz Iḥyāʾ al-Turāth al-Maghribī, 1988), 73, question 6.

46. For pre-Islamic Palermo, see Guiseppe Agnello, *Palermo Bizantina* (Amsterdam: A. M. Hakkert, 1969); and Ferdinando Maurici, "Sicilia Bizantina: Gli insediamenti del Palermitano," *Archivio Storico Siciliano* 20 (1994): 27–93. For the Muslim capture of Syracuse, see Bruno Lavagnini, "Siracusa occupata dagli Arabi e l'epistola di Teodosio Monaco," *Byzantion* 29/30 (1935 / 1936): 267–279; and Carlo O. Zuretti, "La espugnazione di Siracusa nell'880," in *Centenario della nascita di Michele Amari* (Palermo: Stabilimento Tipigrafico Virzi, 1910), 165–184.

located in the city.[47] This half-century period provides a concrete example of the blurred line between Christian and Muslim worlds of the medieval Mediterranean. Participating in both the Greek Christian and Ifrīqiyan Muslim worlds simultaneously, Sicily maintained political, social, and economic ties with both spheres and also continued communication with the Latin world of Europe.

Further campaigns were conducted against cities in the center and north of the island over the ensuing years. For the first several years of the conquest period, these attacks were conducted solely by the original invading force, before more ships could arrive from North Africa with reinforcements. In 830, the Aghlabid *emīr* Ziyādat Allāh sent Ifrīqiyan troops to support the conquest effort; I find no evidence of such support vessels arriving during the intervening three years. Andalusī Muslim fighters also came to Sicily in order to aid the conquest.[48] The influx of foreign warriors may indicate that the conquest of Sicily had been framed in terms of *jihād* on a regional level and that a call for participation had gone out widely among the Muslim territories of the western Mediterranean. Aghlabid troops were sent to help those fighters already on the island a few more times during the conquest period, although the majority of the original campaigns in Sicily's interior were conducted by the forces that landed on its shores in 827/828. Communications between the troops on the island and their commanders in Qayrawān were thus clearly unreliable and inconsistent, and it is possible that these Muslim forces were unable to rebuild their ships after the fleet's destruction in 827; nonetheless, news of the advancing conquests on the island had clearly reached Ifrīqiya by 830. Even with the arrival of support troops in that year, it appears as though the Aghlabid *emīr* could only partially commit to the attempt on the island, and shipments of supplies and support troops from North Africa arrived only irregularly. Political communication between the Muslim forces in Sicily and the government at Qayrawān only appears in the sources after the establishment of the provincial administration at Palermo.

---

47. For the circulation and minting of coins in Byzantine Sicily, see A. Cutroni Tusa, "Monetazione e circolazaione monetaria nella Sicilia bizantina," in *Byzantino-Sicula IV: Atti del I Congresso Internazionale di Archeologica della Sicilia Bizantina (Corleone, 1998)*, ed. Rosa Maria Carra Bonacasa (Palermo: Istituto Siciliano di Studi Bizantini e Neoellenici, 2002), 413–438; and D. Ricotti Prina, "La monetazaione Siciliana nell'epoca Bizantina" *Numismatica* 16 (1950): 26–60. The Muslims adapted a type of Greek coin (the *tremissis*) already in circulation in Sicily, creating a new denomination of coin called the quarter dinar. For more on this coinage, see chapter 3 and figure 6.

48. See al-Daʾūdī, *Kitāb al-amwāl*, 73, question 6, for the detail about *mujāhids* arriving from al-Andalus to join in the fighting in Sicily during the conquest period. This is one of the very few pieces of evidence I have found for early medieval communication between al-Andalus and the Muslims of Sicily.

The majority of the towns in Sicily had been subjected to Muslim rule by the year 902. The full completion of the Muslim conquest of Sicily, however, would take a total of one hundred and thirty years, as there were a number of uprisings and reversals along the way. The Greek population, occasionally aided by forces from Constantinople or Byzantine Calabria, regularly reclaimed towns and formed pockets of resistance to the invaders, but eventually all of the towns submitted to Muslim rule. The conquest that started in Māzara in 827 ended finally with the fall of Taormina (see figure 3) in 902 (although the Muslims needed to reconquer Rometta in 965, which was one of many towns whose Greek Christian population had seized their city from its Muslim overlords and was then resubdued by Muslim armies). Greek uprisings were particularly frequent in the eastern part of the island because of the varied terrain there; hilltop towns were difficult to capture and hold.

Despite the seemingly tepid defense of Sicily offered by Constantinople in the ninth century, the empire occasionally attempted to regain the island from Muslim rule during the tenth century. Even up to the first third of the eleventh century, the Byzantines at times launched naval forces in order to recapture the island, as political stability and will in Constantinople allowed. For example, Greek Christians in the city of Rometta appealed to the Byzantine emperor Nicephorus Phocas for aid in uprising against their Muslim overlords in 964/965. He sent a fleet, under the command of Nicetas, which met the forces of the Fatimid caliph al-Muᶜizz (953–975). Nicetas was captured, and Rometta was returned to Muslim rule.[49] A similar attempt later served as a precursor to the Norman conquest of the island. In 1038, a Greek navy led by a general named Maniakes was sent to Sicily, where it was joined by Apulian and Calabrian soldiers as well as those of the Lombard prince Guaimar. This campaign was mentioned by Amatus of Montecassino for the year 1039, at which time William of Hauteville, recently arrived from Normandy, was the captain of Prince Guaimar's forces.[50] The gains made by this combined Christian army were reversed when Maniakes was recalled to Constantinople. Despite this and other occasional attempts to restore Byzantine rule on the island, the Greek empire's western holdings were greatly diminished after the fall of Sicily to the Muslims.

Shifting from a political allegiance to Constantinople to a dependence upon Aghlabid North Africa brought Sicily new economic, cultural, and spiritual con-

49. Ibn al-Athīr, *al-Kāmil fī al-tārīkh*, *BAS* Arabic, rev. ed., 1: 263ff.; *BAS* Ital., rev. ed., 1: 342ff.

50. Amatus of Montecassino, *Storia de'Normanni*, ed. Vincenzo de Bartholomeis (Rome: Fonti per la storia d'Italia, 1935), 2.8. Translation in Amatus of Montecassino, *The History of the Normans*, trans. Prescott N. Dunbar, rev. by G. A. Loud (Woodbridge, UK: Boydell Press, 2004), 66. For more on this event, see chapter 4.

nections to the wider Islamic world; after the tenth century, Sicily joined the expanding Fatimid Caliphate and thus drew politically closer to Egypt, even while it thereby moved farther in distance from its capital at Cairo. During these same centuries, the routine Greek presence in the western Mediterranean, which had characterized the earlier centuries, was also dropping off as the Byzantine Empire contracted into itself. Greek Christian populations survived in Sicily throughout the Muslim period, but I have not been able to find much evidence for how closely they communicated either with Constantinople or with the Greek Christian regions of southern Italy. The simultaneous decrease in the numbers of Christian travelers to Sicily and the increase in Muslim and Jewish ones from the dār al-Islām meant that the nature of multicultural relations in the central and western Mediterranean region was fundamentally changing: Latin, Muslim, and Jewish merchants, pilgrims, and envoys played more prominent roles in regional communication networks, while Greek Christians became far less visible along the routes of communication in and around Sicily.

Diplomatically and politically, too, Sicily was drawn into the dār al-Islām. In contrast to the relatively good data on diplomatic affairs for Byzantine Sicily, however, evidence for Muslim Sicilian envoys, messengers, and diplomats at foreign Christian courts is virtually nonexistent. In addition to a change in the types of sources extant from these years—a change that may help explain this absence of evidence—there was also a shift in the relationship between the Byzantine Empire and the caliphate in regard to the western Mediterranean. Emperors were forced to concentrate their efforts on regions closer to Constantinople, and fewer ships and officials could be sent to Sicily, despite their occasional attempts to recapture the island. However, none of these efforts appears to have ended with a treaty or other diplomatic communication between the Greek and Muslim rulers—at least insofar as the source material can show us. With the rise of Muslim power in the western Mediterranean region and the contraction of Byzantine holdings in the area, there was less of a need for Byzantine-Muslim political treaties concerning Sicily and more of a focus on eastern Mediterranean lands.[51] At the same time, the Muslim conquest of the island spelled the end of Latin papal estates and churches on

51. Evidence exists for peaceful relationships and missions of diplomacy between emperor and caliph concerning other regions. For diplomatic relations between Muslim states and Byzantium generally, see Marius Canard, "Les Relations Politiques et Sociales entre Byance et les Arabes," *Dumbarton Oaks Papers* 18 (1964): 33–56; Kennedy, "Byzantine-Arab Diplomacy"; Yaacov Lev, "The Fatimids and Byzantium, 10th–12th Centuries," pts. 1 and 2, *Graeco-Arabica* 6 (1995): 190–209 and *Graeco-Arabica* 7/8 (1999/2000): 273–282; and Amin Tibi, "Byzantine-Fatimid Relations in the Reign of Al-Mu'izz Li-Din Allah (r. 953–975 A.D.) as Reflected in Primary Arabic Sources," *Graeco-Arabica* 4 (1991): 91–107.

Sicily (there is no evidence of a remaining Latin Christian population in Muslim Sicily, as there is for a persistent Greek Christian community) and thus a diminished need for European powers to send envoys regularly to the island as they had done in the earlier centuries. Additionally, there may have been little need for diplomatic treaties between the Muslim island and other territories of the dār al-Islām, since the island's primary political affairs were usually directed through its capital (either at Qayrawān or, later, at Cairo). Alternatively, envoys carrying news and directives from North Africa, Spain, or the central Islamic lands may have made the journey without appearing in the source record. Therefore, unlike the relatively busy diplomatic scene in Sicily during the period of Greek administration, there is little evidence that the Muslim rulers of the island used it as a site of regular political or diplomatic meetings or as the crossroads for broader official communications.

Economic Connections with North Africa

During these years of both violence and diplomacy, from the first seventh-century raids through the ninth-century conquest, Sicily and the Islamic world also began to exchange material goods and economic products, but to a far less measurable degree. Despite the hints that merchants sailed between North Africa and Sicily, both when it was a Greek Christian island and when it came under Muslim dominion, it is important to note that the true level and scope of trade cannot be measured with any kind of accuracy for this period. Nonetheless, it is instructive to examine the interconnection between Sicily and North Africa in terms of the products that moved back and forth between them because, as we will see below, the slight evidence for Muslim economic interest in Greek Sicily is followed in the Islamic centuries (ninth through mid-eleventh centuries) by an explosion of economic data showing a wide variety of goods traveling to and from Sicily within the economic orbit of the dār al-Islām.

Plunder, the most visible form of goods that moved between the island and the northern shores of Africa, could take the form of either material or human spoils. During the Muslim raids on Byzantine Sicily, attackers collected both material goods and humans for export to North Africa. The booty gathered on the island could have been later sold at market in addition to being distributed among the participating warriors. Human cargo, either as purchased slaves or as captives after war or a raiding expedition, appears relatively rarely in the sources, but it is widely assumed that slaves were traded throughout Europe, across the Mediterranean, and along the long-distance trade routes that connected West and East. As Michael McCormick has pointed out, slaves are not typically visible in economic data from the European Middle Ages, but that fact does not mean that they did not constitute one of the products within the system of early medieval commercial exchange.[52] There is little remaining evidence for Christian slave trading taking place on the island of Sicily itself, but we do know that Christian ships gathered humans for sale from the early medieval Mediterranean in general.[53] The Greek hagiographical sources also include many stories of Greek Christians who were captured in Sicily during the regular Muslim raids of the seventh and eighth centuries, most of whom, like Elias the Younger, as discussed in chapter 1, would likely have ended up as slaves in the Muslim world.[54] Stories like Elias's may have been more typical of Sicilian Christian experiences during Muslim raids than our sources allow us to see in detail. Evidence in Latin sources shows that Christians, too, captured humans for the slave trade in the Mediterranean, even if we cannot see this happening on the island itself, which may represent a more widespread practice in the central Mediterranean region. For example, the *Liber Pontificalis* contains a story of Venetian traders who went to Rome and set up market there. They purchased slaves whom they intended to sell to Africa, but Pope Zachary manumitted the slaves and forbade the trade in human life.[55] Thus some numbers of Christians found themselves enslaved in North Africa, but the extent of the slave trade between Sicily and the Muslim world cannot be definitely known.

Other evidence for human and material goods that moved from Sicily to North Africa as a result of these raids is found in Latin, Greek, and Arabic sources. Arabic chronicles that contain accounts of the raids against Sicily often include lists of the riches—notably including ornate icons, coins, and human captives—that were brought back to North Africa. From the very

---

52. For example, it is well known that early Muslim North Africa was a center of the slave trade, in particular exporting slaves from the Sudan to the Islamic East. Elizabeth Savage has suggested that Berber slaves were one of the initial sources of wealth in North Africa that spurred further Islamic conquests in the region. See Elizabeth Savage, "Berbers and Blacks: Ibadi Slave Traffic in Eighth-Century North Africa," *The Journal of African History* 33 (1992): 351–368.

53. Michael McCormick has collected references to Christian slavers in Italy. One example concerns Byzantine slave ships sailing along the Italian coast trying to buy Christians for sale to Muslims. See McCormick, *Origins*, 877–878 passim. The biography of Gregory of Agrigento (ca. 559–630) suggests that Sicily was a common source of slaves in the late Roman (and pre-Muslim) world, as Gregory's first trip from the island to Carthage was upon a ship whose captain intended to sell him there upon arrival. Leontios, *Vita S. Gregorii Agrigentini*, c. 7–8. For slavery in the Mediterranean more widely, see Youval Rotman, *Byzantine Slavery and the Mediterranean World* (Cambridge, MA: Harvard University Press, 2009).

54. For more on Muslim raids aimed at capturing slaves and the Greek Christian responses, see Conant, "Anxieties of Violence."

55. *Life* of Pope Zachary, *LP* I.433.14–19.

start of the Muslim raids on Sicily, treasure and slaves were an important part of the recorded accounts in the Arabic sources in particular, demonstrating how economically important Sicily would become for the North African state. The chronicle of al-Nuwayrī provides one account of this valuable plunder, during what was possibly the first Muslim incursion into Sicily in the year 653/654.[56] Led by ʿAbd Allāh ibn Qays, the raid was successful, leading to both military success and the capture of valuable goods. ʿAbd Allāh returned to Ifrīqiya, al-Nuwayrī explained, with human prisoners and treasure, including "idols" ("aṣnām") made of gold, silver, and jewels. While this episode does not constitute trade per se, it does show the movement of valuable goods from the Christian island to the Muslim mainland and the chronicler's interest in detailing the profitable nature of these raids. Such valuable goods captured from Sicily may have suggested to the North African governors that the island was a wealthy place worth their continued investment of military resources in exchange for the lucrative yield in slaves and booty.

Greek saints' lives from the Byzantine period are the most important sources we have for stories of saints who were enslaved during Muslim raids, some of whom escaped by miraculous means. The most notable of these saints from Greek Sicily is St. Elias the Younger of Enna (823–903), whose *bios* describes his double capture from Sicily during the course of different Muslim raids on the island.[57] His first period in Muslim captivity ended when a Byzantine ship intercepted the one on which he was being transported to North Africa. He was able to return home to Greek Sicily, only to be recaptured in a subsequent Muslim attack on the island. The second time, he was taken to Ifrīqiya and sold into a Christian household from which he eventually escaped. Another Sicilian saint, Joseph the Hymnographer (d. ca. 886), was captured by Muslim "pirates" and enslaved, though he was sailing in a different part of the Mediterranean.[58] Traveling between Constantinople and Rome, Joseph's ship was captured and he was taken to Crete; there he was eventually ransomed. Although this anecdote does not directly involve Sicily, it shows pirate activity in the central and eastern Mediterranean during the Byzantine period and the enslavement of Christians. Sicily, both before and after the Muslim conquest, participated in this lucrative slave trade within the wider Islamic world, first as a source of Christian slaves and later as a transit point and naval port for

56. "Awwal man ghazā jazīrat Ṣiqiliya fī al-Islām." al-Nuwayrī, *Nihāyat al-arab*, *BAS* Arabic, 425. See also Ibn al-Athīr, *al-Kāmil fī al-tārīkh*, year AH 31, *BAS* Arabic, 215; *BAS* Ital., 2: 296.

57. *Vita Eliae Iunioris* (*BHG* 580), *AASS* v. 37, August XVII, 479–509; and Giuseppe Rossi Taibbi, *Vita di sant'Elia il Giovane*.

58. Theophanes, *Vita Iosephi hymnographi*, *BHG* 944–947b, in *Monumenta graeca et latina*, vol. 2, 1–14; and *AASS* v. 10, April III, 266–276.

slave-trading ships, but the volume of this trade in unknowable from the extant sources.

Another open question, as discussed in chapter 1, is that of Sicilian wheat and its possible appeal for the Aghlabids. A letter by Pope Leo III contains one piece of evidence suggesting that agricultural goods, such as grain, may have been among the spoils collected in the region by the Muslim raiders. This Latin letter, dated August 26, 812, discussed above as an account of naval warfare on the island of Lampedusa near Sicily, also recounts an anecdote about the Muslim depredations on Ischia, a small volcanic island off the coast of Naples. In this incident, the Muslims left behind the dead bodies of men and horses, along with a stash of looted grain and chaff ("granum et scirpha") that they could not carry with them, which were then found by the Gaetanis.[59] Here we have one bit of anecdotal and secondhand information about the Muslim armies collecting grain and other agricultural or commercial goods on their raids into Christian territory of the central Mediterranean. The later Arabic chroniclers, however, do not appear to have been concerned to note the presence of agricultural goods among the spoils collected in Sicily and southern Italy, instead focusing on high-value goods such as bejeweled icons, gold and silver, and humans intended for the slave market. Nonetheless, grain may have been one of the attractions that the island held for the Aghlabid administration at Qayrawān—surviving textual evidence simply does not tell us, one way or the other, until much later when the Jewish mercantile letters and Muslim legal responsa begin to record evidence of commercial transactions between Muslim Sicily and its political center in North Africa.

What is clear in the ninth century is that Sicily's economic production appears to have been a strong draw for the Aghlabid rulers of Ifrīqiya. The dynamic connections established between the Greek island and Muslim Ifrīqiya across the period of the raids—starting in the seventh century and escalating in the middle of the eighth century—may have contributed to the decision by the Aghlabids to shift from raiding the island to conquering it outright in the ninth century. Even though the official story of the invasion hinges on matters of diplomatic agreements and political expediency, the long record of raiding, and the details provided by chroniclers about the types of plunder acquired, suggests that economic considerations played a role in the decision to attempt to take Sicily as the Aghlabids' own province, rather than simply as a source of continual plunder. As we will see in the following chapter, Sicily under Muslim

59. Leonis III, *Papae Epistolae X, MGH*, Epis. 5, 96.33–97.8. The word *scirpha* appears to be unique to this text. Du Cange defines it as coming from the Greek κάρφος (woodchip) and having the meaning of the Latin *palea*, or chaff. Du Cange et al., *Glossarium mediae et infimae Latinitatis* (Niort: L. Favre, 1883–1887), 7: col. 355c.

administration became closely connected with the trade routes and commercial relationships of both Egypt and North Africa. Trade, in fact, appears in the extant sources—particularly from the Cairo Geniza detailing the activities of Jewish merchants in the central Mediterranean—as the primary way in which Muslim Sicily communicated with the rest of the dār al-Islām. Given that this was the case in later centuries, it likewise may have been true that the Aghlabids of Ifrīqiya foresaw the economic importance that Sicily could hold, both as a source of trade goods and as a shipping hub for items en route to other locales in the Mediterranean. Thus it is possible, but in no way demonstrable, that the Muslims of North Africa wanted Sicily in part because of its economic potential and the role that the island could play in cross-Mediterranean trade.

Population, Settlement, and Resettlement

The final category of communication between Sicily and other regions of the Mediterranean during the period of transition from Greek to Muslim rule is that of the movement of population groups that led to large-scale demographic transformation. The military and economic connections that brought Sicily into the orbit of Muslim Africa in the early Middle Ages also caused population shifts that shaped the human landscape of the central Mediterranean region. These movements of people within the area serve as a further illustration of the ways in which early medieval Sicily functioned as a locus of connection between the Latin, Greek, and Muslim worlds. This type of travel is not that of individuals but of masses of people moving for colonization and migration; likewise, conversion patterns—mostly invisible in the textual sources—helped transform the character, culture, and language of Sicily during these centuries. Attendant upon the many major political and religious shifts that took place in Sicily during the seventh through twelfth centuries were transformations in the language and culture of the island's population. The island both received immigrants from elsewhere and at times saw some of its population leave for other regions. Some of these changes can be traced in the sources, allowing us to understand more fully the ways in which Sicily was affected by broader political and economic trends in the Mediterranean world, while other transformations are only visible in hindsight. Evidence for relocated Sicilians and immigrants to the island also reveals the lands with which Sicily was connected through networks of personal travel and settlement and, thereby, the broad networks of communication that existed between these various regions. These data suggest that Sicily's population shifted not only when the island's dominant political and religious regime changed, but also at times of tumult in the Mediterranean at large. This role of Sicily as a way station for Mediterranean-wide demographic change may speak to the island's significance in wider networks of communication and shipping: the island may have been a convenient place of refuge because of its position along shipping lanes and its numerous ports of call for ships within the wider region.

By the time Sicily experienced its first attacks by the Muslim forces of North Africa in the seventh century, the island's population was a majority Byzantine Greek, although Latin settlements and churches remained.[60] During the ninth-century Muslim invasion of Sicily, the Byzantine population of the island only partly gave way to the invading Muslims—made up of both Berber and Arab factions—and Greek speakers were never completely erased from the island (although I find no evidence for continued Latin population there). To be sure, the centuries of Muslim raids displaced considerable numbers of Greeks who either fled, were killed, or were captured for the slave market. The Greek narratives of saints' lives and their miracles from Sicily and southern Italy that date from the eighth and early ninth centuries record several stories about individual monks and entire monastic communities who escaped the attackers from Muslim North Africa, either temporarily or permanently. In a number of these accounts, the monks moved north to establish new monastic communities outside of the regions under threat of Muslim raids, as we saw in chapter 1. But in other narratives the monks and the Christian inhabitants of besieged towns relocated only temporarily—to cave shelters or into the hills—and returned to their homes after the departure of the Muslim raiders.[61] Some of the conquered Christian population also surely converted to Islam and assimilated into the majority population, but the means and chronology of those conversions are unclear.

However, Greek Christian migration did not exclusively entail movement away from Sicily: in the same centuries that some Christians were departing from Sicily because of Muslim invasions, other Greek migrants arrived in Byzantine Sicily. Fleeing the Muslim incursions into North Africa, some Christians there sought asylum in Sicily. In 697/698, for example, general Ḥassan b. al-Nuʿmān al-Ghassānī captured Carthage, and, according to Ibn ʿIdhārī, some of the Christian and Berber residents of the city took refuge in Sicily, while

60. For two opposing views of this process of Hellenization of Sicily, see Guillou, "La Sicile Byzantine"; and Lynn White Jr., "The Byzantinization of Sicily," *The American Historical Review* 42, no. 1 (1936): 1–21. See also the summary of the historiographical debate and further bibliography in Herrin, "The Process of Hellenization," esp. n. 46.

61. See Costa-Louillet, "Saints de Sicile e d'Italie Méridionale."

others moved to Spain.[62] This confluence of people leaving the island and arriving on it at the same time (and due in part to the same forces acting in different locations) was repeated at other points in Sicily's history and indicates that the island could serve as a transitional spot for those relocating within the western Mediterranean area.

As the Aghlabids exerted greater pressure on Sicily in the ninth century, however, it appears that more Greeks left the island than arrived on it. Saints' lives show that some of the Greek saints and their families left the island for southern Italy or the East due to the invasions and then continued traveling for other reasons. In the 820s, the family of Joseph the Hymnographer (born in Catania and died ca. 886) emigrated from Sicily to the Peloponnesus because of the Arab raids, for example, and from there Joseph moved to Constantinople.[63] Another monk who left Sicily because of attacks from North Africa was Elias Spelaiotes (864–960), who had moved to the island from Reggio Calabria to join a monastery but departed on a pilgrimage to Rome after his friend and fellow monk was killed during a Muslim attack.[64] Elias the Younger also relocated due to Muslim violence: he was born in Enna in central Sicily and early in his life was forced by Muslim attacks to relocate.[65] According to his *bios*, Enna was destroyed by Saracens from Carthage ("Καρχηδονίων . . . Σαρακηνῶν"), forcing the saint's family to move to the castle (κάστρον) of Santa Maria for shelter.[66] These are only individual anecdotes and cannot help us quantify population movements during and after the Muslim raids, but they can show us how some Christian families responded to the Muslim threat by emigrating to different Christian regions with which Sicily had preexisting connections. Notwithstanding these examples of individuals and families who left Sicily because of the Muslim attacks, many Greek Christians must have stayed on the island, given that in the eleventh century, invading Normans discovered Greek communities there. Indeed, some towns and areas of northeastern Sicily maintained their majority Greek Christian character throughout the Muslim period.[67]

---

62. Ibn ʿIdhārī, *Kitāb al-bayān al-mughrib*, *BAS* Arabic, 353; *BAS* Ital., 2: 456.

63. Theophanes, *Vita Iosephi hymnographi*; *AASS* v. 10, April III, 266–276.

64. *Vita S. Eliae Spelaeotae* (BHG 581), *AASS* v. 43, September XI, 848–888.

65. *Vita Eliae Iunioris* (BHG 580), AASS v. 37, *AASS* v. 37, August XVII, 479–509, Giuseppe Rossi Taibbi, *Vita di sant'Elia il Giovane*.

66. *Vita Eliae Iunioris*, c. 3, esp. ll. 55–58. It is not clear where this fortification was located, whether in Sicily or in mainland Italy.

67. Norman invaders encountered Greek Christians in several of the towns they attacked and obviously expected them to support the Christian conquerors. Geoffrey of Malaterra seemed surprised that these Christians would choose to continue to support their Muslim overlords See Geoffrey of Malaterra, *De rebus gestis Rogerii Calabriae et Siciliae comitis et Robertis Guiscardi ducis fratris eius*, ed. Ernesto Pontieri, Rerum Italicarum Scriptores series 2, v. 5 pt. 1 (Bologna: Nicola Zanichelli, 1927),

The accounts of Muslim attacks in the Greek *vitae* of Sicilian saints show the devastation of populations and of the countryside as well as the escapes of the saints and their families. The Greek population of Sicily continued, in the ninth and tenth centuries, to experience Muslim attacks that again forced some people to migrate to other cities in Sicily or to the Italian mainland, further displacing the Christian population, even if temporarily. The *bioi* of SS. Christopher and Makarios (d. 1000) and of St. Sabas (d. 990/901), for example, describe several invasions that destroyed fields and brought on famine, along with the miracles performed by the saints in aid of the people.[68] Many other hagiographies of contemporary Sicilian saints depict similar depredations, both as a prompt for a saint's travels and as an opportunity for miracles. Nonetheless, we can see in these stories the outlines of a pattern of Muslim raids and Christian responses. During each of these invasions, the Greek population sought refuge as in the earlier accounts: at times in hilltop citadels, caves, forests, and monasteries, and at other times in towns further north in Sicily or in mainland Italy. Christopher and his sons and fellow monks, Makarios and Sabas, fled from their monastery of St. Philip of Agira—first to Calabria and then further north to Salerno when the raiders attacked southern Italy. Such progressive migration may have been common among the Greek population at large, but it is also possible that some people who took refuge in temporary shelters later returned to their homes and regular lives after the establishment of a stable Muslim administration; some surely converted to Islam, but we cannot see this happening in the extant sources.

At the same time that the Greek Christians were either moving or converting to Islam, Arabic- and Berber-speaking Muslim populations were colonizing the conquered island. Despite the survival of many Christians in Sicily after the Muslim conquest of the island, a majority of the population during the Muslim period apparently consisted of Arabs and Berbers who migrated there from North Africa after the takeover, along with Jewish inhabitants whose time of arrival in Sicily is unknown.[69] This transformation of the island from a Greek-speaking Christian region to an Arabic-speaking Muslim one is inadequately understood by scholars, as is the later change that took place after the Norman

b. 2, c. 14 and b. 2, c. 29. English translation in Kenneth Baxter Wolf, *The Deeds of Count Roger of Calabria and Sicily and of His Brother Duke Robert Guiscard* (Ann Arbor: University of Michigan Press, 2005), p. 92 and p. 102–104. For more on the later fate of these Greek populations, see Graham A. Loud, "Communities, Cultures and Conflict in Southern Italy, from the Byzantines to the Angevins" *al-Masāq* 28:2 (2016): 132–152.

68. Giuseppe Cozza-Luzi, *Historia et laudes SS. Sabae et Macarii iuniorum e Sicilia auctore Oreste Patriarcha Hierosolymitano* (Rome: Typis Vaticanis, 1893).

69. For information about the earliest history of Jews in Sicily, see Simonsohn, ix-lxxii; and Simonsohn, *Between Scylla and Charybdis*.

invasion and the shift toward a Latin Christian population.[70] It seems likely that these large-scale demographic shifts took place as people slowly converted due to pressures—economic, cultural, or even political—exerted by the dominant culture, and that new settlements by the conquering people gradually replaced the island's previous residents.[71] Nevertheless, minority population groups remained under both regimes—in the case of Greek Christians, throughout the Muslim period in the northeast, and in the case of Muslims, until the final descendants of Sicily's Muslims were expelled from the island under Frederick II in the thirteenth century.[72]

Such trends of movement, population change, and acculturation—of both language and religion in Sicily—across the early medieval centuries demonstrate the complexity of the cross-cultural, political, and economic relationships found in and around Sicily at this time. Multifaceted communications—violent and peaceful, spectacular and mundane—took place on the island involving parties and individuals from the Latin world, the Greek world, and the Muslim world. Many of these communications are visible in the extant sources, but many others can only be surmised from existing evidence. Altogether, however, it is clear that the island was never simply a participant in one empire, religion, language, or culture at a time: the three worlds of the early medieval Mediterranean met, mixed, and collided on Sicily as they did nowhere else.

---

70. On the subject of Sicily's demographic transformations, see Metcalfe, *Muslims and Christians in Norman Sicily*.

71. See Chiarelli, *A History of Muslim Sicily*, for more on the Muslim colonization and the role of the Berbers in Sicilian society.

72. See David Abulafia, "Monarchs and Minorities in the Christian Western Mediterranean around 1300: Lucera and Its Analogues," in *Christendom and Its Discontents: Exclusion, Persecution, and Rebellion, 1000–1500*, ed. Scott L. Waugh and Peter D. Diehl (Cambridge: Cambridge University Press, 1996), 234–263; Eberhard Horst, *Der Sultan von Lucera: Friedrich II. und der Islam* (Freiburg: Herder, 1997); Christoph T. Maier, "Crusade and Rhetoric against the Muslim Colony of Lucera: Eudes of Chateauroux's Sermones de Rebellione Sarracenorum Lucherie in Apulia," *Journal of Medieval History* 21, no. 4 (1995): 343–385; and Jean-Marie Martin, "La colonie Sarrasine de Lucera et son environnement. Quelques reflexions," in *Mediterraneo medievale: Scritti in onore di Francesco Giunta* (Soveria Mannelli: Rubbettino, 1989), 2: 805–808.

Chapter 3

Sicily in the Dār al-Islām

> There are quite a few ribat [fortresses] on the coastline, full of freeloaders, scoundrels and renegades, both young and old, poor and ignorant. These people would pretend to perform their prostrations, standing in order to steal money given to charity, or to defame honorable women. Most of them were pimps and perverts. They sought refuge there because they were incapable of doing anything else, and because they had no place to go. They were low-life and rabble.
>
> Ibn Ḥawqal, *Kitāb ṣūrat al-arḍ*[1]

As we have seen in the previous two chapters, Sicily of the sixth through ninth centuries was a space of multifaceted communications between all three of the major cultural zones of the early medieval world: not only did Byzantine-ruled Sicily participate in transregional communications between the Latin (and Germanic) and Greek Christian worlds, but it did so also, from the mid-seventh century, between these Christian powers and the political and cultural world of Islam as it gained power through the western Mediterranean. At times, in fact, the evidence shows the island in simultaneous communications with Constantinople, Rome, and Qayrawān and as the site of multilateral communications between these parties. Early medieval Sicily thus constituted a space of interaction between Latin Christians, Greek Christians, and Muslims, even as it formed a vital frontier for Byzantium along the edge of the expanding Islamic world. This situation of complex intercultural and interregional communications did not, however, work in the same ways at all times and, from the middle of the eighth century, began to shift fundamentally in favor of Sicily's connections to the Muslim world. As the attacks on Sicily from Muslim North Africa increased, the island

1. Muḥammad Abū al-Qāsim Ibn Ḥawqal, *Kitāb ṣūrat al-arḍ*, 2nd ed, ed. J. H. Kramers, *BGA*, vol. 2. (Leiden: E. J. Brill, 1967), 121. The quoted passage comes from William E. Granara's translation in "Ibn Hawqal in Sicily," *Alif: Journal of Comparative Poetics* 3 (1983): 97.

drew closer—in terms of communications—to the dār al-Islām and, at the same time, further from Constantinople, which had an increasingly difficult time controlling and defending the island, both from internal rebellions and from external invaders. In many ways, then, the Aghlabid conquest of Sicily in the ninth century only confirmed a transition that had been in process for many years. The political conquest of Sicily thus did not create a firm break in the island's history, but rather a transformation of preexisting networks: patterns of travel and communication had indeed linked the island with the Muslim world for many years.

Sicily remained under Muslim control until the middle of the eleventh century CE, first ruled by the Aghlabids of Ifrīqiya and then by the new Fatimid power that was based, from 969, in Egypt. The period of Muslim dominion on Sicily lasted until Christians under Norman leadership invaded the island beginning in 1060. As early medieval Sicily drifted conceptually closer to the dār al-Islām and then entered it, the communications networks with which it was involved, and the uses to which the island was put by its rulers, shifted significantly. If patterns of travel and communication in the early Middle Ages show Sicily as an island at the very overlap between the Muslim and Christian worlds—at once connected to all three major civilizations of the Mediterranean world—in the late ninth and tenth centuries, it was firmly planted within the realm of Muslim northern Africa. By the middle of the ninth century, the majority of the island was under Islamic control, and it soon became clear that Christian rule—despite regular Byzantine attempts at reconquest—had given way to an Islamic administration locally based at Palermo but directed from afar by first Qayrawān and then, from 969, Cairo. This new political orientation toward Muslim northern Africa necessitated the development of new patterns of communication: officials and administrators now arrived from Africa rather than from Constantinople, and trade relations—invisible as they may have been in the earlier source materials—created strong links between Sicily and the ports of Ifrīqiya and Egypt. Likewise, the majority of intellectual and religious visitors traveled to or from other places in the Islamic world, especially via Ifrīqiya and Egypt. The reorientation of Sicily toward the Islamic world does not mean, however, that all links with the Christian regions of the Mediterranean ceased at this time, even if only the slightest and most circumstantial pieces of evidence suggest any type of sustained communications between Sicily and either Greek or Latin domains during these centuries.

Given that Sicily was a late addition to the Muslim world—conquered more than a century after the majority of Muslim political expansion had concluded—it entered into a civilization that had already developed a strong set of intellectual and cultural traditions. The Islamicate civilization was broad and expansive, having incorporated a multitude of cultures, ethnolinguistic groups, and religious minorities as well as diverse regions that had previously been under varied demographic, administrative, and political control. Therefore, by the time of Sicily's conquest, there were established means of intellectually and culturally bringing a location into the Islamic world—geographical, biographical, and cultural scholarship carried out by learned intellectuals who both drew on previous scholarly traditions and traveled broadly in order to further describe and define the spaces of the dār al-Islām.[2] Indeed, many pilgrims and scholars traveled extensively throughout the Islamicate world during the premodern period, many leaving travelogues about all or part of their experiences. These accounts, along with scholarly geographical treatises and cartographical depictions of the world, helped medieval readers to conceptualize the world of Islam and its boundaries and can help us to understand the place of Sicily within that world.

In addition to their intellectual and scholarly importance, geographical and cartographical texts rank among the most abundant written sources extant for the Muslim period of Sicily's history—but, like most of the texts from this period, they do not come from the island itself and thus only allow us to view Sicily from outside. Unfortunately, the two and a half centuries of Muslim rule on Sicily have left to the modern historian very few contemporary accounts of life and culture on the island. The Arabic chronicles, which have been utilized to construct a chronological account of the island's Islamic conquest and administration, were, for the most part, written in North Africa during later centuries, after Sicily had already left the Islamicate world.[3] Economic records are virtually nonexistent outside of the merchant letters from the Cairo Geniza cache, which contain numerous references to trade with Muslim Sicily.[4] Another

2. Indeed, as Houari Touati argues, the boundaries of the dār al-Islām were defined and confirmed through the means of travel and discovery. Touati, *Islam and Travel in the Middle Ages*, trans. Lydia G. Cochrane (Chicago: University of Chicago Press, 2010). See also Zayde Antrim, *Routes and Realms: The Power of Place in the Early Islamic World* (Oxford: Oxford University Press, 2012). On Arabic geographical traditions, see S. Maqbul Ahmad, "Djughrāfiyā," *EI*², 2: 575–587; and Andre Miquel, *La geographie humaine du monde musulman jusqu'au milieu du 11e siecle* (Paris: Mouton, 1967).

3. For an overview of the Arabic sources available for the study of Sicily, see Chiarelli, *A History of Muslim Sicily*, xxvii–xxxii; Jeremy Johns, "Arabic Sources for Sicily," *Proceedings of the British Academy* 132 (2007): 341–360; and Abraham L. Udovitch, "New Materials for the History of Islamic Sicily" in *Del Nuovo sulla Sicilia Musulmana*, ed. Biancamaria Scarcia Amoretti (Rome: Accademia Nazionale de Lincei, 1993), 183–210. The majority of narrative Arabic sources extant from this period of Sicily's history have been collected by Michele Amari, in *BAS* Arabic and translated into Italian in *BAS* Ital. Documentary sources, most of them from the later Norman period, are collected in Salvatore Cusa, ed., *I diplomi Greci ed Arabi di Sicilia*, 2 vols. (Palermo: D. Lao, 1868).

4. Introduction to the Cairo Geniza and its history can be found in the works of S. D. Goitein, esp. "The Cairo Geniza as a Source for the History of Muslim Civilisation," *Studia Islamica* 3 (1955): 75–91, and "Documents of the Cairo Geniza as a Source for Mediterranean Social History," *Journal of*

important type of source that sheds light on economic travel between Sicily and other parts of the dār al-Islām is legal documents, called *fatwās*, that record some, but by no means all, of the acts of travel and trade that occurred between Sicily and Ifrīqiya, both before and after the Norman conquest of the island. These sources, along with geographical descriptions and travel accounts of Sicily, will be used here to reconstruct the island's communication patterns during the centuries of Islamic rule.

One of the most important aspects of the communication systems in the Mediterranean basin during the tenth and eleventh centuries is the rise of very prominent roles played by the Jewish residents of the western Muslim lands. Jews had been resident in Sicily from very early in the millennium (from at least the fourth century), although the date of their original arrival in the western Mediterranean is unknown.[5] Therefore, it is important to note that Jewish traders, artisans, pilgrims, and scholars had likely been active in the travel and communications networks of Sicily prior to the Islamic period, although they are virtually unseen in the surviving sources; what is evident during the tenth and eleventh centuries in the extant sources is the increased visibility of Jews' activity. Indeed, the majority of sources of information about the trade relationships between Sicily and North Africa concern such Jewish merchants, and therefore there is a primary emphasis in this chapter on the role of Jewish travelers. These Jews, living and working in the Muslim world and using Arabic as their daily spoken language, played vital roles in connecting Sicily with both Ifrīqiya and Egypt, due in large part to the fact that these communities lived and did the majority of their business in Fusṭāṭ, Egypt, where the Cairo Geniza documents were preserved. They also traveled widely throughout the Mediterranean, although the focus here will be on the ways in which their activities intersected with Sicilian communication networks.[6] In fact, if it were not for the existence of these Judeo-Arabic merchants' letters, very little would be known about how the various regions of the Muslim-controlled western

the American Oriental Society 80 (1960): 91–100. See also Mark R. Cohen, "Geniza for Islamicists, Islamic Geniza, and the 'New Cairo Geniza,'" *Harvard Middle Eastern and Islamic Review* 7 (2006): 129–145. Digital images of many of the Geniza documents are available at the website of the Cambridge Digital Library of Geniza texts by Cambridge University Library at: http://cudl.lib.cam.ac.uk/collections/genizah. Transcriptions of more than four thousand Geniza documents can be found at the website of the Princeton Geniza Project, https://geniza.princeton.edu/pgp/.

5. For the history of Sicily's Jews, see Simonsohn, *Between Scylla and Charybdis*

6. Much has been written about the Mediterranean-wide connections of this one community of Jewish merchants, notably by the scholar most responsible for bringing the documents of the Cairo Geniza to wide attention, S. D. Goitein. See his six-volume analysis of the lives and activities of this community, *A Mediterranean Society*, 6 vols. (Berkeley: University of California Press, 1967–1993). See also Jessica L. Goldberg, *Trade and Institutions in the Medieval Mediterranean: The Geniza Merchants and Their Business World* (Cambridge: Cambridge University Press, 2012).

Mediterranean were interconnected, especially in terms of economic affairs.[7] To be sure, Muslim merchants and Muslim-owned ships also sailed these routes and linked these places, but there is simply far less evidence preserved with which to recreate their travel patterns.

Possibly because of this accident of source survival, much less is known about Muslim-ruled Sicily's direct contact and communication with Christian Italy or with Muslim al-Andalus—both places with which Muslim Sicily might naturally be presumed to have established communications. Likewise, we find little or no evidence for a connection between Sicily and Constantinople during these years. A substantial population of Greek Christians survived as a religious and linguistic minority throughout the centuries of Islamic rule, but how this community may have maintained contact with the rest of the Greek or Latin Christian worlds is not clear. Muslim Sicily appears to have had some level of trade contacts with Christian southern Italy, but clues to this connection are found primarily in the numismatic evidence that coins, and thus only implicitly other commercial products, traveled from Muslim Sicily to Christian southern Italy. Because this source cannot speak to the type or volume of goods traded, however, we cannot in any way quantify the level or regularity of such economic communications.

Muslim Sicily became integrated into the Islamic sphere, operating again as its frontier with the Christian world, but in a radically different way than it had done under Byzantine rule. While under Greek domination, the island appears in the sources as a nexus of communications that moved in multiple directions toward the Latin, Greek, and Arab Muslim worlds. On the other hand, Sicily during the Islamic period looks more like an edge: a location at the border of the dār al-Islām that helped to protect and defend (and possibly advance) the cultural, political, and economic interests of the polity as a whole, and where there was some, perhaps slight, degree of intercultural interaction. Links to the immediately proximate south Italian mainland did exist during this period, but to an unmeasurable degree. However, such limited porosity of the border does not mean that Muslim Sicily participated in widespread and multidirectional connections within the Mediterranean basin, as it had done in earlier centuries. As it appears in the extant sources, Sicily during the Muslim centuries did not operate as a nodal point in a complex web of intercultural communications, nor did it function as a mediator in political or diplomatic relations between the Muslim and Christian worlds, such as we saw in the earlier centuries. Instead, the bulk of the island's communications

7. For a historiographical overview of the question whether the Jews of the Geniza community can be taken as representative of Muslim trade practices, see Goldberg, *Trade*, 26–29.

were directed to and from North Africa and Egypt and, to a far lesser degree, the eastern Mediterranean and al-Andalus.

Political, Military, and Diplomatic Connections with North Africa

If military forays into Sicily were the means by which the island was initially drawn close to the dār al-Islām, it was political travel that most closely integrated the conquered island into the Aghlabid province of Ifrīqiya. Following the establishment of Islamic rule on Sicily, Muslim officials and political governors (usually referred to as *wālīs* or *emīrs*) regularly traveled from Africa to Sicily in order to govern the island, first from the Aghlabid capital of Qayrawān and, after the late tenth century, from the Fatimid capital at Cairo. Sicily never truly established an independent administration of its own, although the Kalbid dynasty of governors (948–1053) was able to govern with a greater autonomy than those during the Aghlabid period of rule, in part because the Fatimid capital at Cairo was farther away and, ultimately, more concerned with establishing political authority to the East than in Sicily. The provincial and dependent relationship between Sicily and the Islamic powers of northern Africa meant that the majority of the island's administrators and local rulers were assigned by the court at Qayrawān or Cairo, although by the end of the ninth century the governors were being elected by the local population and confirmed in their leadership by the Aghlabid *emīr*. Such an arrangement necessitated a significant level of political travel between Sicily and the power centers in the dār al-Islām, although much of this type of communication is assumed rather than stated directly: in general, we see the effects of the travel, such as a change in leadership, rather than the act of travel itself. In other words, alongside these government officials, there may have traveled letters, news, commercial commodities, and a variety of other people and things that we cannot see in the surviving sources.

As a newly conquered territory, Sicily needed the full range of Islamic administrative personnel and institutions, all of whom had to travel to the island from the capital.[8] Governors, armies, administrative officials, and judges arrived there from Muslim Africa in order to oversee the island; we see little evidence that native Greek administrators were utilized, as had been the case in

8. Two excellent narrative histories of the Muslim period of rule in Sicily exist, so I will not provide here a complete account of the political events during these centuries. See Chiarelli, *A History of Muslim Sicily*; and Metcalfe, *The Muslims of Medieval Italy*.

the earliest Byzantine territories conquered for Islam in Syria. The first several governors of the island doubled as the military commanders leading the conquest efforts. There was significant turnover among this set of leaders, with several of the early commander-governors dying in Sicily after only a short time of service. The earliest long-serving *wālī* of Muslim Sicily was Abū Fihr Muḥammad b. ʿAbd Allāh, who was appointed by his cousin the Aghlabid *emīr* in 832 and served until his death in 851.[9] The next *wālī* was Abū Fihr's brother, Abū al-Aghlab Ibrāhīm b. ʿAbd Allāh, who was also appointed by *Emīr* Ziyādat Allāh, again having been sent to Palermo directly from Qayrawān. A similar pattern of appointments from Qayrawān continued until 909, when the Fatimid forces took over in both North Africa and its province of Sicily; thereafter, Fatimid attempts to impose governors on Sicily were met by resistance and rebellion, and a semi-independent dynasty of governors from the Kalbid family was established on the island by 948.[10]

However, it was not only the highest-level administrators who were appointed to their posts in Sicily from North Africa—so too were the officials who served as civil-religious jurists (*qāḍī*s), important legal experts who managed legal and religious affairs in Muslim communities. One example of a judge appointed directly from North Africa was Abū al-Qāsim al-Ṭarzī, a chief *qāḍī* of Sicily who had earlier been the *muḥtasib* (market inspector) of Qayrawān.[11] Likewise, we have evidence that a later head judge was appointed to Sicily from Ifrīqiya: Abū ʿAmr Maymūn b. ʿAmr b. al-Maʿlūf (d. 928/929) had been *ṣāhib al-maẓālim* (minister of justice) in Qayrawān before he was appointed *qāḍī* in Sicily. He served in Sicily for a time but returned to North Africa after resigning his position and was buried in Qayrawān.[12] North Africa was both the beginning and end point for his career, and his time in Sicily was only one temporary posting. Thus we see that administrators like Abū

9. Ibn ʿIdhārī, *Kitāb al-bayān al-mughrib*, *BAS* Arabic, 356, *BAS* Ital., 2: 7; al-Nuwayrī, *Nihāyat al-arab*, *BAS* Arabic, 431, *BAS* Ital., rev. ed. 2: 119; Ibn al-Athīr, *al-Kāmil fī al-tārīkh*, *BAS* Arabic, 225, 230, *BAS* Ital., rev. ed., 1: 369, 377.

10. For a compiled list of the governors of Islamic Sicily, see Hiroshi Takayama, "The Aghlabid Governors in Sicily: 827–909 (Islamic Sicily I)," *Annals of Japan Association for Middle East Studies* 7 (1992): 427–443; and Takayama, "The Fatimid and Kalbite Governors in Sicily: 909–1044 (Islamic Sicily II)," *Mediterranean World* 13 (1992): 21–30. For the Fatimids' struggle to impose their control on Sicily, see Chiarelli, *A History of Muslim Sicily*, 67–93, and Metcalfe, *The Muslims of Medieval Italy*, 44–69.

11. al-Mālikī, *Riyāḍ al-nufūs*, *BAS* Arabic, 190–191, *BAS* Ital., 1: 255. For other *qāḍī*s appointed to Sicily from Aghlabid Ifrīqiya, see Giuseppe Mandalà, "Political Martyrdom and Religious Censorship in Islamic Sicily: A Case Study during the Age of Ibrāhīm II (261–289/875–902)," *al-Qanṭara* 35 (2014): 151–186.

12. al-Mālikī, *Riyāḍ al-nufūs*, *BAS* Arabic, 191–192, *BAS* Ital., 1: 255–256. According to his biography, Abū ʿAmr Maymūn departed for Sicily from Sūsa and returned to North Africa via that same port.

ʿAmr Maymūn not only arrived in Sicily from North Africa but also often did so after an earlier appointment in North Africa.

It is possible that administrative positions in Sicily were viewed as temporary postings in a frontier zone, meant to either train or reward officials within the wider administrative arena of Aghlabid territory. Most Ifrīqiyan officials who were sent to Sicily apparently did not see their relocation to the island as permanent and often returned to Ifrīqiya at the end of their appointments. There also appears to have been little attempt on the part of the Aghlabids to prepare local Sicilians—either new converts or emigrants to the island from North Africa—for administrative posts by bringing them to Qayrawān for appointments, although the possibility remains that this happened below the surface of the recorded sources. Rather, men who were trained for government service in North Africa could take a—sometimes temporary—position in Sicily as an extension of their public service careers in the Aghlabid state.

These appointments from Qayrawān continued until 909, at which time the ruling Sunni Aghlabid dynasty was overthrown by the newly declared Shiite Fatimid caliphate.[13] The Fatimid foundation of Cairo as their capital city (built 969–972) meant that Sicily's overseers were more distant than previously (and also Shiite, as opposed to Sicily's majority Sunni population). Direct and regular communication between Cairo and Sicily appears to have been a lower priority for the Fatimids, especially after the transfer of the Fatimid capital to Cairo—in large part, perhaps, because of strident Sicilian resistance to Fatimid rule and an entrenched commitment on the island to Sunni religious traditions.[14] The Fatimids did try to enforce their will on the island, but they found little success. Sicily was also no longer a hot spot for Byzantine-Muslim warfare and diplomacy, as it had been during the seventh through ninth centuries, despite occasional Greek attempts to reconquer the island throughout the tenth and into the eleventh centuries.[15]

13. For the Fatimid takeover of northern Africa, see Michael Brett, *The Rise of the Fatimids: The World of the Mediterranean and the Middle East in the Fourth Century of the Hijra, Tenth Century CE* (Leiden: E. J. Brill, 2001).

14. A lot of uncertainty remains concerning the depth of conversion to Shiism in Sicily after the Fatimid revolution. See Antonio Pellitteri, "The Historical-Ideological Framework of Islamic Fatimid Sicily (Fourth/Tenth Century) with Reference to the Works of the Qāḍī al-Nuʿmān," *al-Masāq* 7 (1994): 111–163. For more on the historiographical claims of the persistence of Sunnism, as represented by the prevailing Mālikī school, and countervailing evidence that suggests greater diversity among the legal scholars of Islamic Sicily, see William E. Granara, "Islamic Education and the Transmission of Knowledge in Muslim Sicily," in *Law and Education in Medieval Islam: Studies in Memory of Professor George Makdisi*, ed. Joseph E. Lowry, Devin J. Stewart, and Shawkat Toorawa (Cambridge: E. J. W. Gibb Memorial Trust, 2004), 150–173; and Mandalà, "Political Martyrdom."

15. According to Yaacov Lev, after the Fatimids moved to Egypt, their primary focus was directed toward Syria, and their main conflicts and relations with the Byzantines occurred in that area rather than in the western Mediterranean, where Byzantine influence had all but disappeared. Lev,

Because of the limited involvement of Fatimid rulers in the central Mediterranean, and because of the island's diminished importance for the Islamic confrontation with Greek Christian powers during this period, Sicily was essentially left to manage its own affairs. A semi-independent dynasty of governors from the family of Ḥasan ibn Ali al-Kalbī, known as the Kalbids, exercised a level of self-governance on the island—as did the Fatimid-appointed governors in Ifrīqiya, the Zīrid *emīrs* (973–1148). Nonetheless, the Kalbid governors never officially broke away from North Africa or established an independent state in Sicily, despite several attempts. The final Kalbid governor of a united Sicily was Ḥasan Ṣamṣām al-Dawla (1040–1053), but he was prevented from exercising any real power by a combination of internal divisions within the island and renewed attacks by Byzantine forces attempting to reclaim the island.[16] A period of civil strife ensued at the end of the Kalbid period, and for the next decade numerous petty rulers (*qāʾids*) would vie amongst themselves for control.[17] Thus, although the Aghlabids ruled Sicily as a nearby province that needed regular appointments of officials and administrators—if never as an extension of their own political authority—during the Fatimid period, the island was left to drift even further from the heart of political or diplomatic affairs. Sicily under the Fatimids operated, politically, as a distant frontier—far from the center and, in many ways, left to its own devices.

The highest-ranking Muslim ruler to arrive on Sicily's shores was Ibrāhīm II, the Aghlabid *emīr* who stepped down in favor of his son, Abū Abbas ʿAbd Allāh II, in 902.[18] Upon his retirement, he traveled to Sicily, defeated the Greek resistance in the town of Taormina (see figure 3), and then proceeded to Calabria on the mainland, where he died at Cosenza in October of 902.[19] The purpose of Ibrāhīm's voyage was the prosecution of *jihād*, which was only at that time being brought to an end in Sicily itself. Presumably, Ibrāhīm thought that the time was right for extending the boundaries

"The Fatimids and Byzantium," 6: 198ff. For what evidence there is of direct Fatimid involvement in the western Mediterranean, see Lev, "A Mediterranean Encounter: The Fatimids and Europe, Tenth to Twelfth Centuries," in *Shipping, Trade and Crusade in the Medieval Mediterranean: Studies in Honour of John Pryor*, ed. Ruthy Gertwagen and Elizabeth Jeffreys (Farnham: Ashgate, 2012), 131–156.

16. For the uncertain chronology of the period at the end of the Kalbid dynasty and the years of civil war and political breakup prior to the Norman invasion, see Metcalfe, *The Muslims of Medieval Italy*, 70–87, and Chiarelli, *A History of Muslim Sicily*, 122–132.

17. For the variety of possible meanings and uses of the term "qāʾid" in Muslim and formerly Muslim territories of the western Mediterranean, see R. I. Burns, *Islam Under the Crusaders: Colonial Survival in the Thirteenth-Century Kingdom of Valencia* (Princeton, NJ: Princeton University Press, 1973), 368–373.

18. Ibn al-Athīr, *al-Kāmil fī al-tārīkh*, *BAS* Arabic, 245ff, *BAS* Ital., 2: 326ff.

19. For details and bibliography about the fortress in Taormina, which was used successively by the Byzantines, Muslims, and Normans, see Ferdinando Maurici, *Castelli medievali in Sicilia: dai bizantini ai normanni* (Palermo: Sellerio, 1992), 373.

FIGURE 3. View of Taormina with a fortress dated to the Muslim period (Castello Saraceno) on the peak at the right. Photo by author.

of the dār al-Islām into Christian Italy, or perhaps he personally wanted to end his life as a *mujāhid* (a fighter of the *jihād*). It is notable that Ibrāhīm does not appear to have visited Sicily during his reign as *emīr* but only as a private citizen. Indeed, his military contribution to the expansion of Islam into Italy was not followed up by more official actions. This event may represent only a brief moment of zeal for *jihād* on the part of one individual rather than a consistent official policy.

On the other hand, some evidence does suggest that Sicily was being used as an advance base for *jihād* in Italy for at least the next century, or at least that the infrastructure of *jihād* was in place there. The traveler Ibn Ḥawqal, who visited the island in 973, claimed that *jihād* was being conducted against Italy from Sicily on a regular basis when he visited in the late tenth century. As in the epigraph with which this chapter began, Ibn Ḥawqal described *ribāṭs* (fortifications that housed fighters of the *jihād*, considered a defining characteristic of the frontiers of the dār al-Islām) that lined the shores of Sicily for the purposes of waging war against the nearby Christian lands. However, he was not pleased by what he found there: he castigated the many Sicilians who, he claimed, had become teachers in order to avoid participation in the holy war.[20] He also disdained both the people and their activities in the *ribāṭs* themselves—he thought that they performed neither their religious duties nor their military ones with exactitude. Whatever the legitimacy of Ibn Ḥawqal's complaints, his remarks do show that the infrastructure for *jihād* was in place in tenth-century Sicily. This anecdote shows that the island was perceived by some Muslims as an appropriate site for the expansion of the dār al-Islām, even if the actual effectiveness of raids from Sicily into southern Italy may have been slight.

Muslim forces did attack southern and central Italy at times, but these may have primarily been troops arriving directly from North Africa or from other Muslim-held territories in the region (such as Crete or Fraxinetum), completely bypassing Sicily.[21] I have found only one piece of evidence that definitively shows that Sicilians fought *jihād* against Christians in Italy: Ibn al-Athīr noted a battle in southern Italy between the Sicilians and the Franks under the emperor Otto II as late as 981/982.[22] In other words, Sicily was not a necessary component of Muslim aggression and expansion into Europe—as it had been for Byzantine interests in Italy. Ships could and did sail directly from northern Africa to mainland Italy. And, in many cases, the Muslim military involvement in the chaotic political scene of southern Italy came as a result of alliances with local Christian leaders battling for supremacy in the region, rather than from the Sicilian governors' impetus to conquer Christian territory within Italy.[23] Muslim troops briefly held Brindisi in 838, and in 840 they took Taranto and attacked Bari; these towns were ruled by Muslim *emīrs* from 847.[24] Sicilian Muslims may have participated in these raids on the mainland, although this is not definitively confirmed by the existing sources. These mainland cities, along with the whole of Calabria and Apulia, were regained by Byzantine

20. Ibn Ḥawqal, *Kitāb ṣūrat al-arḍ*, 121. A *ribāṭ* was a fortified site built for the purposes of both defensive and offensive warfare along the boundaries of the dār al-Islām. Some of these coastal fortifications appear to have survived into the Norman period, based on the evidence of Ibn Jubayr, who visited the island in the late twelfth century. See also Metcalfe, *The Muslims of Medieval Italy*, 61–62.

21. For Muslim Crete, see Vassilios Christides, *The Conquest of Crete by the Arabs (ca. 824): A Turning Point in the Struggle between Byzantium and Islam* (Athens: Akademia Athenon, 1984). For the Muslim colony at Fraxinetum in southern France, see Scott G. Bruce, *Cluny and the Muslims of La Garde-Freinet: Hagiography and the Problem of Islam in Medieval Europe* (Ithaca, NY: Cornell University Press, 2015).

22. Ibn al-Athīr, *al-Kāmil fī al-tārīkh*, *BAS* Arabic, rev. ed., 1: 272ff, *BAS* Ital., rev. ed., 1: 346ff.

23. For an attempt to reconstruct a narrative of Muslim involvement and alliances with Lombards and other Christians in ninth-century southern Italy, see Metcalfe, *The Muslims of Medieval Italy*, 16–22.

24. Many historians have claimed that Sicilian fighters established these short-lived emirates. This is a reasonable suggestion, due to proximity, but I have found no direct evidence proving that this was the case. Textual sources that could illuminate the Muslim conquest and rule of these cities are scarce to nonexistent.

forces in the 880s. Muslims from Sicily may also have participated in ravaging Rome in 846 and raiding along the Italian coast during many years of the ninth century. Unfortunately, sources do not allow a complete reconstruction of the patterns of these incursions into mainland Italy or the degree to which these were directed from Sicily or used Sicily as an advance base. The Arabic chronicles that allowed us to see the process of the Muslim subjugation of Sicily do not include detailed information about the raids into southern Italy—suggesting that the chroniclers saw no need to paint Sicily as a base for further expansion into Europe. What does appear to be clear from the scant textual evidence is that Muslim participation in southern Italian affairs was not the result of concerted Aghlabid plans to jump from Sicily to the mainland in an effort to conquer and rule Italy, but rather opportunistic involvement in the local scene.

These data can only suggest that, at some points during Islamic rule on the island, Sicily may have been used as a base from which to mount attacks on Christian Italy—or at least that, as a frontier location, it was considered useful for that purpose. This political and military use of Sicily as an advance base does not appear in the extant sources, however, analogously to the ways in which Sicily was used by Constantinople as an extension of its imperial authority on the mainland. I find no evidence that the island's officials were regularly directed by Qayrawān or Cairo to conquer, rule, or govern territories in southern Italy in the way that the Greek administrators were regularly employed by Constantinople to execute imperial orders in Rome or Ravenna. Under Islamic rule, the Sicilian frontier was a place of theoretical—if not actual—*jihād* for expansion of the boundaries of Islam, rather than a proxy for the central government. That is, neither the Aghlabids nor the Fatimids appear to have systematically used Sicily as a stepping-stone to mainland Italy for the purpose of either conquering Christian territories or maintaining control over Muslim settlements there. Sicily's role in the Mediterranean and within its larger polity shifted fundamentally after its incorporation into the dār al-Islām, which is reflected in the patterns of travel and communication that linked the island to other places in the Mediterranean region.

Intellectual Connections to the Dār al-Islām

Travel in the medieval Islamicate world in general was both a practical occupation—it brought goods to market and pilgrims to shrines, for example—and an important intellectual exercise. Merchants, administrators, and pilgrims needed to move from one place to another in order to deliver goods, news, ideas, or their souls closer to their intended goals, and scholars traveled both to study with masters and to see and experience the world. The fluidity of such travel and communication within the medieval Islamic world has been well studied, as has the impact of this high degree of connectivity—even across political and theological boundaries. At the same time, travel to or geographical description of a place was an intellectual project of "establishing belonging"—a means of understanding, explaining, and interpreting the world for readers and scholars who themselves might not be able to travel to all of the places within or at the edges of the dār al-Islām.[25] Many academic geographers and cartographers, indeed, relied on received traditions in order to describe places they had not personally visited. Taken together, texts by a wide range of travelers and scholars were able to draw a newly conquered location like Sicily into the intellectual and cultural orbit of the Islamic world and to explain and describe it for readers in faraway places, thus potentially bringing the island conceptually nearer to the central Islamic lands. This process also created the possibility of further types of communication between the center and the borderland and between the Muslim and Christian worlds in the Mediterranean region, by establishing connections and pathways of communication to the newly conquered space.

One of the most important ways in which a location was conceptually incorporated into the dār al-Islām is through the cartographical and geographical descriptions found in maps and scholarly treatises describing the world. Numerous descriptions of Sicily appear in Arabic geographies written after the incorporation of the island into the Islamicate civilization in the ninth century. Notably, however, most do not indicate actual travel to the island on the part of the author. Rather, the accounts appear to draw on earlier descriptions and maps within the Arabic scholarly tradition and reflect the desire to describe and to locate places within the wider dār al-Islām. Significantly, neither the majority of the maps nor the geographical descriptions from the ninth through eleventh centuries depict Sicily as a place of central importance. Most early medieval maps and geographical works clearly positioned Sicily on the periphery of the broader Muslim world. Indeed, the one account we have of personal travel to the island during this period, by the Muslim traveler Ibn Ḥawqal, testifies to the marginality of the island—it appeared to him as a strange borderland zone of hybrid Muslim-Christian customs and incomplete Islamization.

The marginality of Sicily in the Muslim imagination of the central Middle Ages is visually apparent in nearly all extant cartographical depictions of the

25. Antrim, *Routes and Realms*, 1.

Mediterranean that were created in the central Islamic lands during these centuries.[26] During the period of Muslim rule on the island, only one known map emerged from the central Islamic lands that placed Sicily with any prominence in the Mediterranean—a map from the recently discovered *Kitāb Gharā'ib al-funūn wa-mulaḥ al-'uyūn*, translated as *The Book of Curiosities*, which is a later copy of a text that was originally produced in the first half of the eleventh century, likely in Egypt.[27] Only in much later centuries, after Sicily became a Christian possession, did maps more generally (both Muslim and Christian) begin to place Sicily prominently in the Mediterranean, in accordance with the transformed position of Sicily in the Latin Christian world (as we will see in chapter 5). On such later maps created in the central Islamic lands, the island appears but is often shown as a circle that lies in a row with the two other islands of Crete and Cyprus, both also shown as circular.[28] Written geographical descriptions of Sicily often discussed its triangularity, but most Muslim cartographers were generally disinterested in accurately representing its shape and size. Even Mount Etna, the most notable feature of the island in the accounts of many Islamic geographers, did not find its way onto maps from the Islamic world at this time.

The author and cartographer of *The Book of Curiosities* included detailed descriptions and images of the Mediterranean and its islands, in particular Sicily and the major ports in Ifrīqiya and Egypt with which the island was

26. For a general exploration of medieval Muslim maps, see Margherita Pinna, *Il Mediterraneo e la Sardegna nella cartografia musulmana (dall'VIII al XVI secolo)* (Nuoro: Istituto superiore regionale etnografico, 1996); Karen C. Pinto, *Ways of Seeing: Scenarios of the World in the Medieval Islamic Cartographic Imagination* (PhD thesis, Columbia University, 2002); and Pinto, *Medieval Islamic Maps: An Exploration* (Chicago: University of Chicago Press, 2016).

27. The extant copy, held at the Bodleian Libraries at the University of Oxford (MS. Arab. c. 90), is a twelfth- or thirteenth-century copy of a treatise that the editors believe was originally composed between 1020 and 1050. The editors of this treatise and its set of maps have noted the uniqueness of the coverage of Sicily and the central Mediterranean region, noting that the author himself was likely from this area and was both particularly knowledgeable about and interested in it. Emilie Savage-Smith and Yossef Rapoport, eds., *The Book of Curiosities: A Critical Edition* (March 2007), www.bodley.ox.ac.uk/bookofcuriosities; and Savage-Smith and Rapoport, *An Eleventh-Century Egyptian Guide to the Universe: The Book of Curiosities* (Leiden: E. J. Brill, 2013).

28. For more on these later Islamic cartographic depictions of the Mediterranean and its islands, and images of what she sees as typical later Mediterranean maps, see Karen C. Pinto, "'Surat Baḥr al-Rum' (Picture of the Sea of Byzantium): Possible Meanings Underlying the Forms," *Eastern Mediterranean Cartographies* 25/26 (2004): 223–241. See also Emilie Savage-Smith, "Cartography," in *A Companion to Mediterranean History*, ed. Peregrine Horden and Sharon Kinoshita (Oxford: Wiley-Blackwell, 2014), 184–199. Savage-Smith attributes the lack of focus on the sea and its islands as a reflection of a particular school of cartography, which was largely concerned with land rather than sea routes and, in particular, those routes across the central Islamic lands (187). For more on this school of cartography, see Gerald R. Tibbetts, "The Balkhi School of Geographers," in *Cartography in the Traditional Islamic and South Asian Societies*, ed. J. B. Harley and David Woodward (Chicago: University of Chicago Press, 1992), vol. 2, bk. 1, 108–136.

economically linked (as we will see in this chapter).[29] The Mediterranean Sea is shown filled with islands (118 in total), most of which are round, but two of which—Sicily and Cyprus—were drawn as long thin rectangles; 121 ports are depicted along the sea's shores.[30] The manuscript also includes an individual map of Sicily itself, which is unique within the extant corpus of medieval Islamic maps from this period (see figure 4). With great detail, this image traces the outlines and major features of the island. Also included are individual maps of the Ifrīqiyan port of al-Mahdiyya and of Tinnīs, an island-city in the eastern Nile River delta.[31] In contrast, the western Mediterranean—al-Andalus and the Maghrib—are passed over with little detail. It is quite certain that the author of this treatise and the cartographer of this manuscript were intensely concerned with the linkages between Sicily and the eastern Mediterranean—in particular, with the trade connections between Muslim Sicily, Ifrīqiya, and Egypt.[32] Sicily's economic, social, and cultural communication patterns in these centuries connected the island very closely to both of these regions, to the apparent exclusion of Christian Italy or Muslim al-Andalus—exactly as this treatise visualizes in its maps.

The Book of Curiosities is anomalous in its intense focus on Sicily and its trade partners in the eastern Mediterranean. On most early Islamic maps, Sicily does not even appear in the Mediterranean Sea. On most such maps, indeed, the Mediterranean appears to be devoid of islands altogether, although islands are usually scattered throughout the eastern seas. The entire Mediterranean region is shown as much smaller than the East, with the economically important Indian Ocean region particularly prominent.[33] In contrast, the later map attributed to al-Idrīsī, the Norman king Roger II's geographer, depicts Sicily as a large triangle located prominently between Italy and Spain (see figure 7). Patronized by the first Norman king and working in Sicily, al-Idrīsī would be expected to have had detailed and firsthand information about Sicily and the western Mediterranean and to have had a vested interest in highlighting

---

29. An extraordinarily detailed map of Sicily (Bodleian Libraries, University of Oxford, MS. Arab. c. 90, fols. 32b–33a) can also be found online: http://cosmos.bodley.ox.ac.uk/hms/mss_browse.php?expand=732,803&state=main&act=chfolio&folio=58.

30. See Emilie Savage-Smith, "Maps and Trade," in *Byzantine Trade, 4th–12th Centuries: The Archaeology of Local, Regional and International Exchange, Papers of the Thirty-Eighth Spring Symposium of Byzantine Studies, St John's College, University of Oxford, March 2004*, ed. Marlia Mundell Mango (Farnham: Ashgate, 2009), esp. 20–25.

31. See the maps of the Mediterranean as a whole (fols. 30b–31a), the island of Cyprus (fol. 36b), the harbor of al-Mahdiyya (fol. 34a), and the island city of Tinnīs (fols. 35b–36a), *The Book of Curiosities*.

32. For the ways in which these maps reflect contemporary trade patterns, see Savage-Smith, "Maps and Trade," esp. 28.

33. Savage-Smith, "Cartography," 189.

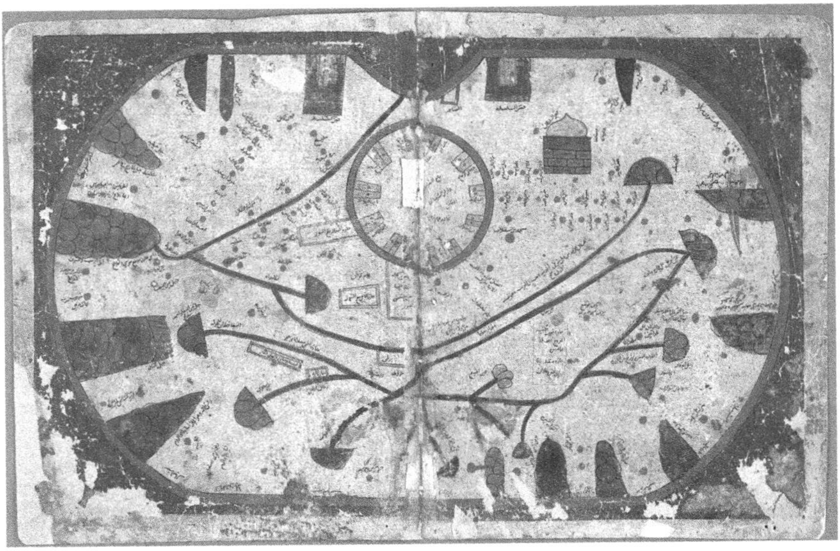

FIGURE 4. Map of Sicily in *The Book of Curiosities*, ca. 12th century. Bodleian Libraries, University of Oxford, MS. Arab. c. 90, fols. 32v–33r.

the domain of his patron.[34] His map, rather than following Islamic cartographical traditions of depicting Sicily, should instead be seen as more representative of later Christian maps that highlight Christian Sicily within the Mediterranean, in line with the greater centrality of the island under Norman rule.

Arabic-language treatises on travel and geography that were written during the period of Muslim dominion on the island also present Sicily as a marginal or relatively insignificant location. Much of the information found in these geographical accounts is brief, general, and indicative of little contemporary familiarity with the island, its people and culture, or its economy—possibly suggesting that this remote island was not considered important enough to investigate more deeply, or perhaps that it was too distant for most geographers to contemplate actually visiting. Descriptions of Sicily in the extant Arabic geographical treatises from this period provide little that could be understood as unique or original information; indeed, many geographers working in the central Islamic lands appear to have known very little about Sicily and often did not distinguish it from the other islands in the Mediterranean. Only three early Muslims, who visited Sicily personally, provided firsthand Arabic accounts about the island: Ibn Ḥawqal (late tenth century),

34. Ibid., 190ff.

al-Idrīsī (mid-twelfth century), and Ibn Jubayr (late twelfth century). Only one of these travelers, Ibn Ḥawqal, visited while the island was controlled by Muslim rulers, while the later two reflect conditions under Norman Christian rule and will be discussed in chapter 5. Such a shortage of contemporary information in geographical treatises also suggests that there was little direct connection between the intellectual circles of Sicily and those of the central Islamic lands.[35] This state of affairs also highlights that most of the Arabic geographers wrote within standard traditions of scholarship, collecting new evidence only about the most significant locations or ones about which too little was known. The basic information about Sicily was clearly considered sufficient for understanding this place, which was not important enough to warrant more detailed or up-to-date descriptions. This dearth of comprehensive representations of Sicily in the works of tenth-century Arabic geographers, along with the island's invisibility on most contemporary Islamic maps, suggests that, for many scholars working in the heart of the central Islamic lands, Sicily was not considered a vital western trading hub, a major political conquest, or a center of thriving Islamic intellectual or cultural life. Nonetheless, it was recognized by some geographers as a part of the Islamic sphere and thus warranted mention, even if brief and vague. It was, however, conceptually located at the remote edge of the dār al-Islām.

The standard pattern of Arabic geographical scholarship presents Sicily as a large inhabited island in the Baḥr al-Rūm (the Sea of the Christians, i.e., the Mediterranean Sea), with little other detail provided. Geographers usually included a list of other places nearby and located Sicily adjacent either to Christian territories (the lands of the Rūmīs or the Faranj) or to the Maghrib—but typically not both—a practice suggesting that these scholars had little information about the island beyond the basic details of its geographical location. None of these early geographers mentions anything about the island's convenient location as a supposed stepping-stone between northern and southern shores of the Mediterranean basin. Instead, the island was placed in proximity to either one or the other shore and linked with its religious-cultural civilization. Sicily was rarely, if ever, given a separate section within a geographical treatise, despite its size and supposed importance in economic systems of the Mediterranean (with *The Book of Curiosities* again being the sole exception). In fact, cartographers often listed Sicily as just one among the many islands of the Mediterranean, of which it was the largest but not necessarily the most famous; many geographers knew far more about Cyprus

35. A paucity of connection between Sicily and the central Muslim lands exists despite the travel of some Muslim scholars from Sicily to Egypt or North Africa for both intellectual purposes and migration.

in the eastern Mediterranean. Those authors who did have a little more contemporary knowledge about Sicily mentioned its tradition of rich cultivation, whether or not it was currently controlled by Muslims, and included a description of the wondrous volcano Mount Etna.

The *Kitāb al-Aʿlāq al-nafīsa* by Ibn Rustah (fl. 903–913), for example, claimed that there were 162 inhabited islands in the Mediterranean, of which only five were considered important, according to this author. These important islands were Corsica, Sardinia, Crete, and Cyprus, which were all about the same size, and Sicily, which was considerably larger.[36] Thus, relative size was the extent of this early geographer's knowledge of the island: Ibn Rustah did not mention Mount Etna or the agricultural cultivation on the island, both of which details were commonplace among later geographical treatments of Sicily. He even seems not to have known that Sicily was at the time controlled by Muslims, a detail suggesting that he relied on an earlier source for his information about the island.[37] In a similar manner, al-Muqaddasī (d. ca. 990) placed Sicily in a group of three populated islands in the Mediterranean. Of these, he noted, Sicily was close to the Maghrib, Crete faced Egypt, and Cyprus was positioned close to Syria.[38] He gave no further information about Sicily—not even the fact that it was a Muslim-controlled territory, indicating that he, too, probably relied on scholarship that had been written prior to the Muslim conquest of the island. Such writers, for whom Sicily was a far-distant island on the periphery of the world, along the divide between the Islamic and Christian realms, were not even aware that the island was by then a part of the Muslim world. Or perhaps their accounts were cursory simply because Sicily was considered to be so peripheral and remote a location that no effort was made to obtain more comprehensive information about it. As a small place on the edge of that larger civilization, it did not warrant fuller or more detailed treatment.

A few early Muslim geographers did include bits of further detail about Sicily, but most of this knowledge centered on Mount Etna (see figure 5). The spectacle created by the huge volcano, which was also mentioned in many Christian visitors' accounts, was an exemplar of the strange and marvelous sights to be found in the world. Although al-Masʿūdī (d. 956) included a sec-

36. Aḥmad ibn ʿUmar ibn Rustah, *Kitāb al-Aʿlāq al-nafīsa*, ed. M. J. de Goeje, *BGA*, vol. 7 (Leiden: E. J. Brill, 1967). French translation available in *Les Atours Précieux*, trans. Gaston Wiet (Cairo: Société de Géographie d'Égypte, 1955), 93.

37. Not all but a majority of the island had been conquered by Muslim forces by the time that Ibn Rustah was likely writing, but that news must not have been of widespread knowledge or importance in the central Islamic lands.

38. Shams al-Dīn Abū ʿAbdallāh Muḥammad al-Muqaddasī, *Kitāb Aḥsan al-taqāsīm fī maʿrifat al-aqālīm*, ed. M. J. de Goeje, *BGA*, vol. 3 (Leiden: E. J. Brill, 1967), 12.

FIGURE 5. Southern flank of Mount Etna showing lateral cones and flow from the eruption of 2001. Photo by Wilson44691, Wikimedia Commons, Public Domain.

tion on Sicily in his treatise on history and geography, the *Kitāb Tanbīh wa al-ishrāf*, the majority of his entry about the island concentrated on Mount Etna (Jabal al-Burkān).[39] He mentioned that within the Baḥr al-Rūm there were several noteworthy islands: Cyprus, Crete, and Sicily (which he spelled Siqilliya as opposed to the more common Ṣiqilliya). He provided no details about Crete or Cyprus, and Sicily was distinguished only by the legends surrounding the volcano that spewed fire and rocks from its crater. According to al-Masʿūdī, the fire from this volcano was visible from a great distance, and the rocks that were ejected from the volcano's mouth were said to have unique properties. Otherwise, he had no specific information about the island or its culture. Likewise, writing roughly a century after the end of Muslim rule on the island, al-Qazwīnī (d. 1283) knew only that Sicily was shaped like a triangle, that Mount Etna was its most famous distinguishing feature, and that it had a number of cities and villages, but he mentioned little else.[40] The brevity of these descriptions may be attributed to the geographers' reliance on earlier

39. Abu al-ḤasanʿAlī ibn al-Ḥusayn al-Masʿūdī, *Kitāb al-Tanbīh wa'l-ischrāf*, ed. M. J. de Goeje, *BGA*, vol. 8 (Leiden: E. J. Brill, 1967). For the Mediterranean, see 57–60; for Sicily and Mount Etna, see 59. Other authors, including Ibn Jubayr, referred to Etna as the "Mountain of Fire" ("Jabal al-Nar"). Muḥammad ibn Aḥmad ibn Jubayr, *Riḥlat Ibn Jubayr* (Beirut: Dār Ṣādir, 1964), 301.

40. Zakarīyā ibn Muḥammad al-Qazwīnī, *Āthār al-bilād wa akhbār al-ʿibād* (Beirut: Dār Ṣādir, 1969).

sources with a similar unfamiliarity with or a paucity of contemporary information about the island; either way, it did not appear to them as a place of political or cultural significance.

A Persian geography from the late tenth century contains information similar to that in the Arabic treatises. This information transfer likely demonstrates the spread of scholarship and scholars to the East rather than regular travel between Persian lands and Sicily, of which I have found no documented evidence. The anonymous *Ḥudūd al-ʿĀlam* (982) lists Sicily as one of six inhabited islands in the Christian Sea.[41] All of the six inhabited islands are described in this text as well cultivated and containing many towns, thriving populations, merchants, armies, and considerable wealth. These six islands as a group were referred to as the most prosperous and productive islands in all the world, but within this group no one island was distinguished for its particular wealth or agricultural capacity. Sicily was described only as located close to the land of Christians and encircled by a high mountain (perhaps an inaccurate reference to Mount Etna). This text also provides one small reference to the island's (perhaps false) history, when it claimed that Roman treasure had been stored on the island because it was considered such a secure stronghold.

There is one Arabic treatise that displays more thorough information about the culture of Sicily despite no evidence that the author himself visited it. Written in the first half of the tenth century, the *Kitāb masālik al-mamālik* by al-Iṣṭakhrī (d. 957/958) includes some details about the island's agriculture and society and its location on the Muslim-Christian border.[42] The section on Sicily begins by noting that the Mediterranean contains large islands, small islands, and mountains. He identified Sicily as the largest of the inhabited islands, followed in size by Crete and Cyprus. Lying next to the Christian regions, he stated, the Sicily of this account was fertile and rich with grain, livestock, and slaves. In addition to this reference to its agricultural capacity, al-Iṣṭakhrī also described the island's population as a unique product of the borderland: he referred to the inhabitants of both Sicily and Crete as "people of the *ghazw*" ("raiders" or "those who wage war for Islam").[43] This reference to the military activities of Sicily's inhabitants may indicate that he considered the island to be an important locus for the advance of the power and religion of

41. As I do not know Persian, I have relied on an English translation of this geographical treatise. *Ḥudūd al-ʿĀlam: 'The Regions of the World,' a Persian Geography, 372 A.H. / 982 A.D.*, 2nd ed., ed. C. E. Bosworth, trans. V. Minorsky (London: E. J. W. Gibb Memorial Trust, 1970), 59–60.

42. Abū Isḥāq al-Iṣṭakhrī, *Kitāb masālik al-mamālik*, ed. M. J. de Goeje, *BGA*, vol. 1 (Leiden: E. J. Brill, 1967). For the Baḥr al-Rūm in general, see 68–71; for Sicily, in particular, see 70.

43. Ibid., 70.

Islam in the Mediterranean. However, al-Iṣṭakhrī also was aware that not all of Sicily's population had been converted to Islam; he informed his readers that a small community of Christians lived on the island alongside the Muslim inhabitants. He also noted that similar situations had been found in some other Muslim lands, an observation indicating that Sicily was known not to be unique in having two religious cultures under one political regime. He summed up his brief segment on Sicily by reporting that both Muslim and Christian ships sailed in the waters of the Mediterranean and that at times they engaged in naval warfare in the region—perhaps a reference to the regular attempts on the part of Constantinople to recover Sicily or to local Italian merchant ships that sailed in the region. Al-Iṣṭakhrī's description thus locates Sicily as a significant space on the frontier between the two religious cultures, their economies, and the military conflicts in which they sometimes engaged—but not necessarily as a conduit for other communications between them. For al-Iṣṭakhrī, the island was a site of the advance of Islam against Christian Italy, a forum for interreligious conflict, and, at the same time, a place with a religiously mixed borderland culture.

While al-Iṣṭakhrī's account of Sicily was unique in its thorough description of the island, there is no evidence that he personally traveled there. In contrast, the three most detailed and informative Arabic geographical accounts of Sicily were written by authors who had personally traveled to Sicily and were therefore more familiar with the island and its cultures. The earliest of these travelers, Ibn Ḥawqal, who visited the island beginning in April of 973, was the only one to arrive during the period of Muslim rule on the island.[44] Ibn Ḥawqal visited the island in the course of his travels as a geographer and possibly as a merchant and Shiite missionary, and Sicily appears to have been the final place he visited. His account is a scathing depiction of the island and its lands, people, and economy. Nonetheless, this text has some utility for historians, and it may be that the very negativity of his experience there can help us to understand what it meant for Sicily to be a remote borderland on the periphery of the dār al-Islām.

Ibn Ḥawqal presented an image of Sicily as a hybrid cultural zone, one where Islam had failed to effectively take root. He began his account in the *Kitāb al-masālik wa al-mamālik* (also known as the *Kitāb ṣūrat al-arḍ*) in a manner similar to previous scholarly geographical treatments of the island, perhaps

44. For background on Ibn Ḥawqal, see Francesco Gabrieli, "Ibn Hawqal e gli Arabi di Sicilia," in *L'Islam nella storia* (Bari: Dedalo, 1966), 57–67; Miquel, *La geographie humaine*, 299–309; and Abderrahman Tlili, "La Sicilia descrita della penna de un autore del X secolo: Ibn Hawqal," *Sharq al-Andalus* 6 (1989): 23–32.

indicating a reliance on earlier treatises.[45] He informed his readers that Sicily was shaped like an isosceles triangle ("ʿalā shakl muthallath mutasāwī al-sāqayn") with its apex in the west and that it was located facing Spain, the Maghrib, Constantinople, and Rayū (Reggio Calabria, the toe of mainland Italy).[46] Having himself been to the island, he was thus aware of its geographical position between the mainlands of both Europe and Africa. He noted, too, that almost all of Sicily was inhabited, cultivated, and mountainous. It was full of castles and fortresses but, in his opinion, the only prominent and famous city was the capital, Palermo.[47] Unlike earlier academic geographies, however, Ibn Ḥawqal showed a significant level of awareness of the island's history and made comparisons—always unfavorable—between the island and other western Muslim polities. Indeed, Ibn Ḥawqal conveyed an almost uniformly negative view of the society and people of Sicily. He expressed disdain for the people, the buildings, the customs, and even the environment and landscape that he found on the island. He claimed that Sicily produced nothing—or very little—of economic value or importance and that it served only as a market center for the trade of goods produced elsewhere.

Ibn Ḥawqal disparagingly compared tenth-century Sicily's landscape and culture both to those of Spain and to the ones of the island's own past. In his view, Sicily's basic conditions could be compared to Spain's in terms of its excellent agricultural land and the lushness of its fields, but he claimed that the lands were not being utilized correctly and that even the soil itself was in a state of decay. Despite the numerous rivers, streams, and irrigation systems that Ibn Ḥawqal described, he asserted that not a year passed without the grain harvests spoiling. The current agricultural output of the island was much diminished from ancient times, he claimed, and so, therefore, was the country's income. The government in previous centuries was able to bring in much revenue from the island, from taxes, income from the harvest, and tribute levied on Calabria (suggesting that he was comparing the island not to the ancient past, but to an earlier period of Islamic rule), but this was no longer the case. He maintained that, in the (unspecified) past, Sicily's agricultural produce and the fertility of the land, with its great variety of foods and drinks, made Sicily one of the most fertile and prosperous regions of the ancient world. But when Ibn Ḥawqal visited, in the late tenth century, he argued that it had passed from a situation of ease and comfort to one of misery. Certainly, this screed against Muslim Sicily should be understood as a literary, rather than as a strictly

45. Ibn Ḥawqal, *Kitāb ṣūrat al-arḍ*. For his visit to Sicily, see 118–131.

46. Ibid., 118.

47. Ibid., 118–119.

accurate, depiction of life and customs on the island, but, at the same time, it may represent Ibn Ḥāwqal's unease with being at the edge of civilized life within the dār al-Islām. He saw Sicily as a retrograde location—economically, agriculturally, culturally, and politically—the very opposite of a space that was considered vital to the workings of the Islamic world as a whole. And if there was any truth to his criticisms about contemporary land use and the economy, it may indicate that the Fatimid rulers were neglecting the island's infrastructure and environment.

The Sicilian people, too, he claimed, were stupid and slovenly, practiced a poor version of Islam, and spoke a bastardized dialect of Arabic.[48] His indictment of the Muslim population of Sicily may possibly indicate a relatively shallow process of religious education and Arabicization of the population, or it may simply reflect the high proportion of recent converts, both Berber and Greek, among the Sicilian Muslims. In either case, Ibn Ḥawqal reeled off a litany of complaints about this people and their culture: the Sicilians were deaf and dumb (possibly referring to their nonstandard dialect of Arabic); they were not mentioned in any books (claiming that the culture of the island neither was famous nor deserved to be widely known); they were like beasts in their understanding; they were negligent of their obligations in regard to commerce; they held assertions contrary to the truth and treated strangers and travelers very badly; and, generally, the Sicilians lacked all awareness of proper social behavior.[49] Altogether, according to Ibn Ḥawqal, the Sicilian people were stupid, backward, and wrongheaded, due in part to their food choices (they ate too many raw onions, which, he asserted, they did regularly, to the detriment of both their taste buds and their brains) and in part to their pride and laziness.[50]

The Sicilian community was so backward, he added, that they even had among them an entirely different sect of Muslims: ones who displayed a type of borderland culture that may have resulted from a blend of Islamic traditions and the local customs of the Berber and Greek converts. These "bastardized Muslims" ("mushaʿmiḍūn"), as he referred to them, lived in fortresses, rural places, and villages—as opposed to cities, of which Palermo was the only notable one on the island—and coexisted to an uncomfortable (to him) degree with the island's Christian population.[51] Indeed, he claimed that they practiced intercultural marriage: they believed, he wrote, that it was acceptable to marry Christian women as long as their sons were raised as Muslims, while

48. Ibid., 128–129.
49. Ibid., 130.
50. Ibid., 123–124.
51. Ibid., 130.

daughters could be raised Christian.[52] Sicilian Muslims did not pray, Ibn Ḥawqal asserted, nor did they perform ablutions; they were not circumcised, did not give alms, or go on pilgrimage. Indeed, they were, in his mind, even losing the knowledge of the Arabic language and of proper Islamic customs—that is, they were drawing farther away from the central Islamic lands, culturally and intellectually, rather than moving closer. Ibn Ḥawqal's vitriol may have been a product of his political and religious allegiances—he was a Shiite while Sicily retained much of its Sunni culture even after the Fatimids took over the island's administration—but it may also have been a reaction to the mixed culture on an island that never became fully integrated into the culture of the dār al-Islām despite the military and political conquest. Thus, his view provides perhaps one glimpse of a liminal culture, in a peripheral location—one that would have seemed nearly unrecognizable to a reader from the central Islamic lands.

The island was not completely unrecognizable to him as a Muslim space, however. Despite his negative assessment, Ibn Ḥawqal did present aspects of Palermo, and a few details about the rest of the island, that indicate widespread Muslim institutions paralleling those in other parts of the Muslim world—but, again, in pale imitation, according to his opinion. In fact, his description provides the most complete picture we have of the Sicilian capital as it developed under Muslim rule, and he described it as having characteristically Muslim urban amenities, including mosques, baths, shops, and military garrisons.[53] He informed his reader that Palermo was a walled city with nine gates and composed of several distinct quarters: a port district (which was separated from the rest of the city by a stream), a main central area, and an adjoining suburban district.[54] Also, a part of greater Palermo was a smaller adjoining city, called Khāliṣa, with its own walls. This was the location of the governor's headquarters and his military garrison, as well as administrative offices, markets, baths, and a central mosque that was smaller than that in the main city of Palermo. In its center, Palermo was bisected by a wide paved boulevard, along which were found markets and other commercial establishments. A river ran parallel to this road, and alongside the river there were vegetable gardens, orchards, and many mills.[55] Ibn Ḥawqal's critical pen, however, was quick to note that

52. Ibid., 129–130.

53. Archaeological investigations on the Islamic layer of Palermo have begun to yield important contributions to our knowledge of the city and island during this period. See Alessandra Molinari, "La Sicilia islamica: Riflessioni sul passato e sul futuro della ricerca in campo archeologico," in "La Sicile à l'époque islamique. Questions de méthode et renouvellement récent des problématiques," special issue, *Mélanges de l'école Française de Rome, Moyen Âge* 116, no. 1 (2004): 19–46.

54. Ibn Ḥawqal, *Kitāb ṣūrat al-arḍ*, 119–120.

55. Ibid., 122.

despite this apparent productivity, these gardens and mills provided the people with only a small income.

This portion of his account is very valuable to historians interested in the economy and trade connections of Islamic Sicily, as Ibn Ḥawqal extensively described the markets of Palermo, the many types of products and services to be found there, and the good prices that these goods fetched.[56] However, he also made sure to point out that Sicily itself did not produce any of these commodities, except for some wheat, wool, wine, sugar, and cloth.[57] Otherwise, despite its grand past as a source of abundant wheat crops, he wrote, Sicily's people currently depended fully on foreign merchants whom, he claimed, they mistreated. But, he conceded, the Sicilians produced textiles that were incomparable and of good market value. For example, one type of ordinary (not luxury) fabric was sold for around 50–60 *rubāʿī* (quarter dinars) per piece and was superior to a similar product from Egypt sold at 50–60 dinars.[58] Other than this cloth and some papyrus ("al-bardū")—grown on the island and used primarily for making ropes for ships, but also for rolls of paper ("ṭawāmīr al-qarāṭīs"), which were utilized only by the local administration and not exported—all other necessary commodities had to be imported to the island and transported within it.[59] His complaints aside, Ibn Ḥawqal shows us that Islamic Sicily was commercially integrated into the wider economy of the Muslim Mediterranean—a view, indeed, that other economic records reinforce, as we will see below.

Ibn Ḥawqal also described, but, again, criticized, the institutions of Islamic society that he saw on Sicily, such as mosques, schools, and military establishments. The central mosque of Palermo he described as huge, presenting an image of opulence and great wealth that Ibn Ḥawqal claimed was unsupportable by the reality of the island's economic output. In addition to this main mosque, which he estimated would hold around 7,000 worshipers, Ibn Ḥawqal claimed to have counted around three hundred smaller mosques in the metropolitan area. This abundance of mosques led Ibn Ḥawqal to criticize the Sicilian people once again.[60] In his view, there were so many small places of worship because the Sicilian Muslims were full of vanity—each wanting to have his own private mosque rather than joining other believers for prayer as in a proper Muslim city. In addition, he claimed that there were

56. Ibid., 121.
57. Ibid., 131.
58. Ibid., 131.
59. Ibid., 122–123.
60. Ibid., 120–121. These numbers are of course no more accurate than those given in any other medieval source; they are simply a reflection of Ibn Ḥawqal's desire to portray the hubris and laziness of the Sicilian population.

about three hundred schools in the city, but he considered them equally useless, along with what he referred to as their incompetent, stupid, and insane schoolteachers. There were so many schools, in Ibn Ḥawqal's opinion, because the schoolmasters wanted to avoid participating in the military expeditions of *jihād*, which Ibn Ḥawqal claimed was being waged against the Christians in Europe only ineffectively, given the lack of tribute payments coming into the island from the mainland. Ibn Ḥawqal was no more pleased with the edifices built for carrying on this war, the coastal *ribāṭs* that housed the warriors.[61] The very presence of *ribāṭs* signifies this space as a frontier, as these were traditionally built along the border of the dār al-Islām as both a line of defensive fortresses and a shelter for frontier fighters who were tasked with expanding the area under Muslim political control. In these Sicilian *ribāṭs*, Ibn Ḥawqal claimed that he encountered men whom he described as being full of hypocrisy, vulgarity, and villainy. Some of them even worked as pimps, he asserted, rather than being serious men engaged in holy war on behalf of Islam. In all, Ibn Ḥawqal determined that these were institutions based not on piety but rebelliousness. That is, they had been built in order to defend and expand the borders of the Islamic world, but Ibn Ḥawqal judged them as failing to live up to these expectations. Thus, even as a frontier of the dār al-Islām, Sicily was deemed a failure.

It may be easy to dismiss Ibn Ḥawqal's account as too biased to be useful, but I think we can glean from it important information about his perspective on Sicily as a borderland. Ibn Ḥawqal's negative assessment of Sicily appears to have hinged on his unpleasant experiences with the culture and attitudes of the people he found there but may also have been informed by his political or religious allegiances. While we cannot expect a Shiite promoter to provide a fair assessment of a Sunni-dominated island with a mixed Muslim-Christian population, his account does offer a number of points of entry for thinking about tenth-century Sicily as a border zone on the periphery of the broader Islamic world. Ibn Ḥawqal noted the prevalence of Muslim institutions, such as mosques, religious schools, and *ribāṭs*, and of merchants who came to the island's markets from around the Muslim-controlled Mediterranean—all clearly denoting that this was a location situated firmly within the Islamicate arena, no matter his opinion of the institutions' effectiveness or rectitude. But he also categorized the island as something of an anomaly, both geographically and culturally at the distant edge of the dār al-Islām—a culturally hybridized space with nonstandard forms of language, religion, and family structure. Supposed customs such as the one that allegedly permitted Christians and

61. Ibid., 121.

Muslims to marry and raise children in joint households seemed very peculiar to him. Therefore, this was not a location that had been culturally drawn into the center, in the eyes of this observer, but remained on the periphery, both geographically and culturally. Indeed, Ibn Ḥawqal seemed to have believed that he would find an island that lived up to his expectations, based on his knowledge of its glorious past, but instead discovered that the island had suffered a downgrade. Not only had it lost all of its earlier riches and luxury and not flourished as a center of Islamic culture, but also, in his opinion, Sicily had surrendered its claims to fame and relevance in terms of economy, agriculture, and even environment. Rather than integrating a wealthy island into the broader culture of Islam, or bringing the Arabic language and Muslim culture to a productive economy, therefore, the incorporation of Sicily into the dār al-Islām had, for Ibn Ḥawqal, simply created a confusing border culture with a mixture of Muslim and Christian customs. Ibn Ḥawqal's excoriation of the frontier and its people also depended on the assumption that very few of his readers had been to Sicily. Indeed, the success of such a negative appraisal both relied on and reinforced the marginality of the island—a space that he deemed both geographically distant and conceptually insignificant, a semi-Muslim place at the edge of the Islamic world.

Nearly invisible on maps, treated only lightly by geographers, and reviled by Ibn Ḥawqal, tenth-century Sicily may appear to have been completely detached from the intellectual currents of the dār al-Islām. Yet this was not entirely the case. Sicily is known to have had a tradition of Arabic scholars (*ʿulamāʾ*) and poets, many of whom studied with masters or worked for eminent patrons in other parts of the Islamic world; however, the breadth and depth of this tradition are unknown. Extant biographies of men whose scholarly careers saw them traveling to or from Sicily during the years of Muslim rule on the island are few and often incomplete. Throughout the centuries of Islamic culture on Sicily, in fact, there is more abundant data for scholars leaving the island than for those arriving or living there—likely because the majority of sources from this period originate from outside the island. Only rarely does our evidence show a student traveling to Sicily to study with a master (although we do know of a few who did so), and most intellectuals of Sicilian origin are known for the works they produced after leaving the island. In fact, several of the biographical dictionaries of famous scholars contain stories about men whose ancestral origins lay in Sicily but whose academic or literary careers took place long after their families' departure from the island. While there are hints of a larger school of Arabic poets and scholars in Sicily during the Muslim period, most of their works are lost, and thus we cannot gauge their impact in the literary circles of the central Islamic lands.[62]

Some references in the evidence do suggest the existence of a stronger scholarly tradition on the island, one in close connection with the intellectual systems of North Africa. We have brief notices that some scholars traveled to the island for study, but our knowledge of their intellectual networks is insufficient. For example, one student who visited Sicily for the purposes of study was Abū Saʿīd Luqmān b. Yūsuf al-Ghassānī (d. 930/931 in Tunis), a polymath who spent fourteen years there teaching al-Mālikī's text *al-Mudawwana*.[63] This lengthy period of legal work in Sicily possibly indicates that there was an important school for Malīkī legal thought on the island.[64] However, this reference to a scholar traveling to Sicily in order to study Mālikī legal texts with a master is unique among my findings. It is possible that there was an established network of Mālikī learning that involved Sicilian masters, with perhaps many more scholars like this one traveling there for similar intellectual purposes, but we cannot know for sure. Evidence for other types of scholarship on the island comes from the biographical dictionaries of illustrious men. For example, the entry on Ibn al-Qaṭṭāʿ (1041–1121), found in the collection of Ibn Khallikān, mentions that this scholar studied in Sicily with a teacher named Ibn al-Birr, who, it is written, was known as the greatest scholarly master on the island.[65] Unfortunately, we cannot fully recreate his network of students and colleagues, but we can see that some important (though now lost) intellectual works must have been produced in Muslim Sicily. Likewise, Ibn Ḥawqal, visiting in 973, claimed to have found numerous religious schools in Sicily, but it is not clear whether these were small foundations attached to mosques for

62. There were certainly more texts written in Arabic about Sicily than are extant; for instance, Ibn Ḥawqal noted that he had written an entire history of the island, but that text is lost to us. For more on the intellectual community of Muslim Sicily, see Iḥsān ʿAbbās, *Mu'jim al-ʿulamāʾ wa al-shu'ra' al-saqilliyin* (Beirut: Dār al-Gharb al-Islāmī, 1994); Andrea Borruso, "Su una antologia di poeti arabi siciliani medievali," *Annali, Istituto universitario orientale* 48, no. 1 (1988/1989): 63–70; Borruso, "Poesie Arabe en Sicile," *al-Masāq* 4 (1991): 17–34; Chiarelli, *A History of Muslim Sicily*, 295–311; Granara, "Islamic Education"; Annliese Nef, "Les élites savantes urbaines dans la Sicile islamique d'après les dictionnaires biographiques arabes," in "La Sicile à l'époque islamique: Questions de méthode et renouvellement récent des problématiques," special issue, *Mélanges de l'École Française de Rome, Moyen Âge* 116, no. 1 (2004): 451–470; and Umberto Rizzitano, "Un compendio dell'Antologia di Poeti Arabo-Siciliani," *Atti della Accademia Nazionale dei Lincei* 8, no. 5 (1958): 335–379.

63. al-Mālikī, *Riyāḍ al-nufūs*, *BAS* Arabic, rev. ed., 223–224, *BAS* Ital., 1: 256–257.

64. Sicily, as has long been recognized, was dominated by the Mālikī legal school. For more detailed examination of Islamic education in Sicily, see Granara, "Islamic Education," and Mandalà, "Political Martyrdom."

65. For more on both of these men and the other scholars who migrated from Sicily, see Metcalfe, *The Muslims of Medieval Italy*, 122–123.

the purpose of local religious education or outposts of a more thriving intellectual culture.

Other pieces of similar information show that Sicily's intellectuals themselves were closely connected to the broader literary and scholarly cultures of Ifrīqiya, Egypt, and, to a lesser degree, al-Andalus, through travel, work, and study in those places. Among the scholars whose biographies we have are several intellectuals who carried out part of their careers in Sicily while at the same time participating in the more well-known court cultures outside of the island. Many *ʿulamāʾ* were associated with Sicily in the biographical dictionaries because they ended their lives there, yet these men had important connections to North Africa, Spain, and the central Islamic lands. An example of such a career trajectory is that of Muḥammad b. Khurāsān, a grammarian (*naḥwī*) who studied in Egypt and then went to Sicily to teach *ḥadīth* to religious students there. He was not originally from Sicily but traveled there to live and work; he died in Sicily in 996/997 at the age of seventy-six. Another intellectual born outside the island who ended his career in Sicily was Abū al-ʿAlāʾ Ṣāʿid b. al-Ḥasan b. ʿĪsā al-Rabaʿī al-Baghdādī. He was a lexicographer (*lughawī*), originally from Baghdad, who traveled to Spain in 990/991 and served under the *ḥājib* al-Mansūr.[66] According to his biography, he died in Sicily in 1026/1027, after he fell out of favor with al-Mansūr. We have no account of his migration from Spain to Sicily, but it is possible that he was seeking a new patron on the island. The literary culture of al-Andalus was by far the most famous in the medieval western Mediterranean, and it appears that Sicily's school of poets and scholars was much smaller. Nonetheless, this example of an act of scholarly travel may reflect a deeper intellectual connection between Sicily and al-Andalus than can be seen in the extant sources.

Scholarly links between Sicily and other regions of the Muslim Mediterranean are also revealed through the biographies of Muslim scholars who were born or began their careers in Sicily but became famous elsewhere. The preponderance of such scholars moved from Sicily to Ifrīqiya in order to advance their careers, although some are known to have migrated to Spain or Egypt. For example, the famous poet (*shāʿir*) Abū Muḥammad ʿAbd al-Jabbār b. Abī Bakr b. Muḥammad b. Ḥamdīs al-Ṣiqillī (known as Ibn Ḥamdīs) was born in Sicily but moved to Spain in 1078/1079 and thence to al-Mahdiyya, where he served at the court of the Zīrid *emīr* Tamīm ibn al-Muʿizz. He died either in Mallorca or Bougie in 1132/1133.[67] His biographical entry in the

66. Ibn Khallikān, *Wafayāt al-aʿyān wa-anbāʾ abnāʾ al-zamān*, 8 vols., ed. Iḥsān ʿAbbās (Beirut: Dār Ṣādir, 1968–1977), 2: 488–489. The official known as a *ḥājib*, or chamberlain, was similar to a vizier.

67. Ibn Khallikān, *Wafayāt*, 3: 212–215.

dictionary of Ibn Khallikān does not explicitly state the reason for his departure from the island, but the timing makes it likely that he moved due to the invasions of the Normans (Palermo fell in 1072), in which case Ibn Ḥamdīs would be one of the most notable representatives of such émigrés.[68] Although his poetic corpus was written entirely in al-Andalus and Ifrīqiya, many of his poems, including the one quoted in his biography, refer to Sicily and his longing for the island.[69]

Like Ibn Ḥamdīs, several other scholars made their way from Sicily to North Africa by way of al-Andalus, while other Sicilian scholars traveled directly from the island to Ifrīqiya. Among the most famous of these was Ibn al-Qaṭṭāᶜ, a writer and philologist who was born in Sicily but lived, worked, and died in Egypt.[70] He was born in 1041 and studied literature (*adab*) under several teachers in Sicily, including the Sicilian master Ibn al-Birr. He left the island because of the Norman invasion and traveled first to al-Andalus and then to Egypt. His biography explicitly mentions that he departed when the Christians were on the verge of gaining complete control of Sicily, as opposed to Ibn Ḥamdīs's biography, which does not explain the precise reason for the poet's migration from Sicily. In 1106/1107 Ibn al-Qaṭṭāᶜ arrived in Egypt and taught there before he died in 1121/1122.[71] This pattern of emigration to al-Andalus and thence to northern Africa is likely due to an established tradition of intellectual and political communication between the two regions. Scholars and other members of the Sicilian Muslim elite who emigrated from the island thus would have found not only political refuge but also patrons, friends, and associates who could assist them in securing patronage and setting up their new lives in al-Andalus, Ifrīqiya, or Egypt.

Several other scholarly connections to Sicily are only visible much later, after one or more generations had passed since the scholar or his family had emigrated. One well-known scholar of the twelfth century who had Sicilian ancestry but whose entire career was conducted in North Africa was Abū ᶜAbd Allāh Muḥammad b. ᶜAlī Umar b. Muḥammad al-Tamīmī al-Māzarī, known as Imām al-Māzarī, a Mālikī expert in the traditions of the Prophet

68. William Granara argues that Ibn Ḥamdīs left Sicily for the Iberian court in order to further his career as a poet and then was prevented from ever returning to his homeland because of the Norman conquests. See William E. Granara, "Ibn Ḥamdīs and the Poetry of Nostalgia," in *The Literature of al-Andalus*, ed. Maria Rosa Menocal, Raymond P. Scheindlin, and Michael Sells (Cambridge: Cambridge University Press, 2000), 388–403.

69. William E. Granara, "Remaking Muslim Sicily: Ibn Ḥamdīs and the Poetics of Exile," *Edebiyāt* 9 (1998): 167–198. A few of Ibn Ḥamdīs's poems have been translated by Karla Mallette in her *The Kingdom of Sicily, 1100–1250: A Literary History* (Philadelphia: University of Pennsylvania Press, 2005), 131–138.

70. Ibn Khallikān, *Wafayāt*, 3: 322–324.

71. Ibid.: "rahalaᶜan Ṣiqilliya lamma ashraf ᶜalā tamallakhān al-Faranj, wa waṣala ilā Misr."

("al-faqīh al-Mālikī al-muḥaddith"). Ibn Khallikān called him "one of the most distinguished of such experts in regard to knowledge of the *ḥadīth* and his teaching on that subject."[72] Imām al-Māzarī's name is derived from the southwestern Sicilian coastal town of Māzara (modern Mazara del Vallo), a port in frequent connection with North Africa. Nevertheless, al-Māzarī seems to have lived and pursued his career exclusively in North Africa, and he died in al-Mahdiyya in 1141. It is not clear whether he himself was born on the island before the family migrated, or if he was the descendant of one of the families who fled the Norman invasion. What we do know is that his name indicates that he was commonly identified as a Sicilian and that he maintained an interest in the island. To wit, several of his legal pronouncements concerned Muslims remaining in Sicily, North Africans who traveled to Sicily, or Sicilians who had migrated to North Africa. Even if he never personally set foot on the island, his career highlights the close connection between Ifrīqiya and Sicily and an important association with the island, its people, and its affairs even after it became a Christian territory. Several of the *fatwās* of Imām al-Māzarī will be discussed below as evidence for continued trade between Muslim Ifrīqiya and Christian Sicily in the twelfth century. At the same time, his life and career show that maintaining an identity as "a Sicilian" could have value for an intellectual in North Africa even several generations removed from the island itself.

As a whole, the Muslim scholars of Sicily participated in the wider networks of *ʿulamāʾ* that radiated out of the central Islamic lands, having particularly close associations with the intellectual circles of Ifrīqiya and al-Andalus. Sicily itself may have had a more thriving scholarly culture than we can see in the surviving sources, but, at the same time, all of these scholars moved regularly throughout the western Mediterranean—so that it can be difficult to separate one regional intellectual tradition from those of its neighbors. Nonetheless, the overall image that can be gleaned from the extant geographical treatises, maps, and scholars' biographies is that Muslim Sicily was closely integrated with other Muslim societies in the western Mediterranean. At the same time, it may have been commonly viewed in the central Islamic lands as a remote, marginal, or even backward place with a hybridized multicultural population. Nonetheless, at times scholars traveled to or from Sicily during their careers of study and literary output, linking the island, to some degree, into the larger intellectual trends of the Muslim western Mediterranean.

72. Ibn Khallikān, *Wafayāt*, 4: 285: "āhad al-aʿlām al-mushār ilayhim fī ḥifẓ al-ḥadīth wa al-kalām ʿalayhu."

Economic Connections with Egypt and Ifrīqiya

Given Ibn Ḥawqal's focus on Sicily's agricultural produce and mercantile wealth (or lack thereof, in his view), it may not be surprising that the most significant role played by the island in the dār al-Islām appears to be an economic one. Indeed, commercial travel is the single largest source of information about travel between Sicily and the Muslim world during the two centuries of Islamic rule on the island. The prevalence of these economic data, in turn, is thanks in large part to the discovery of a cache of documents referred to as the Cairo Geniza, which includes a large number of letters to and from Jewish merchants active in the central Mediterranean during the years of Muslim power in the region.[73] Additional information—especially helpful for the period of Sicily's history after the end of Muslim dominion, as we will see in chapter 4—comes from North African legal sources called *fatwās* that record some of the conflicts and concerns of Ifrīqiyan traders doing business in and around Sicily. Some of these decisions settled disputes between partners, while others resolved conflicts about payment of sailors' salaries or the freight costs on a ship after the vessel had been wrecked or the voyage abandoned due to poor weather. That the *fatwās* only record conflicts arising in the midst of commercial journeys suggests that they account for only a few of the far greater number of trips that took place between Sicily and North Africa during that period but left no record. There must have been many more business deals that were successful or in which conflicts were resolved without the mediation of a *faqīh* (Islamic legal expert). Additionally, there may have been legal cases for which the *fatwā* is either unrecorded or lost. Thus, although these *fatwās* are few in number, there is good reason to believe that they represent much broader patterns of commercial travel and exchange.

Combined, these sources show that Sicily during the centuries of Islamic dominion—particularly in the eleventh century—often served as a transit spot for merchants who imported goods to the island, sold them there for a profit, and then purchased other merchandise for export to another place. In this manner, the island was much like its trade partners of Egypt and North Africa, which also featured markets where merchants bought and sold products for import and export.[74] In the case of Sicily, however, the regions from which it imported and to which it exported goods appear to be limited primarily

73. For an introduction to the contents of the Cairo Geniza materials and the society that created them, see *Medit. Soc* and Goldberg, *Trade*.

74. On the "trade triangle" between Sicily, Ifrīqiya, and Egypt, see S. D. Goitein, "The Unity of the Mediterranean World in the 'Middle' Middle Ages," in *Studies in Islamic History and Institutions* (Leiden: E. J. Brill, 1966), 296–307; "Medieval Tunisia: The Hub of the Mediterranean," in *Studies in*

to Egypt and North Africa. Very little evidence exists to suggest that merchants from al-Andalus or the Christian West visited Sicily's markets or that traders active in Sicily moved goods to those places. That is, Sicily served as a site of important markets for the regional Mediterranean trade conducted by both Muslims and Jews, but it did not operate as a meeting point for merchants from the Arabic-speaking world and those from the Latin world. This is likely due in large part to the fact that southern Italian mercantile cities, such as Amalfi, Genoa, Salerno, and Naples, had already established their own trading connections directly with the southern shores of the Mediterranean.[75] Italian merchants had no need for intermediary markets in Sicily when they were themselves capable of sailing directly to Egypt or the eastern Mediterranean for trade purposes; only the slightest evidence of Sicily-Italy trade exists. Instead, Sicily's markets seem to have been frequented most often by Jewish and Muslim merchants from Egypt and Ifrīqiya because that was the preferred pattern for mercantile communications in the Muslim Mediterranean. Trade took place within overlapping regional zones that combined to create far broader networks of exchange, in which individual merchants usually did not have to make the entire journey from the central Mediterranean to the Near or Far East.

One example from the Geniza letters will serve as an introduction to the variety of products and markets involved in Sicily's economic networks. At some time in the eleventh century, a Jewish trader named Mūsā b. Isḥāq b. Ḥisda wrote a letter to his senior partner, the prominent merchant Yūsuf b. ʿAwqal.[76] Mūsā, at the time located in the Ifrīqiyan city of al-Mahdiyya, sent this note to Yūsuf in Fusṭāṭ, Egypt, to inform him about a shipment of raw hides that he had purchased in Sicily and that he owned in partnership with Yūsuf.[77] As Yūsuf's agent, Mūsā had taken the bales of goods from Sicily to al-Mahdiyya hoping to sell them there at a profit, but the ship's cargo was mostly destroyed by water damage. Mūsā assured his partner that everything they were able to salvage would bring a profit for them and that God would

Islamic History and Institutions (Leiden: E. J. Brill, 1968), 308–328; and "Sicily and Southern Italy in the Cairo Geniza Documents," *Archivio Storico per le Sicilia Orientale* 67 (1971): 9–33.

75. Armand O. Citarella, "The Relations of Amalfi with the Arab World before the Crusades," *Speculum* 42, no. 2 (1967): 299–312; Citarella, "Patterns in Medieval Trade: The Commerce of Amalfi before the Crusades," *The Journal of Economic History* 28 (1968): 531–555; and Barbara M. Kreutz, "Ghost Ships and Phantom Cargoes: Reconstructing Early Amalfitan Trade," *Journal of Medieval History* 20 (1994): 347–357.

76. University of Oxford, Bodleian Libraries, MS. Heb. c. 27.82; Ben-Sasson, 214ff.; Simonsohn, doc. 33.

77. For more on this merchant and his family, see Norman A. Stillman, "The Eleventh Century Merchant House of Ibn ʿAwkal (A Geniza Study)," *Journal of the Economic and Social History of the Orient* 16, no. 1 (1973): 15–88; and Goldberg, *Trade*, esp. 38–39, 308–315.

provide compensation for the rest. So the traveling merchant Mūsā, present in Sicily while conducting business on behalf of himself and his partner back in Egypt, had purchased goods on the island and then sailed to Ifrīqiya, where he hoped to sell those goods and purchase others with the proceeds; other commodities purchased in Sicily were sent directly to Egypt. This letter thus documents commercial travel between Sicily and Ifrīqiya (directed from Egypt), as well as between Sicily and Egypt and between Ifrīqiya and Egypt, all of which was connected and mediated through the commercial and personal relationships that spanned three separate regions of the central Mediterranean.[78] Neither of these merchants lived permanently in Sicily, but they were conversant with the mercantile environment there and had easy connections with both Ifrīqiya and Sicily, to and from where they sailed regularly from their home base in Egypt. When the traders themselves were not sailing back and forth to Egypt, they were able to send letters like this one via ships that were making the journey across the Mediterranean. This pattern of commerce and communication linking Islamic Sicily with Egypt and Ifrīqiya is repeated in numerous Geniza letters from the tenth through twelfth centuries.

Medieval interregional commerce, such as in this example, was carried out by investors and traveling merchants like Mūsā and Yūsuf who formed partnerships in order to transport goods and money to markets throughout the Mediterranean and invested capital and resources to fund these commercial exchanges.[79] Such partnerships are represented both in Latin commercial contracts from Europe and in the Judeo-Arabic letters of the Cairo Geniza, as well as in some of the judicial opinions (*fatwās*) from the Islamic world. Because of the nature of the sources, then, the traveling merchants who appear in the Geniza letters and the *fatwās* were primarily Jews and Muslims, with Christians showing up far less frequently. These letters predominantly feature Jewish merchants and their business deals, although they occasionally include

78. Mūsā's letter, which came to Fusṭāṭ from al-Mahdiyya, almost certainly traveled on a merchant ship. Sicily does not appear as an important stop along the route of the *barīd*, which was a primarily overland route by which news and instructions traveled throughout the Sunni caliphal lands; there is no evidence of *barīd* routes extending into the seas. See Adam J. Silverstein, *Postal Systems in the Pre-modern Islamic World* (Cambridge: Cambridge University Press, 2007).

79. Much has been written on the medieval mercantile system of contracts and agency. See Robert S. Lopez and Irving W. Raymond, *Medieval Trade in the Mediterranean World* (New York: Columbia University Press, 1955), pt. 3, for an overview of contracts as well as examples in translation. See also *Medit. Soc.*, 1: iii, B, pp. 164–186; Goldberg, *Trade*, esp. 123–150; H. R. Idris, "Commerce maritime et ḳirāḍ en Berbérie orientale," *Journal of the Economic and Social History of the Orient* 4 (1961): 225–239; and Abraham L. Udovitch, "At the Origins of the Western Commenda: Islam, Israel, Byzantium?" *Speculum* 37, no. 2 (1962): 198–207.

references to partnerships with Muslim businessmen or shipowners.[80] In similar fashion, the Islamic judicial opinions from North Africa provide data almost exclusively about Muslim mercantile activity, including several partnerships formed for the purpose of obtaining goods from Sicily. None of the sources for the Islamic period of Sicily, therefore, present a complete picture of the people and places involved in cross-Mediterranean trade at the time, but, taken together, they show a mercantile environment heavily dominated by Jews living in the Arab Muslim world. As depicted in the Geniza documents, this Mediterranean trade was directed and carried out by a mobile and adaptable community primarily of Jews living in Egypt, Ifrīqiya, and Sicily, who also traveled throughout the Mediterranean and beyond.[81] Muslim merchants were likely just as prominent in these networks of commercial travel, as evidenced by the legal sources depicting trade disputes between Muslims; their activities may have followed patterns similar to those of the Jewish merchants, but the information about Muslim mercantile travel is much more scant than that about Jewish commercial activity. Overall, what is clear is that the majority of the trade with Islamic Sicily was conducted with both Ifrīqiya and Egypt. Commercial affairs linked the island closely to its nearest neighboring Muslim regions, with goods, people, letters, and ships moving quickly and frequently between them in what has been referred to as a kind of commercial triangle.[82]

When viewed through the lens of the North African Islamic sources alone, however, Sicily's closest commercial partner appears to have been Ifrīqiya itself, with Egypt rarely figuring in these accounts of commercial travel; such a disparity highlights our dependence on sources that present only a limited cross section of the historical reality, much of which is thus lost to us. One *fatwā* from the tenth century illustrates the types of transactions and legal disputes that were involved in business carried out by Muslim merchants between Sicily

80. The Arabic and Judeo-Arabic sources of the North Africa *fatwās* and Cairo Geniza only rarely mention Christian merchants, who are known from other sources to have operated in Egypt and North Africa.

81. We do know that some Sicilian merchants (most likely Jewish) had established a semipermanent trading community in Fusṭāṭ, but there are few other references to native Sicilian merchants traveling through the Mediterranean on commercial business. Cambridge, T-S 12.371; Ben-Sasson, 439ff.; Simonsohn, doc. 76.

82. The concept of a Sicily-Egypt-Ifrīqiya trade triangle may be too oversimplified, especially if the Geniza evidence is examined in detail. Goldberg breaks down more closely the types of routes preferred by individual travelers and those originating in particular regions and the changes in these preferred routes over time. She found that many traders remained in regional networks like those we see between Sicily, Egypt, and Ifrīqiya. See Goldberg, *Trade*, esp. 261–276. For our purposes here, it is sufficient to note the high degree of interconnection between the regions without needing to specify whether the traders traveled in uni- or multidirectional routes during particular decades.

and Ifrīqiya. Issued in the tenth century at Qayrawān by Abū Saʿīd b. Akhī Hisham (d. 981 or 983), the opinion treats the resolution of a contract that was not fully executed due to a shipwreck.[83] This *fatwā*, like several other similar ones, describes a commercial transaction that involved travel from Sicily to Ifrīqiya for the purpose of selling goods there, although the exact commodities traded are not specified. It is likewise unclear whether these merchants were native Sicilians or Ifrīqiyans, or possibly foreign merchants taking advantage of the ships that sailed frequently between Sicilian and North African ports. They were almost certainly Muslims, due to the fact that their commercial dispute was being adjudicated in the court of a *qāḍī*.[84] The description of the question states that some travelers chartered a ship to sail from Sicily to Sūsa, but the ship made it only as far as Tunis when weather conditions made it necessary for the merchandise to be unloaded there. The ship was unable to re-embark for Sūsa, and no land route was offered as an alternative. Now that the final destination for the merchandise was unreachable by sea, the businessmen were concerned that they might end up having to pay the full freight charges for the journey to Sūsa, which would create a loss for them if their goods sold for less at Tunis than they would have brought at Sūsa. The Qayrawān-based Abū Saʿīd b. Akhī Hisham was consulted on the case, and he declared that if the profits from the sale at Tunis were higher than at Sūsa, then the freight fee should be increased, while if the profits were less, the freight should be decreased and the original contract voided.[85]

A similar tenth-century situation, also found in the *fatwā* compilation of al-Wansharīsī, involved another ship traveling from Sicily to Sūsa with merchandise aboard. This ship, too, stopped short of Sūsa, in the vicinity of Tunis, but in this case the captain offered to transport the merchants by land to their final destination. Similar questions about freight costs were asked by the disputants. This question was decided by the jurist Ibn Siblūn, also based in Qayrawān (d. 999), and in this case he decided in favor of having the merchants pay the entire freight costs, since land transportation to Sūsa was

83. al-Wansharīsī, 8: 310.

84. On the other hand, medieval people living in multicultural environments often sought legal opinions from judges in faith traditions other than their own, in the hopes of receiving a more favorable decision. This process, known as "forum shopping," has been studied by legal scholars and experts on religious minorities, for example those involved in RELMIN, the Legal Status of Religious Minorities in the Euro-Mediterranean World (5th–15th centuries) project. See, for example, John Tolan, "The Infidel before the Judge: Navigating Justice Systems in Multiconfessional Medieval Europe," in *Religiöse Vielfalt und der Umgang mit Minderheiten. Vergangene und gegenwärtige Erfahrungen*, ed. Dorothea Weltecke (Konstanz: UVK, 2014), 57–79.

85. Qayrawān was the location of a great school of Mālikī jurisprudence during the Middle Ages. See Idris, "Commerce maritime," 225–228.

available.[86] These two examples demonstrate that Muslim merchants were indeed sailing between Ifrīqiya and Sicily and that they were bringing goods from Sicily to sell in various North African markets. The origin of these goods is unclear—they may have been Sicilian products or those imported from elsewhere to be sold in the island's markets—but the economic importance of Sicily to Ifrīqiya emerges from these and similar legal sources. So even though neither the island's rulers in Ifrīqiya nor those in Egypt used Sicily as an extension of their political power as Constantinople had done in earlier centuries, Sicily was deeply embedded in both of their economic systems. Indeed, Sicily's markets, the commodities sold there, and the ports to and from which goods were shipped offer us an opportunity to glimpse the significant economic role that Sicily played in the Muslim Mediterranean.

Commodities sold in the island's markets represent the full range of products that were traded across the medieval Mediterranean, from foodstuffs and spices to raw materials and coins. Perhaps the most important item of food in the economy, particularly in reference to Sicily, was wheat—although it shows up as a commodity in the Geniza letters far less frequently than we might expect. Although Sicily was a significant source of wheat in the ancient economy, the degree to which Sicily's wheat cultivation remained an important economic factor under Byzantine rule is unclear from the existing sources. However, from the time that Sicily begins to appear in the Geniza documents, in the tenth century CE, we can resume discussion of the trade in wheat; quantitative assessments are still impossible due to the limited nature of the surviving evidence, but we can at least see wheat being traded during these centuries alongside many other products originating in both the Near East and central Mediterranean regions. However, wheat was not, by any means, the only or even primary commodity named in the sources as an object of trade between Sicily, Ifrīqiya, and Egypt in the tenth through thirteenth centuries: it was one among many foodstuffs, raw materials, and textiles that traveled along these routes.

When grain appears in the letters of the Geniza that relate to trade to and from Sicily, it is usually mentioned only in requests for prices of wheat, not in reference to cargoes of grain being shipped or received. For example, one letter written from Alexandria to Fusṭāṭ that discussed the commercial trade in coins and cloth in great detail mentioned wheat only in a final sentence requesting news about the current quality of water and price for wheat in

86. al-Wansharīsī, 8: 299–300.

Fusṭāṭ.[87] It was an important commodity, clearly, but no more significant than the coins and cloth in this letter. Wheat appears in other Geniza letters in similar ways, as a product traded, shipped, or purchased, but in no case is this grain exclusively a Sicilian agricultural product. Since wheat was harvested widely throughout the Muslim Mediterranean and the Christian West, the grain shipments in question could have originated from many locations.[88] One example shows a merchant declaring his intention to sell various goods in Palermo and then purchase wheat, but it is not clear whether he intended to purchase Sicilian produce or simply grain that was for sale there but that had been shipped to the island from elsewhere, like many other commodities were.[89]

Rather than being discussed as a specific product of Sicilian cultivation, then, grain and bread were mentioned by these authors as part of general discussions of the conditions of life in various places throughout the Mediterranean basin. It was a fundamental part of the daily food supply of the Mediterranean population and a vital aspect of the medieval economy of both Christian and Muslim regions. For example, one author in Alexandria provided the prices of wheat in various places along with the fact that his family had put some sacks of new wheat into storage for the winter.[90] These regular references to the price of wheat suggest that it was considered a key indicator of the relative strength of a local or regional economy at a given time. References in Geniza letters to the price of wheat often appear to stand in for evidence of the current troubles afflicting certain locales. Many authors wrote that the situation in a particular city was terrible, a comment followed immediately by mention of the current prices of wheat and oil, suggesting that these prices were high because of political turmoil.[91] One example of this practice is found

87. Cambridge, T-S 13J28.9, Ben-Sasson, 579ff.; Simonsohn, doc. 65, line 11. Nothing in the text indicates that wheat needed to be imported into Egypt from Sicily or from anywhere else. This letter is dated to August 1054. See also Moshe Gil, "Sicily 827–1072, in Light of the Geniza Documents and Parallel Sources," in *Italia Judaica: Gli ebrei in Sicilia sino all'espulsione del 1492, Atti del V convegno internazionale, Palermo, 15–19 giugno 1992* (Rome: Ministero per i beni culturali e ambientali, 1995), 132; and *Medit. Soc.*, 1: 100, 229, 324.

88. For the diffusion of hard wheat through the Islamic world to the Christian West, see Watson, *Agricultural Innovation*, 20–23.

89. St. Petersburg, INA D-55 No. 14; Ben-Sasson, 57ff.; Simonsohn, doc. 127, ll. 29–31.

90. New York, Jewish Theological Seminary, Adler Coll. NS 2(I).13; Simonsohn, doc. 145, right margin l. 3. Again, there is no reason to suspect that this is anything other than locally grown wheat, but it is not specified.

91. A notable example of this association between high wheat prices and political upheaval is the Geniza letter in which a Sicilian merchant who had left Sicily due to the Norman invasion described the violence and disruptions wrought on the island by this turmoil. After recounting the bloodshed attendant upon the Norman takeover of Palermo, he noted that the price of bread had risen and that bread was also difficult to procure. Cambridge, T-S 13J13.27, fol. 1a, ll. 13–16.

in a letter in which the author, located in al-Mahdiyya, noted the price fluctuations over recent months of both wheat and oil. This statement occurred in the context of his lament about the disastrous violence occurring in the region: he noted that Qayrawān was deserted and destroyed and that both North Africa and Sicily were suffering political violence (the former due to Bedouin invasions and civil wars, the latter due to the Norman invasion).[92]

Taken together, the evidence presented in the letters of the Geniza does not point to wheat as the trade commodity of singular importance in relation to Sicily but rather as one of many products bought and sold when conditions presented themselves as good for business. On the other hand, there are several legal pronouncements from tenth- through twelfth-century North Africa that shed light on the direct trade in grain and other merchandise between there and Sicily. They indicate that wheat may have been an especially important product in the direct Sicily-Ifrīqiya trade, both before and after the Norman invasion of the island. Several of these *fatwās* record deals concluded between North Africans for the purpose of traveling to Sicily to do business there. Some do not specify the cargo sought, but the ones that do mention the commodity either name wheat (*qamḥ*) or use the general term for food (*ṭaʿām*), which may refer to wheat. In each of the *fatwās*, the transaction proceeded generally as follows: two or more partners created a contract to pool resources for the purchase of Sicilian grain, which one or more of them would travel to the island to procure. Trade using coinage, rather than barter in commercial goods, seems to have been most common among these Ifrīqiyan Muslim businessmen, although in a few cases the *fatwās* explicitly mention that North African goods were taken to Sicily for trade.[93] Those *fatwās* that specifically mention Ifrīqiyans seeking grain from Sicily date from the tenth to the twelfth centuries, both before and after the Norman conquest, which fact will be discussed in more detail in chapter 4. For much of this period of political and economic upheaval, North Africa was experiencing famine, drought, and disruptive nomadic migrations, making it possible (or indeed likely) that Sicily became an even more important source of food.[94]

---

92. Cambridge, T-S 16.179; Ben-Sasson, 36ff.; Simonsohn, doc. 122.

93. For example, one *fatwā* specifies that the partners contributed, in total, two donkeys and a measure of sumac.

94. See chapter 4 for the background to the Bedouin invasion that has traditionally been thought to have caused the famine in North Africa. For the climatological changes that may actually have caused drought and famine in these decades, see Ronnie Ellenblum, *The Collapse of the Eastern Mediterranean: Climate Change and the Decline of the East, 950–1072* (Cambridge: Cambridge University Press, 2012), 147–159. Details about the hardships in eleventh-century Ifrīqiya are also found in some of the letters from the Cairo Geniza. Cambridge, T-S 12.372; Ben-Sasson, 552ff.; Simonsohn, doc. 111, fol. 1b, ll. 1–4. In this letter the author relayed information from North Africa about the difficulties of

Two *fatwās* issued by the Ifrīqiyan jurist al-Qābisī (d. 1012) illustrate commercial journeys originating in North Africa with the purpose of buying and importing Sicilian wheat. In the first of these two cases, al-Qābisī's advice was sought concerning a gift given by a ship's captain to a man who was operating as his brother's agent in a commercial venture.[95] The case states that the partner who traveled to Sicily from Qayrawān was given some dinars by his brother in order that he procure Sicilian wheat ("qamḥ").[96] The second case involved a group of investors who rented a ship for the trip to Sicily to buy food ("ṭaʿām") and found that when their traveling partner returned, he had kept the entire cargo for himself.[97] This legal case centered on whether or not the man was required to pay back the costs of renting the ship or only the freight charges (as he in fact did). In both of these examples one can see that Sicilian wheat and other foodstuffs were desired in Ifrīqiya, either to meet immediate food needs or to profit from the investment.[98]

Wheat, however, was by no means the only food product that we see traveling between Sicily, Ifrīqiya, and Egypt and beyond. Other foodstuffs, such as olive oil and wine, along with spices, fruits, nuts, and cheese, were also distributed along these Mediterranean trade routes.[99] Olive and grape products were important in the Mediterranean diet and economy, and Roman Sicily and North Africa are known to have produced large amounts of both, enough that

---

finding food in Qayrawān: "The situation in North Africa is deplorable. Wheat fetches three in Qayrawān, oil is in short supply." Translation is Simonsohn's. See also Cambridge, T-S13J16.19; Ben-Sasson, 539ff.; Simonsohn, doc. 112. This letter notes specifically that there was famine in Alexandria, stemming from the problems in the West, and that "there is a water shortage and wheat costs three for a gold coin and (is sold) secretly" (translation is Simonsohn's, doc. 112, line 28). These problems also affected the prices of other items, including textiles, which, the author noted, could not be sold for a profit (he stated that one lost on the resale). Letter from Alexandria, November 1056, Cambridge, T-S 10J15.15. See also Simonsohn, doc. 114: "people are caught between violence and famine" (lines 4–5) and "a terrible epidemic is raging throughout the coastal towns" of North Africa (line 14). A 1064 letter from a Jewish merchant who had recently traveled from Ifrīqiya to Sicily provides a first-hand account of the military conflicts occurring in the region of Sfax at the time and their effects on business, Philadelphia, Dropsie College 389; Ben-Sasson, 65ff.; Simonsohn, doc. 151, fol. 1a, ll. 57–58.

95. al-Qābisī (d. 1012), al-Wansharīsī, 9: 114–115.

96. Upon the ship's return to Ifrīqiya, the captain gave back a portion of the freight to the traveling brother, who then wondered if he could keep the money (or give it back to his brother) without telling the captain who had originally contributed the funds for the journey. Al-Qābisī counseled in favor of honesty.

97. al-Wansharīsī, 9: 117.

98. See also chapter 4 on goods that were transported to or from Sicily after the Norman conquest of the island, at which time North Africa was suffering a long famine. That situation may have increased both need and profits in the wheat trade.

99. For the trio of olive, grape, and wheat as foodstuffs uniquely characteristic of Mediterranean cultures and climates, see Braudel, *The Mediterranean*, 1: 236. Geniza letters make it clear that the medieval Mediterranean diet was far richer than the common idea of this trinity suggests.

they were exported in some quantities to Italy and beyond.[100] Wine and olive oil appear in our sources as having been shipped to and from Sicily, although the degree to which either was a major export commodity from the island is not clear—it is possible that, as with many of these other products, Sicily's markets acted as depots and trading stations for goods moving along longer-distance trade routes.[101] Olive oil was highly desirable, both for human consumption and as a fuel for lamps and an ingredient in soaps and other personal products.[102] In many of the letters written by Jewish merchants, we see oil purchased, sold, and stored in various locations.[103] In a court decision from Fusṭāṭ, settling a dispute over a business deal in Sicily, for example, we learn of a shipment of sixty jars of oil purchased in Qayrawān with the proceeds of a sale of indigo from Sicily. The dispute arose between Sahlān and Salman, two merchants based in Sicily who claimed shares in the oil and the proceeds from it.[104] An additional letter, this one written in Alexandria in 1056, recounts the voyage taken by a shipment of one hundred containers of oil. The shipment, which also included silk cloth, dresses, and other fabric goods, was loaded onto a ship in al-Mahdiyya.[105] From there, the ship sailed toward Sicily and

100. For oil production and export in one region of northern Africa during the Roman period, see D. J. Mattingly, "Olive Oil Production in Roman Tripolitania," in *Town and Country in Roman Tripolitania*, ed. D. J. Mattingly and D. J. Buck (Oxford, 1985), 27–46; "The Olive Boom: Oil Surpluses, Wealth and Power in Roman Tripolitania," *Libyan Studies* 19 (1988): 21–41; and "Oil for Export? A Comparison of Libyan, Spanish and Tunisian Olive Oil Production in the Roman Empire," *Journal of Roman Archaeology* 1 (1988): 33–56. Mattingly suggests that olive oil, used as food or fuel and for personal hygiene, was in such demand in the ancient Mediterranean that the production requirements may have been in the range of 500 million to one billion liters per year. Mattingly, "The Olive Boom," 22. Some of Tripolitania's oil was exported to Rome as part of the *annona*, but Mattingly believes that olive oil was also a potential commodity for free market trade in the Roman period. Mattingly, "Oil for Export?," 54–56. For more on African oil export during the Roman period, see also Henriette Camps-Fabrer, *L'olivier et l'huile dans l'Afrique romaine* (Algiers: Imprimerie officielle, 1953); and Anthony King and Martin Henig, eds., *The Roman West in the Third Century*, BAR Intl. Series 109 (Oxford: B.A.R., 1981).

101. For olive groves in the Geniza, see Cambridge, T-S 20.71; Ben-Sasson, 459ff.; Simonsohn, doc. 81, line 17: "This year there was a great olive harvest" (al-Mahdiyya, second half of the eleventh century). See also Simonsohn, doc. 145, line 16. For olive oil in later medieval Italy, see Allen J. Grieco, "Olive Tree Cultivation and the Alimentary Use of Olive Oil in Late Medieval Italy (ca. 1300–1500)," in *La production du vin et de l'huile en Méditerranée*, ed. Marie-Claire Amouretti and Jean-Pierre Brun (Paris: École Francaise d'Athenes, 1993), 297–306.

102. *Medit. Soc.*, 1: 120.

103. Oil purchased in Sicily: Cambridge, T-S 20.127; Ben-Sasson, 245ff. (Palermo, second quarter of the eleventh century); Simonsohn, doc. 51.

104. Mosseri Collection A 101 (VII 101); Ben-Sasson, 363ff. (February, 1040); Simonsohn, doc. 60. See also the transcription from the Princeton Geniza Lab: https://geniza.princeton.edu/pgp/index.php?a=document&id=2729.

105. Cambridge, T-S 12.372; Ben-Sasson, 552ff.; Simonsohn, doc. 111, fol. 1a, ll. 7–13. See below for analysis of this same episode in relationship to the silk itself.

was attacked by enemy forces near Agrigento, in the south of the island.[106] The bundle of textiles was stolen by the assailants, but the merchants were allowed to keep the oil, which arrived safely at Māzara. Once there, the jars of oil were loaded onto two different ships for distribution in Egypt.

Wine, another typical medieval commodity, on the other hand, is found very rarely in evidence for trade with Muslim Sicily, presumably because during the centuries of Muslim rule the consumption of alcohol would have been curtailed.[107] Nonetheless, there are references to vineyards on the island, both during the Islamic period and after the Norman takeover. Ibn Ḥawqal, the Muslim traveler who visited Sicily in the tenth century, during Kalbid rule, also claimed that Sicily produced wine ("al-khamr") along with a limited number of other items.[108] In addition, one mid-eleventh-century Geniza letter mentions the purchase in Sicily of grapes for making wine, but it is unclear whether this letter dates from before or after the Norman conquest; in either case, the vineyards must have been tended during the Islamic period, given that it takes years for grapevines to mature.[109] The Arabic geographer Ibn Jubayr, who visited twelfth-century Norman Sicily, also recounted seeing vineyards among the various types of orchards and gardens in Sicily.[110] To be sure, many of these grapes may have served for juice or raisins, both of which were also traded in the Mediterranean economy.

Other food items were transported to or from the island as well, some of which were produced on the island. For example, cheese appears to be one important foodstuff from Sicily and at some point became associated with the island, indicating that some of Sicily's mountainous regions were being used for grazing.[111] A

---

106. The soldiers are described as being loyal to Ibn al-Thumna, the Muslim *emīr* who joined forces with the Norman invaders and aided their conquest of the island in the 1060s.

107. For the comparable situation in medieval Islamic Spain, a location that, despite a similar prohibition, appears to have been known for its wine production even before the thirteenth century, see Constable, *Trade and Traders*, 184–185, 230–231. For wine in ancient Italy, see Nicholas Purcell, "Wine and Wealth in Ancient Italy," *Journal of Roman Studies* 75 (1985): 1–19.

108. Ibn Ḥawqal, *Kitāb ṣūrat al-arḍ*, 131.

109. Cambridge, T-S 13J13.27; Ben-Sasson, 24ff.; Simonsohn, doc. 131, right margin, ll. 1–7.

110. Ibn Jubayr wrote that in Cefalù (Shafludī) there were abundant vines and other trees ("ʿashjar al-aʿnāb wa ghayrhā"). *Riḥlat Ibn Jubayr*, 301.

111. Goitein has noted that cheese, being one of the staple foods of poor Mediterranean peoples, formed a significant part of the trans-Mediterranean commerce in foodstuffs. Cheese was an export commodity from thirteenth-century Christian Europe, as well as from Sicily, Crete, and particular regions of Egypt, and may have been exported from pre-Norman Sicily as well. *Medit. Soc.*, 1: 46, 124. For Sicilian cheese as an ingredient in a recipe in Arabic cookbooks, see Maxime Rodinson, A. J. Arberry, and Charles Perry, *Medieval Arab Cookery* (Devon: Prospect Books, 2001), 449–450; and Charles Perry, "Sicilian Cheese in Medieval Arab Recipes," *Gastronomica* 1 (2001): 76–77. The Geniza records also include two thirteenth-century kosher certificates for Sicilian cheese imported to Egypt. See Cambridge, T-S 12.620; Simonsohn, doc. 218; and Cambridge T-S 13J4.8; Simonsohn, doc. 220.

letter from the Geniza dated to October 1030 mentions that among other items arriving in Alexandria from Sicily—such as flax, wheat, oil, and pepper—thirty containers of cheese had been shipped there from Palermo on a boat that took twenty-nine days to make the trip.[112] We also see sacks of rice and some pumpkin seeds in a bundle of goods that washed up on the shore in Māzara after having been shipped from Palermo. These goods were intended for North Africa and shipped from Sicily but may have been grown elsewhere, using Sicily as a stopover point.[113] Rice is also found in a bale together with twelve bottles of fruit juice that a Jewish merchant in Māzara wrote about in the mid-eleventh century, and barley appears in another letter together with figs, pepper, and wheat.[114] Honey, sugar, fruit juices, and fruit—particularly dried fruits such as figs, raisins, and prunes—as well as nuts, including pistachios, hazelnuts, and almonds, were all important food items traded in the region.[115] Even if they were not harvested on the island, fruits and nuts certainly were sold in the island's markets, according to the list of prices given by Jacob b. Ismaʿīl al-Andalusī, a Sicily-based Jewish merchant. His list of prices "in town" (presumably Palermo) included spices (of which he claimed there was a shortage), flax, indigo and other products for the textile industry, perfumes, metals, shelled almonds, and prunes.[116] Nuts also

112. Cambridge, T-S13J17.11; Ben-Sasson, 226ff.; Simonsohn, doc. 53.

113. Cambridge, T-S 20.122, fol. 1a, l. 34; Ben-Sasson, 340ff.; Simonsohn, doc. 103. Rice was introduced early into the medieval Islamic world from the East and was diffused by Muslims to Egypt, the Maghrib, and Spain in the West, according to Andrew Watson. See his *Agricultural Innovation*, 15–19. See *Medit. Soc.*, 1: 119 for other references to rice in the Geniza. According to al-Idrīsī, rice, along with wheat and barley, was grown in North Africa. Al-Idrīsī, *Description de l'Afrique et de l'Éspagne*, ed. Reinhart Pieter Anne Dozy and Michael Jan de Goeje (Leiden: E. J. Brill, 1968), 61–62 (Arabic), 71–72 (French trans.).

114. For the rice, see Cambridge, T-S 12.366; Ben-Sasson, 520ff.; Simonsohn, doc. 137, fol. 1b, l. 3. For the barley, see Cambridge, T-S NSJ566; Simonsohn, doc. 61, fol. 1a, ll. 13–18. See also *Medit. Soc.*, 1: 118–119.

115. For honey, see *Medit. Soc.*, 1: 125. On honey's use as an aphrodisiac and medicinal, see Efraim Lev, "Drugs Held and Sold by Pharmacists of the Jewish Community of Medieval (11–14th Centuries) Cairo according to Lists of *Materia Medica* Found at the Taylor–Schechter Genizah Collection, Cambridge," *Journal of Ethnopharmacology* 110 (2007): 279. Fruit juices are found, in particular, in the letter mentioned above in which a combined bale of rice and fruit juice were found in Māzara. Cambridge, T-S 12.366, fol. 1b, l. 3. Citrus fruits were one of the most common characteristics of Islamic gardens, and thus it is assumed that the Muslims of Sicily introduced citrus to the island. For the very slim evidence for this, see Watson, *Agricultural Innovation*, 42–50, esp. 46 and 168, n. 21. Likewise, sugar cultivation was brought to Sicily by the Muslims, and sugarcane was apparently grown around Palermo from at least the tenth century. Watson, *Agricultural Innovation*, 28–29 and 161, n. 3. Mention of a cargo of sugar, along with cinnamon and ammoniac, in Palermo is found in a mid-eleventh-century letter from al-Mahdiyya. Cambridge, T-S 12.794; Ben-Sasson, 316ff.; Simonsohn, doc. 119, fol. 1b, l. 17.

116. Mid-twelfth century: Cambridge, T-S 20.76; Ben-Sasson, 259ff.; Simonsohn, doc. 83. For the almonds, which were specified as a gift for the letter's recipient rather than a commercial product, see Simonsohn, doc. 83, fol. 1b, ll. 2–3. Later, in the late eleventh century, Ibn Jubayr reported seeing orchards of apples ("al-tuffāḥ"), chestnuts ("al-shah ballūṭ"), hazelnuts ("al-bunduq"), pears ("al-ijjāṣ"),

appear in a list of prices from Māzara along with the regular spices, flax, indigo, etc.[117] Another merchant specified that he traveled to Māzara in order to buy almonds there.[118]

Spices—the most expensive and important commodity for long-distance trade in the Middle Ages—were also commonly traded in Sicilian markets during the centuries of Islamic dominion.[119] Pepper may have been the most commonly imported spice in the Middle Ages, and the most lucrative: it certainly appears in Geniza mercantile letters more often than any other spice. For example, a Sicilian merchant wrote in one letter that he had sold some pepper and bought almonds and silk with the proceeds, which he then loaded on a ship for export.[120] Another merchant in the mid-eleventh century claimed in a letter to have shipped pepper from al-Mahdiyya to Palermo on behalf of the letter's recipient.[121] Many other spices besides pepper also appear in lists of items shipped to Sicily for sale there. For instance, one merchant in Qayrawān informed his letter's recipient both that spices were in demand in North Africa and that pepper specifically was highly sought after in Sicily.[122] His letter also includes prices for cinnamon, asafoetida, senna, cardamom, cloves, and other spices and sums up with the following request: "For my dirhams, bring me only spices."[123] Another letter from mid-eleventh-century Palermo mentions that spices were selling well on the island at the time: "If you plan to travel, you had better come to Palermo, because eastern spices sell well over here."[124] A similar reference to the market for spices in general is found in a letter from al-Mahdiyya to Fusṭāṭ in which the author provided prices for both al-Mahdiyya and Sicily, stating that "all spices were in great demand because there was a shortage."[125]

---

and other fruits in the mountainous areas near Messina, although he did not mention whether these items were harvested for export or only for local consumption, and we cannot know if these orchards predated the Norman occupation or were planted by the Normans. *Riḥlat Ibn Jubayr*, 297.

117. Cambridge, T-S 12.366, upper margin; Ben-Sasson, 520ff., Simonsohn, doc. 137, upper margin.

118. Philadelphia, Dropsie College 389; Ben-Sasson, 65ff.; Simonsohn, doc. 151, fol. 1b, l. 46.

119. The category of "spices" is broad and includes items used in food preparation, as medicinals or perfumes, and in the dyeing or preparation of textiles. For the place of spices, as a general category, in both medieval trade and culture, see Michel Balard, "Les épices au Moyen Âge," *Temas medievales* 5 (1995): 91–100; and Paul Freedman, *Out of the East: Spices and the Medieval Imagination* (New Haven, CT: Yale University Press, 2008). For medicinal uses of spices according to Geniza records, see Lev, "Drugs," 275–293. See *Medit. Soc.*, 1: 220–222 for the price of pepper in the letters of the Geniza.

120. Cambridge, T-S Misc. 28.37d; Ben-Sasson, 288ff.; Simonsohn, doc. 78, fol. 1a, ll. 7–9.

121. Cambridge, T-S; Ben-Sasson, 316ff.; Simonsohn, doc. 119, fol. 1a, ll. 11–15.

122. Cambridge, T-S 12.251; Ben-Sasson, 238ff.; Simonsohn, doc. 86, fol. 1a, ll. 3–4.

123. Cambridge, T-S 12.251; Ben-Sasson, 238ff.; Simonsohn, doc. 86, fol. 1a, l. 20.

124. Cambridge, T-S 13J26.10; Simonsohn, doc. 138, ll. 24–25. Translation is Simonsohn's. See also the transcription by the Princeton Geniza Lab, https://geniza.princeton.edu/pgp/index.php?a=document&id=3379

125. Cambridge, T-S 16.163; Ben-Sasson, 393ff.; Simonsohn, doc. 150, right margin, ll. 13–14.

Textiles and raw materials for textile production also appear regularly in Geniza letters about trade with Sicily. Indeed, the island became famous for its production of silk cloth in particular, although it also produced some wool and was known later, in the twelfth century, for its export of cotton.[126] At the same time, silk and other textiles were not unique to Sicily: a wide variety of flax, cloth, and silk from different regions appear in the source record, where they were given different names based on origin and quality of material. Within this range of high- and low-quality silks, cloths embroidered, dyed, cut to length, or sewn into veils, coats, and dresses, however, several Sicilian products appear to have been especially important. Of all the raw materials shipped to and from the island, flax and indigo (used in dying cloth) are most commonly found in merchant letters and lists. Like many other products in this cross-Mediterranean trade, however, the majority of raw materials for the textile industry (with the exception of raw silk) did not originate in Sicily. Rather, they were shipped to Sicily for production or for sale on the island and reexport to other parts of the Mediterranean commercial world. Among the finished goods, silk cloth and garments appear most frequently to have been exported from Sicily for sale in other markets.

Of the various materials related to textile production, our sources indicate that flax was the item most commonly shipped to Sicily. Flax has a long history in the Mediterranean economy and was an important commodity in both local and interregional networks of trade.[127] Egypt was the primary exporter of flax, in all of its varieties, although not the only one.[128] For example, one writer, a merchant based in Ifrīqiya, specified which types of flax he wanted

126. Maurice Lombard covers the Mediterranean textile trade in his *Les textiles dans le monde musulman du VIIe au XIIe siècle*, vol. 3 of *Études d'économie médiévale* (Paris: Éditions de l'EHESS, 2002). Lombard also reports the existence of a Sicilian wool industry, of which little mention is made in the Geniza records (54ff). Ibn Ḥawqal also reported that tenth-century Sicily produced wool, but did not specify whether it was for local use only or also for commercial export. Ibn Ḥawqal, *Kitāb ṣūrat al-arḍ*, 131. For the cotton trade in later medieval Sicily, see Abulafia, *The Two Italies*, 38, 48. For Goitein's assessment of the "international" flavor of the cloth and textile trade, see *Medit. Soc.*, 1: 49–51.

127. Moshe Gil has provided a brief history of flax cultivation in the Mediterranean in his "The Flax Trade in the Mediterranean in the Eleventh Century A.D. as Seen in Merchants' Letters from the Cairo Geniza," *Journal of Near Eastern Studies* 63, no. 2 (2004): 81–96. Gil concludes that the eleventh-century Mediterranean trade in flax was entirely carried out by Jewish Maghribī merchants (93).

128. There is also a Geniza reference to sales of flax from Europe. See Cambridge, T-S 20.127; Ben-Sasson, 245ff.; and Simonsohn, doc. 51, fol. 1b, ll. 3–4, for the detail that customers were at that time seeking only Egyptian flax, in the absence of Neapolitan flax. On both Egyptian and North African flax production, see Lombard, *Les textiles*, 47–51. For Egyptian flax sales, see Oxford, Bodl., MS. Heb. d. 65.17; Ben-Sasson, 219ff.; Simonsohn, doc. 34; Cambridge, T-S 12.124; Simonsohn, doc. 45; Cambridge, T-S 13J29.9; Ben-Sasson, 230ff.; Simonsohn, doc. 46; Mosseri Coll. VIII, 476.1; Ben-Sasson, 574; Simonsohn, doc. 56.

his letter's recipient to purchase in Egypt for him and where they should be obtained. He later listed market prices in Ifrīqiya for the different types of flax from various regions in Egypt.[129] Flax bound for Sicily is also found in a 1027 letter from Fusṭāṭ, in which a merchant apologized for having put the merchandise on a boat to Qayrawān but then diverting the shipments to Sicily instead. This merchandise consisted of twenty bales of flax, a bale of high-quality silk, and four packages of pepper. The majority of the flax was intended for Sicily, according to the author, while other merchandise needed to go to North Africa, with the exact destination depending on market conditions. Indeed, the high demand for flax in Sicily was shown in a letter from around 1050 in which a merchant in Alexandria counseled his son in Būṣīr, one of the primary flax-growing regions of Egypt, to purchase flax carefully, since it was the only product desired on the island's markets at that time.[130] A merchant in Māzara in ca. 1060 also recounted the demand for flax in Sicily's markets, asking that the letter's recipient send some flax and specifying a certain type because it was "in fashion here at present."[131] In another letter, the merchant Salāma b. Yūsuf al-Ghazzāl mentioned that he had attempted to sell flax in North Africa but that the market there had not proven profitable.[132] Therefore, he packed up his wares and sailed for Sicily, where he was able to sell the flax and make a profit. This merchant's experience demonstrates the variability in markets in the Mediterranean commercial world and the fact that good prices in one town did not necessarily mean favorable prices everywhere.

If flax was the most common product shipped to Sicily according to the Geniza letters, silk was the primary textile product exported from Sicily.[133]

---

129. For more information about flax production in Egypt, including estimates of annual export volume, see Abraham Udovitch, "International Trade and the Medieval Egyptian Countryside," in *Agriculture in Egypt: From Pharaonic to Modern Times*, ed. Alan K. Bowman and Eugene Rogan, vol. 96, *Proceedings of the British Academy* (Oxford: Published for the British Academy by Oxford University Press, 1999), 267–285. For a list of the most common varieties of flax, see Gil, "Flax Trade in the Mediterranean," 84.

130. Cambridge, T-S 10J20.12; Simonsohn, doc. 101, fol. 1a, ll. 12–13.

131. Cambridge, T-S 12.366; Ben-Sasson, 520ff.; Simonsohn, doc. 137, fol. 1a, ll. 13–14. Flax was not the only commodity for sale listed in this letter in Sicily. The merchant also provided current prices for cinnamon, indigo, nuts, brazilwood, sugar, mastic, incense, food products, soap, and various spices. On mastic, see Paul Freedman, "Mastic: A Mediterranean Luxury Product," *Mediterranean Historical Review* 26 (2011): 99–113.

132. Cambridge, T-S Ar. 5.1; Ben-Sasson, 210ff.; Simonsohn, doc. 48.

133. Moshe Gil, "References to Silk in Geniza Documents of the Eleventh Century A.D.," *Journal of Near Eastern Studies* 61, no. 1 (2002): 31–38. For the Sicilian silk industry, see Andre Guillou, "La soie Sicilienne au Xe–XIe s.," in *Byzantino-Sicula II* (Palermo: Istituto Siciliano di Studi Bizantini e Neoellenici, 1975), 285–288; David Jacoby, "Seide und seidene Textilien im arabischen und normannischen Sizilien: der wirtschaftliche Kontext," in *Nobiles Officinae: Die königlichen Hofwerkstätten zu Palermo zur Zeit der Normannen und Staufer im 12. und 13: Jahrhundert*, ed. Wilfried Seipel (Milano: Skira, 2004), 61–73; and Lombard, *Les textiles*, 100–104. Goitein asserts that Sicilian Jews were foremost in the is-

Sicilian silk appears frequently in records of trade deals in the central Mediterranean, and Sicily's silk industry, as evidenced by the Geniza letters, was present on the island at least from the Islamic period, if not from the Byzantine era of rule, and remained famous into the Norman period. Tracing the path of one bundle of silk found in a mid-eleventh-century Geniza letter written by a merchant in North Africa can help us to understand some of the ways in which Sicily was connected to other regions in the medieval Mediterranean silk trade.[134] These fifty-four measures of silk originated in Val Demone, the region of eastern Sicily encompassing Messina and its environs (see map 1). From there, the silk and other goods were intended to arrive in Palermo, where one Sulayman b. Ya'qub was to deliver the package to a man named Sulayman b. Saul al-Andalusī al-Wadayshī. Al-Wadayshī was then supposed to take the silk along with a consignment of quarter dinars to Māzara and deliver them to another partner, Mūsā, who had already departed from Palermo and was headed east. When al-Wadayshī did not find Mūsā in Māzara (a port often used as a stopover point for ships sailing from Palermo to Egypt), he sent the money and the silk with another merchant on his way to Egypt. When the silk arrived in Alexandria, it was discovered that Mūsā's boat had sunk and that he had drowned. The man in possession of the cloth attempted to sell it in Alexandria but, finding no buyer there, took it to Fusṭāṭ, where he successfully

land's many textile-related industries and that Mediterranean Jews generally were prominent in silk production, either because it had been an ancient specialty in Palestine, or because the Jewish merchants had the opportunity to travel to China and thus carry back knowledge of silk production. See *Medit. Soc.*, 1: 100, 104. See for example Cambridge, T-S NSJ274v and T-S 6J5.6v; Simonsohn, doc. 66, ll. 23–26. For more details on the range of sale prices for silk in Geniza letters, see *Medit. Soc.*, 1: 222–224. Sicily became famous for certain types of silk produced there: *lāsīn* was a silk fabric of lower quality produced primarily in Sicily and sometimes referred to in modern scholarship as "Sicilian silk." For the forced relocation of Byzantine silk workers by Norman kings and the introduction of silk to the island in the ninth century, see David Jacoby, "Silk Economics and Cross-Cultural Artistic Interaction: Byzantium, the Muslim World, and the Christian West," *Dumbarton Oaks Papers* 58 (2004): 197–240, esp. 200–201, 226–227. For the Mediterranean silk industry in general and the local industries of Spain, Sicily, and Ifrīqiya, see *Medit. Soc.*, 1: 101–102; Lombard, *Les textiles*, 79–104; and Isabelle Dolezalek, "Textile Connections? Two Ifrīqiyan Church Treasuries in Norman Sicily and the Problem of Continuity across Political Change," *al-Masāq* 25: 1 (2013): 92–112. For prices of silk as reflected in the Geniza record, see *Medit. Soc.*, 1: 222ff. and 454, n. 53. For the production and distribution of silk in al-Andalus, see Lombard, *Les textiles*, 95–100; Constable, *Trade and Traders*, 173–181; and Florence May, *Silk Textiles of Spain: Eighth to Fifteenth Century* (New York: Hispanic notes & monographes, 1957). Goitein's assessment is that North Africa, although mentioned often in regard to shipments of silk cloth and clothing, was a redistribution point rather than a source of locally produced silk goods. On the other hand, Lombard attributes to Ifrīqiya a smaller-scale silk production industry of its own. On North Africa's silk industry, see Lombard, *Les textiles*, 94–95; *Medit. Soc.*, 1: 84. Al-Idrīsī describes plantations of date palms, figs, olives, and mulberry trees in Libya, the latter of which suggests the existence of a silk industry in the region. See al-Idrīsī, *Description de l'Afrique et de l'Éspagne*, 122 (Arabic), 143–144 (French).

134. Cambridge, T-S 20.4; Ben-Sasson, 453ff.; Simonsohn, doc. 67.

sold it along with some of his own silk. This one bundle of silk fabric thus traveled first from the east to the west of Sicily and then to the southwestern part of the island. From there it traveled first to Alexandria and then to Fusṭāṭ, where it was sold and thus leaves our sight. This is not the only possible path for Sicilian silk, but this itinerary was typical for many similar packages of silk, whether raw or in the form of cloth or finished clothing, that were exported from the island.

Aside from raw silk, finished clothing is one of the most common items described in the merchant letters as having been purchased on the island for export to Egypt and North Africa. Much like for finished silk cloth, demand was high in the Mediterranean for Sicilian-made items.[135] For example, an account list for items purchased in mid-eleventh-century Sicily includes turbans, blue sashes, a silk sash, a garment, a load of silk cloth, and several silk kerchiefs.[136] Another letter, this one sent from Fusṭāṭ to Alexandria in the middle of the eleventh century, mentions ships arriving from Sicily on which cloth and finished clothing were expected to arrive.[137] The author asked his partner to purchase both cloth and coats and to bring them to him for his own use. Other Sicilian fabrics and clothes were shipped to Egypt for sale there. One merchant located in Sicily wrote to his partner in Egypt listing the textiles he had recently shipped to him from the island.[138] These included lengths of fabric, a cotton kerchief, a blue veil, five dresses, two mantles, and several other garments. Sicilian garments were also redistributed from Egypt to other places, such as Palestine, but through the mediation of markets in Africa.[139] That is, Sicily's commercial relationships may have linked it more broadly with

---

135. For textiles arriving in Egypt from Europe in the middle of the eleventh century, see Cambridge, T-S 8J20.2; Ben-Sasson, 535ff.; Simonsohn, doc. 113, fol. 1b, l. 5, in which the author notes that a boat arrived from Amalfi loaded with honey and textiles. For one account of Spanish silks and garments for sale in Egypt ca. 1060, see Cambridge, T-S 24.40; Simonsohn, doc. 140.

136. Cambridge, T-S Ar. 54.88; Ben-Sasson, 337ff.; Simonsohn, doc. 73.

137. Cambridge, T-S 13J18.8; Ben-Sasson, 514ff.; Simonsohn, doc. 79, fol. 1a, ll. 29–30.

138. Cambridge, T-S 10J5.24; Simonsohn, doc. 146. All of the textiles listed by the author as having been recently shipped to Egypt from Sicily were purchased, he says, with the proceeds of the sale of pearls on the island.

139. See the letter from Tyre to Egypt from ca. 1060 in which the author requests that Sicilian cloth be sent along from Egypt to him in Palestine. Oxford, Bodl., MS. Heb. c. 28.20; Ben-Sasson, 284ff.; Simonsohn, doc. 142. It is important to point out that none of the Geniza letters appear to have been sent directly between regions in the Far East and territories in the West (e.g., we have no letters sent from Spain to Egypt, even though trade with Spain and in Spanish goods is visible in Egyptian markets), and that individual merchants would have rarely traveled the entirety of a long-distance trade route. Rather, most medieval commercial journeys were regional, and trade goods would be sent on from one region to another. For more details on trade routes in the Geniza, see *Medit. Soc.*, 1: 213–214.

the entire Mediterranean world, but only indirectly. The island's direct commercial links were primarily with Egypt and Ifrīqiya.

In addition to finished silk cloth and clothing, raw materials for the dyeing and production of garments are found in abundance in records concerning Sicily's commercial relationships in the Mediterranean.[140] A number of mercantile letters from the Cairo Geniza refer to the shipment or sale of indigo to Sicily, such as the eleventh-century account ledger from North Africa that mentions the demand for indigo (and henna) to be shipped from Tripoli to Tunis and from there to Palermo.[141] Another letter deals with a load of indigo shipped to Sicily for sale there and damaged en route.[142] The merchant who wrote this letter complained of the difficulties he encountered trying to sell this waterlogged cargo on the island.[143] Other disputed shipments of indigo appear in a 1040 court document from Fusṭāṭ that records a conflict between two merchants, Khalaf b. Mūsā al-Barqi and Salman b. Da'ūd b. Simon.[144] This document again demonstrates the intricate relationships between the commercial centers of North Africa and Sicily, showing bales of indigo shipped from al-Mahdiyya to Sicily and stored in a warehouse on the island before they were removed and sold. The seller then purchased sixty containers of oil with the proceeds, and the dispute between the Sicilian and North African merchants concerned the shares of the oil due to each. Part of the indigo was sold in Palermo, but an unsold portion was taken to Qayrawān and given to another merchant there, and some of the financial profit from the Palermitan sale was taken to a merchant in Sfax. Thus one load of indigo was involved in transactions in three North African cities and one Sicilian city. This, and

140. For a general account of the variety of colors of fabric and clothing, as well as the Geniza evidence for clothing styles and fashions, see *Medit. Soc.*, 1: 106–108. An in-depth study of the trousseau lists found in the Geniza and what they tell us about medieval clothing styles has been done by Yedida K. Stillman, "The Importance of the Cairo Geniza for the History of Medieval Female Attire," *International Journal of Middle East Studies* 7 (1976): 579–589; Stillman, *Arab Dress: A Short History from the Dawn of Islam to Modern Times* (Leiden: E. J. Brill, 2000); R. B. Serjeant, *Islamic Textiles: Material for a History up to the Mongol Conquest* (Beirut: Librairie du Liban, 1972), 191–192.

141. Cambridge, T-S 3.36; Ben-Sasson, 243ff.; Simonsohn, doc. 31, ll. 2–4. For more on the trade in indigo, particularly in the eastern Islamic lands, see W. Heyd, *Histoire du commerce du Levant au moyen-âge* (Leipzig: O. Harrassowitz, 1885–1886; repr., Amsterdam: Adolf M. Hakkert, 1959), 2: 626–629. Page numbers refer to the 1959 edition.

142. Indigo must have been a common product on ships sailing to Sicily, for in many of these Geniza records we find bales of it damaged or stolen along the route. One of the reasons that merchants had so many problems with indigo was the possibility of spoilage, as seen in a merchant's account of his voyages in the Mediterranean during which he was forced to ship his bale of indigo to the west rather than to Palermo because he could not find a ship sailing to the island in time. See Philadelphia, Dropsie College 389; Ben-Sasson, 65ff.; Simonsohn, doc. 151, fol. 1a, ll. 17–18. See also Cambridge, T-S 20.122; Ben-Sasson, 340ff.; Simonsohn, doc. 103, fol. 1a, ll. 19–20.

143. Cambridge, T-S 10J6.1; Simonsohn, doc. 32.

144. Mosseri Coll. A 101 (VII 101); Ben-Sasson, 364ff.; Simonsohn, doc. 60.

other similar routes taken by merchants and materials, demonstrates the close connections Sicily's merchants maintained with the markets of Ifrīqiya and the way that Sicily's markets acted in some ways as extensions of those in Ifrīqiya.

A wide variety of other products also traded in these markets, showing the full integration of Sicily into the Mediterranean-wide economic system. While foodstuffs and textile products formed the bulk of the trade with Sicily, the Geniza records also reveal that the business of the Egyptian, North African, and Sicilian merchants included a significant number of other products, including metals and a variety of raw materials. Occasional references are also found to a Sicilian trade in tar (used in the shipbuilding industry), soap, wax, camphor, and sulphur.[145] Other dyestuffs, medicinals, and products used for tanning leather also traveled to and from Sicily, including lac, brazilwood, vermillion, sumac, and saffron.[146] Tin, copper, lead, and mercury are among the metals found in different Geniza accounts of trade with Sicily, and there is some indication that metals were mined on the island during the medieval period.[147] Pearls also appear in some Geniza letters as commodities sold in Sicily to fund the purchase of silks and clothing for export from the island, and coral

---

145. For camphor in medieval commerce, see Heyd, *Histoire du commerce*, 2: 590–595. For camphor as a medicinal, see Lev, "Drugs," 279. In one letter we see wax that traveled with hides. See Cambridge, T-S 13J16.23; Ben-Sasson, 241ff.; Simonsohn, doc. 35.

146. On sumac, see E. García Sánchez and L. Ramón-Laca Menéndez de Luarca, "Sebestén y Zumaque, Dos Frutos Importados de Oriente Durante la Edad Media," *Annuario de Estudios Medievales* 31 (2001): 867–881. On saffron, see David Abulafia, "Crocuses and Crusaders: San Gimignano, Pisa and the Kingdom of Jerusalem," repr. in David Abulafia, *Italy, Sicily and the Mediterranean, 1100–1400* (London: Variorum, 1987), XIV. For saffron used as a common medicinal, see Lev, "Drugs," 281 and 289. For more on lac, see Heyd, *Histoire du commerce*, 2: 624–626. For accounts that include prices for lac in Sicily, see Cambridge, T-S 12.372; Ben-Sasson, 552ff.; Simonsohn, doc. 111; and New York, Theol. Sem., Adler Coll. NS 18.24; Ben-Sasson, 431ff.; Simonsohn, doc. 97. For brazilwood, see for example the list of prices for Palermo in Cambridge, T-S 12.251; Ben-Sasson, 238ff.; Simonsohn, doc. 86. The author suggests that spices were the item of greatest profit on the island at the time, which was some point in the middle of the eleventh century. Another eleventh-century letter stated that brazilwood was going for high prices in Sicily, but that it was only available from one merchant, which fact drove up the price. Cambridge, T-S 20.76; Ben-Sasson, 259ff.; Simonsohn, doc. 83, fol. 1b, ll. 5–12. Another account of brazilwood fetching high prices is in New York, Theol. Sem., Adler Coll. NS 18.24; Ben-Sasson, 431ff.; Simonsohn, doc. 97, fol. 1b, ll. 14–15.

147. For instance, Ibn Ḥawqal indicated the existence of an iron mine in Sicily, near the towns of Gharbiya and Balhara, belonging to the government, which provided iron for the needs of the navy and its ships. See also Simonsohn, xxx. For mining and metal usage in the early medieval period, see Maurice Lombard, *Les métaux dans l'ancien monde du Ve au XIe siècle*, vol. 2 of *Études d'économie médiévale* (Paris: Mouton, 1974). Mining in Sicily is also mentioned by the twelfth-century geographer al-Idrīsī, who is discussed in chapter 5. See also David Abulafia, "Local Trade Networks in Medieval Sicily: The Evidence of Idrisi," in *Shipping, Trade and Crusade in the Medieval Mediterranean: Studies in Honour of John Pryor*, ed. Ruthy Gertwagen and Elizabeth Jeffreys (Farnham: Ashgate, 2012), 157–166.

and other beads are mentioned as well.[148] Sicily's economic networks at this time thus clearly involved the transportation and sale of a wide variety of products, some made in Sicily and others in Egypt or Ifrīqiya and still others imported into the Mediterranean from farther east by merchants in wider networks of exchange. Sicily, as a key market and depot for goods in the central Mediterranean network, was thus deeply—if indirectly—connected to the broader economy of the Arab Muslim world.

In a number of instances, we find animal hides originating on Sicily and transported to other markets for sale, a fact suggesting that hides may have been a widely known Sicilian product. Ibn Ḥawqal, the tenth-century visitor to Sicily who disparaged the island's agricultural productivity, admitted that the island's animal skins were one of its very few commodities of significance.[149] In an early-eleventh-century Geniza letter, Mūsā b. Isḥāq b. Ḥisda, a Jewish merchant writing from al-Mahdiyya to his partner, Yūsuf b. ʿAwqal, in Egypt, detailed the goods that he had shipped to him from the island before he left there for North Africa.[150] He reported that he purchased 700 hides all at the same price and shipped them from the island on a boat owned by one Ibn Makhluf. The shipment contained three bales of hides in partnership between Yūsuf and a man named Abū Isḥaw, a bale of hides for Faraḥ b. Judah, and a bale of wax that Mūsā owned privately. Of the cargo of hides, Mūsā specified that the one labeled for Faraḥ contained ninety-five Syracusan hides,

148. For the medieval trade in pearls and gemstones, see Heyd, *Histoire du commerce*, 2: 648–658. For both pearls and coral as pharmacological agents, used particularly in the treatment of eye diseases, see Lev, "Drugs," 279. Cambridge, T-S 13J8.5; Ben-Sasson, 482ff.; Simonsohn, doc. 77. For one bundle containing both saffron and pearls, see Cambridge, T-S 20.76; Ben-Sasson, 259ff.; Simonsohn, doc. 83, fol. 1b, ll. 1–2. Pearls for sale in Sicily are also mentioned in a list in a mid-eleventh-century letter from Trapani: New York, Theol. Sem., Adler Coll. NS 18.24; Ben-Sasson, 431ff.; Simonsohn, doc. 97. The prices for pearls were given in a letter from Palermo dated ca. 1065: Oxford, Bodl., MS. Heb. c. 28.61; Ben-Sasson, 275ff.; Simonsohn, doc. 156, fol. 1a, l. 15. One letter contains an account of transactions in Egypt in the mid-eleventh century, which notes that silk was transported there from Sicily after having been purchased with the proceeds of pearl sales. New York, Theol. Sem., Adler Coll. 3014.3; Ben-Sasson, 603ff.; Simonsohn, doc. 128, ll. 16–20. Another letter, from Sicily ca. 1060, lists a variety of textiles dispatched to Egypt that the author asserts were purchased with the profit from the sale of some pearls. Cambridge, T-S 10J5.24; Simonsohn, doc. 146. Sicily may have gained a reputation in the Islamic world as a source of particularly fine coral, since Sicilian coral is mentioned in several later texts. See al-Idrīsī, *Description de l'Afrique et de l'Éspagne*, 116 (Arabic), 135 (French). The pharmacologist and botanist Ibn al-Bayṭār (d. 1248) noted that coral, used for treating medical ailments including eye and heart problems, was found in abundance near Syracuse. ʿAbd Allāh ibn Aḥmad ibn al-Bayṭār, "Traité des Simples," trans. Lucien Leclerc, *Notices et extraits des Manuscrits de la Biblioteque Nationale* 23 (1877); 25 (1881); 26 (1883): vol. 23: 223–225; and Shams al-Dīn al-Dimashqī, *Manuel de la Cosmographie du Moyen Age*, trans. August Ferdinand Michael Mehren (Paris: 1874), 83. See also *Medit. Soc.*, 1: 47.

149. Ibn Ḥawqal, *Kitāb ṣūrat al-arḍ*, 131.

150. Oxford, Bodl., MS. Heb. c. 27.82; Ben-Sasson, 214ff.; Simonsohn, doc. 33.

half of which he had purchased directly from their producers.[151] A number of other references to Syracusan hides also suggest that there was perhaps a central market on the island for the selling of animal skins or that the hides from that region of Sicily had a particularly high reputation.[152]

A final example will serve to illustrate the multidirectional commercial travel that radiated from Egypt to Sicily and elsewhere in the Mediterranean. In this letter, the merchant Ibrahīm b. Faraḥ wrote to his partner explaining what he had done with the goods entrusted to him.[153] Among the shipments he recorded were several bales intended for Sicily, on board three separate ships. The goods loaded onto these Sicily-bound boats consisted of flax and spices (generally), while a more varied list of goods were dispatched to al-Mahdiyya, including pepper, indigo, clothing, and quicksilver. Wide varieties of products thus moved in multiple directions at the same time, traveling between Sicily, Ifrīqiya, and Egypt.

All of these exchanges also involved coinage (either in specie or as credit)—specifically the gold dinars and silver dirhams of the Muslim monetary system, along with their fractions, as minted by various authorities. Coins themselves are also a very conspicuous item of commercial exchange in the letters of the Geniza, and they were often traded like commodities by the same merchants who dealt in other goods.[154] One example, from a note written in mid-eleventh-century al-Mahdiyya, illustrates some of the complex monetary exchanges revealed in Geniza letters.[155] The author reported that he conducted a sale of goods to some Rūmīs (Christians) in dirhams, which he then took to the money changer in order to trade them for dinars, because the exchange rate was rising quickly. He then promised that he would sort through the old dirhams he had, send the good ones on to his partner in Fusṭāṭ, and try to sell the bad ones. He added that he had been collecting these old dirhams for the last year because these silver coins were in demand in North Africa. Later in the letter, the author assured the recipient that one of their partners, named Mūsā, had shipped some dirhams from Palermo to Egypt. Here we see coins themselves serving as a commodity: judged by quality, stored until the ex-

---

151. Simonsohn, doc. 33, l. 4.

152. Cambridge, T-S Ar. 54.88; Ben-Sasson, 337ff.; Simonsohn, doc. 73, fol. 1a, ll. 1–3. Leather also appears as a packing material for bales of goods, along with cloth, as in Cambridge, T-S 20.122; Ben-Sasson, 340ff.; Simonsohn, doc. 103, l. 23.

153. Cambridge, T-S 13J26.8; Ben-Sasson, 592ff.; Simonsohn, doc. 159.

154. Udovitch asserts that this demand for coins among the Geniza merchants was a result of the competition for high-quality merchandise, in particular flax, the demand for which was greater than the supply. Merchants needed to have on hand sufficient reserves of cash in locally accepted issues in order to purchase flax from the growers. See Udovitch, "International Trade," 274–278.

155. Cambridge, T-S 12.794; Ben-Sasson, 316ff.; Simonsohn, doc. 119.

change rate was favorable, and shipped to other regions for sale or use there.[156] This letter also allows us to see Christian merchants who had sailed directly to Ifrīqiya on commercial voyages and who were conducting their trade using Islamic coins, which held far more value in the region than any coins from western Christendom. The gold coins from Muslim Sicily were considered of such superior value that they were imitated by some Christian cities in southern Italy and reproduced widely throughout the Muslim Mediterranean.

Altogether, great quantities of goods and money moved between Sicily and its regional trading partners of Ifrīqiya and Egypt. This rich trade relationship created a pattern of ship traffic that appears to have attracted the attention of pirates who were active in the region. The Strait of Sicily is narrow, separating the island from Ifrīqiya by only about ninety miles, meaning that merchant vessels could be trapped there by privateers more easily than when sailing in open waters. In addition, this appears as one of the most active regions of mercantile shipping in the tenth and eleventh centuries, which fact itself would have drawn pirates into the area. Several North African *fatwās* deal with cases of merchant ships attacked by pirates or enemy navies taking advantage of this lucrative trade route. In one example, a *fatwā* issued by Abū ʿImrān al-Fāsī (d. 1038) at Qayrawān states that a ship loaded with merchandise was seized by pirates ("luṣūṣ") of unknown origin, and the vessel was abandoned after the pirates took all of the goods on board.[157] Then some Rūmīs (Christians), also of unstated origin, came along and seized the ship, a situation that prompted the merchants to seek legal advice concerning whether they still owed the original freight charges.[158] Al-Fāsī answered that, in his judgment, when the Christians arrived after the pirate attack and appropriated the vessel, this caused the freight charges to be annulled. A similar legal response, also from al-Fāsī, concerned a ship that was attacked by Rūmīs while in the port at Tunis.[159] This ship had been loaded and docked but had not yet set sail when the Christians attacked and captured the ship's captain and part of the merchandise. The captain purchased his freedom and demanded that the sailors return a portion of their wages. Not all pirates in the region were Christians,

156. Many of these coins would have circulated in purses rather than as loose coins, which were traded by weight. See for example a mid-eleventh-century letter from al-Mahdiyya that mentions a purse filled with 2,000 Sicilian *zaytūnī* dirhams, worth fifteen dinars according to Egyptian weight: Cambridge, T-S 20.69; Ben-Sasson, 501ff.; Simonsohn, doc. 69, fol. 1b, l. 20.

157. al-Wansharīsī, 8: 302.

158. The generic Arabic term Rūmī may refer to any type of Christian: Byzantine Greeks, Sicilians, Normans, or sailors from the maritime cities of mainland Italy. When "enemies" are mentioned as the attackers, it is not clear where they originated or on whose behalf they attacked the merchant ships.

159. al-Wansharīsī, 8: 297–298.

surely, but these two cases show that some Christian vessels in the region attacked ones on which Muslim merchants transported their goods. Christian merchants and ships were already active in the central Mediterranean—an activity that would continue to increase across the eleventh and twelfth centuries—and sailed directly to Ifrīqiya and Egypt from a variety of places, such as Venice, Pisa, Naples, and Amalfi.

A third *fatwā* from Abū ʿImrān al-Fāsī further demonstrates both that ships were regularly assailed by pirates while pursuing cross-Mediterranean commercial journeys and that the region between Sicily and the coast of Africa may have been a hot spot for such activity.[160] In this case, several boats, one from Alexandria and the rest from al-Mahdiyya, were sailing in convoy. Near the coast of Barqa, they were attacked by enemy ships (not identified), and many of the people aboard were killed and the survivors taken captive, along with their vessels.[161] The attacking ships were intercepted by vessels from Sicily, who saved both the survivors and their fleet. The beleaguered ships were then guided to Sicily, where the passengers disembarked. The ensuing legal questions related to whether the payment of a fee or gift was due to the Sicilian rescuers and whether the salvaged ships became the property of the Sicilians or should revert to their original owners. Al-Fāsī decided in favor of the original owners, although he allowed that a gift could be given to the Sicilians in return for their efforts. This *fatwā* shows pirate ships and merchant vessels—including ones identified as Sicilian—operating simultaneously along the routes between North Africa and Sicily, marking this as a particularly active area for commercial travel.

Other sources show that Sicilians themselves were sometimes the ones stealing goods from others' ships. One Geniza letter shows North African silk that was in transit from North Africa to Egypt but was intercepted and stolen by Sicilian soldiers off the island's southern coast.[162] This letter, written from Alexandria to Fusṭāṭ in 1056 and discussed above in relation to its shipment of oil, relays the information that a merchant named Abraham had departed from al-Mahdiyya with a package containing bundles of silk, a finished cloak, silk dresses, and flax.[163] The ship he was on sailed eastward and was attacked near Agrigento by the forces of Ibn al-Thumna, who took the bundles of cloth and

160. Ibid., 302–304.

161. Barqa is identified as the modern city of al-Marj, on the Libyan coast. It is not specified whether the ships were sailing east or west on this trip and what their final destination was.

162. Cambridge, T-S 12.372; Ben-Sasson, 552ff.; Simonsohn, doc. 111, fol. 1a, ll. 6–13.

163. It is not specified in the letter whether this silk was produced in North Africa or simply purchased there, having been first imported from elsewhere.

even the hat off Abraham's head.[164] They left him with the one hundred containers of oil he was also transporting, and he managed to find a ship from Māzara on which he could send the oil to Egypt. This theft—specifically of silk, with the oil left ignored—suggests that silk and cloth were considered very valuable and profitable; they also were probably much easier to carry off than jugs of oil.

These and other accounts of both trade and piracy in the waters near Sicily show that the region was well known as a location for regular commerce, since pirates go where the goods are. Many types of goods traveled across this stretch of water between Sicily and Ifrīqiya and between Sicily and Egypt, connecting these three places in a web of commercial travel that would have been attractive to privateering vessels or enemy warships, which could make a profit off the economic activities of merchants in the region. Sicily was a very active market for regional commerce in the western Islamicate world—in particular in the specific regional markets of the central Mediterranean trade and travel routes between Sicily and the northern coast of Africa. The island may have lain at the edge of the dār al-Islām, but it was obviously central to the economies of other places within the Muslim Mediterranean and remained in close commercial contact with the ports of northern Africa.

Sicily's Connections with the Wider Mediterranean Region

The multitude of economic records from Sicily's Muslim centuries thus shows the island closely connected to the economies of Ifrīqiya and Egypt. However, compared with the frequency with which the trade triangle between Sicily, North Africa, and Egypt is depicted in the Geniza letters and *fatwās*, only limited information is available in the extant sources to illuminate the relationship of Islamic Sicily with the westernmost Islamic regions of al-Andalus and the Maghrib, with the eastern Mediterranean (outside of Egypt), or with Latin Europe.[165] Some level of communication between Islamic Sicily and al-Andalus clearly took place, although the scarce evidence for these links makes it

164. Ibn al-Thumna was the Muslim Sicilian leader (*qa'id*) who joined forces with the Normans during their conquest of the island in the 1060s, giving them inside information and aiding in their takeover of Muslim territories. See chapter 4.

165. Patricia Skinner asks a similar question about why more southern Italian merchants from Amalfi, who were very active in the eastern Mediterranean, do not show up in the sources from al-Andalus in her "Amalfitans in the Caliphate of Cordoba—Or Not?" *al-Masāq* 24:2 (2012): 125–138. Lev Kapitaikin has sought to link Sicily more closely with al-Andalus in terms of artistic and architectural traditions, although the preponderance of his evidence dates from the later Christian Norman period.

impossible to form a complete picture of the purposes and value of their relationship. Some data suggest that Muslim warriors from al-Andalus participated in the initial Aghlabid conquest of the island, and these efforts may have established connections that do not appear in the later sources. However, I have found no confirmation that Andalusī Muslims continued to arrive in Sicily to wage *jihād* into Christian southern Italy during the ninth or tenth centuries or that they maintained notable diplomatic or political relations with the island.

Some—though comparatively very few—pieces of evidence do suggest commercial links between Sicily and al-Andalus during these centuries.[166] One ninth-century *fatwā* issued in Ifrīqiya by Yahya bin ʿUmar (b. al-Andalus 828, d. Ifrīqiya 901) demonstrates that commercial ties may have existed between the island and Spain, as this legal opinion uses the route from Sicily to al-Andalus as one example of cross-Mediterranean trade.[167] The question to the jurist contains no specific details of an actual suit, but it involves issues similar to those found in other, more detailed cases: a group of partners who had hired a ship that was forced by the wind to stop short of the intended destination asked what fees were then due for the trip and whether they should have been adjusted. The jurist's response presented several possible examples of commercial sea journeys, each with a different resolution to the dispute. The first instance cited is an open-sea journey, exemplified by the trip from Ifrīqiya to Sicily or from al-Andalus to Sicily, and the other example is a coastal voyage, like that from Egypt to Ifrīqiya. The use of a direct Spain–Sicily voyage as a juristic example demonstrates that the trip was theoretically possible, and perhaps more common than we can see, in the ninth century.[168]

The jurist Ibn Siblūn was responsible for the decision in a case that provides an actual piece of evidence for commercial travel from Sicily to al-Andalus.[169] The *fatwā* in question cites a ship that had been contracted to transport goods from Sicily to al-Andalus during the safe season for sailing the Mediterranean, but the ship only made it to the North African coast before opposing winds halted the journey. The navigable season then ended, and a disagreement resulted about the status of the contract, which had not been fulfilled. The ship's

---

See Lev Kapitaikin, "'The Daughter of al-Andalus': Interrelations between Norman Sicily and the Muslim West," *al-Masāq* 25, no. 1 (2013): 113–134.

166. A number of seaborne commercial journeys from al-Andalus that stopped in Sicily are cited in Constable, *Trade and Traders*, esp. 34–35, 240–245.

167. al-Wansharīsī, 8: 310–311.

168. It is also possible that this *fatwā* represents a scholastic question rather than an actual case that appeared before the judge. In either event, commercial travel between Sicily and al-Andalus was at least deemed possible by this jurist, even if not common.

169. al-Wansharīsī, 8: 299–300.

owner wished to be absolved of his contractual obligation to complete the trip to al-Andalus (presumably during the next sailing season), and Ibn Siblūn agreed. This legal case demonstrates that commercial voyages between Sicily and Spain did occur, although they were apparently less common than voyages between Sicily and Ifrīqiya, which show up much more often throughout the source record. Without more evidence, we cannot accurately measure the proportion of trade carried out between Sicily and al-Andalus to that conducted between Sicily and Ifrīqiya or Egypt, since the strong imbalance in the source record may reflect reality, or it may only reflect source survival. At the very least, we can see that merchants and merchandise did sometimes sail between these two lands of the western dār al-Islām. It is perhaps simply an unfortunate result of the accidents of record survival that we do not see more instances of direct trade between Muslim Sicily and al-Andalus; these few anecdotes may represent a phenomenon more common than can be detected in the extant sources.

Western Muslim pilgrims also may have used the route through Sicily on their voyages to the holy sites of the eastern Islamic Mediterranean; more often, however, they apparently took the overland route through northern Africa. We see Maghribī and Andalusī pilgrims who sometimes passed through Sicily on the journey to Mecca, even though this was considered by many to be a dangerous route for the *hajj*.[170] For example, one *fatwā* in al-Wansharīsī's collection provides evidence that some Spanish Muslims stopped in Sicily en route to Mecca but that this route was not the preferred one. According to the text of an opinion issued by Saḥnūn (d. 854)—a jurist in Qayrawān and a leading figure of the Mālikī legal tradition—an Iberian Muslim pilgrim died on the return from Mecca.[171] Upon his death, the *hajjī*'s belongings were entrusted to a fellow Andalusī in the group, who was tasked with distributing them to the man's heirs back in al-Andalus. This second traveler took a route through Sicily, and while there, he lost the goods that he was transporting to the man's heirs, although we are not told if this loss was the result of theft or neglect. After a consultation with the experts ("ahl al-maʿrifa"), it was decided that this man himself was liable for the cost of the deceased *hajjī*'s goods because he chose the most dangerous route for his journey. It is not stated why Sicily

170. Sea travel in general was prohibited by some legal experts, despite widespread evidence that medieval Muslims sailed around the Mediterranean for religious, commercial, and personal reasons. Hassan Khalilieh has examined a series of opinions issued on the subject of the sea route for the *hajj* in which sea travel was condemned as dangerous and its obligation postponed until the journey could again be considered safe. Khalilieh, "The Legal Opinion of Maliki Jurists regarding Andalusian Muslim Pilgrims Travelling by Sea during the Eleventh and Twelfth Centuries CE," *Mediterranean Historical Review* 14, no. 1 (1999): 59–69.

171. al-Wansharīsī, 9:. 85.

was perceived to be a dangerous place for the traveler (as it in fact turned out to be), only that the perils of stopping there were supposed to have been widely known. Sicily may have been a necessary and convenient route for Muslim pilgrims traveling on Christian ships, but at least some Islamic legal experts considered it an unsafe way to get to the Holy Land and preferred the overland route via northern Africa.[172]

At the same time, little evidence exists for political or diplomatic relationships between Muslim Sicily and other Islamic regions of the western Mediterranean, perhaps contrary to expectations. This, too, may well be an accident of the survival of textual sources, or it may indicate that the political relationships between Sicily and other places were primarily mediated through the island's capital at, initially, Qayrawān and, later, Cairo. One brief reference to a Sicilian messenger at the tenth-century Spanish court of ʿAbd al-Raḥmān III (*emīr*, 912–929, caliph, 929–961) indicates that these two regions may have sent envoys back and forth with news and requests for aid that do not show up more widely in the sources.[173] Ibn Ḥayyān tell us that a message was sent from Palermo to the *emīr*'s court in 915 seeking aid for a Sicilian rebellion against the Fatimid caliph.[174] In this anecdote, Sicily was seeking to act independently from the new political power rising in North Africa, the Fatimids. It is unclear whether Andalusī reinforcements were in fact sent to help the revolt. The Fatimid forces quashed the insurrection after a few years of battle, during which the rebels used the Sicilian naval fleet to attack Fatimid-held ports in North Africa.[175] This diplomatic appeal to an Andalusī ruler may have been one desperate measure to find an ally against the much stronger power of the Fatimids, or it may reflect a longer tradition of political connections between Sicily and al-Andalus that is otherwise invisible to us. The fact that this was a rebellion, and thus an exceptional situation, as well as the fact that Ibn Ḥayyān saw fit to note the ambassador's arrival in his chronicle, may indicate that direct diplomatic relationships between Sicily and al-Andalus were not common—and were thus remarkable enough to document. On the other hand, it is possible that the

172. Certainly some later Iberian *hajjīs* and travelers passed through Sicily during its period of Latin Christian rule; Benjamin of Tudela and Ibn Jubayr, both of whom visited Sicily in the twelfth century, are prominent examples, although their trips do not necessarily mean that similar journeys were common in the tenth or eleventh centuries. Lev Kapitaikin has found a few other examples of Muslim pilgrims from al-Andalus passing through Sicily, although most of these anecdotes also date from the Norman period rather than before it; see Kapitaikin, "'The Daughter of al-Andalus,'" esp. 119.

173. See Abū Marwān Ḥayyān ibn Ḥayyān, *al-Muqtabas*, vol. 5, ed. P. Chalmeta and F. Corriente (Madrid: Instituto Hispano-Arabe de Cultura, 1979), 101.

174. For more on this revolt against the Fatimids, see Chiarelli, *A History of Muslim Sicily*, 76–81.

175. *Cronica di Cambridge*, *BAS* Arabic, 228; Ibn al-Athīr, *al-Kāmil fī al-tārīkh*, *BAS* Arabic, rev. ed., 1: 332;. Ibn ʿIdhārī, *Kitāb al-bayān al-mughrib*, *BAS*, rev. ed., Arabic, 471.

dispatch of this messenger reflected a more entrenched tradition of communications between Muslim Sicily and Spain but one that is difficult to recreate from existing sources. Taken together, however, these small pieces of evidence for communications and exchange—religious, economic, or political—between Sicily and al-Andalus are far less apparent in the sources than the well-established relationships between Sicily and Ifrīqiya and Egypt. This imbalance either represents a weaker network of direct communications between Sicily and the western Mediterranean or results from the mediation of their interaction through the more powerful political and commercial centers of the African coast.

Likewise scarce is the evidence for direct connections between Muslim Sicily and the eastern Mediterranean. A few Geniza letters refer to relationships between the Sicilian Jewish community and their coreligionists in Jerusalem or Baghdad; it is not clear whether these letters traveled on ships sailing from Sicily to the eastern Mediterranean or via the overland route through northern Africa—we see little evidence of direct shipping from Muslim Sicily to the Levant. Several Geniza letters mentioned charitable collections taken in Sicily for the aid of Palestinian Jews, suggesting the existence of an established pattern of communication with Jerusalem, at least as far as Sicily's Jews were concerned. In one such letter, written from Palermo to the leader of the Jerusalem academy, the author Abū al-Ḥay b. Ḥākim excused his community for the lack of response to an earlier letter (which, he said, they had received and read out to the congregation in the local synagogue) by noting that they were under dire financial pressure in Sicily and could not send a donation along with this written response.[176] The poll tax (*jizya*) imposed on religious minorities by the Islamic government of the island had risen, he stated, which caused impoverishment and even emigration by some members of the Sicilian Jewish community. He wrote that some Sicilian Jews had escaped "overseas," although we are not told to which regions they had moved.[177] It is also clear in this letter that, whatever the number of families who moved their residence from the island, many Jews remained in Sicily. The author promised that when the community came together to celebrate the upcoming holidays, he would do his best to raise the funds and send a response to Jerusalem along with their donation.[178] Thus we see a clear spiritual and social connection between the Jewish communities of Sicily and the Levant, although we cannot tell whether their correspondence traveled directly or, more likely, via Egypt. Likewise, I

176. New York, Theol. Sem., Adler Coll. 4009.4; Ben-Sasson, 145ff.; Simonsohn, doc. 39.

177. It is possible that they moved to the Italian mainland, where communities of Jews are also known to have lived.

178. Simonsohn, doc. 39, ll. 21–25.

have found no record of Muslims from Sicily sailing directly to the lands of the eastern Mediterranean, a fact indicating either that the sources for these trips have been lost or that the majority of Sicilian travel—perhaps both Muslim and Jewish—to or from the eastern Mediterranean was carried out via Egypt or Ifrīqiya.[179] The mediation of Sicily's communications with the eastern Mediterranean (or, at least, of the interaction between the Jewish communities in these two places) via Egypt would certainly fit within the larger picture we get of the island as lying politically, intellectually, and culturally at the periphery of the Mediterranean system in these centuries.

Connections between Muslim Sicily and Latin Europe are equally difficult to locate in the existing sources. While it is clear that occasional military raids were conducted in southern Italy during the period of Muslim rule, it is less certain whether these were intended as raids for booty or as attempts at territorial conquest. In addition to hostile relationships, circumstantial information suggests some kind of commercial exchange between the island and the nearby Italian mainland, and we know that at times Sicilian Muslims served as mercenaries in southern Italian Christian armies.[180] Economically, the island's links with Christian southern Italy show up only through the evidence of coins. All of the merchandise discussed above as moving through these Mediterranean networks of exchange was paid for either with credit or in coinage. The basic monetary system in use in the network of trade between Ifrīqiya, Sicily, and Egypt was that of the Islamic world—based on a gold dinar and silver dirham and fractions thereof, issued by various governments in the Mediterranean.[181] One of the most widely utilized coinages in the regional trade at this time was one minted at Sicily, which was a unique denomination called a quarter dinar (*rubāʿī*) (see figure 6).[182] First issued in ninth-century Sicily by the

179. The emigrations of Muslim scholars (more in chapter 4) from Sicily during or after the Christian invasion of the island in the eleventh century confirm the pattern: they arrived in the central Islamic lands only after departing first for Egypt, Ifrīqiya, or al-Andalus.

180. Tehmina Goskar makes the argument that Christian southern Italy participated in the wider culture of fashion and material culture of the Muslim central Mediterranean region, although the evidence for direct communications between the Christian region and the Muslim island is lacking. Goskar, "Material Worlds: The Shared Cultures of Southern Italy and Its Mediterranean Neighbours in the Tenth to Twelfth Centuries," *al-Masāq* 23, no. 3 (2011): 189–204.

181. On the medieval Islamic monetary system, see Andrew S. Ehrenkreutz, "Monetary Aspects of Medieval Near Eastern Economic History," in *Studies in the Economic History of the Middle East*, ed. M. A. Cook (Oxford: Oxford University Press, 1970), 37–50. For a description of lead and copper seals from ninth- and tenth-century Sicily, possibly produced in Ifrīqiya and brought to Sicily, see Paul Balog, "Dated Aghlabid Lead and Copper Seals from Sicily," *Studi Maghrebini* 11 (1979): 125–132.

182. For more on the coins of medieval Sicily and southern Italy, see Philip Grierson and Lucia Travaini, *Medieval European Coinage: With a Catalogue of the Coins in the Fitzwilliam Museum, Cambridge*, vol. 14, *Italy (III) South Italy, Sicily, Sardinia* (Cambridge: Cambridge University Press, 1986); Philip Grierson, "The Coinages of Norman Apulia and Sicily in Their International Setting," *Anglo-Norman*

FIGURE 6. Quarter dinar minted in Sicily during the reign of the Fatimid caliph Al-ʿAziz (975–996). *A*, obverse; *B*, reverse. Fitzwilliam Museum, Grierson Collection, CM.PG.11262-2006.

Aghlabids and based on the Byzantine *tremissis* (one-third of a *solidus*) that had been produced at Syracuse until the Muslim conquest, the *rubāʿī* became one of the most widely used coins in Mediterranean trade and came to be minted widely across the Mediterranean world.[183] While the quarter dinar was a coin with origins in the Muslim world (Sicily itself), and thus with Arabic inscriptions and imagery, it also found popularity on the Christian mainland, particularly in the Greek commercial city-states of southern Italy. By the tenth century, the Sicilian quarter dinar was in wide use in Italian cities

Studies 25 (1992): 117–132; Lucia Travaini, "Le monete in Italia meridionale e in Sicilia dal X al XII secolo," in *Il Mediterraneo I Luoghi e la Memoria* (Taranto: Taranto-Castello Aragonese, 1989), 2: 55–64; and Travaini, "La riforma monetaria di Ruggero II e la circolazione minuta in Italia meridionale tra X e XII secolo," *Rivista Italiana di Numismatica e Scienza Affini* 83 (1981): 133–153.

183. Michael L. Bates, "The Introduction of the Quarter-Dinar by the Aghlabids in 264 H. (A.D. 878) and Its Derivation from the Byzantine Tremissis," *Revista Italiana di Numismatica e Scienze Affini* 103 (2002): 115–128. It is unclear precisely why the Aghlabids chose the Byzantine *tremissis*—a gold coin equaling one-third of a Byzantine *solidus* and minted during the ninth century only at Syracuse, as it had fallen out of use in the East—as the basis for their new issue, but it is strongly likely that they wished to maintain continuity with the economic system already in existence on the island. Given the dearth of evidence for trade during the Byzantine period of Sicily, we do not know what kind of use and circulation *tremisses* enjoyed beyond the island. For the Byzantine *tremissis*, see Philip Grierson, ed., *Catalogue of the Byzantine Coins in the Dumbarton Oaks Collection and in the Whittemore Collection*, vol. 3, pt. 1, *Leo III to Nicephorus III, 717–1081* (Washington, DC: Dumbarton Oaks Research Library and Collection, 1973), 82. This instance of one regime adopting and changing the coinage of its predecessor would be repeated later when the Norman rulers adapted the gold *rubāʿī* as the coinage of their kingdom and called it the *tari* in Latin. On the *tari*, see Vincenza Grassi, "Tari," *EI*[2], 10: 238–240; Philip Grierson and W. A. Oddy, "Le titre du tari Sicilien du milieu du XIe siècle a 1278," *Revue Numismatique* 16 (1974): 123–134; and S. M. Stern, "Tari: The Quarter-Dinar," *Studi Medievali*, 3rd ser., 11, no. 1 (1970): 177–207.

such as Salerno and Amalfi, and, by the mid-eleventh century, those cities were minting their own versions of this coin, complete with fake Arabic inscriptions meant to visually resemble the authentic Sicilian coins.[184] In the eleventh century the Normans in turn would adopt this gold coin, calling it the *tari* and using it to promote their economy and their self-presentation as "Mediterranean" rulers. The attraction to such a coinage is obvious: a gold coin (at a time when Latin Christian coinages were all in silver) was connected to the far wealthier and more heavily monetized society of the dār al-Islām. At the same time, the very fact that Christian cities of southern Italy borrowed such a coin from Muslim Sicily must have meant that some level of exchange linked the island with those cities and their economies. Unfortunately, textual sources have not been found that would help to illuminate these patterns of commercial or other peaceful communications between Islamic Sicily and Christian southern Italy, although they must have existed to some degree.[185]

At the same time, it is strongly evident that Muslim Sicily's weightiest connections were those it maintained with its closest neighbors in the Muslim central Mediterranean, Ifrīqiya and Egypt. To a lesser extent, Sicily also conducted communications with al-Andalus and the western Mediterranean. While this particularly strong connection with Muslim northern Africa was partly due to political need—officials and armies were sent from either Qayrawān or Cairo to impose order on the island—it was also in part a result of the development of common patterns of intraregional trade carried out by the Muslim and Jewish merchants active in the region. While Sicily during the Byzantine period could function as an extension of Constantinople's political authority and a meeting ground for travelers from both the Latin and Muslim worlds, during the Islamic period it operated more as a true boundary of the dār al-Islām: an important location for the enhancement of power and economic gain, but one on the periphery of the Muslim world. Sicily was conceptually valuable for its role in *jihād* and the fight to expand the boundaries of Islam—while practically this effort was more or less stalled—and as a militarized frontier rather than as a proxy for caliphal or other political authority. Muslim Sicily maintained strong communications networks within the central Mediterranean, but they were primarily regional connections with other Muslim territories, and

---

184. The issue copied by the cities of Salerno and Amalfi was that of the Fatimid caliph al-Muʿizz (953–975). William R. Day, "The Fatimid Quarter-Dinar in Southern Italy and the Imitation Tari of Salerno and Amalfi" (paper presented at American Numismatic Society, New York, 1995), 1–17; Philip Grierson, "The Salernitan Coinage of Gisulf II (1052–77) and Robert Guiscard (1077–85)," *Papers of the British School at Rome* 24 (1956): 37–59.

185. Paul Arthur has found some archaeological evidence to suggest trade between tenth-century Sicily and Byzantine Apulia. See Arthur, "Economic Expansion in Byzantine Apulia," *Collection de l'Ecole française de Rome* 363 (2006): 389–405.

the island does not appear in the extant sources to have operated as a meeting point for merchants or other travelers from both the Muslim and Christian worlds. As we will see in the next chapter, however, the Latin Christian invaders of the mid-eleventh century began to adopt and adapt these preexisting connections to the Muslim world in order to create for themselves an island kingdom that they sought to locate at the center of both the Mediterranean and the world as a whole.

Chapter 4

Sicily from the Dār al-Islām to Latin Christendom

> There was an emperor who was called Otto, and he was the second emperor to bear that name. This Emperor of Rome, with an army of all the Germans in Italy and with all his power, was unable to tame or subjugate the evil of the Saracens. These pagans came from beyond the sea to fight him, captured him, and defeated his host and all his knights. The Emperor of Constantinople similarly fought for a long time against the Saracens of Sicily, depleting his treasury which had been acquired over a long period of time. He took the island of Sicily, but shortly thereafter lost it. But Duke Robert, who was glorious in all his deeds, captured Palermo in five months, between the month of August, when he crossed the sea, and the Nativity of Jesus Christ. . . . There is no record of the number of Saracens who were slain, captured, or sold.
>
> Amatus of Montecassino, *Storia de'Normanni*[1]

After nearly two and a half centuries of Muslim rule, and following several Byzantine attempts at reconquest, Latin Christians from northern Europe invaded and gained control of Sicily during the second half of the eleventh century. These conquerors—called Normans because many of their leaders came from prominent families in the Duchy of Normandy—took advantage of internal divisions within the fractured political landscape of post-Kalbid Sicily (united rule had dissolved in 1053) to bring the island under their control between 1061 and 1091.[2] Having first served as mercenar-

1. Amatus, *Storia de'Normanni*, 6.22; *History of the Normans*, 159.

2. I use the term "Norman" here to describe the Christian conquest and rule of Sicily despite very real concerns about this application of an ethnic identity to a mixed group of warriors. I employ it here simply because the term is widely used and thus easily identified with this particular time and place, but it is important to keep the caveats in mind. See T. S. Brown, "The Political Use of the Past in Norman Sicily" in *The Perception of the Past in 12th-Century Europe*, ed. P. Magdalino (London: Ham-

ies for various local Greek and Lombard rulers in the south of Italy (notably, the 1038 Byzantine campaign in Sicily itself), the brothers Roger and Robert de Hauteville eventually gained supremacy over many of the towns of southern Italy, whence they proceeded to Sicily.[3] Roger soon took command of the island's conquest, while Robert, as the older brother, stayed on the mainland and consolidated power there. Over the course of the next thirty years, Roger and his forces steadily conquered the towns and fortresses of the island, establishing a comital capital in Palermo in 1072. In 1130, Roger's descendant Count Roger II declared his territory to be the Kingdom of Sicily, uniting the island and the mainland territories under his rule from Palermo. Famed for its multicultural royal court and the construction of splendid Greek- and Muslim-influenced art and architecture, the Norman kingdom marked the end of Muslim political dominance on the island, but not of Muslim habitation: populations of Arabic-speaking Muslims lived in Sicily until the 1220s.

The pro-Norman chronicler Amatus of Montecassino presented the Norman success in Sicily, as in the epigraph above, within a context of multilateral Christian attempts to take the island from the Muslims. Referring to both the tenth-century campaign in southern Italy by the German emperor Otto II, during which he died in 982, and the repeated offensives against the island by the Byzantine emperors, Amatus argued that the small band of Normans, because of their superior martial strength, were able to do what two emperors had not been able to accomplish. At the same time, he pointed to a state of interreligious warfare in which both Greek and Latin forces tried to take the island from the "pagans"—who were supported by others arriving "from beyond the sea"—and in which the Normans were motivated by hatred of the "pride" of the Saracens, whom Amatus accused of having "taken the island from Christian hands."[4] This presentation of their religious motivations in no way prevented the Normans from battling against various Christian

---

bledon Press, 1992), 191–210; Joanna H. Drell, "Cultural Syncretism and Ethnic Identity: The Norman 'Conquest' of Southern Italy and Sicily," *Journal of Medieval History* 25, no. 3 (1999): 187–202; Ewan Johnson, "Normandy and Norman Identity in Southern Italian Chronicles," *Anglo-Norman Studies* 27 (2005): 85–100; Johnson, "Origin Myths and the Construction of Medieval Identities: Norman Chronicles 1000–1200," in *Texts and Identities in the Early Middle Ages*, ed. R. Corradini, et al., Forschungen zur Geschichte des Mittelalters, vol. 12 (Vienna: Verlag der Österreichischen Akademie der Wissenschaften, 2006), 153–164; G. A. Loud, "The 'Gens Normannorum'—Myth or Reality?," *Anglo-Norman Studies* 4 (1982): 104–116, 205–209, repr. in ibid., *Conquerors and Churchmen*, I; and Loud, "How 'Norman' Was the Norman Conquest of Southern Italy?," *Nottingham Medieval Studies* 25 (1981): 13–34, repr. in ibid., *Conquerors and Churchmen in Norman Italy*, II.

3. Roger is commonly known as Count Roger of Sicily, and Robert is referred to as Robert Guiscard. They both came from the family of Tancred de Hauteville of Normandy (ca. 990–1057).

4. Amatus, *Storia de'Normanni*, 5.9; *History of the Normans*, 136.

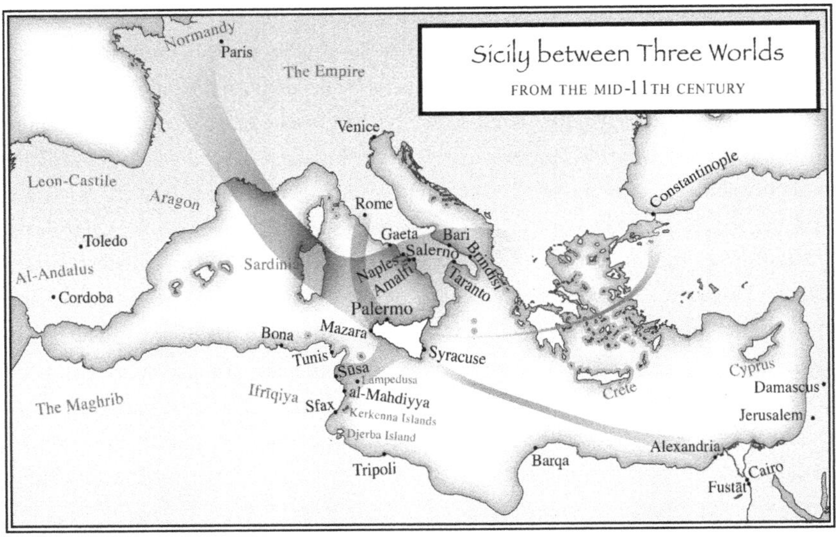

Map 4. Sicily between three worlds, from the mid-eleventh century

powers in southern Italy and employing the insider information of Muslim *qāʾids* from Sicily, but it may help us to understand the variety of contemporary Christian (Norman, Greek, and local southern Italian) perspectives on the nature of the Muslim-Christian border in the region (see map 4). Although that line was not a clearly demarcated one—Amatus himself noted that Muslims lived alongside Christians in mainland Reggio Calabria and that the Salernitans had for many years owed tribute to the Muslims of Sicily—it may be the case that anti-Muslim propaganda helped to spur the Norman invasion of the island, or that, at least in retrospect, interreligious warfare appeared to provide a valuable justification for their actions.

It is certainly the case that the Normans obtained papal approval of their efforts. They received the blessings of Rome, along with papal concession of the lands that the Normans had conquered in southern Italy, after they triumphed over allied forces under Pope Leo IX (1048–1054) at the Battle of Civitate (1053) and, six years later, signed the Treaty of Melfi with his successor Nicholas II (1059–1061), which recognized the Norman right to rule in the region.[5] In this 1059 treaty, Robert Guiscard was invested by the pope with

5. Malaterra, *De rebus gestis*, 1.14; Amatus, *Storia de'Normanni*, 3.39–42; and William of Apulia, *De rebus gestis Roberti Wiscardi*, bk. 2, ed. Marguerite Mathieu (Palermo: Istituto Siciliano di Studi Bizantini e Neoellenici, 1961), 180–256.

authority not only over the Calabrian lands he had conquered but also over Sicily, which at the time was still ruled by various Kalbid *emīrs*. However, as kings of Sicily, the Normans later made themselves enemies of the popes and acted in their own interests over and against those of any other party or ally.

Despite this papal approval for some of the Normans' early activities in southern Italy and Sicily, however, these adventurers appear to have had no clear ideological agenda fueling their invasion of the island. At least, religious motivations do not appear very often in the Latin sources, and when they do so, it is alongside other, more pragmatic considerations such as financial gain or glory. On the whole, pro-Norman chronicles present the conquest as something of a logical extension of the Normans' efforts to gain authority in the southern mainland. Likewise, they were aware that Sicily offered them wealth and an extension of their dominion into the Mediterranean, along with the opportunities for Mediterranean-wide trade and conquest that might arise as a consequence of their control over the largest Mediterranean island, centrally located and with historical ties to both Byzantium and Muslim northern Africa. According to Geoffrey of Malaterra, the motivation for Sicily's conquest was twofold: both spiritual and material gain would accrue to Roger if he could "appropriate for himself the fruits and revenues of the land, which had been usurped by a people disagreeable to God, and dispose of them in the service of God."[6] The Latin chroniclers of Norman activities in Sicily and southern Italy generally suggest that assisting in Byzantine endeavors to regain the island had provided the Hautevilles with their initial exposure to the island of Sicily and had taught them about its military and political weaknesses.

Whatever its initial motivations, the Norman invasion of Sicily has been seen as a watershed event in Mediterranean history, particularly for the relationship between Christendom and the lands of Islam. Sometimes viewed as the moment at which Sicily was removed from the Islamic world and firmly—and irrevocably—attached to the Latin Christian world, the Norman invasion is often heralded as a key juncture in the shifting balance of power between Muslims and Christians in the Mediterranean region. Some scholars have viewed this conquest as part of a larger movement of Latin Christians southward and eastward—into the Levant and the Muslim Mediterranean during the Crusades and during the "Reconquista" in Iberia—that resulted from a

6. Malaterra, *De rebus gestis*, 2.1, trans. in *The Deeds of Count Roger of Calabria and Sicily and of His Brother Duke Robert Guiscard*, trans. Kenneth Baxter Wolf (Ann Arbor: University of Michigan Press, 2005), 85–86. See also Huguette Taviani-Carozzi, "Léon IX et les Normands d'Italie du Sud," in *Léon IX et son temps*, ed. Georges Bischoff and Benoît-Michel Tock (Turnhout: Brepols, 2006), 299–329.

vaguely described expansionist impulse within Latin Christendom as a whole.[7] Thus the Christian takeover of Sicily is held to have created both a religious and a political boundary separating the northern and southern shores of the Mediterranean, shifting northward the dividing line between Islam and Christianity that would play a role in the greater Muslim-Christian conflicts of the coming centuries. Hindsight certainly makes this interpretation seem credible: given Sicily's increasing incorporation into the Latin Christian world, and its union with the southern Italian mainland from 1130, it may seem inevitable that this moment of Christian military and political push south into the formerly Muslim-dominated Mediterranean Sea be viewed as decisive. It is also true that the conquest introduced Latin Christianity to an island that had been populated by Muslims and a minority of Greek Christians and Jews. However, the Norman takeover of Sicily was, at the time of its occurrence over thirty years of the mid-eleventh century, neither a certainly assured success nor a necessarily long-lasting indicator of things to come. In fact, the thirty-year period of the conquest itself and the decades following the Norman triumph were marked by reversals, uncertainty, and, most significantly, a continuation of strong connections between the island and Muslim North Africa that had been established during the preceding centuries.

In addition to seeing the invasion as a tipping point in history, many scholars have investigated the ways in which the Norman rulers of Sicily continued to emulate the Muslim world in cultural terms—for example, royal patronage of Arabic scholarship and poetry, decoration with Islamic artistic and architectural motifs, and employment of Muslim cooks, bodyguards, and even concubines. Indeed, one of the most famous aspects of Norman rule in Sicily is the kings' cultural appropriation of artistic, linguistic, and administrative models taken from the subject Muslim and Greek cultures.[8] In addition, recent scholarship on the Norman period in Sicily has demonstrated important ways in which these Latin Christian rulers looked to emulate the

---

7. For an example of this sentiment, see the remark by David Jacoby that the Norman conquest of Italy and Sicily, the Crusades into the Levant, and the growth of Christian economic activity in the Mediterranean were all part of the "thrust of a rejuvenated West, announcing its imminent military, economic, and demographic expansion." David Jacoby, "The Encounter of Two Societies: Western Conquerors and Byzantines in the Peloponnesus after the Fourth Crusade," *The American Historical Review* 78, no. 4 (1973): 873.

8. For just a few examples of the extensive scholarship on Islamicate cultural elements as utilized by the Norman rulers of Sicily, see Karen C. Britt, "Roger II of Sicily: Rex, Basileus, and Khalif? Identity, Politics, and Propaganda in the Cappella Palatina," *Mediterranean Studies* 16 (2007): 21–45; Lev Kapitaikin, "The Twelfth-Century Paintings of the Ceilings of the Cappella Palatina, Palermo," (PhD thesis, Oxford University, 2011); Mallette, *The Kingdom of Sicily*; and William Tronzo, *The Cultures of His Kingdom: Roger II and the Cappella Palatina in Palermo* (Princeton, NJ: Princeton University Press, 1997).

Fatimid rulers of Africa in some aspects of law and administration.[9] The Normans consciously sought models for their political rule and artistic and intellectual culture among the regional Mediterranean powers, particularly in Byzantium and Muslim Egypt and North Africa. These appropriations, however, do not constitute "toleration," a virtue that is often ascribed to the Norman rulers both for their appreciation of Muslim and Greek cultural elements and for the continued presence in Christian Sicily of a mixed population of Greeks, Jews, and Muslims. Rather, the Normans used Islamic and Greek cultural forms to establish their identity as "Mediterranean" rulers and to assert their own power by utilizing local and regional cultural idioms. Artistically, economically, and politically, the Normans capitalized on the preestablished networks that linked their new island capital with the economic, cultural, and political power of the rest of the Mediterranean world, all as part of a larger attempt to entrench and expand their own power within the Mediterranean basin.

Imitation, appreciation, and appropriation of cultural elements, however, do not prove active communication and continued contact; they may suggest that Norman Sicily maintained travel and communication networks with the Muslim world, but proof must be sought from other sources. Economic connections can provide one lens through which to view the questions of when the relationship between Sicily and the Muslim-dominated southern shore of the Mediterranean Sea, as detailed in chapter 3, was severed and by what means Sicily eventually shifted toward northern Italy and the Latin Christian world. This form of communication—which had been one of the most regular and fluid types of travel and contact between Sicily and the Muslim world in the preceding centuries—eventually linked Sicily much more closely to the Italian mercantile cities of Christian Italy. So the question is: How soon can we think of Sicily as leaving the Islamic sphere and entering the Christian one—at the time of the Norman conquest or sometime much later? This chapter will discuss the position of Sicily vis-à-vis the Muslim and Christian worlds during the eleventh and early twelfth centuries in light of three aspects of cross-Mediterranean communication: naval travel during the period of the conquest, the impact of the Norman takeover on trade between Sicily and the Muslim Mediterranean, and the resulting population movements (simultaneous emigration and immigration) across the newly developing Muslim-Christian boundary. Continuity in these forms of communication shows that the island of Sicily remained closely connected to—and in some ways still a

9. Jeremy Johns, *Arabic Administration in Norman Sicily: The Royal Dīwān* (Cambridge: Cambridge University Press, 2002).

part of—the Islamic world for many years after the Christian Normans took political control of the island.

Military, Diplomatic, and Political Connections

As noted above, several decades before the 1060 invasion, the Normans' involvement with Sicily began with their participation in Byzantine attempts to restore Greek power in the region. Indeed, the very first documented presence of Norman fighters on the island came during a Byzantine effort to recapture Sicily in 1038. Constantinople had launched naval attacks on the island at somewhat regular intervals throughout the late tenth and early eleventh centuries—for example in the years 964, 1025–1027, and 1030—and in 1038 the Greeks again prepared an assault on Sicily, with Normans serving alongside other mercenaries.[10] They made a few gains in the region of Messina but quickly lost them. While the Greek campaign was thwarted, the experience presented the Norman fighters with a glimpse of a place that offered them an opportunity to exercise their own power. Post-Kalbid Sicily was politically fractured but also wealthy and deeply connected with the economy and power structure of the Muslim Mediterranean—a perfect location for the realization of Norman ambition.

The earliest arrivals of Normans into southern Italy occurred in the early eleventh century, when young men from the Duchy of Normandy began arriving in southern Italy and interfering in local conflicts. The region was already fraught with disorder, being split between multiple Lombard princes, Byzantine *catepans* (governors of naval themes), and independent cities such as Amalfi, Salerno, Naples, and Gaeta.[11] The motivations behind this migration of young men from northern France into southern Italy are not perfectly understood or agreed upon among scholars. Some of the Latin sources describe the Normans passing through the area on the way back home from pilgrimage to Jerusalem and being sought out by the prince of Salerno, who was at the time being besieged by tribute-seeking Muslims.[12] An alternate expla-

10. See Archibald R. Lewis, *Naval Power and Trade in the Mediterranean, A.D. 500–1100* (Princeton, NJ: Princeton University Press, 1951), 194–197; and Jonathan Shepard, "Byzantium's Last Sicilian Expedition: Scylitzes' Testimony," *Rivista di studi bizantini e neoellenici*, n.s., 14–16 (1977–1979): 145–159.

11. For the political situation in pre-Norman southern Italy, see Kreutz, *Before the Normans*, and G. A. Loud, *The Age of Robert Guiscard: Southern Italy and the Norman Conquest* (New York: Longman, 2000).

12. This is the "Salerno tradition" of historiography on the Normans' entrée into southern Italian politics and represents the story as told by Amatus of Montecassino. In this version of events, the Normans aided Prince Guaimar III of Salerno due to their love of God and hatred for the "arrogance

nation is that the Norman pilgrims were visiting the shrine of St. Michael on Monte Gargano in Italy when they met a man who asked for their help fighting against the Byzantine authorities of Apulia.[13] Another motivation is suggested by Geoffrey of Malaterra, who depicted Tancred de Hauteville as recognizing that the patrimony for his twelve sons would be too small to support them and recommending that they should each "seek their fortune in various places through exercise of arms."[14] The common elements among these various explanations for Norman interference in southern Italy are two: one, that the Normans were not originally acting on their own initiative, but always as mercenaries for one or another of the local power players, and two, that the Normans were sought out as fighters because of their military prowess, but that they eventually overtook their patrons through a combination of military skill and political acumen. Among the earliest of the Normans in southern Italy were a man named Richard—later known as Richard of Aversa, the duke of Capua—and several members of the Hauteville family, some of whom would later come to rule as kings of the Two Sicilies. Richard was the first of these Normans to carve out a place for himself on the chaotic political scene, first by means of mercenary activity on behalf of one or the other of the players and, later, by leading bands of warriors against various territories

of the Saracens" but returned to Normandy after this one battle. However, the lure of profit and adventure called many of them back to Italy around the year 1000, which marks the beginning of their full-scale involvement in the political events in the region. See Amatus, *Storia de'Normanni*, 1.17.

13. This is referred to in contemporary scholarship as the "Gargano tradition" and is based on the chronicles of William of Apulia and the later Alexander of Telese. These events have been connected with the Lombard attack on Byzantine Apulia in 1017, much later than the dating of ca. 1000 by those in the "Salerno tradition." Some scholars have sought to reconcile these two historiographical traditions into one coherent explanation for the advent of the Normans in southern Italy. See Ferdinand Chalandon, *Histoire de la Domination Normande en Italie et en Sicile*, 2 vols. (Paris, 1907; repr., New York: Burt Franklin, 1960); Chalandon, "The Conquest of South Italy and Sicily by the Normans," in *The Cambridge Medieval History*, ed. J. R. Tanner, C. W. Previte-Orton, and Z. N. Brook (Cambridge: Cambridge University Press, 1964), 167–184. Other scholars have rejected this conflation and sought evidence from different sources to shed light on the reasons for the Normans' advance, concluding that Pope Benedict VIII (1012–1024) was the primary instigator of Norman involvement in the Italian South because of his struggles with the Byzantines there around 1017 and his enlistment of Norman help. See John France, "The Occasion of the Coming of the Normans to Southern Italy," *Journal of Medieval History* 27 (1991): 185–205; and Einar Joranson, "The Inception of the Career of the Normans in Italy—Legend and History," *Speculum* 23, no. 3 (1948): 353–396. One attempt at reconciling these various traditions is that by Graham Loud, who concludes, among other points, that some Normans were already present in the South—acting in small roles as mercenaries in the Lombard anti-Byzantine efforts—and that they gained more prominent roles due perhaps to the intervention of the pope. According to Loud, the important thing to remember is that the Normans were not directing their own conquest but were taking part in the much larger enterprise of negotiating local power in southern Italy. See Loud, *The Age of Robert Guiscard*, 60–91. Norman self-presentation in the Latin chronicle tradition is covered in depth in Kenneth Baxter Wolf, *Making History: The Normans and Their Historians in Eleventh-Century Italy* (Philadelphia: University of Pennsylvania Press, 1995).

14. Malaterra, *De rebus gestis*, 1.5.

for his own gain. Other Norman individuals also made their fortunes in southern Italy, but the Hauteville family—to which both Robert Guiscard and Roger, the first count of Sicily, belonged—would be the most important for the history not only of southern Italy and Sicily but also of the entire medieval Mediterranean and beyond.

Members of the Hauteville clan first became involved in Sicilian affairs as early as the 1030s, when several of the brothers served as mercenaries in a Byzantine Italian army. The Latin chroniclers Amatus of Montecassino and Geoffrey of Malaterra tell us that William, son of Tancred (and brother to both Roger and Robert), along with a force of Norman soldiers, served as a mercenary for the Greeks as they attacked and conquered Muslim Sicilian cities from Messina to Syracuse.[15] They participated in this attempt by the Byzantines, under the command of George Maniakes, the *catepan* of Byzantine Apulia and Calabria, to recapture the island from Muslim rule, but they were by no means loyal to the Byzantine authorities. Malaterra's account of this Sicilian expedition ends with the Normans secretly crossing the straits back to the mainland in order to raid the Byzantine territories of Calabria and Apulia in retribution for a perceived slight when Maniakes divided the spoils after the battle at Troina.[16] The expedition was considered a success for both William—who gained a reputation for fierceness in battle—and for Maniakes—who defeated the Muslims in Messina, Syracuse, Troina, and several towns in the area. This Greek-Norman gain was quickly reversed, however, as had been the other Byzantine attempts at regaining territory on Sicily or fomenting local rebellions there. Nonetheless, Norman bands continued to participate in many of the other important battles and political struggles of eleventh-century southern Italy, gaining ever more power for themselves independent of the Lombard or Byzantine authorities. In time, as other members of this family arrived in the region, they would come to take the upper hand in attacks on Sicily, leaving aside the political or military interests of the Byzantines.

15. This William would be named "count" over the Normans in southern Italy in 1042, with his base of power at Melfi, and would be a close companion of Prince Guaimar IV of Salerno. See Amatus, *Storia de'Normanni*, 2.29. Together they would also attack Byzantine-held Bari in 1043. Amatus's chronicle depicts Guaimar and the Normans cooperating in their assistance to the Greeks, while Geoffrey's has Guaimar foisting the Normans onto Maniakes in an attempt to get them out of his regions and make them no longer a concern of his. Amatus, *Storia de'Normanni*, 2.8; Malaterra, *De rebus gestis*, 1.7–1.9.

16. After the 1038 victory in Sicily and the Normans' secretive return to Italy, the Greeks and Normans found themselves on opposite sides of the battle for political control of southern Italy. In 1041 the Norman bands ravaged the Byzantine provinces of Calabria and Apulia. See Amatus, *Storia de'Normanni*, 2.19ff., and Malaterra, *De rebus gestis*, 1.8–1.10, for the subsequent conflicts between the Byzantine emperor and the Normans in and around the city of Melfi, which was to come under the control of William of Hauteville in 1042.

By the middle of the eleventh century, both Robert and Roger de Hauteville had migrated from Normandy to southern Italy. It was these two men who eventually pushed from the mainland of Italy into Muslim Sicily. There, they took advantage of internal divisions among the Sicilian Muslims to eventually gain mastery over the entire island. Robert Guiscard appeared in the South sometime between 1045 and 1049 and was given command over the territory of Calabria by his elder brother Drogo, who had become leader (*comes*) of all the Normans in southern Italy after the death of William.[17] Robert spent several years attempting to subdue Calabria and bring it under Norman control, aided for a time by his youngest brother, Roger, who would later be given command of the Sicilian expedition. Roger de Hauteville had arrived in Italy around 1057 and served under his brother Robert on the mainland before moving on to conquer the island of Sicily.[18] Their relationship, initially close, broke down over matters of power and dominance, and the brothers spent a period warring against one another rather than together.[19] They eventually reunited, and Roger and Robert together attacked and captured the city of Reggio in 1059, thus securing Calabria for the Normans and (in hindsight, at least) opening the door to the island of Sicily, which lay just across the Straits of Messina from Reggio.

Much like the traditional narrative of the Islamic conquest of Sicily, the story told by Latin chroniclers of the Norman invasion involves a traitorous local official who gave aid and advice that facilitated the conquest of the island by outsiders. In 1060/1061 a Sicilian Muslim named Ibn al-Thumna, called Betumen in the Latin chronicles, approached Roger in Reggio di Calabria, and according to the account in the history by Malaterra, "with repeated entreaties, he encouraged the count to attack Sicily."[20] Ibn al-Thumna, one of several regional

17. For Robert's early career in southern Italy, see Amatus, *Storia de'Normanni*, 2.46 and 3.6ff., and Malaterra, *De rebus gestis*, 1.12 and 1.16ff.

18. Malaterra, *De rebus gestis*, 1.19ff.

19. Ibid., 1.23–1.26. Geoffrey tells his readers that he highlighted Roger's youthful poverty in order to provide a stark contrast with the great riches and power he would attain as count of Sicily.

20. Ibid., 2.3. See also Ibn al-Athīr, *al-Kāmil fi al-tārīkh*, *BAS* Arabic, rev. ed., 1: 318–319; *BAS* Ital., rev. ed., 1: 447. Moshe Gil has reexamined the events of the invasion through a reading of the Geniza letters alongside the Arabic chronicles and concluded that the traditional dating of this invasion to the early 1060s, which I have followed here, is incorrect, and the first incursion should be dated earlier, to around 1056. See Moshe Gil, *Jews in Islamic Countries in the Middle Ages*, trans. David Strassler (Leiden: E. J. Brill, 2004), 549–555. He points to Geniza letters from the 1050s that depict naval warfare by Christians in the region of Sicily well before the traditional invasion date of 1060/1061, as well as dating mistakes that appear in Ibn al-Athīr's chronicle. Jeremy Johns explains away these mistakes in his *Arabic Administration*, 32, n. 7, and, indeed, Gil's redating seems to be unable to withstand scrutiny. My argument—that communications between Sicily and the Islamic world continued despite the disruption of invasion and warfare—does not depend on adherence to the traditional time frame, nor does it falter if this timing is overturned. I have chosen to employ the traditional time frame primarily

rulers (*qā'ids*) in Sicily, who was based in the eastern region of the island near Syracuse, had reportedly killed the brother of one of the other local leaders and thus asked the Normans for protection in exchange for providing them with entry to the island.[21] He acted as guide, informant, interpreter, and ambassador for the Normans as they made their way across the island. Roger also often left Ibn al-Thumna as his representative on Sicily when he returned to mainland Italy. During his trip to Calabria in 1061, for example, Ibn al-Thumna remained on the island to form alliances on behalf of the Normans with Muslim leaders throughout Sicily and to attack those who did not submit.[22]

The thirty-year conquest of the island was carried out by means of a series of campaigns directed initially from the Norman strongholds in mainland Italy.[23] The invasion began in 1060, with a small reconnaissance force attacking the city of Messina, killing some of the city's defenders, and collecting spoils. The city itself was not taken, but Roger's men pushed its inhabitants back into the city walls after they had come out to do battle.[24] In the spring of 1061, Norman forces again attempted to conquer Messina, amassing ships and men to sail from Reggio. They were met by a navy from Palermo, which was sent by the new Muslim ruler of Palermo, "Sausane" (Ṣamṣām al-Dawla), according to Amatus, although Malaterra claims that it was "Belcamet" (Ibn al-Ḥawwās) who heard about the Normans' plan to attack Messina and ordered ships to aid in its defense. The Norman vessels were able to evade these Muslims ships and land in Sicily, and once on shore, Roger's troops defeated those of the *qā'ids* of Palermo who had arrived to help defend the city. When the Muslims of Messina discovered that these reinforcements from Palermo had been slaughtered, they all fled and the city was entered and easily taken.[25] From there, the Normans proceed to Rometta, where they also quickly gained the surrender of the population.[26] With this foothold now established in Sicily, Roger carried out the rest of the island's conquest, which

because it is still the most widely accepted one and because it fits with other known dates such as that of Roger's arrival in southern Italy around 1057.

21. For the association of the Latin Betumen with the Arabic Ibn al-Thumna, see Amari, *Storia dei Musulmani di Sicilia*, 3: 63–89.

22. Malaterra, *De rebus gestis*, 2.22.

23. The full account of Norman progress across the island will not be covered here, as it has been amply treated in a number of other works of scholarship. See in particular Loud, *The Age of Robert Guiscard*.

24. Malaterra, *De rebus gestis*, 2.1; Amatus, *Storia de'Normanni*, 5.10.

25. Malaterra, *De rebus gestis*, 2.8–12; Amatus, *Storia de'Normanni*, 5.12–19.

26. Malaterra, *De rebus gestis*, 2.13; Amatus, *Storia de'Normanni*, 5.20.

was completed in 1091, when he overcame the last Muslim resistance, in the town of Noto.

Not content simply to establish control over the island, the Normans quickly took to the sea in order to extend their power into the Mediterranean. In fact, Norman efforts to subdue the island not only featured a land-based military effort but also included significant seaborne attacks. Even though Christian troops came to Sicily from the nearby mainland of Italy—only around two and a half miles from the northeast tip of Sicily across the Strait of Messina—ship transport was required that could accommodate men, weapons, and horses; these vessels could also have been used to sail further into the Mediterranean, as they apparently soon did.[27] Reports of naval activity in the region—of both a commercial and a military nature—suggest that the Normans took to the sea even earlier than 1060 and, perhaps, independently of their advances on Sicily. Some Geniza letters suggest that there was Christian (possibly Norman, but possibly also Byzantine or southern Italian) seaborne activity disrupting trade patterns already in the 1050s and 1060s. Other sources show that during the conquest (1060–1091), the Norman forces attacked the island by both land and sea, and sometimes simultaneously. By means of such naval activities were the Norman rulers able to begin the process of taking over not only the island itself but also its networks of communication in the Mediterranean.

Often, the Normans clashed with armies and navies sent from Ifrīqiya who fought alongside the residents of the island. Ifrīqiyan authorities occasionally dispatched ships to aid in the island's defense, but there is only slight evidence to suggest that the Fatimids, or the dynasty of provincial governors in Ifrīqiya who ruled initially as their agents, called the Zīrids (973–1148), exerted a significant effort to reconquer Sicily once it was lost to the Normans.[28] The Latin chroniclers described several land battles in which Sicilian Muslim troops were reinforced by troops and ships sent from Ifrīqiya. According to Malaterra's chronicle, ground troops were dispatched "from Arabia and Africa" to aid the

27. See Matthew Bennett, "Norman Naval Activity in the Mediterranean c.1060–c.1108," *Anglo-Norman Studies* 25 (1992): 41–58; and D. P. Waley, "'Combined Operations' in Sicily, A.D. 1060–78," *Papers of the British School at Rome* 22 (1954): 118–125. For discussion of horse transport on medieval ships, see Lillian Ray Martin, "Horse and Cargo Handling on Medieval Mediterranean Ships," *International Journal of Nautical Archaeology* 31 (2002): 237–241; and John H. Pryor, "The Naval Architecture of Crusader Transport Ships and Horse Transports Revisited," *The Mariner's Mirror* 76 (1990): 255–273.

28. The Zīrids gained independence from the Fatimids in 1048 and established their allegiance to the Abbasid caliphs in Baghdad. Independent Zīrid power was destroyed within a century, however, by a combination of the invasions of tribal forces under the Banū Hilāl and attacks by the Normans from Sicily. See H. R. Idris, *La Berbérie orientale sous les Zirides, Xe–XIIe siècles* (Paris: Adrien-Maisonneuve, 1962).

Sicilians in various important battles. However, these North African soldiers were ineffective against Roger's forces, particularly during the first battle of Castrogiovanni (Enna) in 1061 and the major battle at Cerami in 1063.[29] Even though the Zīrid governors of Ifrīqiya were, in the mid-eleventh century, themselves under attack by Bedouin tribes, they nonetheless undertook to defend Sicily by sending warships and troops to fight against the Latin Christians.[30] The Zīrids, having broken away from Fatimid control in 1048, were not officially responsible for overseeing Sicily and were experiencing warfare, political turmoil, and famine during the period of the so-called Hilālian invasion. They abandoned their capital city of Qayrawān in 1057 to these Bedouin invaders and moved to al-Mahdiyya but, nonetheless, thought it important to keep Sicily under Muslim dominion and attempted to aid their coreligionists in Sicily against the encroaching power of the Christians. Their primary interest in Sicily may have been an economic one, though, as the island continued to be an important source of food for the North African population well into the twelfth century—and increasingly so as their economy declined due to drought, famine, and invasions.

One notable sea battle featuring North African ships was waged for Palermo in 1071–1072, but the presence of these supporting vessels did not prevent a Norman victory. Amatus of Montecassino and Geoffrey of Malaterra described the fight for Sicily's capital as having taken place simultaneously on land and at sea, while William of Apulia mentioned that during the naval skirmishes the Sicilian Muslim fleet was joined by ships sent by the Zīrid rulers of North

29. Malaterra, *De rebus gestis*, 2.17, 2.32–33.

30. In the mid-eleventh century the nomadic tribe of the Banū Hilāl were supposedly invited by the Fatimid vizier to enter Ifrīqiya to raid there. This move was said to be in response to the Zīrid *emīr* al-Muʿizz b. Bādīs's resistance to Fatimid authority and allegiance to the Abbasid caliph instead. The resulting incursion of tribal groups, traditionally known as the Hilālian invasion, wrought havoc on North African cities, government, and agriculture, causing widespread famine among the populace. H. R. Idris, "L'invasion hilālienne et ses conséquences," *Cahiers de civilisation médiévale* 43 (1968): 353–369. The violence inflicted by these Bedouins in Ifrīqiya is described in a Geniza letter from 1053, in which we learn that Jews and Muslims from Qayrawān who were attempting flee the city were killed and their stomachs searched because it was suspected that they had swallowed coins in order to smuggle them out (London, British Museum, Or. 5542.9, fol. 1a, ll. 10–13). These invasions also dislocated but did not immediately topple the Zīrid administration. In 1057 the Zīrid capital of Qayrawān surrendered to the Banū Hilāl, and by the middle of the twelfth century the Zīrid dynasty had been destroyed. Michael Brett suggests that the Banū Hilāl had been present and migrating within the region for decades and that the claim of Fatimid agency in this story was crafted to slander them. See Michael Brett, "The Way of the Nomad," *Bulletin of the School of Oriental and African Studies* 58 (1995): 251–269, repr. in *Ibn Khaldun and the Medieval Maghrib* (Aldershot: Variorum, 1999); "Fatimid Historiography: A Case Study—the Quarrel with the Zīrids, 1048–58," in *Medieval Historical Writing in the Christian and Islamic Worlds*, ed. David Morgan (London: School of Oriental and African Studies, 1982), 47–59, repr. in *Ibn Khaldun and the Medieval Maghrib*. See also Ellenblum, *The Collapse of the Eastern Mediterranean*, 147–159.

Africa. Nevertheless, Christian ships managed to break the defensive chain placed across the harbor of Palermo, allowing the Normans to take the city and set up their own administration in the former Muslim capital of the island.[31] Again paralleling the Muslim conquest of Sicily from the Byzantines, efforts to protect and defend the island from invaders came at the same time that forces were already taxed by warfare on the mainland. Like the Greek defense in the ninth century, the Muslim efforts in the eleventh century were largely ineffective, and the battle for Palermo was a decisive one in favor of the Normans. The conquest of Palermo led to the establishment of the Norman comital capital there, and thence to the rapid conquest of much of the remainder of the Muslim-held towns on the island. From 1072 until 1091, the Normans used Palermo as a base from which to carry out their raids on settlements that resisted Christian rule or revolted against the Normans and had to be re-subdued. The former Greek capital, Syracuse, was a late Muslim holdout, falling to the Normans only in 1086. Still, with the Latin Christians in control of the capital at Palermo, the important southwestern port at Māzara, and a large part of the rest of the island, 1072 is often marked as the decisive date in the Norman takeover of Sicily.

Zīrid ships were also sent to Sicily from Ifrīqiya several times during the later stages of the Norman advance, indicating that the North Africans remained committed to maintaining Muslim control over the island despite the advances of the Christians. Likewise, some Zīrid ships harassed the people and ships on Sicily's shores. Geoffrey of Malaterra twice referred to ships that were sent to Sicily in the 1070s from Zīrid North Africa as acting "like pirates" in their manner of sailing and lying in wait to ambush passing vessels. They may have been dispatched in order to wage their defensive war on the sea, since by that time much of the Sicilian territory was under Norman control. They may also have been trying to disrupt Norman commercial shipping or to profit from the enslavement of the new Christian population. In 1074 the *emīr* Tamīm b. al-Muʿizz ordered a fleet from al-Mahdiyya to sail to the island, where it approached the city of Nicotera during the night, took advantage of citizens celebrating the vigil of St. Peter, and killed or captured many of them.[32] They plundered and burned the fortress, but the next morning offered some of the younger and less valuable captives back to the city for ransom. Malaterra claimed that those who were not ransomed were taken back to North Africa

---

31. Apulia, *De rebus gestis Roberti Wiscardi*, bk. 3, 176–178, ll. 225–254. See also Amatus, *Storia de'Normanni*, 6.16; Malaterra, *De rebus gestis*, 2.45.

32. The Latin text has Thimin, for *Emīr* Tamīm b. al-Muʿizz, the fifth Zīrid ruler of Ifrīqiya (1062–1108).

to be sold as slaves.[33] Again the next year, Ifrīqiyan ships sailed toward Māzara with similar aims. This time, however, Roger was able to rout the enemy and send the Africans back to the *emīr* with "painful news."[34] Both of these incidents may have been attempts by the Ifrīqiyan navy to aid native Muslims in the defense of the island against the Norman invaders, but neither was successful, and Tamīm later declared that his intentions toward the Normans were peaceful.[35]

Nonetheless, evidence suggests that some Muslim North African ships continued to make the journey to Christian Sicily for various reasons for about the next century. The majority of evidence for Muslims sailing from Ifrīqiya to Sicily points to trips taken for economic reasons. Indeed, the trade in foodstuffs between Sicily and North Africa continued long after the establishment of Norman administration on the island. Far less evidence indicates that regular trips were taken from Ifrīqiya to Sicily for military or diplomatic purposes. One example, which suggests but does not prove that military travel between Ifrīqiya and Norman Sicily took place, is found in a *fatwā* from the twelfth century. In this legal decision, we learn that a man from al-Mahdiyya named ʿAbd Allāh al-Raʾīs granted his wife, ʿĀʾisha bint ʿUthmān b. Ṭayyib al-Anṣārī, a provisional divorce in the event that he departed with the navy ("marākib al-sulṭān") and did not return for more than four months. As it happened, ʿAbd Allāh had signed the act in April 1121, and in September/October of that same year, he indeed sailed off to Sicily. After he had sent no word to his wife for more than four months, the dissolution of the marriage was pronounced.[36] It is unclear from the *fatwā* record what the *emīr*'s ship was doing in Sicily or what befell the husband. It may be that this anecdote reflects one attempt on the part of the Zīrid governors to reconquer Sicily, in the same manner that Byzantine naval forces tried to retake the island several times after it fell into Muslim hands, or these may have been government-directed commercial voyages. In any event, there continued to be Muslim populations on the island and an enduring economic connection

---

33. Malaterra, *De rebus gestis*, 3.8.

34. Ibid., 3.9.

35. Malaterra wrote that in 1079 ships on orders from *Emīr* Tamīm arrived near Taormina, again "roaming the seas in the manner of pirates." This time, however, Roger sent an envoy to the ship, who returned with the message that the Muslim vessels claimed they had been sent "to chase pirates from the sea if they could find any, and were prepared to assist the count if necessary." With this oath of nonaggression against the Normans, the two parties agreed to a truce, but then the wind sent the ships back out to sea, and they were not seen again. Malaterra, *De rebus gestis*, 3.17, trans. in Wolf, *Deeds of Count Roger*, 147–148. Malaterra later indicated that Roger considered that truce to be valid, as he refused to join with the Pisans in attacking al-Mahdiyya, the capital residence of *Emīr* Tamīm. Malaterra, *De rebus gestis*, 4.3.

36. al-Wansharīsī, 3: 311–312.

between Ifrīqiya and Norman Sicily, and thus this one North African husband could have been sailing to Sicily for any number of reasons.

Economic Connections with the Dār al-Islām

Indeed, the most common motivation for communications between Muslim North Africa and newly Christian Norman Sicily appears to have been trade. The large body of evidence for continued commercial sea travel between Ifrīqiya and the island under Christian rule demonstrates the long tradition of economic interdependence between the two places, which endured despite the change of regime and religion in Sicily. We have already seen the fluidity of travel—particularly that conducted for economic purposes—in the central Mediterranean of the tenth and eleventh centuries, as depicted in the documents written by Jewish merchants and found in the Cairo Geniza, as well as in the Islamic legal sources documenting relationships between trading partners. These letters, business accounts, and court documents reveal significant connections between the merchants and markets of Egypt, Sicily, and Ifrīqiya during the period of Muslim rule on the island. Using such evidence, S. D. Goitein claimed that during the eleventh century Sicily was at the heart of intra-Mediterranean trade but that the island lost its importance during the twelfth century—almost immediately upon the Norman conquest of the island.[37] In specific, we actually see a change in Geniza documentation already in the later eleventh century. Geniza letters that refer to trade between Sicily and the Muslim world abound from the period up through the 1060s, while their numbers drop off significantly after 1072. The Norman conquest of Sicily was not fully complete until after thirty years of Christian activity on the island, but many scholars point to the year 1072 as the decisive one—this was the year in which both Māzara and Palermo, the island's two most active ports, were conquered, and the Norman capital was established at Palermo. This concurrence of military conquest and a sharp reduction in the evidence for cross-Mediterranean trade has led some to suggest that the Norman takeover of Sicily resulted in a real decline in trade between the island and its Muslim neighbors in Africa. Despite the appearance of causality, however, other evidence demonstrates that the commercial relationship between Christian Sicily and Muslim North Africa continued to operate on some level, despite the creation of this new religiopolitical boundary in the Mediterranean.

37. Goitein, "Sicily and Southern Italy," 9–33.

During the Islamic period of rule on Sicily—particularly the tenth and first half of the eleventh century—the island's economy did not function independently of that of North Africa. While we cannot quantitatively measure the degree to which the economies of Sicily, Egypt, and Ifrīqiya relied on the trade in raw materials, finished products, and foodstuffs that circulated between them, we can clearly see that Sicily was closely linked into the Islamicate world of the Mediterranean region through webs of commercial relationships that were mutually beneficial and interdependent. The significant drop-off in the Geniza documentation—our primary, but not sole, source of information for such trade and communication—in the second half of the eleventh century does appear to coincide perfectly with the onset of Norman rule on the island. And the idea that a thriving trade among three neighbors within the dār al-Islām ended when one of those partners fell into Christian hands accords with common sense, especially in light of the common view that the Latin conquest caused the island and its culture, economy, and communication networks to become reoriented toward the Latin Christian world. This conclusion makes sense if we consider the Norman invasion to have been creating a new boundary line dividing the Muslim and Christian worlds: the drawing of a new border, many miles south of the previous line, could be imagined to have cut off the trade connections that linked the island with its previous trading partners among coreligionists.

However, other sources of evidence show that the cessation of these connections was neither immediate nor complete. Trade and communication between newly Christian Sicily and Muslim North Africa persisted, both during and after the Norman conquest. Latin domination of this formerly Muslim island did not, in fact, create a sharp dividing line between northern and southern shores of the Mediterranean Sea. By looking not only at the evidence found in Geniza documents but also at the North African *fatwās*, we find that commercial and social connections endured between Sicily and parts of North Africa both during and after the Norman takeover of the island, meaning that the creation of a new political and religious boundary did not prevent a certain type of unity from remaining in the central Mediterranean region. Therefore, the change in Geniza evidence must have resulted from other factors, such as the emigration of many of Sicily's Jews or a slowdown in trade with Egypt (where the Geniza community was based), even while Sicily continued trading with Ifrīqiya. That is, the apparent change in commercial traffic after the Norman invasion may really only reflect a shift in the types of sources that record this traffic. Trade, particularly in wheat, between Norman Sicily and Muslim North Africa in fact persisted well into the twelfth century, roughly one hundred years after the Normans' initial incursion into Sicily. By the thirteenth century, however, it had become clear that the Mediterranean world had been transformed fundamentally, as Sicily was increasingly left behind by the northern Italian merchants who dominated cross-Mediterranean trade.[38]

This persistence of trade despite interreligious warfare can be witnessed even during the Norman invasion. The Geniza letters document continued communication in the years of fiercest fighting in the 1060s, amid frequent land and naval battles and rapid Norman advances. In fact, merchant letters found in the Cairo Geniza were written to, from, and about Sicily throughout the thirty-year conquest, even though some letters noted the disruptions caused by the fighting.[39] Several of these merchant-authors explicitly mentioned the progress of the Christian forces in Sicily and the deleterious effects that warfare was having on its population as well as on markets, prices, and the availability of foodstuffs. At the same time, these letters also contain references to shipments of merchandise arriving at Sicilian ports and business transactions taking place on the island. Such sources thus show both the disorder caused by foreign invasion and the continuity of commerce and communication between the island and the mainland of Africa—letters, people, and merchandise clearly found ways to get back and forth to Sicily despite the turmoil and possibilities of danger.

Several Geniza letters from the 1060s refer to trade deals carried out without any mention of interference by Norman naval or military activity. For example, a load of lac can be followed on a route from Egypt to Sicily and from there to Ifrīqiya in the early 1060s. Mentioned by a merchant named Yūsuf b. Mūsā in a letter written from al-Mahdiyya and dated to 1063, this shipment of lac had been dispatched from Egypt and had caused the author much trouble; after expending considerable effort, he had been unable to get ahold of it.[40] It arrived from Egypt at the southwestern Sicilian port of Mazara del Vallo, but from there it was sent on to Palermo against Yūsuf's wishes. Yūsuf claimed that he had written several times, asking that the cargo be sent to him in North Africa, but that his request had not yet been fulfilled. This one bundle

---

38. See Abulafia, *The Two Italies*, and Backman, *The Decline and Fall*. For the modern legacies of this notion of economic and social decline in southern Italy and Sicily, see Lucy Riall, "Which Road to the South? Revisionists Revisit the Mezzogiorno," *Journal of Modern Italian Studies* 51, no. 1 (2000): 89–100.

39. This evidence prompted Abraham Udovitch to remark that although the transfer of Sicily from Muslim to Christian rule was significant within the larger picture of the medieval Mediterranean, "its immediate impact on many areas of Sicilian life and of Sicily's relationship to other parts of the Mediterranean were neither very dramatic nor disruptive." Abraham L. Udovitch, "New Materials for the History of Islamic Sicily," in *Del Nuovo sulla Sicilia Musulmana*, ed. Biancamaria Scarcia Amoretti (Rome: Accademia Nazionale de Lincei, 1993), 196.

40. Cambridge, T-S 13J233.18, T-S AS 145.81; Ben-Sasson, 292ff.; Simonsohn, doc. 149.

thus traveled from Egypt to two different ports in Sicily, and it was intended to travel further, to North Africa. Norman military forces had been active on the island for around three years at that point, but the troubles Yūsuf experienced with his load of lac appear to have had nothing to do with invasion and warfare; instead, he experienced difficulties in his interpersonal relationships with his business partners.

Likewise, the merchant Salāma b. Mūsā Safāqusī ("the Sfaxian") wrote a letter from Māzara to Egypt in 1064.[41] In this missive he reported that he had left a cargo of flax in Palermo to be sold for him over the winter, but when he arrived back in that city, he found it unsold. The price of flax had dropped from seventy to forty dinars in the meantime, and Salāma could not find a buyer. He also recounted, later in the letter, that he then shipped the cargo to the port of Sfax, in North Africa, where demand had been on the rise—before the arrival of a shipload of flax that caused a glut on the market and a drop in prices. He was able to sell it there, however, and to make a profit, despite the flooding of the markets in both Palermo and Sfax.[42] Letters such as these recount the common struggles involved in transregional commerce but make no mention of Norman advances in Sicily or Christian naval activity disrupting such trade.

On the other hand, some Geniza letters do explicitly describe the effects of the Norman invasion on their authors' commercial endeavors. One such letter was written in the first half of the 1060s, again by the merchant Salāma, and sent from Māzara to his business partner in Egypt, Yehūda b. Moshe b. Sigmar.[43] Salāma informed his partner that he had suffered a year of great difficulties in the business of importing goods to Sicily from North Africa and had relocated from Sfax to Māzara by means of a perilous sea crossing.[44] As one example, he detailed the trouble he had experienced in carrying out a clandestine import of indigo, for which he was denounced to the "sultan" (Muʿizz ibn Badis, the Zīrid *emīr* of Ifrīqiya) and which he was then required to smuggle to the Maghrib rather than Palermo because he could not find a ship sailing directly to the Sicilian port. He finally arrived in Palermo without any goods or cash and found prices there extremely low, the port blocked, and all of his own money tied up in partnerships with other Jews and with Muslims.

41. Philadelphia, Dropsie College 389; Ben-Sasson, 65ff. Simonsohn, doc. 151.

42. See also Salāma's subsequent letter for more information about this load of flax: Philadelphia, Dropsie College 414; Ben-Sasson, 89ff.; Simonsohn, doc. 152.

43. Philadelphia, Dropsie College 389; Ben-Sasson, 65ff. Simonsohn, doc. 151.

44. Transcription and translation in Moshe Gil, "The Jews in Sicily under Muslim Rule, in the Light of the Geniza Documents," in *Italia judaica, Atti del I Convegno internazionale, Bari 18–22 maggio 1981* (Rome: Ministero per i beni culturali e ambientali, 1983), 87–134.

Things only got worse from there: Salāma put a cargo of oil onto a ship to Māzara (in partnership with a Muslim merchant) that was then to be sent to his partner in Egypt. That ship was "driven away by the enemy" at al-Shāqqa (Sciacca) and then it sank.[45] The Muslim in charge of the ship then stole the oil and sold it for his own profit. In the following lines Salāma went on to mention that the fleet at al-Mahdiyya had mobilized and sailed to Sfax (which then caused ships in that port to be seized and stripped of their merchandise).

In this letter we see that trade and commerce certainly could be disrupted during this time of naval attacks by both Muslim and Christian vessels, but that movements of goods, people, and information did not cease. Norman blockades of the port of Palermo and the sinking of commercial ships on the southern coast of the island were matched by the seizure of such ships by the fleet of the ruler of Ifrīqiya. Merchant vessels had to skirt around danger areas and find alternate ports, but businessmen like our author persisted, and ships continued to sail. Salāma's letter went on to detail shipments arriving by boat in Māzara and the revenues he collected from their sale. His personal travels, combined with those of his merchandise and missives, included stops in al-Mahdiyya, Sfax, Sūsa, Palermo, Māzara, Fusṭāṭ, and Alexandria, as well as encounters with various enemy ships at sea and in port. This juxtaposition of war and trade in a single letter highlights the fact that the Mediterranean Sea in the area around Sicily and Ifrīqiya was a violent place during the 1060s but could nonetheless prove profitable. Despite the obvious disruption caused by the enemy warships and the depressing effect that the conquest had on commerce in Palermo, business and communication between Sicily, Egypt, and Ifrīqiya continued.

Other Geniza letters dated to the 1060s similarly recount the devastating results of Norman activity on the island. One Jewish merchant, a native of Sicily who had fled to Tyre, wrote to a relative in Fusṭāṭ with a personal tale of the destruction taking place in Sicily at the time.[46] The author described rampant violence and illness, the plundering of his warehouses, and the sharp increase in prices, especially of foodstuffs. Another such letter explicitly mentions the fall of Messina to the Normans in 1061.[47] Written by the chief Jewish judge of al-Mahdiyya and sent to Nahray b. Nissīm in Fusṭāṭ, the missive reveals both the news of the advance of Norman troops in Sicily and the consequences of this violence for food supplies in Ifrīqiya. Both Muslims and Jews had been

---

45. Philadelphia, Dropsie College 389, l. 31. Transcription and translation of this letter in Gil, "The Jews in Sicily," 113–126.

46. Cambridge T-S. 13J 3, fol. 27.

47. St. Petersburg, Institute Narodov Azii, D-55, n. 13. See also S. D. Goitein, *Letters of Medieval Jewish Traders* (Princeton: Princeton University Press, 1973), 163–168.

killed and taken captive, the author wrote, and everyone on the island lived in fear of the advancing Normans: "The situation deteriorates constantly, and everyone is terribly disturbed about the progress of the enemy, who has already conquered most of the island. . . . Twelve families of our coreligionists have been taken captive, and countless numbers of Muslims."[48] The author also noted that prices in al-Mahdiyya were rising because "this place must rely for its supply of grain entirely on Sicily."[49] Sicily's grain cultivation was a significant part of the economy and subsistence of Muslims in Ifrīqiya during the ninth and tenth centuries, when grain was a regular commodity in intra-Mediterranean trade, and continued to be important in the eleventh and twelfth centuries. This letter, along with other, later *fatwā* evidence, suggests that the Ifrīqiyan reliance on Sicily's grain yield may even have been increasing in the late eleventh and twelfth centuries. Famine, rampant violence, and political upheaval made Ifrīqiyans ever more in need of foodstuffs from Sicily, in the midst of active warfare and under threat of the island falling under Christian control and, later, despite the Islamic legal prohibition against trade with infidels.[50]

A final set of examples will suffice to underscore the persistence of trade despite, and amid, violence and disorder in the wake of the Norman advances. A Geniza letter written sometime in the second half of the 1060s noted that many of the island's inhabitants were fleeing to Ifrīqiya because of the Norman victories.[51] The overall situation in Sicily was deemed horrible: prices were high, people were seeking escape, and the Christians held most of the island (outside, the author noted, of Palermo, Māzara, and Castrogiovanni). Additionally, the author wrote that he had heard that prices of wheat in Ifrīqiya were exorbitant, likely as a result of the shortfall in imports from Sicily. But still, shortfalls and rising prices do not mean that there was a complete cessation of trade and shipping. Indeed, the very fact of these letters' arrival demonstrates that information was traveling across this militarized boundary—the letters sailed on ships alongside both people and commodities. Another document from around 1065 was written from Muslim-controlled Palermo to

48. Goitein, *Letters*, 167.

49. Ibid.

50. Eleventh-century Ifrīqiya was experiencing a food shortage and famine caused in part by the destruction following invasions by Bedouin tribes. Agricultural fields had been destroyed, the Zīrid government had fled from its capital at Qayrawān, and some among the Muslim and Jewish population were fleeing. North Africans who stayed were thus dependent on outside regions for grain because local cultivation had become difficult. This upheaval of Ifrīqiyan political and agricultural systems may have caused some of the people represented in these *fatwās* to invest in commercial journeys to Sicily for the purpose of purchasing food.

51. Mosseri Coll. II, 128 (L 130)2, S. 158.

a business partner in Fusṭāṭ, detailing various transactions and the merchandise that had been sold in Sicily. This cargo included pearls, flax, silk, and indigo, that is, both luxury goods and raw materials for the textile industry, all common items of trade found in Geniza letters from the earlier decades. Examples such as these persisted in the Geniza evidence throughout the 1060s, demonstrating that commerce continued in the years preceding and during the Norman takeover. Violence on land and at sea disrupted prices, demographics, and personal experiences of travel and commercial exchange, but ships kept sailing between Sicily and the southern shores of the Mediterranean, and those trips were documented by letters found in the Cairo Geniza. Correspondence, money, and news traveled to and from Sicily on the ships arriving and departing its shores, indicating a somewhat regular communication between the island and other regions of the Mediterranean, despite the invasion and its disruptions. However, very few Geniza letters about Sicilian trade or affairs exist from after 1072—the year in which the two most important Sicilian ports, Palermo and Māzara, were transferred to Christian control. One such later Geniza document, from the middle of the twelfth century, shows that some Jewish merchants continued to import spices to Sicily after the Norman conquest. This letter notes the shipment of a quantity of pepper and ginger intended for sale on the island.[52] Other merchants from the Geniza community may also have maintained trade connections with Christian Sicily, but the records from after 1072 are far less numerous than those from the previous years.

The trade record from the late eleventh and early twelfth century may be scarce in the Geniza documents, but evidence for exchange does exist in several *fatwās* issued by North African jurists of the period. Based in Zīrid Ifrīqiya, these Islamic legal experts answered questions and adjudicated disputes about a wide variety of issues of concern to Muslims from their region. Many legal responsa addressed matters related to trade, especially in food items. A number of the texts deal specifically with commerce between Sicily and Ifrīqiya in the decades following the transfer of the island into Christian hands. For the century during and after the Norman invasion, the *fatwās* of Imām al-Māzarī (ca. 1061–1141) are particularly helpful in proving that North African merchants continued to carry out exchanges in Sicily in order to obtain food, especially wheat. One of the *fatwās* that we will examine below directly addresses the question of the legality of such trade with the Christian infidels, demonstrating that the practice was controversial, although considered necessary by many

52. Cambridge, T-S 12.337; Simonsohn, doc. 178, fol. 1a, ll. 26–28.

people in this famine-ravaged region.[53] This set of sources, then, establishes that the drop-off in Geniza documentation of trade between Muslim North Africa and newly Christian Sicily must have resulted from forces other than the cessation of commercial relations between the two places, which had formerly been so closely connected economically. It may indeed have resulted from migration: Jewish emigration to North Africa or Egypt may have redirected most of the commercial activity that had been carried out on the island by this one community of Jewish merchants. Such migration would have effectively ended the Geniza record of trade with the island even if the trade itself did not collapse. Another possible cause of this change in documentation may be that the trade between Sicily and Egypt (where the Geniza records were located) did experience a significant decline, while that with Ifrīqiya continued; the legal records that show Muslims traveling to Latin Christian Sicily for commerce only apply to trade with Ifrīqiya, while the Geniza letters documented the activity of Jews with connections to Egypt. It may also be that the Zīrid lands, experiencing famine and invasion by Bedouin groups, depended on Sicily for grain imports in ways that Egypt did not. In any case, it is clear that economic connections to Muslim Ifrīqiya were maintained not only at the time of the Norman invasion of Sicily but also in the decades following the consolidation of their rule. They were not unaltered, but they were also not severed.

Many of these twelfth-century legal sources provide only the barest details about the economic exchange involved, instead focusing on the dilemma that led the disputants to bring their question before the *qāḍī*. What we learn from these *fatwā*s in general is twofold: one, that merchants and other people in Muslim Ifrīqiya continued to sail to Christian Sicily seeking, primarily, foodstuffs, and two, that such economic voyages must have happened with some regularity, since they appear to have been a topic of much discussion in contemporary Ifrīqiya. Although, again, we cannot quantify these exchanges with any exactitude, we can surmise that they must have been fairly frequent, both because the extant sources only record commercial journeys that experienced a problem (and only a portion of such legal responses were collected and survived) and because one case, discussed below, directly addressed the regularity of such trade. The majority of these *fatwā*s, however, mention trade with Latin Christian Sicily simply by way of explaining the legal dispute and its

53. Although the dating of these *fatwā*s is not specific, we know they were issued before al-Māzarī's death in 1141, and thus it seems more than likely that they were delivered subsequent to the major Norman conquests in Sicily. In 1072 al-Māzarī would have been eleven years old and probably was not issuing learned legal judgments yet.

resolution, so it is merely an accident of source survival that we learn of these exchanges at all.

One such case featured an association between three partners who contributed goods in kind (sumac and donkeys) for exchange in Sicily.[54] Their ship was pushed back by the wind to the port of al-Mahdiyya, and the journey was declared unsuccessful, so al-Māzarī pronounced the dissolution of their contract. We do not learn what product(s) they sought in Sicily, or whether the partnership was re-formed for a second attempt at the exchange. Another similar case is that of an investor who provided money (in *murabiṭūns*, or Almoravid gold dinars) to a traveling merchant for the trip to Sicily, but an encounter with enemy ships wreaked havoc on their business partnership.[55] The traveler reached the island, purchased some goods with that money, and boarded a ship to return to Ifrīqiya. However, a problem arose on this return journey when the ship's passengers were informed of the presence of a nearby enemy vessel and were thus forced to disembark, at which point all of the goods were surrendered to the commander of a nearby fortress.[56] We learn neither what products were sought from Sicily nor for whom those "enemy ships" were working (we might presume that they were Norman vessels, but many other ships would also have been active in the region at the time, including many privateers). This case again demonstrates that, although commercial voyages to Christian Sicily carried both the possibility of physical dangers and the risk of losing one's investment, such business ventures continued to occur with some frequency: investors supported these journeys, merchants remained willing to embark on such a trip, and ships still sailed between Muslim North Africa and Christian Sicily.

We see this continuance of trade yet again in another legal case decided by Imām al-Māzarī. This conflict involved a ship chartered in Sicily for the journey to North Africa and a dispute over the intended destination and freight charges.[57] This *fatwā* states that a boat ("qārib"), belonging to two unnamed associates, was hired in Sicily and arrived at al-Mahdiyya, although some of those on board the ship insisted that the original destination had been Gabes. One of the partners agreed with this assertion, while the other claimed that the goal of the trip had always been al-Mahdiyya. Al-Māzarī adjusted the freight charges based on the ship's actual destination of al-Mahdiyya, whether

54. al-Wansharīsī, 8: 181–182.

55. al-Wansharīsī, 8: 207–208. For more on Mediterranean trade in these Almoravid dinars, see Constable, *Trade and Traders*, esp. 50 and 202–203.

56. The exact location of the fortress is not stated, but I read this as meaning that it was on the southern shores of the Mediterranean Sea.

57. al-Wansharīsī, 8: 305–306.

or not it was the originally intended port of disembarkation.[58] This case is intriguing for its Sicilian point of origin; most of the other journeys found in these *fatwās* sailed to Sicily from North Africa. Presumably the ship's passengers were either Sicilian Muslims or North African ones who had earlier sailed to Sicily and were returning home. Either way, this piece of evidence reveals, at the very least, that merchants were at that time still able to find passage on ships sailing from Norman Sicily to Muslim Ifrīqiya.[59]

A third legal case adjudicated by Imām al-Māzarī demonstrates that the desire for wheat from Sicily may have been widespread among the Ifrīqiyan population and, therefore, that such commercial journeys may have been quite common. The *fatwā* presents the case of a woman who had provided some of her personal jewelry as part of a commercial partnership aimed at procuring foodstuffs ("ṭaᶜām," likely indicating wheat) from Sicily.[60] The woman, acting through an agent, handed over a ring and a silver bracelet to be sold and exchanged for the Sicilian commodity, which was to be shipped to the Ifrīqiyan port of al-Mahdiyya. There, the profits were to be split in half by the two parties; however, when the wheat arrived in al-Mahdiyya, it was sold by the agent. A dispute arose between the merchant and one of the woman's family members, who claimed that the wheat (specified here as merchandise, "biḍāᶜa") had not been intended for sale by the agent but rather by the woman's family.[61] It is uncertain whether this case represents the search for food by a family in North Africa or a shrewd investment at a time when Sicilian grain was considered an expensive and desirable commodity. As with many of the other *fatwās*, this commercial exchange cannot be dated precisely, but since al-Māzarī was born in 1061 and died in 1141, it is certain that this response was given some time after the Norman takeover of Sicily. The important conclusions to be drawn from this anecdote are that a woman in late-eleventh- or early-twelfth-century Ifrīqiya was able to find an agent who would trade her silver for wheat in Christian Sicily and that Sicilian wheat was considered to be a profitable investment when sold in al-Mahdiyya. Like the other such cases, all of which can be dated only generally to after the inception of the Norman conquest of Sicily, this example helps to demonstrate that ships could be found sailing between Sicily and various North African ports, and that Mus-

58. al-Wansharīsī, 8: 305–306.

59. Later in the twelfth century, Ibn Jubayr, whose visit to Sicily in 1184–1185 is discussed in chapter 5, stated that Sicily's Muslims were under a travel ban that prohibited them from freely departing the Latin Christian island.

60. al-Wansharīsī, 8: 208.

61. Claiming to act in the name of the owner of the jewels, the questioner asserted that the jewels had been given to her nearest relative, who was entitled to sell the merchandise ("biḍāᶜa") as part of the services relatives owed each other. Imām al-Māzarī, al-Wansharīsī, 8: 208.

lim merchants and investors continued to form partnerships for the exchange of goods in Sicily, despite the island's transfer to Christian rule and the flight of many Arabic-speaking Jews and Sicilian Muslims away from it. The fact of such interreligious trade appears to be unproblematic in these brief notices about commercial exchanges gone wrong. The legality of the trade, in these particular *fatwās*, was not the question that elicited the legal intervention.

However, alongside these cases is one *fatwā* that reveals the fragile and contentious nature of the continued link between Norman Sicily and Muslim Ifrīqiya, in the form of a religious-legal debate about conducting commerce across the Muslim-Christian border. Dating from the late eleventh century, this case, like those above, presents an example of the enduring trade links between the two regions even after the fall of Sicily to the Normans. In addition, it records evidence of a public deliberation over the legality of such commerce with infidels and of the opposition of many prominent Ifrīqiya jurists to maintaining this connection with newly Christian Sicily.[62] The *fatwā* begins like the ones discussed above, with the details of a commercial partnership intended to obtain merchandise in Sicily and the ensuing conflict among the partners. It is stated that ships departing from al-Mahdiyya and sailing to Sicily contained the belongings and gold dinars of a large and varied group of people (many of them identified as regular people rather than as professional merchants), a cargo meant to be exchanged for food supplies ("aqwāt") in Sicily.[63] The individual investors had pooled their resources in the coinages of both Tripolitan and Almoravid gold dinars.[64] However, because of the minting practices of the head of the Norman Sicilian mint, there was confusion about the exchange rate and the resulting prices of the wheat, and thus the share each person was due from the partnership. In particular, the investors discovered that when their gold dinars arrived in Christian Sicily, the mintmaster melted down their gold and mixed it with silver. The business deal was then carried out in the debased Sicilian currency (the quarter dinar, known in Norman Sicily as the *tari*).[65] This process of forcing monetary exchange and alloying the coins then resulted in disagreement among the investors as to how to divvy up the purchased supplies

---

62. Although the *fatwā* is not dated, it must have been issued sometime before 1093 CE, the date of the death of Abu al-Hamid, one of the jurists involved in the public discussion recorded in the *fatwā*.

63. al-Wansharīsī, 6: 317–318, 7th question.

64. The Almoravids had been advancing across northwestern Africa since the 1050s, conquering the Maghrib and, by the late eleventh century, al-Andalus; their dynasty was replaced by that of the Almohads in 1147.

65. For more on the *tari* as an adaptation of the earlier Sicilian Muslim quarter dinar, see chapter 3.

when the ship returned to al-Mahdiyya with its cargo. The *qāḍī* was asked to adjudicate the dispute, but before answering the question, Imām al-Māzarī took the opportunity to condemn both this voyage and commercial interaction with Sicily in general, claiming that economic travel between Muslim and Christian lands was opposed to Islamic law and harmful to Muslim societies.[66]

In addition to an outright condemnation of trade with Christian Sicily, about which Imām al-Māzarī had pronounced judgments several times (without recording any opposition to it), the *fatwā* went on to describe a meeting of jurists in Qayrawān who debated the legality of commercial voyages to Christian Sicily. The response states that in previous pronouncements (which are apparently lost to us) Imām al-Māzarī had declared that Muslims should not travel to Sicily due to the prevailing infidel (Christian) law, to which those Muslims would be subject upon arrival on the island. This ruling was obviously not universally agreed upon, however, since the *fatwā* records that the sultan then gathered all of the local *qāḍīs* to decide upon the problem of food supplies from Christian Sicily and the necessity of trade with infidels and travel to Christian lands. In the midst of this meeting a contentious debate broke out between the assembled jurists, who were at odds over the prescriptions of Islamic law (*fiqh*) and the best way to reconcile legal reasoning with the need for sustenance for the hungry population of Ifrīqiya. Imām al-Māzarī, despite his other judgments on several cases in which Muslim North Africans sailed to Sicily for food and commercial goods (without, so far as we can tell, remarking on the legality of the trips), declared that Muslims should never willingly enter an infidel land and subject themselves to infidel law, regardless of the urgency of their necessity for food.[67] Other legal scholars opposed this opinion—presumably because they recognized that the urgency was so great—and the assembly then consulted the aged jurist ʿAbd al-Hamid b. al-Saʾigh (d. 1093 CE). He supported and clarified al-Māzarī's position with the explanation that if Muslims purchased goods on the Christian island, prices there would rise, and the Sicilian infidels would then be able to raise large sums of money with which to wage war against Muslim regions (which they in fact did in the second half of the twelfth century).

There are indications in this *fatwā* that such interfaith trade was well known and of widespread concern in late eleventh-century Ifrīqiya. Imām al-Māzarī's response to the question about Sicilian minting practices states that he had previously and on numerous occasions forbidden travel to Sicily—despite the fact

66. al-Wansharīsī, 6: 317–318, 7th question.

67. See chapter 5 for a comparison of this legal injunction with Imām al-Māzarī's position on the legality of native Sicilian Muslims continuing to live on the island after the Norman takeover.

that we know that he also adjudicated disputes concerning several such journeys. His objection was based on the laws of the infidels to which such traveling Muslims would be subjected when entering a non-Muslim territory, rather than on the legality of interreligious trade itself. It is possible that the rulings discussed above were among the *fatwās* referred to here, without leaving an account of his objections, and it is equally probable that many similar cases took place but do not show up in the extant records. The few examples here, of continued trade links and a reliance on Sicily for food in North Africa, may well represent only the tip of an iceberg of trade between Muslim North Africa and Christian Sicily. In any event, the reference to al-Māzarī's repeated opposition to Muslims traveling to Christian Sicily suggests that a number of local people were investing in trade with Sicily and that ships were sailing there on a regular basis, either ignoring or ignorant of these legal pronouncements against such trade. Clearly, therefore, the above examples of commercial voyages to Sicily are not only isolated cases of small-scale investors who engaged in cross-cultural overseas trade between Ifrīqiya and Norman Sicily but rather represent a much more widespread phenomenon. Indeed, the number of such cases must have been relatively high to have inspired the assembly called by the sultan and to have prompted repeated condemnations by al-Māzarī.

The fact that evidence for commercial journeys between Ifrīqiya and Norman Sicily remains, despite such reproach, also demonstrates that, during a time of crisis in North Africa, some individuals were willing to risk censure by their religious officials to obtain profitable commodities (especially, as in this case, food) from wherever they could, even if that was a Christian land. It is clear, therefore, that people were traveling back and forth between Christian Sicily and Islamic North Africa with some regularity, even in periods of political and religious turmoil. This evidence also reveals that Sicily had been—and remained—a vital economic resource for North Africa. Muslim merchants and investors in these deals faced the disapproval of some religious and legal leaders, but either the desire for profit or the need for food at a time of famine and food shortages spurred them to continue doing business in Christian Sicily. The island clearly still received ships from Muslim North Africa, and vice versa. We see no evidence that travelers had difficulty finding passage on ships bound for Sicily. Ifrīqiyan merchants, investors, and citizens obviously looked to the Christian island—even in the face of judicial objection—as a profitable place to do business or as a source of grain, especially important during a famine at home.

Thus it appears that the mid-eleventh-century creation of a new political and religious boundary in the Mediterranean was not paralleled by the formation of an economic divide, despite the sometimes-problematic nature of traveling across the religiopolitical line. Instead, we find a permeable boundary across which, despite numerous difficulties and potential obstructions, a type of unity in communications continued. Although the Norman conquest of Sicily created the potential for a cessation of the shipping and commercial exchange between the island and North Africa, it is clear that some level of exchange persisted—and that it was vital for the Ifrīqiyan, and also the Sicilian, economy. The centuries following the Norman takeover witnessed major changes in the patterns of interregional commerce, the types of goods exchanged, the merchants who conducted the business, and the documentation by which we learn of these exchanges. Egyptian Jewish merchants, for instance, clearly visited Norman Sicily far less frequently than before. However, as the *fatwā* evidence demonstrates, the first several decades after the conquest were ones in which ships continued to sail between the island and North Africa in order to transact exchanges of gold, wheat, and other goods, even if this trade was harried by war and the dilemmas involved in interreligious commerce. And, as we will see below, economic exchanges were not the only motivations for travel between Norman Sicily and Muslim Africa: some people moved across this new boundary line in order to flee from the rising power of the Christians and to relocate their families. Travel to and from Norman Sicily was rarely easy or peaceful, but it certainly persisted into the late eleventh and early twelfth centuries.

Population Movements and Demographic Change

When the Normans arrived in Sicily, they encountered a population that was majority Arabic-speaking Muslims (including many who were descended from North African Berbers and converts from Greek Christianity) along with a significant community of Greek Christians who had resisted conversion to Islam and maintained their customs of religious practice and local rule throughout the period of Muslim dominion.[68] Likewise, despite the Norman conquest, Latin Christian Sicily had a majority Muslim population for many years; a significant number of Muslims remained on the island until the first quarter of the thirteenth century.[69] Latin immigration to the island was by no measure

---

68. Norman invaders encountered Greek Christians in several of the towns they attacked and obviously expected them to support the efforts of the Christian conquerors; Geoffrey of Malaterra seemed surprised that these Christians instead chose to remain under their Muslim overlords. See Malaterra, *De rebus gestis*, 2.14 and 2.29.

69. David Abulafia has estimated the island's population at the time of the Norman conquest to have been roughly 250,000 Muslims. See David Abulafia, "The End of Muslim Sicily," in *Muslims*

systematic or rapid, and the Normans had an economic interest in maintaining a population of Muslims for work in the agricultural fields. The continuance of Muslim habitation in Christian Sicily does not mean that there was stasis in Sicily's demographics, however: Sicily's Muslim community was steadily eroded over the course of the twelfth century, presumably due in part to invisible processes of acculturation and conversion and in part to Latin immigration and Muslim emigration.[70] Flight of Muslims from Sicily to the dār al-Islām certainly began the process of demographic change, but large-scale population movement was halted by the Normans after the imposition of a travel ban in the twelfth century. We have evidence that, during and after the Latin Christian conquest, both Muslims and Jews who had lived and worked on the island emigrated to Egypt and other Mediterranean Muslim lands, fleeing the onset of foreign dominion. However, patterns of migration at this time do not show a simple, unidirectional move away from an island that was falling increasingly into Christian hands. Ifrīqiya itself was experiencing the upheaval of invasion, migrations, famine, and political disorder, and we see some Muslims and Jews moving away from cities there and into Sicily, despite the Christian advances on the island. Having operated for around two centuries as an integral node in the communication networks of the Muslim central Mediterranean, Sicily would have continued to be a natural option for Muslims and Jews seeking refuge from Ifrīqiya. Ships regularly sailed between the two locations for commercial purposes and could also have been used by those seeking to flee to the island. And it may not have been immediately apparent to the inhabitants of the central Mediterranean region that the Christian invaders of Sicily were there to stay and to create an enduring Christian polity; land invasions and naval disruptions were a relatively common part of life in the region and not necessarily indicative of large-scale transformations in the regional balance of power. The drawing of the new religious and cultural boundary line between Latin Christendom and the dār al-Islām, in other words, was not a sudden and clear-cut process, and the movements of

---

Under Latin Rule, 1100–1300, ed. James M. Powell (Princeton, NJ: Princeton University Press, 1990; reprint, David Abulafia, *Commerce and Conquest in the Mediterranean, 1100–1500*, London, 1993.), 104. Graham Loud has pointed out the difficulty of determining population numbers either at the time of the conquest or during the thirteenth-century deportations. See Loud, "Communities, Cultures and Conflict," 149ff. For more on this community and the Islamic legal perspective on Muslims living under "infidel" rule, see chapter 5.

70. Some scholars have suggested that Muslim conversion to Christianity at this time was effected through the Greek Church and, perhaps, signalled reconversion to the faith of their distant ancestors who had converted to Islam after the Muslim conquest. See Jeremy Johns, "The Greek Church and the Conversion of Muslims in Norman Sicily?" *Byzantinische Forschungen* 21 (1995): 133–157. For another approach, albeit inconclusive, to this question, see Loud, "Communities, Cultures and Conflict." The issue of Muslim conversion will also be addressed in chapter 5.

migrants demonstrate the fluidity of travel that was maintained throughout the eleventh century.

It can be difficult to trace the exact patterns of Muslim emigration from Sicily or to determine the proportions of those who departed and those who stayed to live under Christian rule. Some pieces of direct evidence point to an exodus of Muslims from Sicily at the time of the Norman invasion, but the majority of emigrants to North Africa are known only by the indirect evidence of their family names and *nisbas* (a *nisba* is akin to a nickname by which an individual would be identified in association with a specific location, role, or other characteristic of importance to his identity). Biographical dictionary entries for a number of North African and Egyptian scholars, poets, and jurists with Sicilian heritage provide details about their lives, births, or activities on the island, but far more of the entries about people known as "Sicilians" contain no suggestion that the person in question ever set foot in Sicily. Rather, the only reason one has to suspect Sicilian ancestry is the survival of the *nisba* "al-Ṣiqillī," "the Sicilian," which typically indicated that the man's father or grandfather was known to have come from the island and that this bit of information remained an important identifier for the family. Although the biographical entries for most of these notable men do not directly inform us that their ancestors fled Sicily because of the Norman conquest, the dating of many of these lives suggests this to be the case.

In other words, there appear in biographical dictionaries a significant number of men with the identifier "al-Ṣiqillī" whose lives and careers in the dār al-Islām date from after the Norman takeover (in the eleventh, twelfth, and even thirteenth centuries)—in some cases one or more generations later. This persistence of "the Sicilian" as part of these men's identities likely indicates that their ancestors had originated on the island, had fled during or after the Norman takeover, and had maintained an association with the island—or at least a conceptual association through identification with it as a place of origin. Many such scholars retained that identifying nickname for another generation or even more, even though there is no evidence that they themselves ever traveled to the island.[71] Examples of elite North African men known as "Sicilians" but whose own personal lives did not intersect with the island itself include at least five known scholars whose lives dated from the twelfth

71. It is naturally possible for a person whose primary residence was Sicily to travel elsewhere and receive the nickname "the Sicilian." One example might be Abū al-Ḥasan al-Ṣiqillī, al-Ḥarīrī (d. 931/932), whose *nisba* is unexplained in his biography but who lived during the period of Muslim dominion and may have lived in or visited the island.

and thirteenth centuries.[72] The biography of the latest such scholar, Muḥammad al-Qurashī al-Ṣiqillī, who was born in Damascus in 1217 and died in Cairo in 1300, notes that his family fled from Sicily to North Africa and then traveled from there to the central Islamic lands, either immediately or after staying in the West for a time.[73] The persistence of identification as "the Sicilian" among some of the island's Muslim descendants living in North Africa and Egypt implies that, at least for some of the families who migrated, their Sicilian heritage remained a source of distinctive identity, one that could be inherited by sons who had no personal association with Sicily.

Some biographical dictionary entries suggest that their subjects' flight from the island was a result of the Norman invasion. Several famous scholars and poets are included among those Sicilian Muslims for whom there is direct evidence of their emigration from Sicily. Muḥammad b. al-Ḥasan b. ʿAlī, Abū Bakr al-Rabʿī al-Girgantī ("al-Girgenti," signifying a person associated with the southern Sicilian city of Agrigento) was a Mālikī jurist who taught in Sicily and in North Africa before moving to Alexandria, where he died in 1142/1143.[74] His biography, found in the work of al-Maqrīzī, does not explain the reason for the migration of this native Sicilian to the mainland of Africa. However, the date of his death suggests that he spent part of his career in Sicily under the Norman occupation before leaving for Egypt and left sometime after the takeover of the island.[75] Likewise, the most famous Arabic poet from Sicily, known as Ibn Ḥamdīs, was born in Sicily but moved to Spain in 1078/1079 and from there to al-Mahdiyya, where he served at the court of the Zīrid *emīr* Tamīm ibn al-Muʿizz, never returning to Sicily.[76] His biographical entry in the dictionary of Ibn Khallikān does not state the reason for his leaving the island, but the year of his departure from Sicily makes it clear that he moved due to the

72. Abū ʿAmr ʿUthmān b. ʿAlī al-Ṣiqillī (fl. 1100s), Muḥammad b. Ibrāhīm b. Mūsā Abū Bakr al-Tamīmī al-Miṣrī al-Ṣiqillī al-Ṣufī (dates unknown), Muḥammad b. Abī Bakr b. ʿAbd al-Razzāq Sharaf al-Dīn Abū ʿAbd Allāh al-Ṣiqillī (b. 1224/1225, d. in Cairo), Muḥammad b. Muḥammad b. Abī al-Faḍl (b. 1211/1212 in Egypt, d. 1293, known as Ibn al-Ṣiqillī), and Muḥammad b. Makkī b. Abī al-Dhikr b. ʿAbd al-Ghanī b. ʿAlī b. Yūsuf b. Ibrāhīm Shams al-Dīn Abū ʿAbd Allāh b. Taqī al-Dīn b. al-Ḥazm b. Abī al-Dhikr al-Qurashī al-Ṣiqillī (b. 1217 in Damascus, d. 1300 in Cairo). See Aḥmad ibn ʿAlī al-Maqrīzī, *Kitāb al-muqaffā al-kabīr*, *BAS* Arabic, 663–664.

73. His full name was Muḥammad b. Makkī b. Abī al-Dhikr b. ʿAbd al-Ghanī b. ʿAlī b. Yūsuf b. Ibrāhīm Shams al-Dīn Abū ʿAbd Allāh b. Taqī al-Dīn b. al-Ḥazm b. Abī al-Dhikr al-Qurashī al-Ṣiqilli. The path of this scholar's travels is not fully known, but it is clear that his family, likely of Sicilian origin, had made it to Damascus by the time of his birth in 1217.

74. The Malikites (or Mālikīs) were scholars adhering to one of the four most prominent Islamic traditions during the Middle Ages; the Mālikī tradition was widespread in the Islamic West, including Spain, North Africa, and Sicily.

75. al-Maqrīzī, *Kitāb al-muqaffā*, *BAS* Arabic, 664.

76. Ibn Khallikān, *Wafayāt*, 3: 212–215.

invasions of the Normans, in which case he would be one of the most notable representatives of such émigrés.[77]

Other biographical dictionaries from North Africa contain a number of entries that explicitly mention the Norman conquest as the reason behind a subject's flight from Sicily. Ibn al-Qaṭṭāᶜ, a writer and philologist who was born in Sicily in 1041, lived, worked, and died in Egypt.[78] Before emigrating from the island, he studied literature (*adab*) under several teachers in Sicily, including the master Ibn al-Birr. He left the island because of the Norman invasion, migrating first to al-Andalus and then to Egypt. His biography states that he departed when the Christians were on the verge of gaining complete control of Sicily, as opposed to Ibn Ḥamdīs's biography, which does not explain but only suggests the reason for his migration from Sicily. In 1106/1107 Ibn al-Qaṭṭāᶜ arrived in Egypt and taught there before he died in 1121.[79] Another scholar, the poet Abū al-ᶜArab al-Zubayrī, was born in Sicily in 1032 and left in 1072, we are told, due to the Norman conquest. Rather than migrating to North Africa, al-Zubayrī went from Sicily to Spain, on the invitation of the Muslim ruler of Seville, Muᶜtamid b. ᶜAbbād.[80] Like Ibn Ḥamdīs's, his route away from Sicily led to al-Andalus rather than to Ifrīqiya—possibly indicating that a stronger network of connection existed between the scholarly communities of the two regions than I have been able to reconstruct. However, it appears that the largest part of the Sicilian Muslims who fled the Norman invasion of Sicily in the eleventh century migrated to North Africa, as did Ibn al-Qaṭṭāᶜ. This pattern is likely due both to the geographical proximity of Ifrīqiya to Sicily and to the tradition of intellectual and political communication between the two regions. Scholars and other members of the Sicilian Muslim elite would have found not only political refuge but also a similar economy and culture, as well as friends and associates who could assist them in locating patronage and setting up their new homes and careers.

In addition to the Muslims who fled the Norman advances, Sicilian Jews also migrated away from the island, mostly also to North Africa, both during

77. William Granara argues that Ibn Ḥamdīs left Sicily for the Iberian court in order to further his career as a poet and then was prevented from ever returning to his homeland because of the Norman conquests. See Granara, "Ibn Ḥamdīs," 388–403. Whether he emigrated because of the Norman conquest or was simply prohibited from going back to Sicily because of it, the establishment of Christian rule in Sicily appears to have been the cause of the poet's relocation.

78. Ibn Khallikān, *Wafayāt*, 3: 322–324.

79. Ibid.: "rahalaᶜan Ṣiqilliya lamma ashraf ᶜalā tamallakhān al-Faranj, wa waṣala ilā Misr."

80. This anecdote is found in the biography of Abū Hasan al-Huṣrī. Ibn Khallikān, *Wafayāt*, 3: 331–334. "Wa ʾamma Abū al-ᶜArab al-Zubayrī fa-ʾinna wulida bi-Siqilliya sana thalāth wa ᶜashrīn wa arbaᶜmiʾa, wa kharaja min-hā lamma taghallaba al-Rūm ᶜalayhā sana arbaᶜ wa sittīn wa arbaᶜmiʾa qāsidan lil-Muᶜtamid b. ᶜAbbād" (334). According to this entry, al-Zubayrī died sometime after 1113/1114.

and after the conquest. Generally, the travel of Jews to and from Sicily during the Islamic and Norman periods of the island's history, as reflected in the letters of the Geniza collection, was relatively fluid, as it related to both commerce and residence. Jewish families appear to have moved somewhat regularly between Sicily and Egypt and North Africa. The origins and earliest settlement of Jews on the island cannot be dated, but it is clear that there were Jewish communities in Sicily from at least the Byzantine period, and likely by as early as the fourth century.[81] Little is known about these communities during the early centuries.[82] Later, the letters preserved in the Cairo Geniza supply scholars with a picture of the lives of some of the Jews who lived in Sicily during the tenth and eleventh centuries.[83] Many of them were connected, through networks of trade and family life, to the Jewish community in Fusṭāṭ, where the Geniza cache was compiled. Therefore, Sicily's Jews are seen through a lens that highlights their travel activities. The majority of the travel represented in the Geniza letters is that conducted for mercantile reasons, although a handful of letters refer to permanent or semipermanent relocations of individuals or families due to political or economic concerns.

The migration patterns of Jews during Sicily's Islamic period appear to go in both directions: we find Jews who relocated to Sicily as well as those who fled from Sicily to either Egypt or North Africa, depending upon the current state of affairs. Thanks to the Geniza evidence, in fact, Jewish migration is better documented than similar movements of Muslims. Some Sicilian Jews began to flee the island already in the late Kalbid period, escaping the turmoil of civil disorder and the economic upheaval that accompanied military conflict and political fragmentation. One of the earliest references to Jews moving away from Sicily dates from the first quarter of the eleventh century and demonstrates the ties between the Sicilian Jewish community and Jerusalem. This relationship is also attested in several later Geniza letters concerning aid collected by the Sicilian Jewish community for the benefit of their coreligionists in Palestine. One letter, discussed in chapter 3, explains the recent decline in donations with rising taxation on the island and the resulting impoverishment of the community, which caused a number of its members to emigrate.[84] Even without specific details of how many families relocated, to where, or how permanently, we can see that some of

---

81. See Simonsohn, ix–xi; see also his *Between Scylla and Charybdis*.

82. For a brief overview of what is known about them, see Nadia Zeldes, "Palermo and Sicily," in the *Encyclopedia of Jews in the Islamic World*, ed. Norman A. Stillman and Phillip Isaac Ackerman-Lieberman (Leiden: Brill, 2010): vol. 4, 1–5.

83. See in particular Gil, "The Jews in Sicily," 87–134; see also his *Jews in Islamic Countries*.

84. New York, Theol. Sem., Adler Coll. 4009.4; Ben-Sasson, 145ff.; Simonsohn, doc. 39.

the island's Jews evidently had the means and desire to leave Sicily when economic and political conditions made life there difficult for them. This freedom of mobility and the openness of borders in the central Mediterranean are themes sustained throughout the Geniza letters of the eleventh century, so it was not necessarily the coming of the Normans that initiated demographic change on the island, but instead the political disorder following the breakup of the Kalbid emīrate.

Later, the Norman invasion provoked even further emigrations of Jews, many of whom left records of the violence and disruption that prompted their flight. Numerous examples show the political and military strife caused by the Norman incursions. In one Geniza letter, for example, a Sicilian merchant recounted the tumultuous affairs of eleventh-century Sicily that forced him to remove his family from the island to Tyre, in the Levant.[85] This family had lived in Palermo, where they witnessed violence, famine, looting, inflation of food prices, and devaluation of land. Another letter refers directly to the Norman occupation of the island and mentions Sicilian Jews relocating to North Africa.[86] The author, Mūsā b. Abū al-Ḥay Khalīla, writing from Alexandria, informed his reader that the "enemy" had taken all of Sicily except Palermo, Māzara, and Castrogiovanni—indicating that he was writing prior to 1071 / 1072. Because of these advances, he wrote, Sicilians were fleeing to the coast of Africa, although he did not mention specific cities in which they were seeking refuge.[87] In another letter, by Ismāʿīl b. Faraḥ, written after his brother had arrived safely in Māzara, the author mentions ships arriving in Alexandria from Sicily, some of which carried refugees "from an accursed land."[88] In all, Ismāʿīl reported on the recent arrival in Egypt of ten ships from Sicily supposedly carrying five hundred people each. Whatever the actual number of refugees, the impression to be gained from this letter is that a large number of people were choosing to relocate from the island in order to escape the advance of the Norman forces. A later epistle from the same author again addressed the subject of the Jewish flight from Sicily. He wrote to his son that a ship carrying Sicilians from Palermo had docked in Alexandria, while a group of Maghribīs had at the same time sailed to Egypt from Māzara.[89] Ismāʿīl went on to say that he had, in the meantime, received another letter from his brother in

85. Cambridge, TS 13 J 13.27; Ben-Sasson, 24ff.; Simonsohn, doc. 131. See also *Medit. Soc.*, 1: 122.

86. Mosseri Coll., II, 128 (L 130)2; Ben-Sasson, 48ff.; Simonsohn, doc. 158. See also *Medit. Soc.*, 1: 100, 126.

87. Trans. in Simonsohn, doc. 158, ll. 17–18.

88. New York, Theol. Sem., Adler Coll. 2727.38; Ben-Sasson, 544ff.; trans. in Simonsohn, doc. 100, l. 5.

89. Cambridge, TS 10 J 20.12; Simonsohn, doc. 101.

Māzara, who reported that conditions on the island were terrible. This same letter stated that Ismāʿīl's sister and her family had fled from Sicily to al-Mahdiyya along with twenty-three other families. In this time of great political turmoil and violence in both North Africa and Sicily, many families appear to have been uprooted and to have moved several times, relying on their network of friends and associates to seek refuge and a safer situation. Although Jewish flight from Sicily began before the arrival of the Normans, the Christians' territorial gains on the island seem to have accelerated the pace and volume of such migration.

Many other documents from the Geniza collection also provide evidence of families split between Sicily and North Africa during the tenth and eleventh centuries, both before and after the Norman invasion of Sicily. Such Geniza letters include references to Sicilians living in Egypt or indications that different members of the same extended family were living in both locations. One such example is found in the record of a court case that settled a disagreement over property between two brothers, one of whom lived in Qayrawān, while the other resided in Palermo, where the disputed land was located. Abū Zikrī, his wife, and his wife's brothers were Jewish residents of eleventh-century Palermo, where Abū Zikrī operated a shop owned by his brother Samuel, who was at that time living in Qayrawān.[90] The document provides no information about the native land of this family or the length of Samuel's residence in Qayrawān. It does, however, demonstrate that Jews could and did move freely from Sicily to North Africa, and families could be found living and owning property in both places at once. Another court case referred to Sicilian merchants residing in Fusṭāṭ, but for how long or under what conditions is not clear. The letter in which this dispute is mentioned displays the close connections between Jewish merchants in Sicily, Ifrīqiya, and Egypt: the letter's author asked that the verdict be signed either by Egyptians who were known by the community of Jews in Sicily or by Ifrīqiyans who commonly traveled to Alexandria; this request suggests that the writer knew that such people would be numerous.[91] Another example of a family split by geography is that of a widow living in the Sicilian town of Ragusa who wrote to her son in Fusṭāṭ, asking him to return to Sicily to comfort her before her death.[92] Taken together, these examples from the Geniza material show not only that members of the larger Mediterranean Jewish mercantile community commonly traveled between Sicily, Ifrīqiya, and Egypt on business and for the

90. Paris, Alliance Israelite Universelle, VII D-108; Ben-Sasson, 121ff.; Simonsohn, doc. 75.

91. Cambridge, TS 12.371; Ben-Sasson, 439ff.; Simonsohn, doc. 76. See also introduction to Simonsohn, xxiii.

92. New York, Theol. Sem., Adler Coll. 3792.4; Simonsohn, doc. 132.

relocation of their families in response to current events, but also that various members of an extended family might live in different polities but remain in close contact via letters.

Sicily was not the only central Mediterranean location under siege in the eleventh century. Ifrīqiya itself was experiencing famine, Bedouin invasions, and political turmoil at the same time. Because of this, even though some Muslims and Arabic-speaking Jews fled from Sicily, others moved to Sicily from North Africa, as documented in a letter dated to September 1064.[93] Salāma b. Mūsā Safāqusī ("the Sfaxian") wrote to his business partner in Egypt from the Sicilian town of Māzara, a frequent place of refuge for those fleeing North Africa as it is directly across the straits from Ifrīqiya. His letter contains a narrative of his escape a year earlier from al-Mahdiyya, a city to which he had traveled on business (from his base at Sfax) and where he had encountered a "terrible situation" and bad business conditions. After shipping his goods to the Maghrib, Salāma sailed to Māzara and remained there during that year. Later in the letter he mentioned the impossibility of returning to North Africa, either to his hometown of Sfax or to one of the nearby port cities of Sūsa and al-Mahdiyya. Because contemporary Ifrīqiya seemed inhospitable, he then related the fact that he had purchased a house in Māzara and sent for his family to join him.[94] Despite the prevailing opinion among the Jews of the Geniza community that the Normans were "the enemy," this particular letter writer appears to have determined that Sicily was preferable to the economic and political chaos in North Africa; he may also have believed that the violence would not soon reach the southwestern part of the island (which did not fall to the Normans until 1072). Sicily could thus be a haven for some refugees, even while other families were moving elsewhere.

Jews represented in the Geniza letters also migrated to Sicily from Ifrīqiya during the same period. A letter from the mid-eleventh century mentions North African Jews fleeing the invasions of the Banū Hilāl Bedouins, some to the Ifrīqiyan coast and others all the way to southern Sicily. The letter's author, Ismāʿīl b. Faraḥ al-Qābisī, writing from Alexandria, informed his correspondent that his brother Sulaymān had fled from Qayrawān to Māzara in order to escape the violence wrought by these invaders and the ensuing economic crisis. Sulaymān and his family had been trying to leave Qayrawān for Sūsa, on the North African coast, for eight months, but had been continuously thwarted. When they finally did make it there, they found that city too

93. Philadelphia, Dropsie College 389; Ben-Sasson, 65ff.; Simonsohn, doc. 151. See also *Medit. Soc.*, 1: 245; 2: 68, 162, 294.

94. Philadelphia, Dropsie College 389; Ben-Sasson, 65ff.; Simonsohn, doc. 151, ll. 37–39

in political turmoil, leading them to travel further, to southern Sicily.[95] The widespread connections maintained by these Arabic-speaking Jews thus allowed them to move freely within the central Mediterranean, but this fact did not necessarily mean that they could easily find a safe location to move their families to during the tumultuous middle of the eleventh century.

It was not only Mediterranean Jews who sometimes made the choice to move away from war-ravaged Ifrīqiya and into Sicily while it was under invasion by the Latin Christians. I have found one anecdote about a Muslim scholar who migrated to Sicily, rather than away from it, in the middle of the eleventh century. Abū ʿAlī al-Ḥasan b. Rashīq al-Qayrawānī was a poet and scholar who was born in North Africa in the year 1000 and who later traveled to Qayrawān, where he composed poems under the patronage of the Zīrid *emīr* al-Muʿizz ibn Bādīs.[96] He left when that city was destroyed by the Bedouin invasions from 1054 to 1057, at which date the *emīr* himself abandoned Qayrawān in favor of al-Mahdiyya. The scholar moved to Māzara, where he died in 1070/1071. That city, so important as a commercial port and as the nearest city to Ifrīqiya, would fall to the Normans in the next year. Their first foray into the island had taken place only a few years after al-Qayrawānī's arrival in Sicily, where the poet lived during the decade of increasing Norman dominance there. The news of Christian advances on the island would not have been unknown in Māzara, and yet this one poet—and perhaps other Ifrīqiyans like him—determined that remaining on the island would be a better choice than returning to war-ravaged Ifrīqiya.

Thus we see that sea travel and the transfer of information continued between North Africa, Sicily, and Egypt despite the violence and political disruption, allowing people to respond to a threat by relocating their families, either temporarily or permanently. Jewish residents of the Mediterranean may have been especially willing or able to travel back and forth between Ifrīqiya, Sicily, and Egypt, given the fluidity of movement described in the Geniza letters. As in the above examples, many of the Jewish merchants represented in the Geniza records frequently moved around the Mediterranean for business or personal reasons—particularly within the triangle of Egypt, Sicily, and Ifrīqiya—and had ties to family members, friends, and business partners in other regions that could be exploited in times of need. They often held stores of merchandise in warehouses of several different cities and had established relationships with the communities in each of these locations, which possibly allowed their financial lives to recover even after the loss of home

95. London, Brit. Mus., Or. 5542.9; Ben-Sasson, 529ff.; Simonsohn, doc. 99.
96. Ibn Khallikān, *Wafayāt*, 2: 85–89.

and stock in one place. So, although individuals or families might have lived temporarily in Sicily or North Africa, their networks of friends and relations could extend throughout this triangle and even farther, to Palestine, the Levant, and sometimes Spain. When military invasion and political upheaval made it necessary to leave one place of residence, these Arabic-speaking Jews moved either to or from Sicily or even farther afield. At the same time, Muslims, too, were clearly migrating to and from Sicily for safety, commercial opportunities, and scholarly patronage. This multidirectional flow of migration, of both Muslims and Jews—as well as the choice by some to stay on the Christian-conquered island, which we will discuss in chapter 5—demonstrates the lack of a drastic or immediately obvious disruption in Mediterranean communications at the time of the Norman invasion of Sicily. Rather, the entire central Mediterranean region was in turmoil during the eleventh century, and despite the warfare, economic difficulties, and the dislocation of families, communications continued to flow between Sicily and its neighbors in the dār al-Islām: letters were sent and received, shipments of commercial goods were bought and sold, and families found new places of residence. Thus, although the Norman triumph would eventually transform the patterns of communication and travel in which Sicily was involved, the eleventh and early twelfth centuries saw a persistence of the networks that had linked the island to the Muslim lands of the Mediterranean and a continuation of the economic, scholarly, and personal connections that had been established during the preceding centuries of Muslim control over the island.

CHAPTER 5

Sicily at the Center of the Mediterranean

> The Muslims of this city [Palermo] preserve the remaining evidence of the faith. They keep in repair the greater number of their mosques, and come to prayers at the call of the muezzin. In their own suburbs they live apart from the Christians. The markets are full of them, and they are the merchants of the place. They do no congregate for the Friday service, since the *khutbah* [Friday sermon] is forbidden. On feast-days (only may) they recite it with intercessions for the ʿAbbasid Caliphs. They have a qadi to whom they refer their law-suits, and a cathedral mosque where, in this holy month, they assemble under its lamps. The ordinary mosques are countless, and most of them are used as schools for Koran teachers. But in general these Muslims do not mix with their brethren under infidel patronage, and enjoy no security for their goods, their women, or their children. May God, by His favour, amend their lot with His beneficence.
>
> Ibn Jubayr, *Riḥlat Ibn Jubayr*[1]

The communication patterns that linked Islamic Sicily to Ifrīqiya persisted for some time after the island fell into Latin Christian hands in the mid-eleventh century. Economically, for instance, Ifrīqiya still depended on Sicily for foodstuffs, even though the continuance of this trade presented problems for some in the religious-legal establishment in North Africa. Trade and communication with Egypt, on the other hand, were radically altered by the Norman invasion: the Jews of the Cairo Geniza community, at least, appear to have significantly curtailed their travel to Sicily for either

1. Muḥammad ibn Aḥmad ibn Jubayr, *Riḥlat Ibn Jubayr* (Beirut: Dār Ṣādir, 1964), 305–306. English translation in R. J. C. Broadhurst, *The Travels of Ibn Jubayr* (London: Jonathan Cape, 1952), 348–349.

mercantile or personal reasons after 1072.[2] That is, Sicily's connections to Muslim northern Africa were transformed in fundamental ways after the Norman takeover, but not through the creation of a thick and impenetrable Muslim-Christian boundary line; communications across political-religious lines did continue for a variety of reasons, even as they began to shift and change. Indeed, the Norman rulers were keen to ensure that Sicily, from the late eleventh through early thirteenth centuries, was broadly connected within the Mediterranean—to the Muslim regions of Egypt, Spain, and North Africa, to the Latin Christian world of Europe, and to the Byzantine- and crusader-controlled lands of the eastern Mediterranean. It is clear, however, that these networks of communication were adapted, established, or maintained by the Normans intentionally, for material or political gain, and either by military force or royal control.

The Normans attempted to use their base on the island as a hub of regional communication and a springboard for conquests in Africa, Greece, and the Balkans in ways that were unique to these rulers and their vision of a pan-Mediterranean kingdom. They utilized and exploited the preexisting networks of connection throughout the region, the island's own Greek and Muslim subjects, their Greek and Arabic languages and administrative practices, and Byzantine and Islamic artistic and cultural styles, all in order to present themselves as powerful kings ruling over a richly multicultural territory. The nature of the boundary between Latin, Muslim, and Greek worlds was thus radically transformed under the Norman rulers, and Sicily operated in far different ways than it had during either the Byzantine or Muslim period of administration. The Norman kings exploited Sicily's economic, diplomatic, and cultural connections to the wider region, as well as its advantageous geographical location, effectively putting the island in an entirely new and different conceptual place than in the previous periods—one intentionally located right at the center of the Mediterranean Sea. The island's centrality was not to last long: by the late twelfth century it was already clear that Italian merchants from mainland Italy could more effectively control cross-Mediterranean trade without utilizing Sicily as a way station.

Although the Norman invasion took place across the years 1060–1091, it would be another four decades before it was declared a kingdom and politically united with southern Italy by Roger II in 1130.[3] Strong Norman rule

2. Of course, we must leave open the possibility that a set of currently unknown sources would reveal continued links in the ways that the Ifrīqiyan *fatwās* have done.

3. For the rule of Roger II and his self-positioning as a king in the "Mediterranean" style, see Hubert Houben, *Roger II of Sicily: A Ruler between East and West* (Cambridge: Cambridge University Press, 2002).

began to decline already at the time of the death of King William II in 1189. When William died without an heir, the kingdom was riven by political upheaval, interreligious violence, and dynastic disorder. Control of the Sicilian kingdom had by 1194 transitioned from the Normans to a German ruling house known alternately as the Hohenstaufen or the Swabian dynasty (*Svevi* in Italian), because they had been dukes of Swabia from the late eleventh century (and kings of Germany from 1138). Hohenstaufen rule would not long outlive Frederick II (1194–1250, King of Sicily from his majority in 1208, King of Germany from 1212, Holy Roman Emperor from 1220, and King of Jerusalem 1225–1228), who, like the Norman kings before him, maintained a circle of scholars and artists at Palermo who drew on the multiple languages and cultures of the Mediterranean. At the same time, for all his apparent appreciation for Islamicate culture, it was Frederick himself who ordered the expulsion of all of Sicily's remaining Muslim population in the 1220s. By 1266, Frederick's descendants were expelled from the Kingdom of Sicily by Charles of Anjou at the request of the pope, a long-standing enemy of the Hohenstaufen imperial family. Thus, in some ways, the reign of Frederick II could be considered in continuity with the Norman kingdom; in other respects, his island, ruled in connection with mainland southern Italy and with increasingly stronger (although often conflictive) relationships with both the German kingdom and the Roman papacy, was, by the dawn of the thirteenth century, being transformed into an entirely different space, with a new conceptual place in the Mediterranean and in the world.

Thus, the Norman period of rule, although relatively brief, has had an extensive impact on scholarship about the medieval Mediterranean. Norman Sicily has received considerable attention from scholars in part because this period has yielded a greater number and variety of extant sources than previous eras.[4] Suddenly, we have at our disposal notarial documents, tax registers, and Latin chronicles of the Norman rulers' activities. This relative wealth of material can help flesh out the Norman period with much more certainty than the patchy source record allows scholars to do for Islamic Sicily's internal culture, economy, and political affairs. At the same time, scholarly interest in Norman Sicily originally sprang from the belief that there was a set of shared institutions between that island and the far more northerly island conquered by Normans in the middle of the eleventh century.[5] This perceived connection with England meant that study of eleventh- and twelfth-century Sicily rose

4. For a historical overview of the Norman period, see Donald Matthew, *The Norman Kingdom of Sicily* (Cambridge: Cambridge University Press, 1992).

5. For one perspective on the dangers of assuming that England and Sicily shared administrative institutions, see Johns, *Arabic Administration*, 1–10.

to popularity within medieval studies long before the advent of the current enthusiasm for Mediterranean studies. Norman Sicily has also left us a rich architectural and artistic heritage of an apparent multiculturalism, which for centuries has drawn the attention of scholars and tourists alike and fits conveniently within current academic interest in cross-cultural environments and the fates of religious minorities. However, in this respect, we see far more discontinuity than continuity, as the Norman regime fundamentally altered life on the island for Muslims and Jews. This chapter will trace the myriad ways in which the Norman rulers of Sicily and southern Italy exploited the island's preexisting connections with the broader Greek and Muslim spaces of the Mediterranean, while at the same time linking the island ever closer to the politics, economy, and culture of Latin Christendom and drawing it further from the dār al-Islām.

Political, Military, and Diplomatic Connections with the Wider Mediterranean World

The conquest of Sicily by the Normans was by no means the end of their military activity in the Mediterranean. Indeed, Norman kings routinely used Sicily as a base for their territorial ambitions in the greater Mediterranean region, routinely attacking both Muslim and Greek Christian lands and establishing power bases (albeit temporarily held) in both Byzantine Greece and Muslim North Africa. Evidence of Norman military ambition on a broad scale appears already at the end of the eleventh century, even before Sicily's new overlords had conclusively consolidated their power in the region. Before they even arrived in Sicily, in fact, the Normans in southern Italy had united under their command the formerly disparate regions of Lombard, Greek, and independent rule and thus had found for themselves a point of connection with the Roman Empire at Constantinople. With the creation of the Kingdom of Sicily in 1130, the Normans joined Sicily to southern Italy politically and administratively for the first time in centuries, but already a half century prior to this they were using their base in southern Italy as a launching pad for conquests in the Mediterranean.[6] Norman forces under Robert Guiscard began attacking Byzantine territories in the Balkans from their southern Italian lands as early as 1081 in what is known as the Battle of Dyr-

6. For more on Norman south Italy, see among others G. A. Loud, *The Latin Church in Norman Italy* (Cambridge: Cambridge University Press, 2007); Paul Oldfield, *City and Community in Norman Italy* (Cambridge: Cambridge University Press, 2009); and Ramseyer, *The Transformation of a Religious Landscape*.

rhachium (Durazzo).[7] Byzantine memory saw this as both territorial aggression and perhaps something more sinister, such as an attempt to overthrow or replace the ruling imperial family.[8] Indeed, Anna Komnene believed that the Normans—both Robert Guiscard, who attacked her father's lands, and his son Bohemond, whom she met during the First Crusade—were seeking greater fame and power for their family. She wrote that Robert Guiscard, "who from a most undignified condition had attained great distinction, having gathered about him powerful forces, was aiming to become Roman Emperor."[9] Despite his failure to hold on to imperial territory, many years later his son "Bohemond arrived and demanded that they should acclaim the emperor *and* his father [Robert Guiscard], but they made fun of his beard."[10] Like the later incursions into North Africa, the territorial gains after the Battle of Dyrrhachium were short-lived. Nonetheless, the Norman leaders of Sicily and southern Italy thus became involved in the broader conflict between Rome and Constantinople and in the complex situation along Byzantium's Balkan frontier. The legacy of Norman attacks on imperial lands was indeed long. Southern Italians who participated in the Crusades, for example, earned the ire of the Byzantine emperors in large part because of the memory of these territorial aggressions. Hostile Greek sources showed the Norman crusaders raiding Byzantine lands again along the crusading journey and linked these attacks to Norman ambitions for greater power and the lack of trustworthiness among Normans as a whole.[11]

7. Vera von Falkenhausen, "I rapporti con Bizanzio," in *I Normanni. Popolo d'Europa 1030–1200*, ed. Mario D'Onofrio (Venice: Marsilio Editori, 1994), 350–355; R. Upsher Smith Jr., "*Nobilissimus* and Warleader: The Opportunity and the Necessity behind Robert Guiscard's Balkan Expeditions," *Byzantion: Revue internationale des études byzantines* 70, no. 2 (2000): 507–526; Stephenson, *Byzantium's Balkan Frontier*, esp. 144–146 and 156–186; and Georgios Theotokis, *The Norman Campaigns in the Balkans, 1081–1108 AD* (Woodbridge, UK: Boydell & Brewer, 2014).

8. Indeed, this may also have been part of the Latin tradition of presenting Norman ambitions in the Byzantine lands. Theotokis points to a twelfth-century Latin chronicler who claimed that it was Robert Guiscard's aim in attacking Dyrrhachium to make Bohemond the emperor of the Romans. See Theotokis, *The Norman Campaigns*, 142–143.

9. Anna Komnene, *The Alexiad*, trans. E. R. A. Sewter and Peter Frankopan (London: Penguin, 2009), 35, bk. 1.12.

10. Ibid. Plenty has been written about the role of Bohemond, Robert Guiscard's son, in the First Crusade. See, for example, Rudolf Hiestand, "Boemondo I e la Prima Crociata," in *Il Mezzogiorno normanno-svevo e le Crociate: Atti delle quattordicesime giornate normanno-svevo, Bari, 17–20 ottobre 2000*, ed. Giosuè Musca (Bari: Edizioni Dedalo, 2002), 65–94; and Jonathan Shepard, "When Greek Meets Greek: Alexius Comnenus and Bohemond in 1097–98," *Byzantine and Modern Greek Studies* 12, no. 1 (1988): 185–278.

11. For example, once established in the crusader Levant as the count of Tripoli, Bohemond of Taranto, Robert Guiscard's son and a participant in the attack of 1081, moved against the Byzantine emperor in what has at times been referred to as the crusade of 1107. On whether this attack should properly be thought of as part of the crusading movement or as part of the longer-running conflict between the Normans and the emperors, see Brett E. Whalen, "God's Will or Not? Bohemond's

Ifrīqiya, both due to geographical proximity and the preexisting networks of economic interdependence with Sicily, may have seemed another natural step in Norman military expansion. Indeed, Norman military activity in the Muslim regions of northern Africa was a regular feature of the twelfth-century Mediterranean. Norman naval forces, along with those of other ambitious Latin Christian powers of the central Mediterranean, such as Pisa and Genoa, invaded Muslim Ifrīqiya numerous times, even as early as 1087.[12] In the course of the twelfth century, Normans attacked and briefly controlled several North African territories such as the island of Djerba (1134–1135), Tripoli (1145–1146), the Kerkennah Islands and al-Mahdiyya, Sfax, and Sūsa (1148–1149). The effects of such raids are recorded in some of the same Arabic sources that helped us understand earlier Muslim military activity in the region. For example, Ibn Khallikān's biographical dictionary reports that King Roger II of Sicily (1111–1154, king from 1130) took Tripoli on June 18, 1146, plundered the city, killed all the men, enslaved women and children, and established a garrison there.[13] Then, on July 1, Roger's forces occupied al-Mahdiyya, which had been evacuated by al-Ḥasan b. ʿAlī—he had fled with all the moveable wealth he could carry, along with the city's stronger inhabitants, leaving the weaker ones to be captured. Roger also found treasure and money, which he also seized. The Norman foothold in Africa was short-lived, however. Ibn Khallikān's account further states that the Franks held these cities only until the Almoravid ʿAbd al-Muʾmin arrived and reconquered al-Mahdiyya on January 21, 1160.[14] The Normans were thus using Sicily as the launching point for further conquests in the Mediterranean and North Africa, but their successes were isolated to a few years in the middle of the twelfth century.[15] Nonetheless, Norman attacks on Muslim lands continued throughout the middle

Campaign against the Byzantine Empire (1105–1108)," in *Crusades: Medieval Worlds in Conflict*, ed. Thomas Madden, James L. Naus, and Vincent Ryan (Farnham: Ashgate, 2009), 111–125.

12. For the joint Pisa-Genoa attack on the Ifrīqiyan port city of al-Mahdiyya, see H. E. J. Cowdrey, "The Mahdia Campaign of 1087," *The English Historical Review* 162 (1977): 1–29.

13. This story appears in the biography of Tamīm b. al-Muʿizz: Ibn Khallikān, *Wafayāt*, 6: 211–218.

14. Ibid., 218.

15. Several scholars have written about the Norman attempts to create a Mediterranean kingdom in Africa from their base in Palermo. See, for example, David Abulafia, "The Norman Kingdom of Africa and the Norman Expeditions to Majorca and the Muslim Mediterranean," in *Anglo-Norman Studies VII: Proceedings of the Battle Conference, 1984*, ed. R. Allen Brown (Woodbridge, UK: Boydell & Brewer, 1985), 26–49; Bennett, "Norman Naval Activity"; Michael Brett, "Muslim Justice under Infidel Rule: The Normans in Ifriqiya, 517–555H/1123–1160AD," *Cahiers de Tunisie* 43 (1995): 325–368; Charles Dalli, "Bridging Europe and Africa: Norman Sicily's Other Kingdom," in *Bridging the Gaps: Sources, Methodology and Approaches to Religion in History*, ed. Joaquim Carvalho (Pisa: Plus-Pisa University Press, 2008), 77–93; and Jeremy Johns, "Malik Ifrīqiya: The Norman Kingdom of Africa and the Fātimids," *Libyan Studies* 18 (1987): 89–101.

and later half of the twelfth century, even as they were pursing diplomatic relationships with both the Fatimids of Egypt and the Almohads of North Africa, the Maghrib, and al-Andalus.[16]

Indeed, wide-ranging diplomatic relations characterize the Norman period. For the first time, envoys traveled to and from Palermo between the papal court and many of the royal courts of Latin Europe.[17] One reason for such diplomacy was royal marriage, which likewise connected the Norman island more closely to the polities of Christian Europe. The Norman kings chose wives from Christian Spain, England, and Burgundy.[18] Marriage alliances such as that between William II and Joan of England, for example, required ambassadorial communications at a very high level. Their marriage also linked Norman Sicily more closely with the English kingdom ruled by Joan's brother, Richard I, who himself wintered on the island en route to the Holy Land for the Third Crusade. At the same time, we find accounts of diplomats from Muslim countries appearing at Sicilian courts in the Norman period, when the island's Latin rulers made a conscious effort to maintain relationships with the Islamic world in cultural, intellectual, and economic matters as well as political affairs. One such example is found in the biography of the poet known as Ibn Qalāqis. He spent a year and a half on the island in the early part of the reign of King William II, and when he left, he sailed as a passenger alongside the ambassador sent by the Fatimid ruler of Egypt to the Norman court. It is well established that the Normans had regular diplomatic contact with the Fatimids, who ruled the most powerful Muslim polity in the central Mediterranean region until the caliphate's dissolution in 1171 by Saladin.[19]

16. Yaacov Lev, "The Fāṭimid Navy, Byzantium and the Mediterranean Sea 909–1036 C.E./297–427 A.H.," *Byzantion* 54 (1984): 220–252; "The Fatimids and Byzantium."

17. For diplomatic relations with England, for example, see G. A. Loud, "The Kingdom of Sicily and the Kingdom of England, 1066–1266," *History* 88 (2003): 550–563. Loud argues that the second half of the twelfth century was a period of increased diplomatic relations between the two islands, but that most people in England continued to view Sicily as a strange and exotic place.

18. For more on the political positioning of Roger II via marriage alliance with Christian Spain, see Dawn Marie Hayes, "Roger II and the Legacy of Alfonso VI of León-Castile: Identity and Aspiration on Europe's Margins in Early Twelfth-Century Europe" (lecture, Medieval Association of the Midwest's 30th Annual Meeting, St. Louis University, Madrid, January 23, 2015). For Roger II's connections with Capetian France, see Hayes, "French Connections: The Significance of the Fleurs-de-Lis in the Mosaic of King Roger II of Sicily in the Church of Santa Maria dell'Ammiraglio, Palermo," *Viator* 44 (2013): 119–149.

19. For further evidence of the relationship between the Norman kings and Egyptian rulers, see Marius Canard, "Une lettre du calife fāṭimite al-Ḥāfiẓ à Roger II de Sicile," in *Atti del Convegno Internazionale di Studi Ruggeriani* (Palermo, 1955, repr., *Miscellanea Orientalia*, London: Variorum, 1973), 125–146; Jeremy Johns, "The Norman Kings of Sicily and the Fāṭimid Caliphate," *Anglo-Norman Studies* 15 (1993): 133–159; and Johns, "Malik Ifrīqiya."

Diplomatic relations between Fatimid Egypt and Norman Sicily were in fact formative for the administrative practices developed by the Normans on the island. Jeremy Johns has demonstrated that the Norman kings intentionally sought both connection with and emulation of the Fatimid administration and its governmental methods, after an initial period of borrowing from the Greeks and their administrative approach on the island.[20] Thus, Johns argues that the choice to make a connection with the Fatimids in Egypt was just that—an intentional decision on the part of the Norman kings to look toward Muslim Egypt for both diplomatic relationships and models for administration. In other words, the preexisting diplomatic and political connections between Sicily and Fatimid Egypt were severed or ignored when the Normans took over in Sicily and were later purposely reestablished in order to suit the Christians' governing strategies. Johns's argument serves as an important reminder about the transition from Islamic Sicily to Latin Sicily: the existence of communication patterns or cultural trends during the period of Norman domination does not necessarily mean that those same conditions can be traced backward to the Islamic period or to the years immediately after the Norman takeover. Rather, the Normans made intentional choices about which connections to maintain, which to adapt, which to sever, and which to reestablish, as suited their particular needs and interests. At the same time, this argument shows the impact of the diplomatic relationship between Norman Sicily and the Fatimids and the intentional choice made by the Normans to look to Fatimid Egypt for role models in governing the mixed population of a Mediterranean kingdom.

Sicily's Muslim Community and Its Connections with the Dār al-Islām

The question of how to govern a multicultural Mediterranean island was especially important because of the continued presence of both Greek Christian and native Muslim populations in Sicily, long after the imposition of Norman rule. Indeed, Muslim communities remained on the island until the 1220s, when Frederick II began expelling its surviving Muslim inhabitants, removing them to the mainland colony of Lucera.[21] Long before this time, how-

20. Johns, *Arabic Administration*.

21. The expulsions took place over many years from the 1220s to 1240s. For more on the colony at Lucera and its destruction by Charles II of Naples in 1300, see Abulafia, "The End of Muslim Sicily"; Abulafia, "Monarchs and Minorities"; Brian Catlos, *Muslims of Medieval Latin Christendom, c. 1050–1614* (Cambridge: Cambridge University Press, 2014), esp. 121–127; Horst, *Der Sultan von Lucera*; John Philip Lomax, "Frederick II, His Saracens, and the Papacy," in *Medieval Christian Perceptions of*

ever, some of the Muslim residents of Sicily had already emigrated to lands within the dār al-Islām at the time of the Christian conquest. However, it is also clear that not all Muslims could or chose to migrate: the existence of a large population of Muslims under Norman rule is attested in a wide variety of sources in both Arabic and Latin.[22] Confirmation that there was a significant and active Muslim community during the Norman period also comes from the eyewitness accounts of twelfth-century travelers such as Ibn Jubayr and Benjamin of Tudela, both of whom found Muslims living and working in Christian Sicily. There were surely many reasons why some Muslim families stayed put even after the Muslim *emīrs* had been replaced by Christians: financial inability to relocate, promises of patronage by the new Christian rulers, the hope for a rapid overthrow of the new infidel regime, or the simple desire to remain in a home they had known all their lives rather than emigrate to an unknown and lonely new land could all prevent some Muslims from leaving this newly Christian place. Thus although Muslim legal thought generally considered it sinful to live in an area conquered by Christians or other infidels, not all of Sicily's Muslim residents would have been financially, emotionally, or physically able to move their families and belongings across the sea.[23]

Islam, ed. J. V. Tolan (New York: Garland, 1996), 175–197; Loud, "Communities, Cultures and Conflict"; Maier, "Crusade and Rhetoric"; Martin, "La colonie Sarrasine de Lucera"; Metcalfe, *The Muslims of Medieval Italy*, 275–298; and Julie Taylor, *Muslims in Medieval Italy* (Lanham, MD: Lexington Books, 2003).

22. On the subject of the Muslim population of Sicily, see Henri Bercher, Annie Courteaux, and Jean Mouton, "Une abbaye latine dans la societe musulmane: Monreale au XIIe siècle," *Annales* 34 (1979): 525–547; Joshua C. Birk, "Sicilian Counterpoint: Power and Pluralism in Norman Sicily" (PhD thesis, University of California, Santa Barbara, 2006); Johns, *Arabic Administration*; Johns, "The Monreale Survey: Indigenes and Invaders in Medieval West Sicily," in *Papers in Italian Archaeology IV*, ed. Caroline Malone and Simon Stoddart, BAR International Series 246 (Oxford: B.A.R., 1985), vol. 4, 215–224; Johns, "The Boys from Messoiuso: Muslim *Jizya*-Payers in Christian Sicily," in *Islamic Reflections, Arabic Musings: Studies in Honor of Professor Alan Jones*, ed. Robert G. Hoyland and Philip F. Kennedy (Oxford: Gibb Memorial Trust, 2004), 243–255; Metcalfe, *Muslims and Christians in Norman Sicily*; Metcalfe, "The Muslims of Sicily under Christian Rule," in *The Society of Norman Italy*, ed. G. A. Loud and Alex Metcalfe (Leiden: E. J. Brill, 2002), 289–317; and Timothy James Smit, "Commerce and Coexistence: Muslims in the Economy and Society of Norman Sicily" (PhD thesis, University of Minnesota, 2009).

23. The Islamic legal injunction commonly referred to as the "obligation to emigrate" dictated that Muslims must depart from a land ruled by non-Muslims and not subject themselves to the dominion of unbelievers. In the medieval Muslim West, jurists and scholars debated the terms under which this obligation might be abrogated. Many legal scholars of the time agreed that potential financial loss (i.e., the forfeiting of land owned in the conquered region) was not a sufficient reason to remain in infidel lands, while a complete lack of financial resources or the physical inability to make the trip could exempt one from blame for continuing to reside under non-Muslim rule. At the same time, individual jurists, such as Imām al-Māzarī, sometimes made decisions to recognize Muslim communities under infidel rule for other reasons. For various perspectives on the juristic debate about Muslim minorities and the "obligation to emigrate," see Khaled Abou El Fadl, "Islamic Law and Muslim Minorities: The Juristic Discourse on Muslim Minorities from the Second/Eighth to the Eleventh/Seventeenth Centuries," *Islamic Law and Society* 1, no. 2 (1994): 141–187; Sarah Davis-Secord, "Muslims

Many of Sicily's Muslims were of lower economic status, working as villeins on agricultural estates controlled by Latin lords.[24] However, evidence suggests that some Muslim elites also remained, both as overseers of Muslim agricultural workers and as staff members of the Norman administration in Palermo.[25] We also know that the Norman rulers permitted some degree of autonomous self-governance, at least at the local level, to these subject Muslims; nevertheless, their community leaders were appointed by the Norman kings and could be dismissed by them. This fact could cause difficulties for Muslims, both in Sicily and overseas, in the dār al-Islām. In addition to the *fatwās* issued by Imām al-Māzarī (d. 1141) that we saw in chapter 4, one of his legal judgments addresses the legitimacy of one such *qāḍī* serving under the Normans.[26] In this case, the questioner asked the jurist whether the decisions ("aḥkām") from the Sicilian judge (the "qāḍī al-Ṣiqilliya," the title of the highest Islamic judge on the island) ought to be obeyed and considered legally valid even though the judge lived and worked while in a state of subjection to Christians, a condition generally considered sinful by many medieval Islamic legal theorists. The *fatwā* states that al-Māzarī was unsure whether the *qāḍī* had refused to move or was forced to stay in Sicily: that is, al-Māzarī made his declaration without knowing whether the judge's situation was intentional and thus whether his motives for living under infidel rule were sinful or pure. Nonetheless, al-Māzarī's judgment was that this *qāḍī*, despite his circumstances and the fact of his appointment by the Christian king, should be treated as though he had been appointed by a Muslim potentate and thus his judgments accepted as legal and valid, not only in Sicily but also in other lands of the dār al-Islām.[27]

---

in Norman Sicily: The Evidence of Imām al-Māzarī's *Fatwās*," *Mediterranean Studies* 16 (2007): 46–66; P. S. van Kongingsveld and G. A. Wiegers, "The Islamic Statute of the Mudejars in the Light of a New Source," *al-Qanṭara* 17 (1996): 19–58; Kathryn A. Miller, "Muslim Minorities and the Obligation to Emigrate to Islamic Territory: Two Fatwās from Fifteenth-Century Granada," *Islamic Law and Society* 7, no. 2 (2000): 256–288; Jean-Pierre Molenat, "Le problème de la permanence des musulmans dans les territoires conquis par les Chrétiens, du point de vue de la loi islamique," *Arabica* 48, no. 3 (2001): 392–400; and Bernard Lewis, "Legal and Historical Reflection on the Position of Muslim Populations under Non-Muslim Rule," *Journal of the Institute of Muslim Minority Affairs* 13, no. 1 (1992): 1–16.

24. Sicilian Muslims were subjected to something much like *dhimmī* status (that is, the subjugated position of religious minorities living in the dār al-Islām) in the Norman kingdom, paying the equivalent of the poll tax (the *jizya*) that religious minorities paid to Muslim rulers in the dār al-Islām—called in Latin the *gesia*. See Johns, "The Boys from Messoiuso," and his *Arabic Administration*.

25. For more on the so-called palace Saracens who served in the courts and administrations of several Norman kings, see Metcalfe, *Muslim and Christians in Norman Sicily*, 46–49; Metcalfe, *The Muslims of Medieval Italy*, 193–208; and Johns, *Arabic Administration*, 212–256.

26. al-Wansharīsī, 10: 107–108.

27. For more on the legal reasoning used by al-Māzarī to support his judgment, see Davis-Secord, "Muslims in Norman Sicily," esp. 57–59. Among other factors, al-Māzarī emphasized that Sicilian Muslims needed legitimate Islamic juridical leadership in order for them to fulfill their civil and religious obligations.

This ruling differed from the judgments of many other western Muslim jurists about the legitimacy of an Islamic judge living in a Christian land and suggested that al-Māzarī, despite his strict prohibition on intentional travel from Ifrīqiya to Christian Sicily for the purpose of trade, as discussed in chapter 4, perceived a valid need for acceptable Muslim leadership even in the dār al-ḥarb.[28]

We can thus see, in the various decisions of this one jurist, a level of ambivalence about how to confront the problem of a newly drawn boundary between Islam and Christianity and the predicament of Muslims living on the "wrong" side of this line. On the one hand, he recognized that all Muslims need proper leadership and guidance in order to carry out the religious and civil obligations involved in living and practicing their Islamic faith—even ones who lived in non-Muslim lands. Given that al-Māzarī himself came from this Sicilian Muslim community, he may, too, have been thinking of friends or family on the island. Without legitimate Muslim leadership, the community would struggle to perform regular acts of Muslim practice, such as marriage, burial, religious education, and the resolution of disputes according to Islamic law. Presumably, this could lead to community disintegration, the loss of a distinctive Islamic religious identity, and acculturation to the majority religion.[29] By the end of the twelfth century, when Ibn Jubayr visited some of these remaining Sicilian Muslims, he found exactly that: a community struggling to survive the stresses and pressures of living as minorities under non-Muslim rule. The decision of al-Māzarī to recognize the legal authority of the *qāḍī al-Ṣiqilliya* may have been partially an effort to stanch such community

---

28. The "dār al-ḥarb" refers to all lands outside of the Islamic domain, that is, regions under infidel rule, against which it was claimed that *jihād* should be constantly carried out. There was a common legal tenet that the boundary between Muslim and infidel lands should not be breached except during wars of expansion. For example, the *fatwās* of the Andalusī jurist Ibn Rushd (d. 1122) express the opinion that Muslims should neither live in nor travel to the dār al-ḥarb, under any circumstances. Ibn Rushd even went so far as to state that Muslims living under non-Muslim law were not to be considered trustworthy as legal witnesses or as leaders of prayer. This so-called uncompromising position is supposed, by some modern scholars such as Khaled Abou El Fadl, to be the fully developed Mālikī position on the subject of Muslim minorities in non-Muslim territories. See Abou El Fadl, "Islamic Law and Muslim Minorities." Several other Mālikī jurists, like Imām al-Māzarī, however, made exceptions for some Muslims to legally remain under infidel rule. See Davis-Secord, "Muslims in Norman Sicily"; Kongingsveld and Wiegers, "The Islamic Statute"; and Miller, "Muslim Minorities." Each stresses the contextualized nature of the response to Muslim minorities by some Islamic jurists: local considerations weighed as heavily for these *qāḍīs* as did strict interpretation of legal tradition. At the same time, a more practical approach to travel and communication across the supposed boundary between the dār al-ḥarb and the dār al-Islām is demonstrated by the numerous historical examples of stabilized borders, cross-border trade, and peace treaties between Muslim and non-Muslim rulers.

29. For a linguistic and religious perspective on the breakdown of Latin Sicily's Muslim population, see Metcalfe, *Muslim and Christians in Norman Sicily*.

disintegration and keep Sicily's minority Muslims conceptually and religiously attached to the dār al-Islām. On the other hand, voluntary travel to the Christian island by Muslims from the dār al-Islām was strictly forbidden by al-Māzarī. That religious and political boundary should not be crossed, he asserted, even when the population of Ifrīqiya was starving and in need of Sicilian grain. So, while Sicily's Muslim communities should, for their own sake, be drawn conceptually nearer to the dār al-Islām, al-Māzarī believed that Ifrīqiya's Muslims should not look at newly Christian Sicily as a location still in the Islamic world or as a licit partner in active communication or exchange.[30] In the eyes of this one jurist, it was, at the same time, both inside and outside of the dār al-Islām.

Indeed, by the end of the twelfth century, we find that the Muslims of an increasingly Latinized Sicily were effectively cut off from active communication with the dār al-Islām. One eyewitness account portrayed the Sicilian Muslim communities at the end of the Norman period as isolated, harassed, and in economic and cultural decline. Abū al-Ḥusayn Muḥammad ibn Aḥmad ibn Jubayr (1145–1217), known as Ibn Jubayr, was a traveler and pilgrim from al-Andalus who stopped in Sicily at the end of his journey, from early December 1184 through early April 1185. He composed his *Riḥla*, or travelogue, after his return from a two-year-long journey from Granada to Mecca and back that included stops in many cities and towns throughout both the Muslim and Christian Mediterranean.[31] Visiting Sicily during the reign of the Norman king William II (1166–1189), he crossed the island from Messina to Trapani, where he caught a ship sailing back to Spain. His lengthy descriptions of the island, its cities and countryside, and the resident Muslims have been discussed at length by many scholars interested in Muslim life under

30. We have seen, however, that trade did continue, at least for some time. By the end of the twelfth century, trade from Sicily was being directed primarily by the Normans and their trading partners from the Italian mainland, but it is not possible for me to say at what precise point the Sicily-Ifrīqiya trade shifted into their control.

31. Ibn Jubayr's visit to Sicily lasted from the month of Ramaḍān (December 6, 1184–January 4, 1185) through the month of Dhū al-Ḥijja (March 5–April 3, 1185). The passages concerning Sicily are found in Ibn Jubayr, *Riḥlat*, 292–316; Broadhurst, *Travels*, 335–360. For the basic description of *riḥla* as a journey in search of knowledge, see Ian Richard Netton, "Riḥla," in *EI*[2], vol. 8 (Leiden: E. J. Brill, 1995), 328; and C. F. Beckingham, "The *Riḥla*: Fact or Fiction?," in *Golden Roads: Migration, Pilgrimage and Travel in Medieval and Modern Islam*, ed. Ian Richard Netton (Richmond, UK: Curzon Press, 1993), 86–94. For Ibn Jubayr's *Riḥla* as a source, see Metcalfe, *Muslims and Christians in Norman Sicily*, 39–41. For further elaboration of the development of this genre and its relationship to Islamic epistemology, see Touati, *Islam and Travel in the Middle Ages*. For more on Ibn Jubayr's biography and journey, see Charles Pellat, "Ibn Djubayr," *EI*[2], vol. 3 (Leiden: E. J. Brill, 1995), 755; Ian Richard Netton, "Ibn Jubayr: Penitent Pilgrim and Observant Traveler," in *Seek Knowledge: Thought and Travel in the House of Islam* (Richmond: Curzon Press, 1996), 95–101; and Netton, "Basic Structures and Signs of Alienation in the *Riḥla* of Ibn Jubayr," in Netton, *Golden Roads*, 57–74.

Norman rule.[32] Ibn Jubayr encountered several settlements of Muslims who were permitted to maintain mosques and, at least in some locations, to hold noisy public religious festivals and broadcast the call to prayer. At the same time, he expressed the fear that the Norman king was exploiting the island's Muslims for financial gain (through payment of the *jizya*, withdrawal of favor from Muslim elites, and confiscations of their property) and for his self-aggrandizement as a pacific and multicultural ruler. Ibn Jubayr also found ships traveling from Sicilian ports to a wide variety of places in the Mediterranean and transporting both Christian and Muslim passengers, but these ships were all owned by Christians. At least from this one perspective, then, twelfth-century Sicily appeared as a transitional space on the Muslim-Christian border—located both in the sphere of Christian political power and, to some degree, in the Islamic sphere of culture and settlement—but one that Ibn Jubayr experienced as shifting decidedly toward Latin Christian dominance.

In general, Ibn Jubayr held a mixed opinion about Norman Sicily and its kings, with much that he found favorable and much that made him fearful. Initially pleased by the reports he had received about Muslims living at the royal court, the king's patronage of Islamic arts and culture, and the freedom of Muslims to live and worship on the island, by the time he departed several months later, however, he had decided that the indignities of life under infidel rule were too much for this community to bear. In positive terms, he portrayed the Christian king as appreciative of Islamicate culture and relatively kind to the secret Muslims among his court staff and concubines. William dressed in silk clothing made by a Muslim tailor, ate food prepared by Muslim cooks, was protected by Muslim bodyguards, and attracted to his court physicians, astrologers, intellectuals, and poets from around the Islamic world; Ibn Jubayr even heard a rumor that William could read and write Arabic.[33] All of these Muslims at the royal court practiced their Islamic faith in secret by necessity. Nonetheless, Ibn Jubayr reported that King William was aware of and tolerated the Islamic religious practice and even proselytization among some of his women and servants.[34] Likewise, William's palaces were lovely and richly appointed, with pleasant gardens and other luxuries. William was known to enjoy a variety

32. See, for instance, Sarah Davis-Secord, "Bearers of Islam: Muslim Women between Assimilation and Resistance in Christian Sicily," in *Gender in the Premodern Mediterranean*, ed. Megan Moore (Tempe: Arizona Center for Medieval and Renaissance Studies, 2017); Mallette, *The Kingdom of Sicily*, 1–3; Johns, *Arabic Administration*; Metcalfe, *The Muslims of Medieval Italy*; and Georges Peyronnet, "Coexistence islamo-chrétienne en Sicile et au moyen-orient," *Islamochristiana* 19 (1993): 55–73.

33. Ibn Jubayr, *Riḥlat*, 298; Broadhurst, *Travels*, 341.

34. For an opposite account, of William forcing the conversion of some of Sicily's Muslim leaders, see Ibn Jubayr, *Riḥlat*, 313–316.

of earthly delights: the pleasures of royal servants, palaces, and gardens, as well as the orderly administration of his realm, the organization of laws and procedures, and splendid ceremonies—all of which earned Ibn Jubayr's praise for ruling "in a manner that resembles the Muslim kings" ("bi-mulūk al-Muslimīn").[35] This image of themselves, indeed, is what the Norman rulers were attempting to promote.

In addition to appreciation for Muslims and their culture at the royal court, Ibn Jubayr found communities of resident Muslims who lived and worked freely on the island, owning lands and running mosques and schools; nonetheless, it became clear to Ibn Jubayr that these Muslims lived under conditions very different from those of their coreligionists in the dār al-Islām. In Palermo, even though Muslim worshipers were only allowed to gather on holy days, and the Friday sermon (*khuṭbah*) was outlawed, the Muslim community was allowed to maintain a *qāḍī*, to whom they were able to take their internal disputes. Rural Muslim communities maintained religious shrines and had imāms who led regular prayers as well as a muezzin to call the faithful to prayer.[36] The sound of the call to prayer, after so many months without hearing it (during his travels through the crusader Levant and while sailing on Christian ships), recalled Ibn Jubayr to the aural culture of the dār al-Islām—reinforcing the notion that he felt, to some degree, as though he was culturally in an Islamic space. "But in general," he continued, "these Muslims do not mix with their brethren under infidel patronage, and enjoy no security for their goods, their women, or their children."[37] That is, even though they were treated relatively well and were allowed certain freedoms of worship, Sicilian Muslims were isolated and lived constantly under the thumb of their powerful Christian lords. Indeed, only forty years later, the remnants of this community would be rounded up and expelled from the island by Frederick II, having been radically diminished in number.[38]

The isolation and disintegration of Sicily's Muslim community appear to have been the primary concerns expressed to Ibn Jubayr and his fellow travel-

---

35. Ibn Jubayr, *Riḥlat*, 298; Broadhurst, *Travels*, 340–341.

36. Ibn Jubayr, *Riḥlat*, 305; Broadhurst, *Travels*, 348. Ibn Jubayr did hear the call to prayer (*adhān*) at least once while in Sicily, when he and his party were at the Muslim settlement at Qaṣr Saʿd, a few miles from Palermo; they also participated in both regular daily prayers and special Ramaḍān services there. See Ibn Jubayr, *Riḥlat*, 303; Broadhurst, *Travels*, 345–346.

37. Ibn Jubayr, *Riḥlat*, 306; Broadhurst, *Travels*, 349.

38. Abulafia believes that, from a quarter million Muslims (representing initially more than half of the island's total population) who lived in Sicily in the mid-eleventh century, only 20,000 were deported to Lucera in the 1220s. This represents a reduction in the island's population by as much as ninety percent in only a century and a half. Abulafia, "The End of Muslim Sicily," 104. Likewise, Taylor estimates an initial Luceran population of between 15,000 and 20,000 Muslims. Taylor, *Muslims in Medieval Italy*, 1 and 41.

ers by members of that community. In Trapani, while waiting for a ship to sail westward, he heard a number of disturbing stories about the life of minorities in Sicily.[39] He was told of the humiliation of paying the *jizya*, which kept many of the island's Muslims impoverished and under financial pressure, and of a travel ban that prohibited Sicilian Muslims from freely communicating with the dār al-Islām. There were more direct pressures as well: Ibn Jubayr learned of Muslim elites—those who had earlier collaborated with the Normans—now being punished and removed from royal patronage; of religious conversions, forced or nearly so, and the consequent transformation of mosques into churches; and of the Norman policies that undercut parental authority and encouraged conversion among Muslim youths by allowing young people in conflict with their families to take sanctuary in churches. By doing so, they could escape punishment by their parents; this Ibn Jubayr saw as an enticement to those children to convert and a subversion of the rightful authority of Muslim mothers and fathers.[40] These and other complaints led Ibn Jubayr to reflect less positively on Norman Sicily at the end of his time there than he had at the beginning. Some Muslims in Sicily felt so oppressed by the indignities and temptations of life under Christian rule, he determined, that one family even requested that someone among Ibn Jubayr's group of pilgrims marry their only daughter so that she could live freely in the dār al-Islām. The family hoped that, once she had successfully relocated to al-Andalus, they could follow her in emigration when the travel ban was lifted. Being cut off from free communication with and travel to the dār al-Islām, Sicily's Muslims felt isolated and pressured into acculturation.[41]

Ibn Jubayr's experiences highlight the distinction between native and foreign Muslims in Sicily. Pilgrims like himself and the foreign scholars patronized by the king were free to come and go, while native Sicilians' movements were restricted and their relations with the dār al-Islām interrupted. While Muslims from North Africa were at some times able to travel to and from Sicily for the purposes of trade, at other times the Normans controlled and restricted the free communication of the island's native Muslim population. Thus, it is not the case that Norman Sicily did not have routine interactions with the Muslim regions of the Mediterranean, but rather that, by the late twelfth century, these connections were being maintained and directed by the Norman rulers themselves, for their purposes and at the expense of organic communication between coreligionists in the wider sphere of the Mediterranean basin. Ibn

39. Ibn Jubayr, *Riḥlat*, 308–316; Broadhurst, *Travels*, 351–361.

40. For more on the variety of forces that led to acculturation and conversion among Norman Sicily's Muslim population, see Metcalfe, *Muslims and Christians in Norman Sicily*.

41. For more on this anecdote and the pressure to convert, see Davis-Secord, "Bearers of Islam."

Jubayr may have felt at times that Sicily was culturally a part of the Muslim world, but he came to understand that the island was in fact solidly and detrimentally located in the Christian sphere of power, with communication and travel directed and controlled by the Normans for their advantage.

Intellectual and Religious Connections to the Dār al-Islām and Latin Christendom

One aspect of King William II's attitude toward Muslims that Ibn Jubayr was most ambivalent about was the king's desire to patronize Muslim scholars. While Ibn Jubayr praised the Norman ruler for employing local Muslims at court and for appreciating Arabic-language intellectual activity, he castigated William for drawing foreign Muslims away from the dār al-Islām and into his—religiously, culturally, and politically Christian—domain. Ibn Jubayr wrote: "He pays much attention to his (Muslim) physicians and astrologers, and also takes great care of them. He will even, when told that a physician or astrologer is passing through his land, order his detainment, and then provide him with means of living so that he will forget his native land. May God in His favor preserve the Muslims from this seduction."[42] On the one hand, he appreciated King William's respect for Islamic culture and learning, but, on the other hand, he feared that royal patronage of Muslim scholars in Palermo could amount to entrapment, drawing them out of the dār al-Islām and thus further fragmenting the Muslim world and its culture.

As we have seen in chapter 3, during the centuries of Islamic dominion, Sicily functioned religiously and intellectually as an extension of North Africa, much as it did in political and economic matters. While we do have knowledge of many Muslim Sicilian scholars, poets, and legal experts, we know about most of them because they left the island to advance their careers in the central Islamic lands. Even those whose careers in scholarship and religious education took place on the island were connected to intellectual circles that encompassed both Sicily and the mainland Islamic societies of Ifrīqiya and, to a lesser extent, those of Egypt and al-Andalus.[43] Muslim religious and intellec-

42. Ibn Jubayr, *Riḥlat*, 298–299; Broadhurst, *Travels*, 341. The word translated as "seduction" is *fitna*, which could also mean any force that threatens to bring disorder to an individual Muslim or to the *umma* (the universal community of Muslims). This word and concept were used frequently by Ibn Jubayr, especially of Christian Sicily as a seductive place for Muslims, where Christian toleration and friendliness might induce conversion and acculturation. For more on this concept, see Davis-Secord, "Bearers of Islam."

43. Examples of men who traveled to Sicily to teach include Muḥammad b. Khurāsān and Abū al-ʿAlā' Ṣāʿid b. al-Ḥasan b. ʿĪsā al-Rabaʿī al-Baghdādī, both discussed in chapter 3. Their travels were undertaken within scholarly networks that originated in the central Islamic lands.

tual figures continued to work in Sicily after the Norman takeover—some as individuals born there who then moved elsewhere and some as scholars attracted to the Christian royal court at Palermo by the patronage of the Norman kings. As we have seen in chapter 4, some native Sicilian *ʿulamāʾ* emigrated from the island at the time of the Christian conquest, while others did not. Several twelfth-century scholars were born in Sicily and died elsewhere, although their biographies do not specify whether they fled the Christian occupation or departed simply to pursue their careers. Several of these men's death dates suggest that they might have been born in a Sicily that had already been taken over by the Normans, and thus that their families were among those who remained after the conquest. For example, the jurist Muḥammad b. al-Ḥasan b. ʿAlī, Abū Bakr al-Rabaʿī al-Girgantī, whose nisba associates him with the Sicilian town of Agrigento, taught in Sicily and in North Africa before moving to Alexandria, where he lived until his death in 1142/1143.[44] Likewise, the Mālikī scholar Muḥammad b. al-Musallam was born in Māzara and went to Alexandria via al-Mahdiyya in order to study with master scholars. He died there in 1136.[45] Abū ʿAbd Allāh Muḥammad b. Abī Muḥammad b. Ẓafar al-Ṣiqillī was another Sicilian intellectual who moved to the central Islamic lands after starting his career in Norman Sicily. He was a scholar and prolific writer who was born in Sicily, went on pilgrimage to Mecca, then moved throughout the dār al-Islām until he died at Hamāt in 1169/1170.[46] His biography also provides further confirmation that intellectual travel between Sicily and North Africa was not cut off after the island transferred to Christian rule, since, according to al-Maqrīzī, Muḥammad b. Ẓafar was living in Sicily again in 1159/1160, when he wrote the *Sulwān al-muṭaʿ* (Solace of the obedient).[47] Each of these biographies suggests that some Muslim scholars born in Sicily in the immediate aftermath of the Norman takeover continued to live there for some time under Norman administration; at the same time, like the *ʿulamāʾ* of the Islamic period, they gained prominence by moving to the central Islamic lands, especially via Ifrīqiya.

As the twelfth century progressed, however, fewer Islamic scholars appear to have arisen from the native Muslim population in Christian Sicily. This situation is a likely result of a general decline in the opportunities for Islamic religious, scientific, or legal education in a Sicily where Latin Christian culture was becoming increasingly dominant through colonization and the establishment of Latin religious foundations along with the contraction of the subject

44. al-Maqrīzī, *Kitāb al-muqaffā*, *BAS* Arabic, 664.
45. al-Maqrīzī, *Kitāb al-muqaffā*, *BAS* Arabic, 667–668, 880–881.
46. Ibn Khallikān, *Wafayāt*, 4: 395–397: "ahad al-ʾadabāʾ al-faḍalāʾ ṣāhib al-taṣānīf al-mimatʿa."
47. al-Maqrīzī, *Kitāb al-muqaffā*, *BAS* Arabic, 665–667, 877–880.

Muslim population via acculturation, conversion, and impoverishment.[48] Indeed, far more of the known intellectuals working in Arabic in Latin Sicily were non-Sicilians who worked under the patronage of Norman and Hohenstaufen kings.[49] Perhaps the most famous example of a nonnative Muslim intellectual patronized by a Norman king is also perhaps the earliest, a Muslim geographer who wrote an account of the world in the Arabic geographical tradition, discussed in chapter 3. Likely a native of Ceuta or al-Andalus, Abū ʿAbd Allāh Muḥammad al-Idrīsī, known as al-Idrīsī, wrote his work under the patronage of the Norman king of Sicily, Roger II (count of Sicily 1112–1130, king of Sicily 1130–1154).[50] This text, known either as the *Kitāb Rujār* (The book of Roger, named for its royal patron) or as the *Kitāb nuzhat al-mushtāq fī ikhtirāq al-āfāq* (The book of entertainment for he who longs to travel the world), was completed in 1154 and purported to describe the entire known world. Unlike earlier Arabic geographies, however, which were notable for their lack of detail about Sicily, al-Idrīsī's work is packed with information about towns throughout the island, both large and small. Also in contrast to the overwhelmingly negative views of Sicily presented by the tenth-century visitor Ibn Ḥawqal, the description of Sicily in al-Idrīsī's book is notable for its unstintingly positive

---

48. For remnants of Islamic sciences in Latin Sicily, see Francesco Barone, "Islām in Sicilia nel XII e XIII secolo: Ortoprassi, scienze religiose e tasawwuf," *Incontri mediterranei. Rivista semestrale di storia e cultura* 6, no. 2 (2003): 104–115.

49. Frederick II is known for his patronage of scholars and artists in a wide variety of languages, his own fluency in Arabic, and the deportation of Sicily's Muslims to the mainland colony of Lucera. The Hohenstaufen's reign and the court culture he fostered at Palermo are complex subjects that have been well covered by other scholars. A basic biography is found in David Abulafia, *Frederick II: A Medieval Emperor* (Oxford: Oxford University Press, 1988); the court culture in Palermo is found on pp. 251–289 and in Andrea Borruso, "Federico II e la tradizione culturale arabo-islamica," in *Federico II: Immagine e Potere*, ed. Maria Stella Calo Mariani and Raffaella Cassano (Venice: Marsilio, 1995), 15–19; and William Tronzo, ed., *Intellectual Life at the Court of Frederick II Hohenstaufen* (Washington, DC: National Gallery of Art, 1994). A good account of the cultural and linguistic changes that took place during Frederick II's reign is found in Mallette, *The Kingdom of Sicily*, 47–64. Mallette argues that it was really under Frederick II that Latin and Romance became the primary cultural languages at court and that Arabic culture, while still valued intellectually, was "shifted from being a living and productive culture to a textual culture . . . the object of translation" (64).

50. For an introduction to al-Idrīsī's biography and works, see S. Maqbul Ahmad, "Cartography of al-Sharīf al-Idrīsī," in *The History of Cartography*, vol. 2, bk. 1, *Cartography in the Traditional Islamic and South Asian Societies*, ed. J. B. Harley and David Woodward (Chicago: University of Chicago Press, 1992), 156–174; Allaoua Amara and Annliese Nef, "Al-Idrīsī et les Hammūdides de Sicile: Nouvelles données biographiques sur l'auteur du Livre de Roger," *Arabica* 67 (2000): 121–127; Annliese Nef, "Al-Idrīsī: Un complément d'enquête biographique," in *Géographes et voyageurs au Moyen Age*, ed. Henri Bresc and Emmanuelle Du Mesnil (Nanterre: Presses universitaires de Paris Ouest, 2010), 53–66; G. Oman, "Notizie bibliografiche sul geografo arabo al-Idrīsī (XII secolo) e sulle opere," *Annali, Istituto Universitario Orientale di Napoli* 11 (1961): 25–61. Critical Arabic edition in al-Idrīsī, *Opus Geographicum*. The section on Sicily is found in fasc. 5, 583–626. Partial French translation in Dozy and De Goeje, *Description de l'Afrique et de l'Espagne*. Complete French translation in al-Idrīsī, *La Première géographie de l'Occident*, trans. by Henri Bresc and Annliese Nef (Paris: Flammarion, 1999).

portrayal of the island under the author's patron, King Roger II. He depicted Sicily as lush, well watered, and abundantly productive. Unlike the earlier account by Ibn Ḥawqal and the twelfth-century one by Ibn Jubayr, however, al-Idrīsī's did not provide many observations about the life of the Muslim population under Norman rule, instead focusing on topography and settlements, following the traditions of Arabic geography. To accompany this text, al-Idrīsī also is said to have produced a world map (a later copy of which is found in figure 7) in the style of earlier Islamic maps.[51] Not surprisingly, this map depicts Sicily as a large triangular island in the middle of the Mediterranean, unlike the earlier map attributed to Ibn Ḥawqal, which omitted visual depiction of the island altogether. Roger II, the first king of Sicily, apparently thought that the best way to celebrate his island was to commission an Arabic-language geography and a map in the Islamic style showing Sicily as one place among many in the world. It is not precisely clear whether Roger intended the geography and map as a message to the local Muslim population—for instance, a message of power that would be easily recognizable within their cultural expectations—or to the wider Muslim world. What is evident is that Roger's royal self-presentation included the production of a book and map in a language that was not his own but that was the lingua franca of the larger region in which he ruled; he thus styled himself as a truly Mediterranean king, one suited for power in a location at once politically Christian and culturally Muslim.[52] His material culture could speak this lingua franca even if he himself could not.

Later Norman kings continued this tradition of patronizing Arabic-language arts and scholarship. Another famous foreign Muslim intellectual drawn to the Norman royal court was a poet known as Ibn Qalāqis (1137–1172). Born in Alexandria and educated in Cairo, he was known for traveling widely throughout the Islamic lands writing poems. On one such trip in 1168, he went to Sicily (during the early part of the reign of King William II), where he met the

51. The original map that may have accompanied al-Idrīsī's manuscript, which was said to have been engraved on silver, does not survive. There are a number of later copies of both the text and the map, dating from the fourteenth to sixteenth centuries, that contain both world maps and sectional maps based on al-Idrīsī's text. For details on these copies and their maps, see Ahmad, "Cartography of al-Sharīf al-Idrīsī" and Pinto, *Medieval Islamic Maps*, 23–25.

52. Another object produced for Roger II in an Islamicate style is his famous red silk "coronation" robe with Arabic *ṭirāz* inscriptions produced in 1133/1134. This object is, as Joshua Birk has put it, "another attempt by the Norman court to make use of a long standing Islamic tradition to communicate royal power." Birk, "Sicilian Counterpoint," 172. For a catalog and analysis of Norman luxury silks and other high-value material goods, many of which displayed links to artistic traditions in the Islamicate world, see Wilfried Seipel, ed., *Nobiles Officinae: Die königlichen Hofwerkstätten zu Palermo zur Zeit der Normannen und Staufer im 12. und 13. Jahrhundert* (Milano: Skira, 2004).

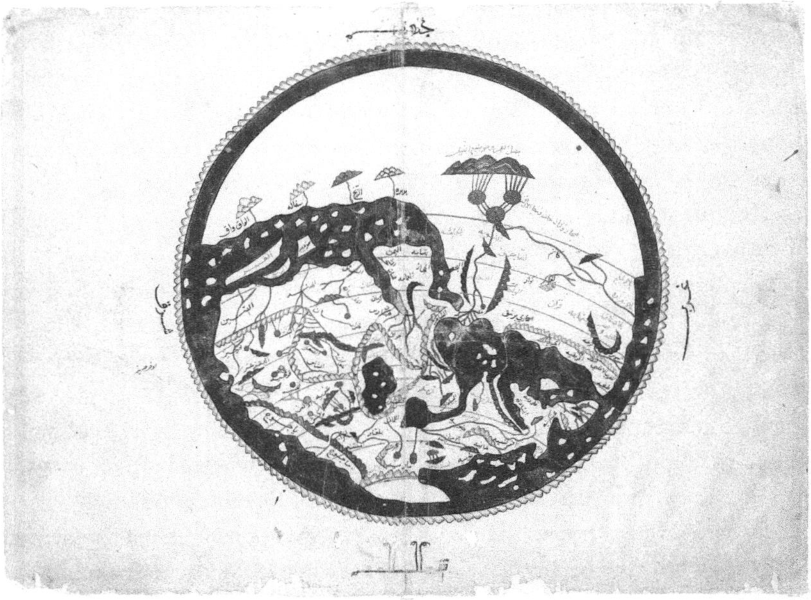

FIGURE 7. World map copy based on one attributed to al-Idrīsī, 1553. Oriented with the south at top. Bodleian Libraries, University of Oxford, MS. Pococke 375, fols. 3v-4r.

qāʾid Abū al-Qāsim and wrote poetry for him.[53] He then traveled to the court at Palermo, where he worked under the patronage of King William. After a year and a half in Sicily, during most of which time he lived in Palermo at the Norman court, he returned by ship to Egypt alongside a Fatimid diplomat. This double patronage indicates that Islamic arts were supported by both local Muslim leaders and Christian kings in Sicily, but also that a poet like Ibn Qalāqis was allowed free egress from Sicily, contrary to the fears expressed sixteen years later by Ibn Jubayr. At the same time, the stories of these individuals illustrate the Norman kings' increasing control over artistic production, even that in Arabic. By 1185, when Ibn Jubayr met him in Sicily, the Sicilian community leader Abū al-Qāsim had lost his position of royal favor and his wealth and was no longer able to patronize the arts or perform acts of charity toward fellow Muslims in need. In fact, Abū al-Qāsim appeared to the author of the *Riḥla* as an exemplar of the many pressures causing the disintegration of Sicily's Muslim community. Impoverished and defeated, Abū al-Qāsim had

53. Ibn Khallikān, *Wafayāt*, 5: 385–389. For more on *qāʾid* Abū al-Qāsim as the leader of the Sicilian Muslim community at the time, see Metcalfe, *The Muslims of Medieval Italy*, 215–222.

been accused by the king of collaborating with the Almohads to overthrow the Christian rulers of Sicily and stripped of his freedom, cash, and properties as well as his role in the Norman administration; even after he was returned to royal favor, he expressed his wish to leave Sicily even as a slave so that he could live in the dār al-Islām rather than under the oppressions of infidel rule.[54]

At the same time that Sicily's Muslims were being increasingly cut off from organic connections with their coreligionists in the dār al-Islām, the island's Norman rulers were actively establishing and promoting Latin ecclesiastical foundations and Latin arts and scholarship. The process of latinizing the island's population, over and against not only the Muslim but also the Greek Christian inhabitants, has been well studied by, most notably, Graham Loud and his students.[55] Their research shows that, while Greek and Muslim religious establishments were allowed to persist on the island, the larger trend in the Norman period was one of drawing the island closer to the Latin Church at Rome. Churches and monasteries of the Latin rite were founded and endowed, and some preexisting mosques and Greek churches were converted to Latin establishments in the course of the twelfth century (see figure 8).[56] The shrines of Latin saints were promoted in the wider Christian world, and pilgrims from around Latin Christendom were attracted by these shrines to visit Sicily, some as part of their longer journeys to or from Jerusalem.[57] Additionally, the intellectual culture fostered on the island by the Norman kings' patronage of Latin, Greek, and Arabic scholars created a space in which Christians from Europe could interact with, learn from, and copy the texts of intellectuals from throughout the Mediterranean world.[58] Even with Latin

54. Ibn Jubayr, *Riḥlat*, 314–315; Broadhurst, *Travels*, 358–359.

55. Loud, *The Latin Church in Norman Italy*; Paul Oldfield, *Sanctity and Pilgrimage*. See also Lynn White Jr. *Latin Monasticism in Norman Sicily* (Cambridge, MA: Harvard University Press, 1938). For the process of linguistic latinization and the end of Arabic, see Metcalfe, *Muslims and Christians in Norman Sicily*.

56. Ibn Jubayr recorded one example of a mosque converted to a church when the owner of that mosque, an expert in Islamic law named Ibn Zurʿa, apostacized and became an expert in Christian law. Ibn Jubayr, *Riḥlat*, 313; Broadhurst, *Travels*, 357. For more on this man and the conversion of his mosque into a church, see Metcalfe, "The Muslims of Sicily," 307–309.

57. Paul Oldfield has linked the Norman promotion of the cult of St. Agatha in Sicily with the travel and communication networks of crusaders as well as the "international stage" offered by the universalizing claims of the Roman Church. The Normans were intentional, he argues, in using the cult of Agatha in the advancement of a Latin Christian identity on the island. Paul Oldfield, "The Medieval Cult of St Agatha of Catania and the Consolidation of Christian Sicily," *Journal of Ecclesiastical History* 62, no. 3 (2011): 439–456.

58. For the general intellectual culture of Norman Sicily, see Matthew, *The Norman Kingdom of Sicily*, 112–128. For a focus on literature and, in particular, poetry, see Mallette, *The Kingdom of Sicily*. There also emerged a school of Hebrew poets in twelfth-century Sicily. See S. M. Stern, "A Twelfth-

FIGURE 8. Church of San Giovanni dei Lebbrosi, traditionally dated to 1071. Although a Norman foundation, this church and others in Palermo may have been built to visually resemble local mosques. Photo by author.

Christianity on the cultural ascendancy, however, for most of the twelfth century, Sicily acted as something of a meeting space for intellectuals and religious travelers from all of the major civilizations and regions of the broader Mediterranean world.

The Crusades, too, placed Sicily at the nexus between Latin Christendom and the Mediterranean world.[59] Famously in conflict with the growing power of the papacy and its interests in Italy, the Norman kings were also at many times agents of the popes, both on and outside the island; one way they supported wider papal efforts was by participating in the Crusades (although, of course, as Anna Komnene suggested, their crusading activities also suited the Norman goal of encroaching against imperial power). The Norman Kingdom of Sicily served doubly in the crusading project—as a point of origin for some

Century Circle of Hebrew Poets in Sicily," pts. 1 and 2, *Journal of Jewish Studies* 1 (1954): 60–79; 2 (1954): 110–113.

59. See, for example, Salvatore Fodale, "Ruggero II el al seconda Crociata," in Musca, *Il mezzogiorno normanno-svevo e le Crociate*, 131–144; and G. A. Loud, "Norman Italy and the Holy Land," in *The Horns of Hattin: Proceedings of the Second Conference of the Society for the Study of the Crusades and the Latin East*, ed. Benjamin Z. Kedar (Jerusalem, 1992), 49–62.

crusaders and as a stopover for European knights and pilgrims on their journeys to the Levant. Indeed, the Hauteville family from Sicily and southern Italy provided the Crusades with several leaders, such as Bohemond (the son of Robert Guiscard) and his nephew Tancred in the First Crusade. Sicilian and southern Italian ports, importantly eastern ones such as Messina on the island and Bari on the mainland, became famous for housing crusading forces from Latin Europe en route to Jerusalem. The ship on which Ibn Jubayr arrived in Messina, indeed, sailed there from crusader-held Acre, as would have numerous other ships carrying knights and pilgrims on their way to fight or pray in the Holy Land. The crusading forces of Richard the Lionheart spent the winter of 1190 in Messina en route to the Third Crusade, where the English king negotiated matters relating to his sister Joan, who had been queen of Sicily as William II's wife until his death the previous year, and to his own bride, Berengaria of Navarre. Thus, in this one moment, we see simultaneous political and social links being forged between Sicily and Christian Spain, England, and the Levant. The Sicilian connection to the Holy Land and to the crusading effort certainly outlasted this one moment. Indeed, over the next several centuries of crusading, the location of Sicily as a port on the way to Jerusalem would become increasingly important because the sea route between Latin Europe and the Holy Land came to take precedence over the traditional land route through ever more hostile Byzantine lands. The voyages of crusaders through Sicily thus helped to bring the island closer to the Latin Christian sphere, in both Europe and the Holy Land, and to strengthen Sicily's role as a place of connection between the Latin world and the Muslim lands that were the targets of the Crusades.

Economic Connections in the Latin and Muslim Mediterranean

As Norman Sicily gained cultural and spiritual prominence in connection to both Latin Europe and the Muslim territories of the eastern Mediterranean, the Norman rulers sought to promote its economic centrality in the Mediterranean region, particularly as a mediating market for merchants from northern Italy and products from the southern Mediterranean—at least for a few decades.[60] Islamic Sicily was extensively involved in the commercial exchange

60. The economy and wider trade connections of Norman Sicily have been written about extensively by David Abulafia. Among his many important works on this topic are: "The Crown and the Economy under Roger II and His Successors," *Dumbarton Oaks Papers* 37 (1983): 1–14; "Sul commercio del grano siciliano nel tardo Duecento," in *Atti del Congresso sul VII Centenario del Vespro Siciliano / XI*

networks of the Muslim Mediterranean, and in particular with Ifrīqiya and Egypt, and many of these trade routes and traditions of exchange persisted into the twelfth century. The trade in Sicilian grain continued to be of great economic and alimentary importance to Ifrīqiya, well into the time of the Norman kingdom. Commodities and gold from the Muslim Mediterranean thus flowed into Sicily, while the island's grain export grew to even greater economic significance both to the island and to merchants from around the wider Mediterranean region. At the same time, the trade in Sicilian commodities attracted the attention of northern Italian merchants, who had been active in Mediterranean commerce prior to the Norman conquest of Sicily but who could now take advantage both of Sicily's mercantile contacts in the wider Mediterranean and of its geographical location to enhance their own positions in the booming commercial world of the Mediterranean. Indeed, David Abulafia has shown that grain and textiles from Sicily, along with its gold coins (which were not minted in northern Italy or Europe until the middle of the thirteenth century), formed essential imports for the economies of mercantile city-states such as Pisa, Venice, and Genoa.[61] So, while Sicily's economic connections with Muslim northern Africa were vital to the economies of both Muslim Sicily and the island under Norman rule, they were also increasingly profitable for the northern Italian merchants who used the island's ports and traded in its wheat, textiles, and gold. By the end of the Norman period, however, it would be clear that these Italian merchants could access the ports and commodities of the Muslim world directly, with little need for an island as intermediary.[62]

The Norman rulers themselves must have been involved in this trade. Royally owned lands were major producers of wheat, the administration earned taxes on these sales, and we have seen one *fatwā* in which the Norman royal mint was accused of enriching the Christian rulers by alloying the purer Is-

---

Congresso della Corona d'Aragona, Palermo-Erice-Trapani, maggio 1982 (Palermo: Accademia di Scienze Lettere e Arti, 1983), 5–22; "Trade and Crusade, 1050–1250," in *Cross Cultural Convergences in the Crusader Period, Essays Presented to Aryeh Grabois on His Sixty-Fifth Birthday*, ed. Michael Goodrich, Sophia Menache, and Sylvia Schein (New York: Peter Long, 1995), 1–20; *The Two Italies*; and "Pisan Commercial Colonies and Consulates in Twelfth-Century Sicily," *The English Historical Review* 93 (1978): 68–81.

61. See in particular the formulation of this argument in Abulafia, *The Two Italies*.

62. For the transformations in Italian trade patterns, see Romney David Smith, "Calamity and Transition: Re-imagining Italian Trade in the Eleventh-Century Mediterranean," *Past and Present* 228 (2015): 15–56. The trade of Pisans in the western Mediterranean has been studied by Travis Bruce in "The Politics of Violence and Trade: Denia and Pisa in the Eleventh Century," *Journal of Medieval History* 32 (2006): 127–142; and Russell Hopley, "Aspects of Trade in the Western Mediterranean during the Eleventh and Twelfth Centuries: Perspectives from Islamic Fatwās and State Correspondence," *Mediaevalia* 32 (2011): 5–42. For the diffusion throughout the Muslim Mediterranean of institutions that facilitated direct trade by visiting European merchants, see Olivia Remie Constable, *Housing the Stranger in the Mediterranean World: Lodging, Trade, and Travel in Late Antiquity and the Middle Ages* (Cambridge: Cambridge University Press, 2003).

lamic gold coins. The Normans took an increasingly strong hand in managing the means of production on their island and its commercial relationships with other regions. The growing state monopoly on trade may have been one of the factors that shut out the Jewish merchants of the Cairo Geniza community, causing them to shift the focus of their commercial endeavors elsewhere.

Both of our visitors to twelfth-century Sicily, al-Idrīsī and Ibn Jubayr, highlighted the broad connectivity that Sicily enjoyed in the Mediterranean and praised the island's agricultural wealth and productivity and the availability of a variety of goods. Ibn Jubayr claimed that "the prosperity of the island surpasses description. It is enough to say that it is a daughter of Spain in the extent of its cultivation, in the luxuriance of its harvests, and in its well-being, having an abundance of varied produce, and fruits of every kind and species," while al-Idrīsī called it the "pearl of its age" for its bounty, population, and beauty. According to al-Idrīsī, Sicily was renowned both for its noble history and for the great number of travelers and merchants who came to the island from all over the world. His account of Sicily's people, towns, and landscape purports to be exhaustive and certainly shows great familiarity with the island's agriculture and economy. The towns were filled with gardens, streams, vineyards ("kurūm"), trees, and a fishing industry that brought in a large quantity of tuna. The capital city of Palermo is described as a large and lovely city, full of both ancient and modern buildings.[63] It was filled with orchards and gardens and, like the whole of the island, was presented as verdant and well watered. Al-Idrīsī depicted Palermo as divided into two parts, a citadel ("qaṣr") and an adjoining town called Khāliṣa. In the citadel he described many palaces, churches, mosques, hostels, *funduqs* (inns that could also serve as warehouses), baths, markets, gardens, and lovely houses.[64] Khāliṣa contained the Gate of the Sea, the arsenal, and the naval fleet. Al-Idrīsī also described the important eastern seaport at Messina; he called it "the point of anchorage for all of the Christian nations" ("bilād al-Rūm").[65] The port at Messina also received ships from both the Muslim and Christian worlds. Travelers, merchants, and products from many lands arrived in Messina, and Messina's harbor also housed the royal navy.

Ibn Jubayr likewise experienced the port of Messina as filled with ships from around the Mediterranean. Despite being a city attractive to merchants and bustling with ships from throughout the region, however, it was unlivable,

---

63. al-Idrīsī, *Opus Geographicum*, 590–592.

64. For the many uses of a *funduq* and the transmission of this institution around the Mediterranean world, see Olivia Remie Constable, *Housing the Stranger*.

65. Ibid., 593.

according to Ibn Jubayr, because it was a primarily Christian city that smelled bad, and there was no one there who understood his customs or language. Thus, he deemed Messina uninviting and unfriendly, while nonetheless safe for the Muslim traveler. Ibn Jubayr found ample goods for purchase at fair prices in the markets, but these were almost exclusively sold by Christian merchants. Palermo, on the other hand, had many Muslim residents, many of whom were merchants: indeed, Ibn Jubayr said that Muslims formed the majority of the merchants there. The capital city, unlike Messina, was filled with the sights and sounds of Muslim cultural life, even if the Friday sermon (*khuṭbah*) had been outlawed.

Having arrived in Messina on a Genoese ship that had departed from Acre two months earlier, Ibn Jubayr and his fellow passengers—including both Muslim and Christian pilgrims—came to land after their ship was destroyed by the wind and currents in the Strait of Messina.[66] He departed for Spain from the western port of Trapani, again traveling on a Christian ship, sailing in convoy with two others. These experiences with Sicily's ports gave him the opportunity to describe the harbors at Messina and Trapani, both of which he characterized as bustling with ships from all over the Mediterranean. Messina, he stated, was the destination of all vessels in the region, both because of its geographical position and because of the favorable market conditions that prevailed there.[67] He described the deep harbor and the narrow strait separating the island from the mainland, which allowed ships to approach very close to the city itself and made small boats for loading and unloading ships unnecessary; thus he called this port the most remarkable of all maritime ports. The great depth of the harbor also enabled many ships to line up at the quay: when Ibn Jubayr arrived there, it was filled with numerous ships, including those of King William II, who was in the city at the time to oversee the building of his fleet. According to Ibn Jubayr's understanding, the royal navy also docked at Palermo, and he encountered the king's vessels again at Trapani.

Sicily in the late twelfth century apparently had several very active ports, receiving ships from throughout the Mediterranean. When Ibn Jubayr and his party were waiting for their ship to al-Andalus at Trapani, the far western port

---

66. This journey, conducted very late in the year, went from Acre to one of the islands to the east of the Greek archipelago, then passed south of Crete before the ship was pushed back toward Crete by a storm. Ibn Jubayr's vessel eventually found its way and came to dock for a few days at another Greek island, before finally making its way to Messina. There, in the straits separating the island from the mainland, the ship was wrecked, and the passengers, who were hungry and thirsty from the long journey—which had taken more than twice as long as expected—needed to be rescued. Ibn Jubayr had anticipated the trip to last between fifteen and twenty days, but it took two months. Ibn Jubayr, *Riḥlat*, 292–293; Broadhurst, *Travels*, 335.

67. Description of Messina in Ibn Jubayr, *Riḥlat*, 294–297; Broadhurst, *Travels*, 336–339.

city on the island, the geographer witnessed a similarly high level of shipping activity connecting the island to the ports of the western Mediterranean. Also there he encountered the royal navy, which was preparing for action. He heard various speculations about the intended target of King William's naval fleet: he reported that some people thought it was Ifrīqiya, others Mallorca, or Alexandria, or even Constantinople.[68] Ibn Jubayr declared that, like Messina, Trapani was "an excellent harbor, most suited for shipping, and is therefore much used by the Rūm [Christians]."[69] In describing the town and port of Trapani, Ibn Jubayr noted that it was particularly important as a point of embarkation for trips to Africa; he claimed that it was most used by those who sailed from Sicily to western ports in the Mediterranean, many of which were under Muslim control. Indeed, he stated that it only took one day and one night to sail from Trapani to Tunis.[70] Even more significantly, Ibn Jubayr asserted that the sea between the Sicilian and North African ports was navigable in all seasons. Ships did not cease to sail between Sicily and Tunis in either summer or winter, according to his account, but only when strong winds made the voyage impossible.[71] Having arranged for a voyage and paid for the passage to Spain, Ibn Jubayr found himself waiting in the port until the ships were cleared for departure. His trip was delayed, he learned, by the order of the Sicilian king, William II, who needed the port for his naval excursion. After the owner of Ibn Jubayr's ship bribed the local governor, the boats were allowed to depart for Spain—one bound for al-Andalus and one for Ceuta, on which he claimed he had sailed to Alexandria at the start of his journey.[72] Together, then, the ports of Messina and Trapani linked the island with both Christian and Muslim ports throughout the Mediterranean basin.

Ibn Jubayr's account of his voyage home highlights this broad connectivity, but also the fact that by this time most of the ships were owned and captained by northern Italians rather than by Sicilians, Jews, or Muslims. The vessel on which he took passage, piloted by a Genoese captain, departed in convoy with two other Christian ships and sailed to the port of the island of al-Rāhib (Favignana, located about four miles west of Trapani), where they were met by another Christian ship. This fourth vessel was also owned by a Genoese

---

68. Ibn Jubayr, *Riḥlat*, 310–313; Broadhurst, *Travels*, 353–356.

69. Description of Trapani in Ibn Jubayr, *Riḥlat*, 308–313; Broadhurst, *Travels*, 351–356.

70. Ibn Jubayr, *Riḥlat*, 308; Broadhurst, *Travels*, 351.

71. We have already seen several examples of failed and danger-filled journeys between Sicily and the Ifrīqiyan ports of Tunis, Sfax, Sūsa, and al-Mahdiyya, possibly belying the blithe attitude with which Ibn Jubayr presented the ease of sailing between the two lands. It was certainly a shorter and easier journey than many in the Mediterranean, but the trip was not without its difficulties and perils.

72. The destinations of these two ships are mentioned in Ibn Jubayr, *Riḥlat*, 307 and 309; Broadhurst, *Travels*, 350 and 352.

captain, named Marco, and was en route from Alexandria. The four ships, which carried Muslim pilgrims whom Ibn Jubayr recognized from his stay in Mecca, sailed together from al-Rāhib to Spain by way of Sardinia and Khāliṭa (Galita), which he identified as an uninhabited but Christian-owned island. This type of coastal navigation through port hopping (cabotage) was typical of medieval Mediterranean seafaring and enhanced the importance of accessible and geographically advantageous ports like those on Sicily. Here, we see the twelfth-century port of Trapani in connection with Ifrīqiya, Alexandria, and Spain by way of Sardinia. The eastern port of the island, Messina, was connected to the Levant and Constantinople. Thus, we see a Christian Sicily visited by Christian ships sailing from the eastern and western Mediterranean basins, and bustling with fleets of royal vessels that could potentially carry out naval attacks on any of a variety of locations in the wider Mediterranean world. This web of linkages, placing Sicily in the position of a widely connected and centrally located stopover point along an array of short- and long-distance routes, was decidedly to the advantage of the Norman kings. Even more significant, perhaps, is Ibn Jubayr's observation that there were only Christian vessels at these Sicilian ports—most of them owned by Genoese—although the passengers aboard the various ships were Christian and Muslim. Such evidence accords with other scholars' findings that, by the end of the twelfth century, the Mediterranean shipping lanes were primarily sailed by Christian ships, even as they carried Muslim merchants, diplomats, and pilgrims aboard. Although the ports were Sicilian, the ships and their captains were Genoese. This association, likewise, is reflected in the larger economic patterns developing across the twelfth century: although the Normans sought to place their island at the center of the Mediterranean economy, by the thirteenth century, northern Italian merchants—particularly the Genoese, but also the Pisans and Venetians—had taken over the business of trade in Sicily's ports. That is, the island and its ports and goods retained their centrality in wider trade networks, but through the agency (and to the benefit) of northern Italian merchants rather than Sicilian ones.[73]

Sicily's economic links to both the dār al-Islām and Latin Christendom thus continued under Norman rule, but these ties shifted in meaning as the island became a transportation depot and connection point for Christian and Muslim markets in a way that had not been the case in the earlier periods. Politically and diplomatically, Norman Sicily maintained communications with both Byzantine and Muslim lands, but for very different reasons. The island in the twelfth century operated less as a meeting ground for envoys from the Greek,

73. Abulafia, *The Two Italies*.

Latin, and Muslim worlds, as it had done during the Byzantine period, than as a base for military attacks against both the Greek and Muslim polities in the Mediterranean and thereby as a staging ground for the Normans' broader claims to power. At the same time, there continued to be a multicultural population of Muslims, Jews, and Greeks in Norman Sicily, although we see a significant shift in the free communications between those native populations and their broader cultural and religious realms. The Normans used cultural elements of these subject populations to project an image of themselves as powerful kings that would be understood in the various linguistic and artistic idioms of their multicultural Mediterranean surroundings. They thus wished not only to place their island directly at the center of the Mediterranean system but also to represent themselves as rulers located right at the heart of the economic, political, and cultural orbits of this wider Mediterranean world. For these purposes, Sicily's Norman rulers both exploited their territory's historical connections with Muslim and Greek regions of the Mediterranean and maximized the island's geographical location in order to foster, create, or establish new networks of communication during the later eleventh and twelfth centuries.

Conclusion

Later medieval maps help to confirm Sicily's new conceptual place in the Mediterranean—a position that had been crafted by the Norman rulers. These Christian maps not only visually depict Sicily—unlike the earlier Muslim maps that omitted the island altogether—but also give it a position of prominence, quite near to the center of the Mediterranean and, thus, of the world.[1] Thirteenth-century maps, created during and soon after the reign of the Hohenstaufen king Frederick II—who brought even more centrality to Sicily through his simultaneous rule as Holy Roman emperor and king of Sicily, with a famed court culture at Palermo—show Sicily as a large triangle, taking up nearly all the space of the central Mediterranean Sea. For example, the anonymous map known as the Psalter World Map (ca. 1262–1270) (figure 9) shows a Sicily that is quite large, nearly fills the Mediterranean Sea (alongside numerous other islands), and is placed directly in the middle of that body of water.[2] Such increased visual prominence reflects the

1. To be sure, a tradition of Islamic maps of the twelfth and thirteenth centuries also begins to depict Sicily prominently within the Mediterranean, along with Crete and Cyprus. See Pinto, *Medieval Islamic Maps*, 70ff.

2. For more on the tradition of later medieval European maps called *mappae mundi* (maps of the world), see David Woodward, "Medieval *mappaemundi*," in *The History of Cartography*, vol. 1, *Cartography in Prehistoric, Ancient, and Medieval Europe and the Mediterranean*, ed. J. B. Harley and David Woodward (Chicago: The University of Chicago Press, 1987), 286–370.

FIGURE 9. Psalter world map, anon., ca. 1262–1270. Oriented with Jerusalem as the center of the globe. © The British Library Board, Add MS 28681, fol. 9r.

important role that Sicily played in the contemporary political and economic systems of the Latin Christian world. Indeed, Sicily lies almost directly adjacent to Jerusalem, an arrangement possibly signifying Sicily's position as an important stop along the journeys of European pilgrims and crusaders, who, by the end of the twelfth century, consistently preferred the sea voyage to the eastern Mediterranean over the traditional land journey through Byzantine

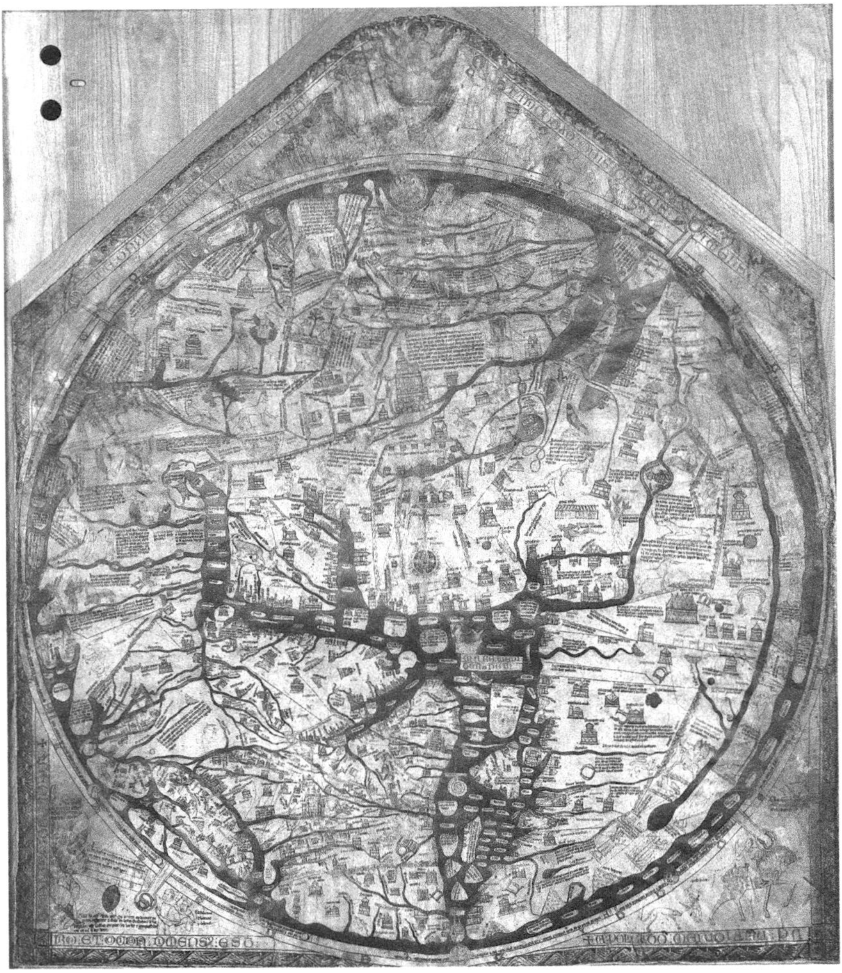

Figure 10. Hereford Mappa Mundi, attributed to Richard de Bello, ca. 1290. Oriented with Jerusalem as the center of the globe. Located in Hereford Cathedral, Hereford, England. Image courtesy of the Hereford Cathedral Library.

and Muslim territory. No viewer of this map could avoid the conclusion that Sicily was an island significant both in its immediate region and in the Christian world as a whole.

This position of centrality is even more apparent in the late thirteenth-century map known as the Hereford Mappa Mundi (ca. 1290) (figure 10). Following medieval Christian cartographic tradition, which placed Jerusalem at the center of the earth—literally as the "navel of the world"—the Hereford map depicts Sicily in closer proximity to this most important of all cities in the

Christian imagination. These two cartographical depictions of Sicily thus help to show that the island had gained a prominent role, both practical and conceptual, in the Latin Christian world that it had not had in earlier centuries. These representations also reveal Sicily to have been closely integrated into larger currents in the political and religious world of Latin Christendom. The Norman kings, despite the brevity of their rule on the island, were primarily responsible for the heightened centrality of Sicily in this conception of the world. They actively worked to exploit their island's location in the Mediterranean and its preexisting economic and cultural connections with both the eastern Mediterranean and Muslim northern Africa in order to create a broader Mediterranean power base for themselves. While their military exploits in Byzantine and Muslim lands saw no lasting success, the efforts themselves demonstrate their intentions of using the island as a launching pad for power on a broader stage.

In contrast, Sicily in previous periods served more peripheral roles in the larger civilizations of which it was a part. But it is important to keep in mind that "peripheral" does not equal "unimportant." Both the Byzantine emperors and the various Muslim dynasties that ruled the island from outside fought strenuously to prevent it from falling into the hands of invaders. The choice to expend resources on defending the island—at times when even the remote capital itself was under siege—indicates that it was perceived as vital to the interests of its distant rulers. Indeed, Constantinople had inextricably bound Sicily to its larger imperial project in the Mediterranean such that the island functioned, in a variety of ways, as an outpost and an arm of central imperial authority. That, indeed, was the role the Byzantines needed Sicily to play in the region, and it was well situated to do so. Sicily was simultaneously far enough from Constantinople and close enough, in terms of communications, that it could serve as a site of exile, a source of representatives to enforce Byzantine will in the region, an arena for diplomatic exchanges with both Latins and Muslims, and even, for a time, the alternate capital of the entire empire. After Sicily's loss to the Aghlabids, Constantinople did not give up the hope of reconquering the island from Muslim control, continuing to launch naval attacks on the occupiers periodically throughout the tenth and early eleventh centuries. Whether in the context of the larger Muslim-Christian contest or because of their ambitions to revive their power in the western Mediterranean, Byzantine emperors thought it essential to attempt to bring Sicily back under Greek control. Even though it lay on the far edge of the empire, it had been of central importance—both at the time of their rule there and in later historical memory.

The Muslim polities that controlled Sicily used the island for far different purposes. In Arabic scholarly geographies and the personal travel account of

Ibn Ḥawqal, Sicily appears as a culturally and conceptually marginal region within the broader expanse of the Muslim world. In addition, Sicily's political and diplomatic role in the dār al-Islām was fundamentally different than it had been under Byzantine administration. Qayrawān, Sicily's conqueror and overseer during the Aghlabid period from the ninth through early tenth century, did not need the island to serve as an extension of its political authority in the same way that Constantinople did. Although Sicily was at times noted for its role in *jihād*—theoretically important for expanding the boundaries of Islam in the world—the actual efforts and successes on that front by Sicilian Muslims were temporary, or focused on spoils of war, and did not result in a significant expansion of the dār al-Islām. Thus, Sicily under Muslim control did not, for practical purposes, lie at the crossing point between a remote capital and the territories in southern Italy. The capital of the *emīrate* was indeed close by in Ifrīqiya, so there was no need for an extended arm of its governing authority from the island and its local leaders, and thus Sicily's role as a regional power base during the Byzantine period was not replicated during the Muslim centuries.

Again, however, this fact does not mean that Ifrīqiyan leaders did not consider Sicily a valuable addition to the lands under their control: after the Fatimid takeover in the early tenth century, a combined force of native Sicilians and the recently overthrown Aghlabids attempted to rebel against Fatimid rule. They, like the Greeks before them, wished to retain the island and regain it after it had been lost. The Fatimids turned away from Sicily, however, and toward the central Islamic lands—allowing a semi-independent dynasty of governors to rule the island—but the governors they appointed to rule in Ifrīqiya, the Zīrids, endeavored to defend the island from Norman invasion. And, like the Byzantines before them, the Ifrīqiyans tried to restore the island to Muslim rule by attacking Latin Christian Sicily, although they were overpowered by the military might of the Normans. At the same time, we have seen that later Arabic chroniclers looked back to the conquest of Sicily with great detail and drama, suggesting that the historical memory of Muslim control over Sicily continued to be vivid and meaningful long after the island fell into Christian hands.

A large part of their desire to keep or restore Sicily to Ifrīqiyan rule may have been due to the outsized importance the island held for the economy and subsistence of Muslim North Africa. Indeed, rather than operating as a meeting place on the border between Christianity and Islam—as Sicily had done in many ways during the Byzantine period—Muslim-ruled Sicily was firmly located in the dār al-Islām and served as a vital market in central Mediterranean trade, as depicted in the Geniza merchants' letters. Even after the Christian conquest of the island, Sicily's grain crop was considered critical for the sustenance of the Ifrīqiyan Muslim population, which was suffering from famine brought on by invasion and disorder. In fact, Sicily's grain was so economically and alimentarily important that some Muslims risked censure from their religious-legal authorities by crossing the border into Christendom even though such journeys had been forbidden. Therefore, although the island may have been geographically peripheral vis-à-vis a wider Islamic world that extended from Spain to central Asia, for the Muslim population in North Africa and its needs, Sicily was absolutely central.

In later centuries, Sicily's place in the trade networks of the central Mediterranean was also crucial to the Norman project of creating a Mediterranean kingdom with a broad economic and political reach and an expansive cultural image. For the first time ruled from a capital internal to the island rather than by a distant set of leaders, Sicily under the Normans moved to the very heart of the Mediterranean as a hub for Muslim-Christian trade, an advance base for far-flung military conquests, and the site of a religiously and linguistically diverse culture that allowed the Normans to promote an image of themselves as powerful kings of a multicultural island. At the same time, their actions and ambitions brought their kingdom ever closer to the politically, culturally, and economically significant spaces of Latin Christendom. Through diplomacy, patronage of Latin ecclesiastical structures, participation in the Crusades, trade with northern Italian merchants, and marriage with the royal houses of Christian Europe, the Norman kings fostered strong connections to Latin Europe and the papacy (even though that particular relationship often proved troublesome). They simultaneously exploited Sicily's economic links to Muslim North Africa and made trade treaties with merchants from northern Italy, which enhanced Sicily's position as an active nexus in Latin-Muslim trade and its role in the larger economic system of the Mediterranean world—but which ultimately led to the ascendancy of those Italian merchants at the expense of the Sicilians, as they came to control the economic pathways that the Norman kings attempted to dominate. In their brief century of rule over Sicily, then, the Norman counts and kings moved their island to the very center of both the Mediterranean world and the Muslim-Christian encounter. This was a project not only of manipulating and creating broad connections but also of conceptually re-centering the world as a whole and Sicily's place within it.

To return, then, to our original question about the "horizons" of medieval Sicily, we must conclude that they shifted and moved significantly over time—but that these transformations were not immediately attendant upon military conquest. Sometimes, indeed, conquest only confirmed a change that had begun long before. Likewise, some political shifts caused only slow alterations in the position of the island and its sphere within the Mediterranean. While

Sicily thus moved, conceptually, to the middle of the Mediterranean only under Norman rule, it was a place that could be, in both the Byzantine and Islamic periods, simultaneously peripheral and central: sometimes a geographical position on the edge could foster a conceptual role for the island that placed it right at the heart of larger political, diplomatic, or economic needs. Sicily's place within larger Mediterranean systems was determined not by its geographical location—either on shipping lanes or as a stepping stone between landmasses—but by larger forces of political change, shifts in the balance of power, and economic need as well as the actions of regular people—merchants, pilgrims, envoys, and others—who traveled to and from Sicily and thus involved the island in patterns of communication, contact, conflict, and exchange. Sicily's conceptual and practical linkages to other spaces in the Mediterranean were manipulated, transformed, severed, or constructed by the Byzantines, Muslims, and Normans in turn, each according to their needs and expectations.

Bibliography

Published Primary Sources

Adamnan. *De locis sanctis*. Edited by Denis Meehan. Dublin: Dublin Institute for Advanced Studies, 1958.

Agnellus, Bishop of Ravenna. *Liber pontificalis ecclesia Ravennatis*. Edited by Claudia Nauerth. 2 vols. Fontes Christiani. Freiburg: Herder, 1996.

Amatus of Montecassino. *Storia de'Normanni*. Edited by Vincenzo de Bartholomeis. Fonti per la storia d'Italia, vol. 76. Rome: Istituto storico italiano, 1935. English translation by Prescott N. Dunbar, *The History of the Normans*, edited by G. A. Loud. Woodbridge: Boydell Press, 2004.

Annales regni Francorum inde ab a. 741. usque ad a. 829. Edited by F. Kurze. *MGH, Scriptores rerum Germanicarum in usum scholarum*, vol. 6. Hannover, 1895.

al-Bakrī, Abū ʿUbayd. *Kitāb al-masālik wa al-mamālik*. Edited by A. van Leuven and A. Ferré. 2 vols. Tunis: al-Dar al-ʿArabiya li'l-Kitab, 1992.

Benjamin of Tudela. *The Itinerary of Benjamin of Tudela*. Edited and translated by Marcus N. Adler and Fuat Sezgin. Frankfurt: Institute for the History of Arabic-Islamic Science, Johann Wolfgang Goethe University, 1995.

Ben-Sasson, Menahem, ed. *The Jews of Sicily 825–1068: Documents and Sources*. Jerusalem: Ben-Zvi Institute, 1991.

Biblioteca arabo-sicula, ossia raccolta di testi Arabici che toccano la geografia, la storia, le biografie e la bibliografia della Sicilia, testi arabici. Edited by Michele Amari. Leipzig: F. A. Brockhaus, 1857–1887. 2nd revised edition by Umberto Rizzitano. 2 vols. Palermo: Accademia Nazaionale di Scienze Lettere e Arti, 1988. Italian translation in *Biblioteca arabo-sicula, ossia raccolta di testi Arabici che toccano la geografia, la storia, le biografie e la bibliografia della Sicilia, versione italiana*. Edited by Michele Amari. 2 vols. Turin and Rome: E. Loescher, 1880–1889. 2nd revised edition by Umberto Rizzitano et al. 3 vols. Palermo: Accademia Nazaionale di Scienze Lettere e Arti, 1997–1998.

Cozza-Luzi, Giuseppe, ed., trans. *Historia et laudes SS. Sabae et Macarii iuniorum e Sicilia auctore Oreste Patriarcha Hierosolymitano*. Rome: Typis Vaticanis, 1893.

Cusa, Salvatore, ed. *I diplomi Greci ed Arabi di Sicilia*. 2 vols. Palermo: D. Lao, 1868.

al-Daʾūdī, Abū Jaʿfar. *Kitāb al-amwāl*. Edited by Riḍā Shahāda. Rabat: Markaz Iḥyāʾ al-Turāth al-Maghribī, 1988.

al-Dimashqī, Shams al-Dīn. *Cosmographie*. Edited by August Ferdinand Michael Mehren. Saint Petersburg: l'Académie Impriale des Sciences, 1866. French translation by August Ferdinand Michael Mehren, *Manuel de la Cosmographie du Moyen Age*. Paris, 1874.

Falcandus, Hugo. *La Historia o Liber de regno Sicilie*. Edited by G. B. Siragusa. Fonti per la Storia d'Italia, vol. 22. Rome: Istituto storico italiano, 1897.

Gregory the Great (Gregorius Magnus). *Registrum espitularum libri*. Edited by Dag Norberg. Corpus Christianorum Series Latina, vols. 140, 140A. Turnhout: Brepols, 1982. English translation by John R. C. Martyn, *Letters of Gregory the Great*. 3 vols. Toronto: PIMS, 2004.

Ḥudūd al-ʿĀlam: 'The Regions of the World,' a Persian Geography, 372 A.H. / 982 A.D. 2nd ed. Edited by C. E. Bosworth. Translated by V. Minorsky. London: E. J. W. Gibb Memorial Trust, 1970.

Huneberc of Heidenheim. "*Hodoeporicon S. Willibaldi*." In *Itinera Hierosolymitana et descriptiones Terrae Sanctae bellis sacris anteriora*, vol. 1, edited by Titus Tobler and Augustus Molinier, 241–281. Osnabrück: Zeller, 1966.

Ibn al-Athīr, ʿIzz al-Dīn. *al-Kāmil fī al-tārīkh*. Edited by Carl J. Tornberg. 12 vols. Beirut: Dār Ṣādir, 1965. French translation by E. Fagnan, *Annales du Maghreb et de l'Espagne*. Algiers: Typographie Adolphe Jourdan, 1898.

Ibn al-Bayṭār, ʿAbd Allāh ibn Aḥmad. "Traité des Simples." Pts. 1, 2, and 3. Translated by Lucien Leclerc, *Notices et extraits des Manuscrits de la Biblioteque Nationale* 23 (1877), 25 (1881), 26 (1883).

Ibn Ḥawqal, Muḥammad Abū al-Qāsim. *Kitāb ṣūrat al-arḍ*. 2nd ed. Edited by J. H. Kramers. *BGA*, vol. 2. Leiden: E. J. Brill, 1967. French translation by J. H. Kramers and Gaston Wiet, *Configuration de la terre*. Beirut: Commission internationale pour la traduction des chefs-d'œuvre, 1964.

Ibn Ḥayyān, Abū Marwān Ḥayyān. *al-Muqtabas*. Vol 5. Edited by P. Chalmeta and F. Corriente. Madrid: Instituto Hispano-Arabe de Cultura, 1979.

Ibn ʿIdhārī, Aḥmad ibn Muḥammad. *Kitāb al-bayān al-mughrib fī akhbār al-maghrib wa al- Andalus*. Beirut: Dār al-Thaqafa, 1967.

Ibn Jubayr, Muḥammad ibn Aḥmad. *Riḥlat Ibn Jubayr*. Beirut: Dār Ṣādir, 1964. English translation by R. J. C. Broadhurst, *The Travels of Ibn Jubayr*. London: Jonathan Cape, 1952.

Ibn Khaldun. *Kitāb al-ʿibar fī ayyām al-ʿarab wa al-ʿajam*. 14 vols. Beirut: Dār al-Kitāb al-Lubnānī, 1983–1986.

Ibn Khallikān. *Wafayāt al-aʿyān wa-anbāʾ abnāʾ al-zamān*. Edited by Ihṣān ʿAbbās. 8 vols. Beirut: Dār al-Thaqāfa, 1968–1977.

Ibn Rustah, Aḥmad ibn ʿUmar. *Kitāb al-Aʿlāq al-nafīsa*. Edited by M. J. de Goeje. *BGA*, vol. 7. Leiden: E. J. Brill, 1967. French translation by Gaston Wiet, *Les Atours Précieux*. Cairo: Société de Géographie d'Égypte, 1955.

al-Idrīsī, Abū ʿAbd Allāh Muḥammad. *Opus Geographicum, sive "Liber ad eorum delectationem qui terras peragrare studeant."* 9 fascs. Edited by Enrico Cerulli and Francesco Gabrieli et al. 2nd ed. Naples / Rome: Istituto Universitario Orientale di Napoli / Istituto Italiano per il Medio ed Estremo Oriente, 1970–1984. Partial Arabic edition and French translation in Reinhart Pieter Anne Dozy and Michael Jan de Goeje, *Description de l'Afrique et de l'Espagne*. Leiden: E. J. Brill, 1968. Complete French translation in al-Idrīsī, *La Première géographie de l'Occident*, translated by Henri Bresc and Annliese Nef. Paris: Flammarion, 1999.

Ignatius the Deacon. *Vita Gregorii Decapolitae*. *BHG* 711. Edition and French translation by Francis Dvornik, *La vie de saint Grégoire le Décapolite et les Slaves macédoniens au IXe siècle*. Paris: Champion, 1926.

al-Iṣṭakhrī, Abū Isḥāq. *Kitāb masālik al-mamālik*. Edited by M. J. de Goeje. *BGA*, vol. 1. Leiden: E. J. Brill, 1967.

Itinerarium Bernardi Monachi Franci. In *Itinera Hierosolymitana et descriptiones Terrae Sanctae bellis sacris anteriora*, vol. 1, edited by Titus Tobler and Augustus Molinier, 307–320. Osnabrück: Zeller, 1966.

Itinerarium S. Willibaldi. In *Itinera Hierosolymitana et descriptiones Terrae Sanctae bellis sacris anteriora*, vol. 1, edited by Titus Tobler and Augustus Molinier, 283–297. Osnabrück: Zeller, 1966.

Leonis III. *Papae Epistolae X*. Edited by Ernst Dümmler and Karl Hampe. *MGH. Epistolae Karolini aevi*, vol. 5, 85–104. Hanover, 1898–1899.

Leontios, Presbyter of Rome. *Vita S. Gregorii Agrigentini*. *BHG* 707. *PG* 98, 550–715. Greek edition and German translation by Albrecht Berger, *Das Leben des Heiligen Gregorios von Agrigent Leontios Presbiteros von Rom: Kritische Ausgabe, Übersetzung und Kommentar*. Berlin: Berliner Byzantinische Arbeiten, 1995. English translation by John R. C. Martyn, *A Translation of Abbot Leontios' Life of Saint Gregory, Bishop of Agrigento*. Lewiston, NY: Edwin Mellen Press, 2004.

Liber Pontificalis. Edited by L. Duchesne. Paris: E. de Boccard, 1955–1957.

Malaterra, Geoffrey of. *De rebus gestis Rogerii Calabriae et Siciliae comitis et Robertis Guiscardi ducis fratris eius*. Edited by Ernesto Pontieri. Rerum Italicarum Scriptores 2nd ser., vol. 5, pt. 1. Bologna: Nicola Zanichelli, 1927–1928. English translation by Kenneth Baxter Wolf, *The Deeds of Count Roger of Calabria and Sicily and of His Brother Duke Robert Guiscard*. Ann Arbor: University of Michigan Press, 2005.

al-Mālikī, Abū Bakr ʿAbd Allāh ibn Muḥammad. *Kitāb Riyāḍ al-nufūs fi tabaqat ʿulamāʾ al-Qayrawān wa-Ifriqīya*. Edited by Bashīr Bakkūsh and Muḥammad al-ʿArūsī Maṭwī. 3 vols. Beirut: Dār al-Gharb al-Islāmī, 1981.

al-Maqrīzī, Aḥmad ibn ʿAlī. *Kitāb al-muqaffā al-kabīr*. Edited by Muḥammad al-Yaʿlāwī. 8 vols. Beirut: Dār al-Gharb al-Islāmī, 1991.

al-Masʿūdī, Abu al-ḤasanʿAlī ibn al-Ḥusayn. *Kitāb al-Tanbīh wa al-ishrāf*. Edited by M. J. de Goeje. *BGA*, vol. 8. Leiden: E. J. Brill, 1967.

al-Muqaddasī, Shams al-Dīn Abū ʿAbdallāh Muḥammad. *Kitāb Aḥsan al-taqāsīm fi ma'rifat al-aqālīm*. Edited by M. J. de Goeje. *BGA*, vol. 3. Leiden: E. J. Brill, 1967.

Narrationes de exilo sancti Martini. *BHL* 5592. Edition and translation by Bronwen Neil, *Seventh Century Popes and Martyrs: The Political Hagiography of Anastasius Bibliothecarius*. Turnhout: Brepols, 2006.

al-Nuwayrī, Aḥmad ibn ʿAbd al-Wahhāb. *Nihāyat al-arab fi funūn al-adab*. Cairo: Dār al-Kutub al-Miṣrīya, 1923.

Peter of Argos. *Epitaphios*. *BHG* 196. *PG* 104, 1365–1380. Greek edition and Latin translation in Giuseppe Cozza-Luzi and Angelo Mai, *Novae patrum bibliothecae*, vol. 9, pt. 3, 31–51. Rome: Consilium propag. christ. nomini, 1888.

al-Qāḍī al-Nuʿmān. *Kitāb Iftitāḥ al-daʿwa*. Edited by Farhad al-Dashrawi. Tunis: al-Sharika al-Tunisiya lil-Tawzīʿ, 1975.

——. *Kitāb al-majālis wa al-musāyarāt*. Edited by al-Habib Faqi et al. 2nd ed. Beirut: Dār al-Gharb al-Islāmī, 1997.

al-Qazwīnī, Zakarīyā ibn Muḥammad. *Āthār al-bilād wa akhbār al-ʿibād*. Beirut: Dār Ṣādir, 1969.

Recueil des Actes des Ducs Normands d'Italie (1046–1127), vol. 1, *Les primiers ducs (1046–1087)*. Edited by Leon-Robert Menager. Bari: Grafica Bigiemme, 1980.

Rogerii II regis diplomata Latina. Codex Diplomaticus Regni Siciliae, 1st ser., vol. 2, bk. 1. Edited by C. R. Bruhl. Cologne: Böhlau, 1987.

Romuald of Salerno. *Chronicon*. Edited by C. A. Garufi. Rerum Italicarum Scriptores, 2nd ser., vol. 7, pt. 1. Bologna: Nicola Zanichelli, 1914–1935.

Simonsohn, Shlomo, ed. *The Jews in Sicily*. Vol. 1, *383–1300*. Leiden: E. J. Brill, 1997.

Theophanes the Confessor. *Chronographia*. Edited by Carl De Boor. Leipzig: B. G. Teubner, 1883. English translation by Cyril Mango and Roger Scott, *The Chronicle of Theophanes Confessor: Byzantine and Near Eastern History A.D. 284–813*. Oxford: Clarendon Press, 1997.

Theophanes the Monk. *Vita Iosephi hymnographi*. *BHG* 944–947b. *AASS* v. 10, April III, 266–276. Edition in "Vie de saint Joseph l'Hymnographe par Théophane." In *Monumenta graeca et latina ad historiam Photii patriarchae pertinentia*, vol. 2, edited by A. Papadopoulos-Kerameus, 1–14. Saint Petersburg, 1901.

Vita Eliae Iunioris. *BHG* 580. *AASS* v. 37, August XVII, 479–509. Greek edition and Italian translation by Giuseppe Rossi Taibbi, *Vita di sant'Elia il Giovane*. Palermo: Istituto Siciliano di Studi Bizantini e Neoellenici, 1962.

Vita Leonis Lucae Corilionensis Abbatis. *BHL* 4842. *AASS*, March I, 98–102. Latin edition and Italian translation by Maria Stelladoro, *La Vita di San Leone Luca di Corleone*. Grottaferrata: Badia Greca di Grottaferrata, 1995.

Vita Leonis Ep. Cataniae. *BHG* 981b. *AASS* v. 6, February XX, 226–229. Greek edition and English translation in A. G. Alexakis, ed., *The Greek life of St. Leo Bishop of Catania (BHG 981b)*. Translated by S. Wessel. Brussels: Société des Bollandistes, 2011. Shorter edition in Acconcia Longo, A, ed.. "La vita di s. Leone vescovo di Catania e gli incantesimi del mago Eliodoro." *Rivista di studi bizantini e neoellenici* 26 (1989): 3–98.

Vita Methodii. *BHG* 1278. *AASS* v. 23, June XIV, 439–447. *PG* 100, 1243–1262.

Vita S. Eliae Spelaeotae. *BHG* 581. *AASS* v. 43, September III, 843–888.

Vita S. Lucae abbatis. *BHL* 4978. *AASS*, October VI, 337–341.

Vita S. Vitalis Abbatis. *AASS*, March II, 26–35.

al-Wansharīsī, Aḥmad ibn Yaḥyā. *al-Miʿyār al-mʿurib wa-al-jāmiʿ al-maghrib ʿan fatāwā ahl Ifrīqiyah wa-al-Andalus wa-al-Maghrib*. Edited by Muḥammad Hajjī. 13 vols. Rabat: Wizārat al-Awqāf wa al-Shuʾūn al-Islāmīyah lil-Mamlakah al-Maghribīyah, 1981–1983.

William of Apulia. *De rebus gestis Roberti Wiscardi*. Edited by Marguerite Mathieu. Palermo: Istituto Siciliano di Studi Bizantini e Neoellenici, 1961.

Secondary Sources

ʿAbbās, Iḥsān. *Muʿjam al-ʿulamāʾ wa al-shuʿarāʾ al-siqilliyin*. Beirut: Dār al-Gharb al-Islāmī, 1994.

Abou El Fadl, Khaled. "Islamic Law and Muslim Minorities: The Juristic Discourse on Muslim Minorities from the Second / Eighth to the Eleventh / Seventeenth Centuries." *Islamic Law and Society* 1, no. 2 (1994): 141–187.

Abulafia, David. *Commerce and Conquest in the Mediterranean, 1100–1500*. Aldershot: Variorum, 1993.

——. "Crocuses and Crusaders: San Gimignano, Pisa and the Kingdom of Jerusalem." Reprinted in David Abulafia, *Italy, Sicily and the Mediterranean, 1100–1400*, XIV. London: Variorum, 1987.

——. "The Crown and the Economy under Roger II and His Successors." *Dumbarton Oaks Papers* 37 (1983): 1–14.

——. "The End of Muslim Sicily." In *Muslims under Latin Rule, 1100–1300*, edited by James M. Powell, 103–133. Princeton, NJ: Princeton University Press, 1990. Reprint, David Abulafia, *Commerce and Conquest in the Mediterranean, 1100–1500*, III.

——. *Frederick II: A Medieval Emperor*. Oxford: Oxford University Press, 1988.

——. *The Great Sea: A Human History of the Mediterranean*. Oxford: Oxford University Press, 2011.

——. "Industrial Products: The Middle Ages." In *Prodotti e tecniche d'Oltremare nelle economie europee, secc. XIII–XVIII. XXIX Settimana dell'Istituto Internazionale di Storia economica 'F. Datini'* 29, 333–358. Florence, 1998.

——. "Introduction: Seven Types of Ambiguity, c. 1100–c.1500." In *Medieval Frontiers: Concepts and Practices*, edited by David Abulafia and Nora Berend, 1–34. Aldershot: Ashgate, 2002.

——. *Italy, Sicily, and the Mediterranean, 1100–1400*. London: Variorum, 1987.

——. "Local Trade Networks in Medieval Sicily: The Evidence of Idrisi." In *Shipping, Trade and Crusade in the Medieval Mediterranean: Studies in Honour of John Pryor*, edited by Ruthy Gertwagen and Elizabeth Jeffreys, 157–166. Farnham: Ashgate, 2012.

——. *A Mediterranean Emporium: The Catalan Kingdom of Majorca*. Cambridge: Cambridge University Press, 1994.

——. "The Merchants of Messina: Levant Trade and Domestic Economy." *Papers of the British School at Rome* 54 (1986): 196–212.

——. "Monarchs and Minorities in the Christian Western Mediterranean around 1300: Lucera and Its Analogues." In *Christendom and Its Discontents: Exclusion, Persecution, and Rebellion, 1000–1500*, edited by Scott L. Waugh and Peter D. Diehl, 234–263. Cambridge: Cambridge University Press, 1996.

——. "The Norman Kingdom of Africa and the Norman Expeditions to Majorca and the Muslim Mediterranean." In *Anglo-Norman Studies VII: Proceedings of the Battle Conference, 1984*, edited by R. Allen Brown, 26–49. Woodbridge, UK: Boydell & Brewer, 1985. Reprint, *Italy, Sicily and the Mediterranean, 1100–1400*, XII.

——. "The Pisan Bacini and the Medieval Mediterranean Economy: A Historian's View-Point." In *Papers in Italian Archaeology*, vol. 4, edited by Caroline Malone and Simon Stoddart, 287–302. BAR International Series 246. Oxford: B.A.R., 1985.

——. "Pisan Commercial Colonies and Consulates in Twelfth-Century Sicily." *The English Historical Review* 93 (1978): 68–81.

——. "Southern Italy, Sicily and Sardinia in the Medieval Mediterranean Economy." In *Commerce and Conquest in the Mediterranean, 1100–1500*, 1–32. Aldershot: Variorum, 1991.

——. "Sul commercio del grano siciliano nel tardo Duecento." In *Atti del Congresso sul VII Centenario del Vespro Siciliano / XI Congresso della Corona d'Aragona,*

Palermo-Erice-Trapani, maggio 1982 "La Societa mediterranea all'epoca del Vespro 2 Communicazioni," 5–22. Palermo: Accademia di Scienze Lettere e Arti, 1983.
——. "Trade and Crusade, 1050–1250." In *Cross Cultural Convergences in the Crusader Period, Essays Presented to Aryeh Grabois on His Sixty-Fifth Birthday*, edited by Michael Goodrich, Sophia Menache, and Sylvia Schein, 1–20. New York: Peter Long, 1995.
——. *The Two Italies*. Cambridge: Cambridge University Press, 1977.
——. *The Western Mediterranean Kingdoms, 1200–1500: The Struggle for Dominion*. New York: Longman, 1997.
Abulafia, David, and Nora Berend, eds. *Medieval Frontiers: Concepts and Practices*. Aldershot: Ashgate, 2002.
Abun-Nasr, Jamil M. *A History of the Maghrib in the Islamic Period*. Cambridge: Cambridge University Press, 1987.
Adelson, Howard L. *Light Weight Solidi and Byzantine Trade during the Sixth and Seventh Centuries*. Numismatic Notes and Monographs no. 138. New York: American Numismatic Society, 1957.
Agius, Dionisius A. *Siculo Arabic*. London: Kegan Paul, 1996.
Agius, Dionisius A., and Ian Richard Netton, eds. *Across the Mediterranean Frontiers: Trade, Politics and Religion, 650–1450*. Turnhout: Brepols, 1997.
Agnello, Guiseppe. *Palermo Bizantina*. Amsterdam: Adolf M. Hakkert, 1969.
Ahmad, Aziz. *A History of Islamic Sicily*. Edinburgh: Edinburgh University Press, 1975.
——. "The Shrinking Frontiers of Islam." *International Journal of Middle East Studies* 7, no. 2 (1976): 145–159.
Albu, Emily. *The Normans in Their Histories: Propaganda, Myth and Subversion*. Woodbridge, UK: Boydell, 2001.
Alexander, Paul Julius. "Les debuts des conquetes Arabes en Sicile et la tradition apocalyptique Byzantino-Slave." In *Religious and Political History and Thought in the Byzantine Empire*. London: Variorum, 1978.
Alvermann, D. "La battaglia di Ottone II contro I Saraceni nel 982." *Archivio storico per la Calabria e la Lucania* 62 (1995): 115–130.
Amara, Allaoua, and Annliese Nef. "Al-Idrīsī et les Hammūdides de Sicile: Nouvelles données biographiques sur l'auteur du Livre de Roger." *Arabica* 67 (2000): 121–127.
Amari, Michele. *Storia dei Musulmani di Sicilia*. 2nd revised ed. by C. A. Nallino. 3 vols. Catania, 1933–1939.
Amoretti, Biancamaria Scarcia, ed. *Del Nuovo sulla Sicilia Musulmana*. Rome: Accademia Nazionale de Lincei, 1993.
Antrim, Zayde. *Routes and Realms: The Power of Place in the Early Islamic World*. Oxford: Oxford University Press, 2012.
Arthur, Paul. "Aspects of Byzantine Economy: An Evaluation of Amphora Evidence from Italy." *Bulletin de Correspondance Hellenique*, supplement 18: *Recherches sur la ceramique Byzantine* (1989): 79–93.
——. "Economic Expansion in Byzantine Apulia." *Collection de l'Ecole française de Rome* 363 (2006): 389–405.
Ashtor, Eliyahu. *East-West Trade in the Medieval Mediterranean*. London: Variorum, 1986.

——. *Levant Trade in the Later Middle Ages*. Princeton: NJ: Princeton University Press, 1983.

Atiya, Aziz Suryal. *Crusade, Commerce, and Culture*. Bloomington: Indiana University Press, 1962.

Aubé, Pierre. *Les empires normands d'Orient: XIe–XIIIe siècle*. Paris: Perrin, 1999.

Auchterlonie, Paul. "Historians and the Arabic Biographical Dictionary: Some New Approaches." In *Islamic Reflections, Arabic Musings: Studies in Honor of Professor Alan Jones*, edited by Robert G. Hoyland and Philip F. Kennedy, 186–200. Oxford: E. J. W. Gibb Memorial Trust, 2004.

Avramea, Anna. "Land and Sea Communications, Fourth-Fifteenth Centuries." In *The Economic History of Byzantium*, edited by Angeliki E. Laiou, 57–90. Washington, DC: Dumbarton Oaks, 2002.

Bacile, Rosa. "Stimulating Perceptions of Kingship: Royal Imagery in the Cathedral of Monreale and in the Church of Santa Maria dell'Ammiraglio in Palermo." *al-Masāq* 16 (2004): 17–52.

Backman, Clifford R. *The Decline and Fall of Medieval Sicily: Politics, Religion, and Economy in the Reign of Frederick III, 1296–1337*. Cambridge: Cambridge University Press, 1995.

Balard, Michel. "Les épices au Moyen Âge." *Temas medievales* 5 (1995): 91–100.

——. "Notes sur le commerce entre l'Italie et l'égypte sous les Fatimides." In *L'égypte fatimide: Son art et son histoire. Actes du colloque organisé à Paris les 28, 29 et 30 mai 1998*, edited by Marianne Barrucand, 627–633. Paris: Presses de l'université de Paris-Sorbonne, 1999.

Balog, Paul. "Contributions to the Arabic Metrology and Coinage." *Annali, Istituto italiano di numismatica* 27/28 (1980/1981): 115–154, plate 119.

——. "Dated Aghlabid Lead and Copper Seals from Sicily." *Studi Maghrebini* 11 (1979): 125–132.

——. "Fāṭimid and Post-Fāṭimid Glass Jetons from Sicily." *Studi Maghrebini* 7 (1975): 125–148.

——. "Nuovi contributi sul contenuto aureo e la tipologica del tari." *Annali, Istituto italiano di numismatica* 27/28 (1980/1981): 155–184, plates 120–129.

Barone, Francesco. "Islām in Sicilia nel XII e XIII secolo: Ortoprassi, scienze religiose e tasawwuf." *Incontri mediterranei. Rivista semestrale di storia e cultura* 6, no. 2 (2003): 104–115.

Bartlett, Robert, and Angus MacKay, eds. *Medieval Frontier Societies*. Oxford: Clarendon Press, 1989.

Basile, David G. "Agricultural Sicily." *Economic Geography* 17 (1941): 109–120.

Bass, George F., and Frederick H. van Doornick Jr. *Yassi Ada: A Seventh-Century Byzantine Shipwreck*. College Station: Texas A&M University Press, 1982.

Bates, Michael L. "The Introduction of the Quarter-Dinar by the Aghlabids in 264 H. (A.D. 878) and Its Derivation from the Byzantine Tremissis." *Revista Italiana di Numismatica e Scienze Affini* 103 (2002): 115–128.

Beckingham, C. F. "The *Riḥla*: Fact or Fiction?" In *Golden Roads: Migration, Pilgrimage and Travel in Mediaeval and Modern Islam*, edited by Ian Richard Netton, 86–94. Richmond, UK: Curzon Press, 1993.

Benin, Stephen D. "Jews, Muslims, and Christians in Byzantine Italy." In *Judaism and Islam Boundaries, Communication and Interaction: Essays in Honor of William M. Brinner*, edited by Benjamin H. Hary, John L. Hayes, and Fred Astren, 27–35. Leiden: E. J. Brill, 2000.

Benjamin, Sandra. *The World of Benjamin of Tudela: A Medieval Mediterranean Travelogue*. Madison, NJ: Fairleigh Dickinson University Press, 1995.

Bennett, Matthew. "Norman Naval Activity in the Mediterranean c.1060–c.1108." *Anglo-Norman Studies* 25 (1992): 41–58.

Bercher, Henri, Annie Courteaux, and Jean Mouton. "Une abbaye latine dans la societe musulmane: Monreale au XIIe siècle." *Annales* 34 (1979): 525–547.

Berend, Nora. "Medievalists and the Notion of the Frontier." *The Medieval History Journal* 2 (1999): 55–72.

Bianquis, Thierry. "Autonomous Egypt from Ibn Ṭūlūn to Kāfūr, 868–969." In *The Cambridge History of Egypt*, vol. 1, *Islamic Egypt, 640–1517*, edited by Carl F. Petry, 86–119. Cambridge: Cambridge University Press, 1998.

Birk, Joshua C. "From Borderlands to Borderlines: Narrating the Past of Twelfth-Century Sicily." In *Multicultural Europe and Cultural Exchange in the Middle Ages and Renaissance*, edited by James P. Helfers, 9–31. Turnhout: Brepols, 2005.

——. "Sicilian Counterpoint: Power and Pluralism in Norman Sicily." PhD thesis, University of California, Santa Barbara, 2006.

Bonner, Michael. *Aristocratic Violence and Holy War: Studies in the Jihad and the Arab-Byzantine Frontier*. New Haven, CT: American Oriental Society, 1996.

——. "The Naming of the Frontier: Awāṣim, Thughūr, and the Arab Geographers." *Bulletin of the School of Oriental and African Studies* 57, no. 1 (1994): 17–24.

——. "Some Observations concerning the Early Development of Jihad on the Arab-Byzantine Frontier." *Studia Islamica* 75 (1992): 5–31. Reprinted in *Arab-Byzantine Relations in Early Islamic Times*, edited by Michael Bonner, 401–427. Aldershot: Ashgate, 2004.

Borruso, Andrea. "Federico II e la tradizione culturale arabo-islamica." In *Federico II: Immagine e Potere*, edited by Maria Stella Calo Mariani and Raffaella Cassano, 15–19. Venice: Marsilio, 1995.

——. "Poesie Arabe en Sicile." *al-Masāq* 4 (1991): 17–34.

——. "Regards sur la civilisation islamique en Sicile au Moyen Age." In *Scholarly Approaches to Religion, Interreligious Perceptions, and Islam*, edited by Jacques Waardenburg, 305–319. Bern: Lang, 1995.

——. "Some Arab-Muslim Perceptions of Religion and Medieval Culture in Sicily." In *Muslim Perceptions of Other Religions: A Historical Survey*, edited by Jacques Waardenburg, 136–142. Oxford: Oxford University Press, 1999.

——. "Su una antologia di poeti arabi siciliani medievali." *Annali, Istituto universitario orientale* 48, no. 1 (1988/1989): 63–70.

Borrut, Antoine, and Christophe Picard. "Râbata, ribât, râbita: Une institution a reconsidérer." In *Chrétiens et Musulmans en Méditerranée Médiévale (VIIIe–XIIIe s.): Échanges et contacts*, edited by Nicolas Prouteau and Philippe Sénac, 33–65. Poitiers: Centre d'études supérieures de civilisation médiévale, 2003.

Borsari, Salvatore. *Il monachesimo bizantino nella Sicilia e nell'Italia Meridionale pre- normanne*. Naples: Istituto italiano per gli studi storici, 1963.

——. "L'amministrazione del tema di Sicilia." *Rivista storica italiana* 66 (1954): 131–158.
Bosworth, C. E. "The Concept of Dhimma in Early Islam." In *Christians and Jews in the Ottoman Empire. The Functioning of a Plural Society*, edited by B. Braude and B. Lewis, 37–51. New York: Holmes & Meier, 1982.
Bougard, François, and André Vauchez, eds. "La Sicile à l'époque islamique. Questions de méthode et renouvellement récent des problématiques." Special issue, *Mélanges de l'École Française de Rome, Moyen Âge* 116, no. 1 (2004).
Braudel, Fernand. *The Mediterranean and the Mediterranean World in the Age of Philip II*. 2 vols. New York: Harper and Row, 1972.
Bresc, Henri. "La Sicile medievale, terre de refuge pour les juifs: Migration et exil." *al-Masāq* 17 (2005): 31–46.
——. "Le serment par le pain des musulmans de Sicilie." *Revue de l'Occident musulman et de la Mediterranee* 35 (1983): 171–174.
——. *Un monde méditerranéen: Économie et société en Sicile, 1300–1450*. 2 vols. Rome: École Française de Rome, 1986.
Brett, Michael. "The Arab Conquest and the Rise of Islam in North Africa." In *The Cambridge History of Africa*, vol. 2, edited by J. D. Fage, 490–555. Cambridge: Cambridge University Press, 1978.
——. "The City-State in Medieval Ifriqiya: The Case of Tripoli." *Cahiers de Tunisie* 34 (1986): 69–94.
——. "Fatimid Historiography: A Case Study—the Quarrel with the Zīrids, 1048–58." In *Medieval Historical Writing in the Christian and Islamic Worlds*, edited by David Morgan, 47–59. London: School of Oriental and African Studies, 1982. Reprinted in *Ibn Khaldun and the Medieval Maghrib*, VIII.
——. "The Fatimid Revolution (861–973) and Its Aftermath in North Africa." In *The Cambridge History of Africa*, edited by J. D. Fage, 589–636. Cambridge: Cambridge University Press, 1978.
——. *Ibn Khaldun and the Medieval Maghrib*. Aldershot: Variorum, 1999.
——. "The Islamization of Egypt and North Africa." Lecture presented at Nehemia Levtzion Center for Islamic Studies, Hebrew University of Jerusalem, January 12, 2005.
——. "Muslim Justice under Infidel Rule: The Normans in Ifriqiya, 517–555AH /1123–1160AD." *Cahiers de Tunisie* 43 (1995): 325–368.
——. *The Rise of the Fatimids: The World of the Mediterranean and the Middle East in the Fourth Century of the Hijra, Tenth Century CE*. Leiden: E. J. Brill, 2001.
——. "The Spread of Islam in Egypt and Northern Africa." In *Northern Africa: Islam and Modernization*, edited by Michael Brett, 1–12. London: Frank Cass, 1973.
——. "The Way of the Nomad." *Bulletin of the School of Oriental and African Studies* 58 (1995): 251–269. Reprinted in *Ibn Khaldun and the Medieval Maghrib*, X.
Britt, Karen C. "Roger II of Sicily: Rex, Basileus, and Khalif? Identity, Politics, and Propaganda in the Cappella Palatina." *Mediterranean Studies* 16 (2007): 21–45.
Broodbank, Cyprian. *The Making of the Middle Sea: A History of the Mediterranean from the Beginning to the Emergence of the Classical World*. Oxford: Oxford University Press, 2013.
Brown, Gordon S. *The Norman Conquest of Southern Italy and Sicily*. Jefferson, NC: McFarland, 2003.

Brown, T. S. "The Political Use of the Past in Norman Sicily." In *The Perception of the Past in 12th-Century Europe*, edited by Paul Magdalino, 191–210. London: Hambledon Press, 1992.

Bruce, Scott G. *Cluny and the Muslims of La Garde-Freinet: Hagiography and the Problem of Islam in Medieval Europe*. Ithaca, NY: Cornell University Press, 2015.

Bruce, Travis. "The Politics of Violence and Trade: Denia and Pisa in the Eleventh Century." *Journal of Medieval History* 32 (2006): 127–142.

Buerger, Janet E. "Morphological Analysis of Medieval Fine Pottery: Provenance and Trade Patterns in the Mediterranean World." In *Archaeological Approaches to Medieval Europe*, edited by Kathleen Biddick, 203–222. Kalamazoo, MI: Medieval Institute Publications, 1984.

Bulliet, Richard W. "A Quantitative Approach to Medieval Muslim Biographical Dictionaries." *Journal of the Economic and Social History of the Orient* 13 (1970): 195–211.

Burns, Robert I. *Islam Under the Crusaders: Colonial Survival in the Thirteenth-Century Kingdom of Valencia*. Princeton, NJ: Princeton University Press, 1973.

——. "The Significance of the Frontier in the Middle Ages." In Bartlett and MacKay, *Medieval Frontier Societies*, 307–330.

Bury, John B. "The Naval Policy of the Roman Empire in Relation to the Western Provinces from the 7th to the 9th Century." In *Scritti per il centenario della nascita di Michele Amari*, 21–34. Palermo: Societá siciliana per la storia patria, 1910.

Cahen, Claude. "Commercial Relations between the Near East and Western Europe from the VIIth to the XIth Century." In *Islam and the Medieval West: Aspects of Intercultural Relations*, edited by Khalil I. Semaan, 1–25. Binghamton: State University of New York at Binghamton, 1975.

——. "Un texte peu connu relatif au commerce oriental d'Amalfi au Xe siècle." *Archivio storico per le province napolitane* 34 (1953/1954): 61–66.

Camps-Fabrer, Henriette. *L'olivier et l'huile dans l'Afrique romaine*. Algiers: Imprimerie officielle, 1953.

Canard, Marius. "Les Relations Politiques et Sociales entre Byance et les Arabes." *Dumbarton Oaks Papers* 18 (1964): 33–56.

——. "Une lettre du calife fāṭimite al-Ḥāfiẓ à Roger II de Sicile." In *Atti del Convegno Internazionale di Studi Ruggeriani*, 125–146. Palermo, 1955. Reprint, *Miscellanea Orientalia*, London: Variorum, 1973.

Capelli, Cristian, et al. "Moors and Saracens in Europe: Estimating the Medieval North African Male Legacy in Southern Europe." *European Journal of Human Genetics* 17 (2009): 848–852.

Carlson, Deborah N., Justin Leidwanger, and Sarah M. Kampbell. *Maritime Studies in the Wake of the Byzantine Shipwreck at Yassiada, Turkey*. College Station: Texas A&M University Press, 2015.

Carver, M. O. H. "Transitions to Islam: Urban Roles in the East and South Mediterranean, Fifth to Tenth Centuries AD." In *Towns in Transition: Urban Evolution in Late Antiquity and the Early Middle Ages*, edited by N. Christie and S. T. Loseby, 184–212. Aldershot: Scholar Press, 1996.

Castro, Francisco Vidal. "Aḥmad al-Wanṣarīsī (m 914/1508). Principales aspectos de su vida." *al-Qanṭara* 12, no. 2 (1991): 315–352.

Catlos, Brian. *Muslims of Medieval Latin Christendom, c. 1050–1614*. Cambridge: Cambridge University Press, 2014.

Ceserani, Giovanna. "The Charm of the Siren: The Place of Classical Sicily in Historiography." In *Sicily from Aeneas to Augustus: New Approaches in Archaeology and History*, edited by Christopher Smith and John Serrati, 174–193. Edinburgh: Edinburgh University Press, 2000.

Chalandon, Ferdinand. "The Conquest of South Italy and Sicily by the Normans." In *The Cambridge Medieval History*, edited by J. R. Tanner, C. W. Previte-Orton, and Z. N. Brook, 167–184. Cambridge: Cambridge University Press, 1964.

——. *Histoire de la Domination Normande en Italie et en Sicile*. 2 vols. Paris, 1907. Reprint, New York: Burt Franklin, 1960.

Chiarelli, Leonard C. *A History of Muslim Sicily*. Venera, Malta: Midsea Books, 2011.

Chibnall, Marjorie. *The Normans*. Oxford: Blackwell, 2000.

Christides, Vassilios. *The Conquest of Crete by the Arabs (ca. 824): A Turning Point in the Struggle between Byzantium and Islam*. Athens: Akademia Athenon, 1984.

——. "Two Parallel Naval Guides of the Tenth Century: Qudāma's Document and Leo VI's Naumachia; A Study on Byzantine and Moslem Naval Preparedness." *Graeco-Arabica* 1 (1982): 51–103.

Ciccaglione, Federico. "La vita economica siciliana nel periodo normanno-svevo." *Archivio Storico per le Sicilia Orientale* 10 (1913): 321–345.

Ciggaar, Krijnie N. *Western Travellers to Constantinople, The West and Byzantium, 962–1204: Cultural and Political Relations*. Leiden: E. J. Brill, 1996.

Cipolla, Carlo M. *Money, Prices, and Civilization in the Mediterranean World*. Princeton, NJ: Princeton University Press, 1956.

Citarella, Armand O. "Patterns in Medieval Trade: The Commerce of Amalfi before the Crusades." *The Journal of Economic History* 28 (1968): 531–555.

——. "The Relations of Amalfi with the Arab World before the Crusades." *Speculum* 42, no. 2 (1967): 299–312.

Cohen, Hayyim J. "The Economic Background and the Secular Occupations of Muslim Jurisprudents and Traditionalists in the Classical Period of Islam (until the Middle of the Eleventh Century)." *Journal of the Economic and Social History of the Orient* 13 (1970): 16–61.

Cohen, Mark R. "Geniza for Islamicists, Islamic Geniza, and the 'New Cairo Geniza.'" *Harvard Middle Eastern and Islamic Review* 7 (2006): 129–145.

Collura, Paolo. "Il monachesimo prenormanno in Sicilia." *Archivio Storico Siciliano*, 4th ser., 8 (1982): 29–45.

Conant, Jonathan P. "Anxieties of Violence: Christians and Muslims in Conflict in Aghlabid North Africa and the Central Mediterranean." *al-Masāq* 27 (2015): 7–23.

——. "Europe and the African Cult of Saints, circa 350–900: An Essay in Mediterranean Communications." *Speculum* 85 (2010): 1–46.

——. *Staying Roman: Conquest and Identity in Africa and the Mediterranean, 439–700*. Cambridge: Cambridge University Press, 2012.

Conrad, Lawrence I. "Islam and the Sea: Paradigms and Problematics." *al-Qanṭara* 23 (2002): 123–154.

Constable, Olivia Remie. "Cross-Cultural Contracts: Sales of Land between Christians and Muslims in 12th-Century Palermo." *Studia Islamica* 85 (1997): 67–84.

——. *Housing the Stranger in the Mediterranean World: Lodging, Trade, and Travel in Late Antiquity and the Middle Ages*. Cambridge: Cambridge University Press, 2003.

——. *Trade and Traders in Muslim Spain: The Commercial Realignment of the Iberian Peninsula, 900–1500*. Cambridge: Cambridge University Press, 1994.

Corsi, Pasquale. "Costante II e Siracusa." *Archivio storico siracusano*, 1985, 157–167.

Cosentino, Salvatore. "Constans II and the Byzantine Navy." *Byzantinische Zeitschrift* 100, no. 2 (2008): 577–603.

Costa-Louillet, G. da. "Saints de Sicile e d'Italie Méridionale aux VIIIe, IXe et Xe siècles." *Byzantion* 29/30 (1959/1960): 89–173.

Cowdrey, H. E. J. "The Mahdia Campaign of 1087." *The English Historical Review* 162 (1977): 1–29.

Curtis, Edmund. *Roger of Sicily and the Normans in Lower Italy, 1016–1154*. London: Putnam, 1912.

Cutroni Tusa, A. "La circolazione monetaria nella Sicilia Bizantina ed il ripostiglio da Castellana (Palermo)." In *Byzantino-Sicula*, 104–110. Palermo: Istituto Siciliano di Studi Bizantini e Neoellenici, 1966.

——. "Monetazione e circolazaione monetaria nella Sicilia bizantina." In *Byzantino-Sicula IV: Atti del I Congresso Internazionale di Archeologica della Sicilia Bizantina (Corleone, 1998)*, edited by Rosa Maria Carra Bonacasa, 413–438. Palermo: Istituto Siciliano di Studi Bizantini e Neoellenici, 2002.

Dalli, Charles. "Bridging Europe and Africa: Norman Sicily's Other Kingdom." In *Bridging the Gaps: Sources, Methodology and Approaches to Religion in History*, edited by Joaquim Carvalho, 77–93. Pisa: Plus-Pisa University Press, 2008.

——. "Medieval Island Societies: Reassessing Insulation in a Central Mediterranean Context." *al-Masāq* 10 (1998): 73–82.

D'Angelo, Franco. "Insediamenti medievali nel territorio circostante Castellammare del Golfo." *Archeologia Medievale* 4 (1977): 340–346.

——. "La ceramica della Sicilia medievale ed i suoi rapporti con la ceramica islamica." *La Ceramica medievale di San Lorenzo Maggiore in Napoli* 2 (1984): 481–487.

——. "La monetazione di Muhammad ibn al-ʿAbbad Amrio ribelle a Federico II di Sicilia." *Studi Maghrebini* 7 (1975): 149–153.

Darling, Linda T. "The Mediterranean as a Borderland." *Review of Middle East Studies* 46, no. 1 (2012): 54–63.

Davis, R. H. C. *The Normans and Their Myth*. London: Thames and Hudson, 1976.

Davis-Secord, Sarah. "Bearers of Islam: Muslim Women between Assimilation and Resistance in Christian Sicily." In *Gender in the Premodern Mediterranean*, edited by Megan Moore. Tempe: Arizona Center for Medieval and Renaissance Studies, 2017.

——. "Muslims in Norman Sicily: The Evidence of Imām al-Māzarī's *Fatwās*." *Mediterranean Studies* 16 (2007): 46–66.

Day, William R. "The Fatimid Quarter-Dinar in Southern Italy and the Imitation Tari of Salerno and Amalfi." Paper presented at American Numismatic Society, New York, 1995.

Decker, Michael. "Frontier Settlement and Economy in the Byzantine East." *Dumbarton Oaks Papers* 61 (2007): 217–267.

De Souza, Philip. "Western Mediterranean Ports in the Roman Empire, First Century B.C. to Sixth Century A.D." *Journal of Mediterranean Studies* 10 (2000): 229–254.

Delano Smith, Catherine. *Western Mediterranean Europe: A Historical Geography of Italy, Spain and Southern France since the Neolithic*. London: Academic Press, 1979.

Delarc, Odon Jean Marie. *Les normands in Italie depuis les premieres invasions jusqu'a l'avenement de S. Gregoire VII*. Paris: E. Leroux, 1883.

Di Gaetano, Cornelia, et al. "Differential Greek and Northern African Migrations to Sicily Are Supported by Genetic Evidence from the Y Chromosome." *European Journal of Human Genetics* 17 (2009): 91–99.

Di Pietro, Robert J., and George Dimitri Selim. "The Language Situation in Arab Sicily." In *Linguistic Studies in Memory of Richard Slade Hassell*, edited by D. G. Stuart, 19–34. Washington, DC: Georgetown University Press, 1967.

Dolezalek, Isabelle. "Textile Connections? Two Ifrīqiyan Church Treasuries in Norman Sicily and the Problem of Continuity across Political Change." *al-Masāq* 25, no. 1 (2013): 92–112.

Douglas, David C. *The Norman Achievement 1050–1100*. Berkeley: University of California Press, 1969.

Drell, Joanna H. "Cultural Syncretism and Ethnic Identity: The Norman 'Conquest' of Southern Italy and Sicily." *Journal of Medieval History* 25, no. 3 (1999): 187–202.

——. "Family Structure in the Principality of Salerno during the Norman Period, 1077–1154." *Anglo-Norman Studies* 18 (1996): 79–104.

——. *Kinship and Conquest: Family Strategies in the Principality of Salerno during the Norman Period, 1077–1194*. Ithaca, NY: Cornell University Press, 2002.

Du Cange et al. *Glossarium mediae et infimae Latinitatis*. 10 vols. Niort: L. Favre, 1883–1887.

Efthymiadis, Stephanos. "Les saints d'Italie méridionale (IXe–XIIe s.) et leur rôle dans la société locale." In *Byzantine Religious Culture: Studies in Honor of Alice-Mary Talbot*, edited by E. Fisher, S. Papaioannou, and D. Sullivan, 347–372. Leiden: E. J. Brill, 2011.

Ehrenkreutz, Andrew S. "Monetary Aspects of Medieval Near Eastern Economic History." In *Studies in the Economic History of the Middle East*, edited by M. A. Cook, 37–50. Oxford: Oxford University Press, 1970. Reprinted in Andrew S. Ehrenhreutz and Jere L. Bacharach, *Monetary Change and Economic History in the Medieval Muslim World*, I. Aldershot: Ashgate, 1992.

——. "Studies in the Monetary History of the Near East in the Middle Ages I: The Standard of Fineness of Some Types of Dinars." *Journal of the Economic and Social History of the Orient* 2 (1959): 128–161. Reprinted in Ehrenhreutz and Bacharach, *Monetary Change and Economic History in the Medieval Muslim World*, VI.

——. "Studies in the Monetary History of the Near East in the Middle Ages II: The Standard of Fineness of Western and Eastern Dinars before the Crusades." *Journal of the Economic and Social History of the Orient* 6 (1963): 243–277. Reprinted in Ehrenhreutz and Bacharach, *Monetary Change and Economic History in the Medieval Muslim World*, VII.

El-Hajji, A. A. *Andalusian Diplomatic Relations with Western Europe during the Umayyad Period (A.H. 138–366 / A.D. 755–976)*. Beirut: Dar al-Irshad, 1970.

———. "Diplomatic Relations between Andalusia and Italy during the Umayyad Period (A.H. 138–366/A.D. 755–976)." *The Islamic Quarterly* 12, no. 3 (1968): 140–145.

El-Hibri, Tayeb. "Coinage Reform under the 'Abbasid Caliph al-Ma'mun." *Journal of the Economic and Social History of the Orient* 36 (1993): 58–83.

Ellenblum, Ronnie. *The Collapse of the Eastern Mediterranean: Climate Change and the Decline of the East, 950–1072*. Cambridge: Cambridge University Press, 2012.

Enos, Richard Leo. "Why Gorgias of Leontini Traveled to Athens: A Study of Recent Epigraphical Evidence." *Rhetoric Review* 11, no. 1 (1992): 1–15.

Ephrat, Daphna. *A Learned Society in a Period of Transition: The Sunni 'Ulama' of Eleventh-Century Baghdad*. Albany, NY: SUNY Press, 2000.

Epstein, Stephan R. *An Island for Itself: Economic Development and Social Change in Late Medieval Sicily*. Cambridge: Cambridge University Press, 1992.

———. "The Textile Industry and the Foreign Cloth Trade in Late Medieval Sicily (1300–1500): A 'Colonial' Relationship?" *Journal of Medieval History* 15 (1989): 141–183.

Falkenhausen, Vera von. "Aspetti economici dei monasteri bizantini in Calabria (sec. X–XI)." In *Calabria bizantina. Aspetti sociali ed economici. Atti del terzo Incontro di studi bizantini, (Reggio Calabria-Bova: 4–5 maggio 1974)*, 29–55. Reggio Calabria, 1978.

———. "Bari bizantina: Profilo di un capoluogo di provincia secoli IX–XI." In *Spazio, societa, potere nell'Italia de Comuni*, edited by G. Rossetti, 195–227. Naples, 1986.

———. "Between Two Empires: Byzantine Italy in the Reign of Basil II." In *Byzantium in the Year 1000*, edited by Paul Magdalino, 135–159. Leiden: E. J. Brill, 2003.

———. "Chiesa greca e chiesa latina in Sicilia prima della conquista araba." *Archivio storico siracusano*, n.s. 5 (1978–1979): 137–155.

———. "Gregor von Burtscheid und das griechische Mönchtum in Kalabrien." *Römische Quartalschrift* 93 (1998): 215–250.

———. "I monasteri greci dell'Italia meridionale e della Sicilia dopo l'avvento dei Normanni: Continuita e mutamenti." In *Il passaggio dal dominio bizantino allo Stato normanno nell'Italia meridionale. Atti del II Convegno internazionale di studio sulla civilta rupestre medioevale nel Mezzogiorno d'Italia (Taranto-Mottola, 31 ottobre–4 novembre 1973)*, edited by Cosimo Damiano Fonseca, 197–219. Taranto: Amministrazione provinciale, 1977.

———. "I rapporti con Bizanzio." In *I Normanni. Popolo d'Europa 1030–1200*, edited by Mario D'Onofrio, 350–355. Venice: Marsilio Editori, 1994.

———. *La dominazione bizantina nell'Italia meridionale dal IX all'XI secolo*. Bari: Ecumenica Editrice, 1978.

———. "La presenza dei Greci nella Sicilia normanna. L'apporto della documentazione archivistica in lingua greca." In *Byzantino-Sicula, IV: Atti del I Congresso internazionale di archeologia della Sicilia bizantina*, edited by Rosa Maria Carra Bonacasa, 31–72. Palermo: Istituto Siciliano di Studi Bizantini e Neoellenici, 2002.

——. "La Vita di s. Nilo come fonte storica per la Calabria bizantina." In *Atti del Congresso internazionale su s. Nilo di Rossano (28 settembre—1 ottobre 1986)*, 271–305. Rossano-Grottaferrata: Università Popolare, 1989.

——. "A Provincial Aristocracy: The Byzantine Provinces in Southern Italy (9th–11th Century)." In *The Byzantine Aristocracy, IX to XIII Centuries*, edited by M. Angold, 211–235. BAR International Series 221. Oxford: B.A.R., 1984.

——. "Reseaux routiers et ports dans l'Italie meridionale byzantine (Vie–XIe s.)." In *Hē Kathēmerinē zōē sto Vyzantio: tomes kai synecheies stēn Hellēnistikē kai Rōmaikē paradosē: praktika tou 1. diethnous symposiou, 15–17 Septemvriou 1988*, edited by Christina G. Angelidē, 709–731. Athens: Kentro Vyzantinōn Ereunōn / E.I.E., 1989.

——. "Taranto in epoca bizantina." *Studi medievali*, 3rd ser., 9 (1968): 133–166.

Fitzgerald, Robert. *The Aeneid*. By Virgil. New York: Vintage Books, 1990.

Fodale, Salvatore. "Herencia y mito de la Sicilia islamica." In *Granada, 1492–1992*, edited by Vincent Bernard and Manuel Barrios Aguilera, 231–240. Granada: Universidad de Granada, 1995.

——. "Ruggero II el al seconda Crociata." In *Il mezzogiorno normanno-svevo e le Crociate: Atti delle quattordicesime giornate normanno-sveve, Bari, 17–20 Ottobre 2000*, edited by Giosuè Musca, 131–144. Bari: Edizioni Dedalo, 2002.

Follieri, Enrica. "I santi della Italia greca." In *Histoire et culture dans l'Italie byzantine: Acquis et nouvelles recherches*, edited by Andre Jacob, Jean-Marie Martin, and Ghislaine Noye, 95–126. Rome: École Française de Rome, 2006.

France, John. "The Occasion of the Coming of the Normans to Southern Italy." *Journal of Medieval History* 27 (1991): 185–205.

Frank, Daniel, ed. *The Jews of Medieval Islam: Community, Society and Identity*. Leiden: E. J. Brill, 1992.

Freedman, Paul. "Mastic: A Mediterranean Luxury Product." *Mediterranean Historical Review* 26 (2011): 99–113.

——. *Out of the East: Spices and the Medieval Imagination*. New Haven, CT: Yale University Press, 2008.

Gabrieli, Francesco. "Ibn Hawqal e gli Arabi di Sicilia." In *L'Islam nella storia*, 57–67. Bari: Edizioni Dedalo, 1966.

——. "La politique arabe des Normands de Sicile." *Studia Islamica* 9 (1958): 83–96.

——. "Un secolo di studi arabo-siculi." *Studia Islamica* 2 (1954): 89–102.

Gabrieli, Francesco, and Umberto Scerrato. *Gli Arabi in Italia: Cultura, contatti e tradizioni*. Milan: Credito Italiano, 1979.

Galatariotou, Catia. "Travel and Perception in Byzantium." *Dumbarton Oaks Papers* 47 (1993): 221–241.

García Sánchez, E., and L. Ramón-Laca Menéndez de Luarca. "Sebestén y Zumaque, Dos Frutos Importados de Oriente Durante la Edad Media." *Annuario de Estudios Medievales* 31 (2001): 867–881.

Garnsey, Peter. "Grain for Rome." In *Trade in the Ancient Economy*, edited by Peter Garnsey, Keith Hopkins, and C. R. Whittaker, 118–130. London: Chatto and Windus, 1983.

Gelfer-Jorgensen, M. *Medieval Islamic Symbolism and the Paintings in the Cefalu Cathedral*. Leiden: E. J. Brill, 1986.

Gertwagen, Ruthi. "Geniza Letters: Maritime Difficulties along the Alexandria-Palermo Route." In *Communication in the Jewish Diaspora: The Pre-modern World*, edited by Sophia Menache, 73–91. Leiden: E. J. Brill, 1996.

Gibb, Hamilton A. R. "Arab-Byzantine Relations under the Umayyad Caliphate." *Dumbarton Oaks Papers* 12 (1958): 219–233.

Gibbins, David. "A Roman Shipwreck of c. AD 200 at Plemmirio, Sicily: Evidence for North African Amphora Production during the Severan Period." *World Archaeology* 32 (2001): 311–334.

Gil, Moshe. "The Flax Trade in the Mediterranean in the Eleventh Century A.D. as Seen in Merchants' Letters from the Cairo Geniza." *Journal of Near Eastern Studies* 63, no. 2 (2004): 81–96.

——. *Jews in Islamic Countries in the Middle Ages*. Translated by David Strassler. Leiden: E. J. Brill, 2004.

——. "The Jews in Sicily under Muslim Rule, in the Light of the Geniza Documents." In *Italia judaica, Atti del I Convegno internazionale, Bari 18–22 maggio 1981*, 87–134. Rome: Ministero per i beni culturali e ambientali, 1983.

——. "References to Silk in Geniza Documents of the Eleventh Century A.D." *Journal of Near Eastern Studies* 61, no. 1 (2002): 31–38.

——. "Sicily 827–1072, in Light of the Geniza Documents and Parallel Sources." In *Italia Judaica: Gli ebrei in Sicilia sino all'espulsione del 1492, Atti del V convegno internazionale, Palermo, 15–19 giugno 1992*, 96–171. Rome: Ministero per i beni culturali e ambientali, 1995.

Gillett, Andrew. *Envoys and Political Communication in the Late Antique West, 411–533*. Cambridge: Cambridge University Press, 2003.

Goitein, S. D. "Cairo: An Islamic City in Light of the Geniza Documents." In *Middle Eastern Cities*, edited by Ira Lapidus, 80–96. Berkeley: University of California Press, 1969.

——. "The Cairo Geniza as a Source for the History of Muslim Civilisation." *Studia Islamica* 3 (1955): 75–91.

——. "Documents of the Cairo Geniza as a Source for Mediterranean Social History." *Journal of the American Oriental Society* 80 (1960): 91–100.

——. *Letters of Medieval Jewish Traders*. Princeton, NJ: Princeton University Press, 1973.

——. "The Main Industries of the Mediterranean Area as Reflected in the Records of the Cairo Geniza." *Journal of the Economic and Social History of the Orient* 4 (1961): 168–197.

——. "Medieval Tunisia: The Hub of the Mediterranean." In *Studies in Islamic History and Institutions*, 308–328. Leiden: E. J. Brill, 1966.

——. *A Mediterranean Society: The Jewish Communities of the Arab World as Portrayed in the Documents of the Cairo Geniza*. 6 vols. Berkeley: University of California Press, 1967–1993.

——. "Mediterranean Trade Preceding the Crusades: Some Facts and Problems." *Diogenes* 59 (1967): 47–62.

——. "Sicily and Southern Italy in the Cairo Geniza Documents." *Archivio Storico per le Sicilia Orientale* 67 (1971): 9–33.

——. "The Unity of the Mediterranean World in the 'Middle' Middle Ages." In *Studies in Islamic History and Institutions*, 296–307. Leiden: E. J. Brill, 1966.

Golb, Norman. "A Judeo-Arabic Court Document of Syracuse, A.D. 1020." *Journal of Near Eastern Studies* 32, no. 1/2 (1973): 105–123.

Goldberg, Jessica L. *Trade and Institutions in the Medieval Mediterranean: The Geniza Merchants and Their Business World*. Cambridge: Cambridge University Press, 2012.

Goskar, Tehmina. "Material Worlds: The Shared Cultures of Southern Italy and Its Mediterranean Neighbours in the Tenth to Twelfth Centuries." *al-Masāq* 23, no. 3 (2011): 189–204.

Gottheil, Richard. "A Distinguished Family of Fatimide Cadis (al-Nuʿmān) in the Tenth Century." *Journal of the American Oriental Society* 27, no. 2 (1906): 217–296.

Granara, William E. "Ibn Ḥamdīs and the Poetry of Nostalgia." In *The Literature of al-Andalus*, edited by Maria Rosa Menocal, Raymond P. Scheindlin, and Michael Sells, 388–403. Cambridge: Cambridge University Press, 2000.

——. "Ibn Hawqal in Sicily." *Alif: Journal of Comparative Poetics* 3 (1983): 94–99.

——. "Ibn Sabīl: Crossing Boundaries in the Biography of Asad." *Scripta Mediterranea* 19/20 (1998/1999): 259–267.

——. "Islamic Education and the Transmission of Knowledge in Muslim Sicily." In *Law and Education in Medieval Islam: Studies in Memory of Professor George Makdisi*, edited by Joseph E. Lowry, Devin J. Stewart, and Shawkat Toorawa, 150–173. Cambridge: E. J. W. Gibb Memorial Trust, 2004.

——. "Jihād and Cross-Cultural Encounter in Muslim Sicily." *Harvard Middle Eastern and Islamic Review* 3, no. 1/2 (1996): 42–61.

——. "Political Legitimacy and Jihad in Muslim Sicily, 217/827–445/1053." PhD dissertation, University of Pennsylvania, 1986.

——. "Remaking Muslim Sicily: Ibn Ḥamdīs and the Poetics of Exile." *Edebiyāt* 9 (1998): 167–198.

Grassi, Vincenza. "Tari." *EI*[2], 10: 238–240. Leiden: E. J. Brill, 2000.

Grew, Raymond. "Review of *A History of Sicily* 3 vols., M. I. Finley and Denis Mack Smith." *American Historical Review* 75 (1969): 537–539.

Grieco, Allen J. "Olive Tree Cultivation and the Alimentary Use of Olive Oil in Late Medieval Italy (ca. 1300–1500)." In *La production du vin et de l'huile en Méditerranée*, edited by Marie-Claire Amouretti and Jean-Pierre Brun, 297–306. Paris: École Française d'Athenes, 1993.

Grierson, Philip. *Byzantine Coins*. Berkeley: University of California Press, 1982.

——. "Carolingian Europe and the Arabs: The Myth of the Mancus." *Revue Belge de Philologie et d'Histoire* 32 (1954): 1059–1074.

——, ed. *Catalogue of the Byzantine Coins in the Dumbarton Oaks Collection and in the Whittemore Collection*. Vol. 3, pt. 1, *Leo III to Nicephorus III, 717–1081*. Washington, DC: Dumbarton Oaks Research Library and Collection, 1973.

——. "Coinage and Money in the Byzantine Empire 498–c. 1090." In *Moneta e scambi nell'alto medioevo*, 411–453. Spoleto: Centro Italiano di studi sull'alto medioevo, 1960.

——. "The Coinages of Norman Apulia and Sicily in Their International Setting." *Anglo-Norman Studies* 25 (1992): 117–132.

——. "Monete Bizantine in Italia dal VII all'XI secolo." In *Moneta e scambi nell'alto medioevo*, 35–55. Spoleto: Centro Italiano di studi sull'alto medioevo, 1960.

——. "The Salernitan Coinage of Gisulf II (1052–77) and Robert Guiscard (1077–85)." *Papers of the British School at Rome* 24 (1956): 37–59.

Grierson, Philip, and W. A. Oddy. "Le titre du tari Sicilien du milieu du XIe siècle à 1278." *Revue Numismatique* 16 (1974): 123–134.

Grierson, Philip, and Lucia Travaini. *Medieval European Coinage: With a Catalogue of the Coins in the Fitzwilliam Museum, Cambridge*. Vol. 14, *Italy (III) South Italy, Sicily, Sardinia*. Cambridge: Cambridge University Press, 1986.

Guérin, Sarah M. "Forgotten Routes? Italy, Ifrīqiya and the Trans-Saharan Ivory Trade." *al-Masāq* 25 (2013): 70–91.

Guichard, Pierre. *L'Espagne et la Sicile Musulmanes aux XIe et XIIe siècles*. Lyon: Presses universitaires de Lyon, 2000.

Guillou, Andre. "Grecs d'Italie du sud et de Sicile au Moyen Âge: Les moines." *Mélanges de l'École Française de Rome* 75 (1963): 79–110. Reprinted in Andre Guillou, *Studies on Byzantine Italy*, XII. London: Variorum, 1970.

——. "La Sicile Byzantine: État de recherches." *Byzantinische Forschungen* 5 (1977): 95–145.

——. "La soie Sicilienne au Xe–XIe s." In *Byzantino-Sicula* II, 285–288. Palermo: Istituto Siciliano di Studi Bizantini e Neoellenici, 1975.

——. "Production and Profits in the Byzantine Province of Italy Tenth to Eleventh Centuries: An Expanding Society." *Dumbarton Oaks Papers* 28 (1974): 89–109.

Haldon, John F. *Byzantium in the Seventh Century: The Transformation of a Culture*. Rev. ed. Cambridge: Cambridge University Press, 1997.

——. "Economy and Administration: How Did the Empire Work?" In *The Cambridge Companion to the Age of Justinian*, edited by Michael Maas, 28–59. Cambridge: Cambridge University Press, 2005.

——. "Some Aspects of Byzantine Military Technology from the Sixth to the Tenth Centuries." *Byzantine and Modern Greek Studies* 1 (1975): 11–47.

Haldon, John F., and Hugh Kennedy. "The Arab-Byzantine Frontier in the Eighth and Ninth Centuries: Military Organisation and Society in the Borderlands." *Zbornik radova Vizantološkog instituta* 19 (1980): 79–116. Reprinted in Hugh Kennedy, *The Byzantine and Early Islamic Near East*, VIII. Aldershot: Variorum, 2006.

Halevi, Leor. "Bernard, Explorer of the Muslim Lake: A Pilgrimage from Rome to Jerusalem, 867." *Medieval Encounters* 4 (1998): 24–50.

Haskins, Charles Homer. *The Normans in European History*. Boston: Houghton Mifflin, 1915.

Haug, Robert. "Frontiers and the State in Early Islamic History: Jihād between Caliphs and Volunteers." *History Compass* 9/8 (2011): 634–643.

Hayes, Dawn Marie. "French Connections: The Significance of the Fleurs-de-Lis in the Mosaic of King Roger II of Sicily in the Church of Santa Maria dell'Ammiraglio, Palermo." *Viator* 44 (2013): 119–149.

——. "Roger II and the Legacy of Alfonso VI of León-Castile: Identity and Aspiration on Europe's Margins in Early Twelfth-Century Europe." Lecture presented at Medieval Association of the Midwest's 30th Annual Meeting, St. Louis University, Madrid, January 23, 2015.

Hendy, Michael F. *Studies in the Byzantine Monetary Economy c. 300–450*. Cambridge: Cambridge University Press, 1985.

Herrin, Judith. "Constantinople, Rome, and the Franks in the Seventh and Eighth Centuries." In *Margins and Metropolis: Authority across the Byzantine Empire*, 220–238. Princeton, NJ: Princeton University Press, 2013.

——. "The Process of Hellenization." In *Margins and Metropolis*, 33–57.

Heyd, W. *Histoire du commerce du Levant au moyen-âge*. 2 vols. Leipzig: O. Harrassowitz, 1885–1886. Reprint, Amsterdam: Adolf M. Hakkert, 1959.

Hiestand, Rudolf. "Boemondo I e la Prima Crociata." In *Il Mezzogiorno normanno-svevo e le Crociate: Atti delle quattordicesime giornate normanno-svevo, Bari, 17–20 ottobre 2000*, edited by Giosuè Musca, 65–94. Bari: Edizioni Dedalo, 2002.

Hodgson, Marshall. *The Venture of Islam*. 3 vols. Chicago: University of Chicago Press, 1974.

Holloway, R. Ross. *The Archaeology of Ancient Sicily*. London: Routledge, 1991.

Holmes, Catherine. "Treaties between Byzantium and the Islamic World." In *War and Peace in Ancient and Medieval History*, edited by Philip de Souza and John France, 141–157. Cambridge: Cambridge University Press, 2008.

Hopkins, Keith. "Taxes and Trade in the Roman Empire (200 B.C.—A.D. 400)." *Journal of Roman Studies* 70 (1980): 101–125.

Hopley, Russell. "Aspects of Trade in the Western Mediterranean during the Eleventh and Twelfth Centuries: Perspectives from Islamic Fatwās and State Correspondence." *Mediaevalia* 32 (2011): 5–42.

Horden, Peregrine. "Poseidon's Oar: Horizons of the Medieval Mediterranean." Lecture presented at Forty-Eighth International Congress on Medieval Studies, Kalamazoo, MI, May 10, 2013.

Horden, Peregrine, and Nicholas Purcell. *The Corrupting Sea: A Study of Mediterranean History*. Oxford: Blackwell, 2000.

Horst, Eberhard. *Der Sultan von Lucera: Friedrich II. und der Islam*. Freiburg: Herder, 1997.

Houben, Hubert. *Roger II of Sicily: A Ruler between East and West*. Cambridge: Cambridge University Press, 2002.

Housley, Norman. *The Italian Crusades: The Papal-Angevin Alliance and the Crusades against Christian Lay Powers, 1254–1343*. Oxford: Clarendon Press, 1982.

Idris, H. R. "Commerce maritime et ḳirāḍ en Berbérie orientale." *Journal of the Economic and Social History of the Orient* 4 (1961): 225–239.

——. *La Berbérie orientale sous les Zirides, Xe–XIIe siècles*. Paris: Adrien-Maisonneuve, 1962.

——. "L'École malikite de Mahdia." In *Études d'Orientalisme dédiées à la mémoire de E. Lévi-Provençal*, 153–163. Paris, 1962.

——. "L'invasion hilālienne et ses conséquences." *Cahiers de civilisation médiévale* 43 (1968): 353–369.

Jacoby, David. "The Encounter of Two Societies: Western Conquerors and Byzantines in the Peloponnesus after the Fourth Crusade." *The American Historical Review* 78, no. 4 (1973): 873–906.

——. "Seide und seidene Textilien im arabischen und normannischen Sizilien: der wirtschaftliche Kontext." In *Nobiles Officinae: Die königlichen Hofwerkstätten zu Palermo zur Zeit der Normannen und Staufer im 12. und 13. Jahrhundert*, edited by Wilfried Seipel, 61–73. Milano: Skira, 2004.

——. "Silk Crosses the Mediterranean." In *Le view del Mediterranean. Idee, uomini, oggetti (secoli XI–XVI), Genova, 19–20 aprile 1994 (Universita degli studi di Genova, Collana dell'Itstituto di storia del medioevo e della espansione europa, n. 1)*, edited by G. Airaldi, 55–79. Genoa, 1997. Reprinted in David Jacoby, *Byzantium, Latin Romania and the Mediterranean*, X. Aldershot: Variorum, 2001.

——. "Silk Economics and Cross-Cultural Artistic Interaction: Byzantium, the Muslim World, and the Christian West." *Dumbarton Oaks Papers* 58 (2004): 197–240.

——. *Trade, Commodities and Shipping in the Medieval Mediterranean*. Aldershot: Variorum, 1997.

James, Edward, Michael McCormick, Joachim Henning, Andreas Schwarcz, Florin Curta, Alan M. Stahl, and David Whitehouse. "Origins of the European Economy: A Debate." *Early Medieval Europe* 12, no. 3 (2003): 259–323.

Jasny, Naum. *The Wheats of Classical Antiquity*. Baltimore, MD: Johns Hopkins Press, 1944.

Jefferson, Rebecca J. W., Erica C. D. Hunter, and Geoffrey Khan. *Published Material from the Cambridge Genizah Collections: A Bibliography, 1980–1997*. 2 vols. Cambridge: Cambridge University Press, 2004.

Jenkins, Kenneth. *Coins of Greek Sicily*. 2nd ed. London: British Museum Publications, 1976.

Johns, Jeremy. *Arabic Administration in Norman Sicily: The Royal Dīwān*. Cambridge: Cambridge University Press, 2002.

——. "Arabic Contracts of Sea-Exchange from Norman Sicily." In *Karissime Gotifride. Historical Essays Presented to Professor Godfrey Wettinger on his Seventieth Birthday*, edited by P. Xuereb, 55–78. Msida: Malta University Press, 1999.

——. "Arabic Sources for Sicily." *Proceedings of the British Academy* 132 (2007): 341–360.

——. "The Boys from Messoiuso: Muslim *Jizya*-Payers in Christian Sicily." In *Islamic Reflections, Arabic Musings: Studies in Honor of Professor Alan Jones*, edited by Robert G. Hoyland and Philip F. Kennedy, 243–255. Oxford: E. J. W. Gibb Memorial Trust, 2004.

——. "The Greek Church and the Conversion of Muslims in Norman Sicily?" *Byzantinische Forschungen* 21 (1995): 133–157.

——. "Malik Ifrīqiya: The Norman Kingdom of Africa and the Fātimids." *Libyan Studies* 18 (1987): 89–101.

——. "The Monreale Survey: Indigenes and Invaders in Medieval West Sicily." In *Papers in Italian Archaeology IV*, edited by Caroline Malone and Simon Stoddart, vol.4, 215–224. BAR International Series 246. Oxford: B.A.R., 1985.

——. "The Norman Kings of Sicily and the Fatimid Caliphate." *Anglo-Norman Studies* 15 (1993): 133–159.

Johns, Jeremy, and Alex Metcalfe. "The Mystery at Churchuro: Conspiracy or Incompetence in Twelfth-Century Sicily?" *Bulletin of the School of Oriental and African Studies* 62, no. 2 (1999): 226–259.

Johns, Jeremy, and Emilie Savage-Smith. "The Book of Curiosities: A Newly Discovered Series of Islamic Maps." *Imago Mundi* 55 (2003): 7–24.

Johnson, Ewan. "Normandy and Norman Identity in Southern Italian Chronicles." *Anglo-Norman Studies* 27 (2005): 85–100.

——. "Origin Myths and the Construction of Medieval Identities: Norman Chronicles 1000–1200." In *Texts and Identities in the Early Middle Ages,* edited by R. Corradini, et al., 153–164. Forschungen zur Geschichte des Mittelalters, vol. 12. Vienna: Verlag der Österreichischen Akademie der Wissenschaften, 2006.

Joranson, Einar. "The Inception of the Career of the Normans in Italy—Legend and History." *Speculum* 23, no. 3 (1948): 353–396.

Kaegi, Walter. *Byzantium and the Early Islamic Conquests*. Cambridge: Cambridge University Press, 1992.

——. *Muslim Expansion and Byzantine Collapse in North Africa*. Cambridge: Cambridge University Press, 2010.

Kampbell, Sarah Marie. "The Pantano Longarini Shipwreck: A Reanalysis." MA thesis, Texas A&M University, 2007.

Kantorowicz, Ernst. *Frederick the Second, 1194–1250*. New York: Frederick Ungar, 1957.

Kapitaikin, Lev. " 'The Daughter of al-Andalus': Interrelations between Norman Sicily and the Muslim West." *al-Masāq* 25, no. 1 (2013): 113–134.

——. "The Twelfth-Century Paintings of the Ceilings of the Cappella Palatina, Palermo." PhD thesis, Oxford University, 2011.

Kapitän, Gerhard. "The Church Wreck off Marzamemi." *Archaeology* 22, no. 2 (1969): 122–133.

Kehr, Karl Andreas. *Die Urkunden der Normannish-Sizilischen Konige: Eine diplomatische Untersuchung*. Innsbruck: Aalen Scientia Verlag, 1962.

Kennedy, Hugh. "Byzantine-Arab Diplomacy in the Near East from the Islamic Conquests to the Mid-eleventh Century." In *Byzantine Diplomacy: Papers from the Twenty-Fourth Spring Symposium of Byzantine Studies, Cambridge, March 1990*, edited by Jonathan Shepard and Simon Franklin, 133–143. Aldershot: Variorum, 1992.

——. "The Muslims in Europe." In *The New Cambridge Medieval History*, vol. 2, edited by Rosamund McKitterick, 249–271. Cambridge: Cambridge University Press, 1995.

——. "Sicily and Al-Andalus under Muslim Rule." In *The New Cambridge Medieval History*, vol. 3, edited by Timothy Reuter, 646–669. Cambridge: Cambridge University Press, 1995.

Khalilieh, Hassan S. "The Legal Opinion of Maliki Jurists regarding Andalusian Muslim Pilgrims Travelling by Sea during the Eleventh and Twelfth Centuries CE." *Mediterranean Historical Review* 14, no. 1 (1999): 59–69.

King, Anthony, and Martin Henig, eds. *The Roman West in the Third Century: Contributions from Archaeology and History*. BAR International Series 109. Oxford: B.A.R., 1981.

Kingsley, Sean. "Mapping Trade by Shipwrecks." In *Byzantine Trade, 4th–12th Centuries: The Archaeology of Local, Regional and International Exchange, Papers of the Thirty-Eighth Spring Symposium of Byzantine Studies, St John's College, University of Oxford, March 2004*, edited by Marlia Mundell Mango, 31–36. Farnham: Ashgate, 2008.

Kislinger, Ewald. "Sightseeing in the Byzantine Empire." In *Hē Epikoinōnia sto Vyzantio: praktika tou [2.] Diethnous Symposiou, 4–6 Oktvriou 1990*, edited by Nikos G. Moschonas, 457–468. Athens: Kentro Vyzantinōn Ereunōn / E.I.E., 1993.

Kitzinger, Ernst. *I Mosaici del Periodo Normanno in Sicilia*, I–VI. Palermo: Accademia nazionale di scienze, lettere e arti di Palermo, 1992–2000.

——. *I Mosaici di Monreale*. Palermo: S.F. Flaccovio, 1960.

——. "Mosaic Decoration in Sicily under Roger II and the Classical Byzantine System of Church Decoration." In *Italian Church Decoration of the Middle Ages and Renaissance. Functions, Forms, and Regional Traditions*, edited by William Tronzo, 147–165. Bologna: Nuova Alfa Editoriale, 1989.

——. *The Mosaics of St. Mary of the Admiral in Palermo*. Washington, DC: Dumbarton Oaks, 1990.

Kolias, Georges. "Le motif et les raisons de l'invasion de Robert Guiscard en territoire byzantin." *Byzantion* 36 (1966): 424–430.

Komnene, Anna. *The Alexiad*. Translated by E. R. A. Sewter and Peter Frankopan. London: Penguin, 2009.

Kongingsveld, P. S. van, and G. A. Wiegers. "The Islamic Statute of the Mudejars in the Light of a New Source." *al-Qanṭara* 17 (1996): 19–58.

Kreutz, Barbara M. *Before the Normans: Southern Italy in the Ninth and Tenth Centuries*. Philadelphia: University of Pennsylvania Press, 1996.

——. "Ghost Ships and Phantom Cargoes: Reconstructing Early Amalfitan Trade." *Journal of Medieval History* 20 (1994): 347–357.

——. "Ships, Shipping, and the Implications of Change in the Early Medieval Mediterranean." *Viator* 7 (1976): 79–109.

Lagardère, Vincent. *Histoire et société en occident musulman au Moyen Âge: Analyse du Mi'yar d'al-Wansarisi*. Madrid: Consejo Superior de Investigaciones Cientificas, 1995.

Laiou, Angeliki E., ed. *The Economic History of Byzantium: From the Seventh through the Fifteenth Century*. 3 vols. Washington, DC: Dumbarton Oaks, 2002.

Laroui, Abdallah. *The History of the Maghrib*. Princeton, NJ: Princeton University Press, 1977.

Lavagnini, Bruno. "Siracusa occupata dagli Arabi e l'epistola di Teodosio Monaco." *Byzantion* 29/30 (1935/1936): 267–279.

Lev, Efraim. "Drugs Held and Sold by Pharmacists of the Jewish Community of Medieval (11–14th Centuries) Cairo according to Lists of *Materia Medica* Found at the Taylor–Schechter Genizah Collection, Cambridge." *Journal of Ethnopharmacology* 110 (2007): 275–293.

Lev, Yaacov. "The Fāṭimid Navy, Byzantium and the Mediterranean Sea 909–1036 C.E./297–427 A.H." *Byzantion* 54 (1984): 220–252.

——. "The Fatimids and Byzantium, 10th–12th Centuries." Pts. 1 and 2. *Graeco-Arabica* 6 (1995): 190–209; 7/8 (1999/2000): 273–282.

——. "A Mediterranean Encounter: The Fatimids and Europe, Tenth to Twelfth Centuries." In *Shipping, Trade and Crusade in the Medieval Mediterranean: Studies in Honour of John Pryor*, edited by Ruthy Gertwagen and Elizabeth Jeffreys, 131–156. Farnham: Ashgate, 2012.

Levi-Provencal, Evariste. "Une herione de la resistance musulmane en Sicile au debut du XIIIe siècle." *Oriente moderno* 34 (1954): 283–288.

Lewicki, T. "Les voies maritimes de la Méditerranée dans le haut Moyen Âge d'après les sources arabes." In *La navigazione mediterranea nell'alto Medioevo*, 447–453. Spoleto: Presso la sede del Centro, 1978.

Lewis, Archibald R. "The Closing of the Mediaeval Frontier 1250–1350." *Speculum* 33, no. 4 (1958): 475–483.

——. *Naval Power and Trade in the Mediterranean, A.D. 500–1100*. Princeton, NJ: Princeton University Press, 1951.

Lewis, Archibald R., and Timothy J. Runyan. *European Naval and Maritime History, 300–1500*. Bloomington: Indiana University Press, 1985.

Lewis, Bernard. "Legal and Historical Reflection on the Position of Muslim Populations under Non-Muslim Rule." *Journal of the Institute of Muslim Minority Affairs* 13, no. 1 (1992): 1–16.

Lo Jacono, Claudio. "La prima incursione musulmana in Sicilia secondo il *Kitāb al- Futūḥ* di Ibn A'tham al-Kūfī." In *Studi arabo-islamici in onore di Roberto Rubinacci nel suo settantesimo cumpleanno*, edited by Clelia Sarnelli Cerqua, 347–363. Naples: Istituto universitario orientale, 1985.

Lomax, John Philip. "Frederick II, His Saracens, and the Papacy." In *Medieval Christian Perceptions of Islam*, edited by J. V. Tolan, 175–197. New York: Garland, 1996.

Lombard, Maurice. *Les métaux dans l'ancien monde du Ve au XIe siècle*. Vol. 2 of *Études d'économie médiévale*. Paris: Mouton, 1974.

——. *Les textiles dans le monde musulman du VIIe au XIIe siècle*. Vol. 3 of *Études d'économie médiévale*. Paris: Éditions de l'EHESS, 2002.

——. "L'or musulman du VIIe au XIe siècles. Les bases monetaires d'une suprématie économique." *Annales* 2 (1947): 143–160.

Lopez, Robert S. "Silk Industry in the Byzantine Empire." *Speculum* 20 (1945): 1–42.

Lopez, Robert S., and Irving W. Raymond. *Medieval Trade in the Mediterranean World*. New York: Columbia University Press, 1955.

Loud, G. A. *The Age of Robert Guiscard: Southern Italy and the Norman Conquest*. New York: Longman, 2000.

——. "Byzantine Italy and the Normans." In *Byzantium and the West c.850–c.1200. Proceedings of the XVIII Spring Symposium of Byzantine Studies*, edited by J. D. Howard-Johnston, 215–233. Amsterdam: Verlag Adolf M. Hakkert, 1988.

——. "Churches and Church Men in an Age of Conquest: Southern Italy, 1030–1130." *The Haskins Society Journal* 4 (1992): 37–53. Reprinted in G. A. Loud, *Conquerors and Churchmen in Norman Italy*, VIII. Aldershot: Ashgate, 1999.

——. "Communities, Cultures and Conflict in Southern Italy, from the Byzantines to the Angevins." *al-Masāq* 28:2 (2016): 132–152.

——. "Continuity and Change in Norman Italy: The Campania during the Eleventh and Twelfth Centuries." *Journal of Medieval History* 22 (1996): 313–343. Reprinted in *Conquerors and Churchmen in Norman Italy*, V.

——. "The Genesis and Context of the Chronicle of Falco of Benevento." *Anglo-Norman Studies* 25 (1993): 177–198.

——. "The 'Gens Normannorum'—Myth or Reality?" *Anglo-Norman Studies* 4 (1981): 104–116, 205–209. Reprinted in *Conquerors and Churchmen in Norman Italy*, I.

——. "How 'Norman' Was the Norman Conquest of Southern Italy?" *Nottingham Medieval Studies* 25 (1981): 13–34. Reprinted in *Conquerors and Churchmen in Norman Italy*, II.

——. "The Kingdom of Sicily and the Kingdom of England, 1066–1266." *History* 88 (2003), 550–563.

——. *The Latin Church in Norman Italy*. Cambridge: Cambridge University Press, 2007.

——. "Monastic Chronicles in the Twelfth-Century Abruzzi." *Anglo-Norman Studies* 27 (2005): 101–131.

——. "The Monastic Economy in the Principality of Salerno during the Eleventh and Twelfth Centuries." *Papers of the British School at Rome* 71 (2003): 147–179.

——. *Montecassino and Benevento in the Middle Ages: Essays in South Italian Church History*. Aldershot: Ashgate, 2000.

——. "Norman Italy and the Holy Land." In *The Horns of Hattin: Proceedings of the Second Conference of the Society for the Study of the Crusades and the Latin East*, edited by Benjamin Z. Kedar, 49–62. Jerusalem: Yad Izhak Ben-Zvi, 1992.

——. "The Papacy and the Rulers of Southern Italy, 1058–1198." In *The Society of Norman Italy*, edited by G. A. Loud and A. Metcalfe, 151–184. Leiden: E. J. Brill, 2002.

——. "Royal Control of the Church in the Twelfth-Century Kingdom of Sicily." *Studies in Church History* 18 (1982): 147–159. Reprinted in *Conquerors and Churchmen in Norman Italy*, X.

Loud, G. A., and Alex Metcalfe, eds. *The Society of Norman Italy*. Leiden: E. J. Brill, 2002.

Luongo, Gennaro. "Itinerari dei santi italo-greci." In *Pellegrinaggi e itinerari dei santi nel Mezzogiorno medievale*, edited by Giovanni Vitolo, 39–56. Europa mediterranea-Quaderni 14. Naples: Liguori, 1999.

Luttrell, Anthony. "L'effritement de l'islam 1091–1282." *Revue du monde musulman et de la Méditerranée* 71 (1995): 49–61.

Mack Smith, Denis. *Medieval Sicily 800–1713*. London: Chatto and Windus, 1968.

Macrides, Ruth, ed. *Travel in the Byzantine World: Papers from the Thirty-Fourth Spring Symposium of Byzantine Studies, Birmingham, April 2000*. Aldershot: Ashgate Variorum, 2002.

Magoulias, Harry. "The Lives of the Saints as Sources of Data for the History of Commerce in the Byzantine Empire in the VIth and VIIth Cent." *Kleronomia* 3 (1971): 303–330.

Maier, Christoph T. "Crusade and Rhetoric against the Muslim Colony of Lucera: Eudes of Chateauroux's Sermones de Rebellione Sarracenorum Lucherie in Apulia." *Journal of Medieval History* 21, no. 4 (1995): 343–385.

Malamut, Elisabeth. *Les îles de l'Empire byzantin: VIIIe–XIIe siècles*. Paris: Universite de Paris, 1988.

——. *Sur la route des saints Byzantins*. Paris: CNRS, 1993.

Malkin, Irad. *A Small Greek World: Networks in the Ancient Mediterranean*. Oxford: Oxford University Press, 2011.

Mallette, Karla. *The Kingdom of Sicily, 1100–1250: A Literary History*. Philadelphia: University of Pennsylvania Press, 2005.

——. "Poetries of the Norman Courts." In *The Literature of al-Andalus*, edited by Maria Rosa Menocal, Raymond P. Scheindlin, and Michael Sells, 377–387. Cambridge: Cambridge University Press, 2000.

——. "Translating Sicily." *Medieval Encounters* 9, no. 1 (2003): 140–163.

Mandalà, Giuseppe. "The Jews of Palermo from Late Antiquity to the Expulsion (598–1492–93)." In *A Companion to Medieval Palermo*, edited by Annliese Nef, 437–485. Leiden: E. J. Brill, 2013.

——. "Political Martyrdom and Religious Censorship in Islamic Sicily: A Case Study during the Age of Ibrāhīm II (261–289/875–902)." *al-Qanṭara* 35 (2014): 151–186.

Mango, Cyril. "On Re-reading the Life of St. Gregory the Decapolite." *Byzantina* 13 (1985): 633–646.

Maqbul Ahmad, S. "Cartography of al-Sharīf al-Idrīsī." In *The History of Cartography*, vol. 2, bk. 1, *Cartography in the Traditional Islamic and South Asian Societies*, edited by J. B. Harley and David Woodward, 156–174. Chicago: University of Chicago Press, 1992.

——. "Djughrafiyā." *EI*^{2}, 2: 575–587. Leiden: E. J. Brill, 1965.

Martin, Jean-Marie. "La colonie Sarrasine de Lucera et son environnement. Quelques reflexions." In *Mediterraneo medievale: Scritti in onore di Francesco Giunta*, vol. 2, 795–811. Soveria Mannelli: Rubbettino, 1989.

——. *Regesti dei documenti dell'Italia meridionale, 570–899, Sources et documents d'histoire du Moyen Âge*, vol. 5. Rome: École Française de Rome, 2002.

Martin, Lillian Ray. "Horse and Cargo Handling on Medieval Mediterranean Ships." *International Journal of Nautical Archaeology* 31 (2002): 237–241.

Martyn, John R. C. *Pope Gregory's Letter-Bearers: A Study of the Men and Women Who Carried Letters for Pope Gregory the Great*. Newcastle: Cambridge Scholars Publishing, 2012.

Masud, Muhammad Khalid. "The Obligation to Migrate: The Doctrine of Hijra in Islamic Law." In *Muslim Travellers: Pilgrimage, Migration, and the Religious Imagination*, edited by Dale F. Eickelman and James Piscatori, 29–49. Berkeley: University of California Press, 1990.

Matthew, Donald. *The Norman Kingdom of Sicily*. Cambridge: Cambridge University Press, 1992.

Mattingly, D. J. "Oil for Export? A Comparison of Libyan, Spanish and Tunisian Olive Oil Production in the Roman Empire." *Journal of Roman Archaeology* 1 (1988): 33–56.

——. "The Olive Boom: Oil Surpluses, Wealth and Power in Roman Tripolitania." *Libyan Studies* 19 (1988): 21–41.

——. "Olive Oil Production in Roman Tripolitania." In *Town and Country in Roman Tripolitania*, edited by D. J. Mattingly and D. J. Buck, 27–46. Oxford, 1985.

Maurici, Ferdinando. *Castelli medievali in Sicilia: dai bizantini ai normanni*. Palermo: Sellerio, 1992.

——. "Sicilia Bizantina: Gli insediamenti del Palermitano." *Archivio Storico Siciliano 20* (1994): 27–93.

——. "Uno stato musulmano nell'Europa cristiana del XIII secolo: L'Emirato siciliano di Mohammed Ibn Abbad." *Acta Historica et Archaeologica Mediaevalia* 18 (1997): 257–280.

May, Florence Lewis. *Silk Textiles of Spain, Eighth to Fifteenth Century*. New York: Hispanic notes & monographes, 1957.

Mazot, Sibylle. "L'Architecture d'influence Nord-Africaine à Palerme." In *L'Egypte fatimide: Son art et son histoire. Actes du colloque organisé à Paris les 28, 29 et 30 mai 1998*, edited by Marianne Barrucand, 665–679. Paris: Presses de l'université de Paris-Sorbonne, 1999.

McConnell, Brian E., and Giuseppe Castellana. "A Rural Settlement of Imperial Roman-Byzantine Date in Contrada Saraceno near Agrigento, Sicily." *American Journal of Archaeology* 94 (1990): 25–44.

McCormick, Michael. "Byzantium on the Move: Imagining a Communications History." In *Travel in the Byzantine World: Papers from the Thirty-Fourth Spring Symposium of Byzantine Studies, Birmingham, April 2000*, edited by Ruth Macrides, 3–29. Aldershot: Ashgate Variorum, 2002.

——. "The Imperial Edge: Italo-Byzantine Identity, Movement and Integration, A.D. 650–950." In *Studies on the Internal Diaspora of the Byzantine Empire*, edited by Hélène Ahrweiler and Angeliki Laiou, 17–52. Washington, DC: Dumbarton Oaks, 1998.

——. *Origins of the European Economy: Communications and Commerce, A.D. 300–900.* Cambridge: Cambridge University Press, 2001.

McQueen, William B. "Relations between the Normans and Byzantium, 1071–1112." *Byzantion* 56 (1986): 427–476.

Menache, Sophia. "Introduction: The 'Pre-History' of Communication." In *Communication in the Jewish Diaspora: The Pre-modern World*, edited by Sophia Menache, 1–13. Leiden: E. J. Brill, 1996.

Menager, Leon-Robert. "Pesanteur et etiologie de la colonisation normande de l'Italie." In *Roberto il Guiscardo e il suo tempo*, 189–214. Rome: Il centro di ricerca, 1975.

Metcalfe, Alex. "De Saracenico in Latinum Transferri: Causes and Effects of Translation in the Fiscal Administration of Norman Sicily." *al-Masāq* 13 (2001): 43–86.

——. *Muslims and Christians in Norman Sicily: Arabic-Speakers and the End of Islam.* New York: Routledge, 2002.

——. *The Muslims of Medieval Italy.* Edinburgh: Edinburgh University Press, 2009.

——. "The Muslims of Sicily under Christian Rule." In *The Society of Norman Italy*, edited by G. A. Loud and Alex Metcalfe, 289–317. Leiden: E. J. Brill, 2002.

——. "Trusting the Text as Far as We Can Throw the Scribe: Further Notes on Reading a Bilingual *Jaridat al-Hudud* from the Royal *Diwan* of Norman Sicily." In *From Al-Andalus to Khurasan: Documents from the Medieval Muslim World*, edited by P. M. Sijpesteijn, L. Sundelin, S. Torallas Tovar, and A. Zomeño, 78–98. Leiden: E. J. Brill, 2007.

Miller, Kathryn A. "Muslim Minorities and the Obligation to Emigrate to Islamic Territory: Two Fatwās from Fifteenth-Century Granada." *Islamic Law and Society* 7, no. 2 (2000): 256–288.

Miquel, Andre. *La geographie humaine du monde musulman jusqu'au milieu du 11e siècle.* Paris: Mouton, 1967.

Molenat, Jean-Pierre. "Le problème de la permanence des musulmans dans les territoires conquis par les Chrétiens, du point de vue de la loi islamique." *Arabica* 48, no. 3 (2001): 392–400.

Molinari, Alessandra. "La Sicilia islamica: Riflessioni sul passato e sul futuro della ricerca in campo archeologico." In "La Sicile à l'époque islamique. Questions de méthode et renouvellement récent des problématiques." Special issue, *Mélanges de l'Éçaise de Rome, Moyen Âge* 116, no. 1 (2004): 19–46.

Momigliano, A. "La riscoperta della Sicilia antica da T. Fazello a P. Orsi." *Studi Urbinati* 52 (1978): 5–23.

——. "The Rediscovery of Greek History: The Case of Sicily." *Studies in XVIIIth Century Culture* 9 (1979): 167–187.

Monneret de Villard, Ugo. *Le pitture musulmane al soffitto della Cappella palatina in Palermo*. Rome: La Libreria dello Stato, 1950.

Morony, Michael G. "Economic Boundaries? Late Antiquity and Early Islam." *Journal of the Economic and Social History of the Orient* 47, no. 2 (2004): 166–194.

Morris, Ian. "Mediterraneanization." *Mediterranean Historical Review* 18, no. 2 (2003): 30–55.

Morrisson, Cecile. *Catalogue des monnaies Byzantines de la Bibliotheque Nationale*. 2 vols. Paris: Bibliotheque Nationale, 1970.

Mostert, Marco. "New Approaches to Medieval Communication?" In *New Approaches to Medieval Communication*, edited by Marco Mostert, 15–37. Turnhout: Brepols, 1999.

Mott, Lawrence V. *Sea Power in the Medieval Mediterranean: The Catalan-Aragonese Fleet in the War of the Sicilian Vespers*. Gainesville: University Press of Florida, 2003.

——. "Serving in the Fleet: Crews and Recruitment Issues in the Catalan-Aragonese Fleets during the War of Sicilian Vespers (1282–1302)." *Medieval Encounters* 13 (2007): 56–77.

——. "The Textile Industry and the Foreign Cloth Trade in Late Medieval Sicily (1300–1500): A 'Colonial' Relationship?" *Journal of Medieval History* 15 (1989): 141–183.

——. "Trade as a Weapon during the War of the Sicilian Vespers." *Medieval Encounters* 9 (2003): 236–243.

Murray, William H. "Do Modern Winds Equal Ancient Winds?" *Mediterranean Historical Review* 2, no. 2 (1987): 139–167.

Muthesius, Anna. "The Byzantine Silk Industry: Lopez and Beyond." *Journal of Medieval History* 19 (1993): 1–67.

Nef, Annliese. "Al-Idrīsī: Un complément d'enquête biographique." In *Géographes et voyageurs au Moyen Age*, edited by Henri Bresc and Emmanuelle Du Mesnil, 53–66. Nanterre: Presses universitaires de Paris Ouest, 2010.

——. "Les élites savantes urbaines dans la Sicile islamique d'après les dictionnaires biographiques arabes." In "La Sicile à l'époque islamique. Questions de méthode et renouvellement récent des problématiques." Special issue, *Mélanges de l'École Française de Rome, Moyen Âge* 116, no. 1 (2004): 451–470.

Netton, Ian Richard. "Basic Structures and Signs of Alienation in the *Riḥla* of Ibn Jubayr." In *Golden Roads: Migration, Pilgrimage and Travel in Mediaeval and Modern Islam*, edited by Ian Richard Netton, 57–74. Richmond, UK: Curzon Press, 1993.

——. "Ibn Jubayr: Penitent Pilgrim and Observant Traveler." In *Seek Knowledge: Thought and Travel in the House of Islam*, edited by Ian Richard Netton, 95–101. Richmond, UK: Curzon Press, 1996.

——. "Riḥla." In *EI*², 8: 328. Leiden: E. J. Brill, 1995.
Nirenberg, David. *Communities of Violence*. Princeton, NJ: Princeton University Press, 1996.
Noble, Thomas F. X. "Greek Popes: Yes or No, and Did It Matter?" In *Western Perspectives on the Mediterranean: Cultural Transfer in Late Antiquity and the Early Middle Ages, 400–800 AD*, edited by Andreas Fischer and I. N. Wood, 77–86. London: Bloomsbury, 2014.
——. *The Republic of St. Peter: The Birth of the Papal State, 680–825*. Philadelphia: University of Pennsylvania Press, 1984.
Oddy, W. A. "The Debasement of the Provincial Byzantine Gold Coinage from the Seventh to the Ninth Centuries." In *Studies in Early Byzantine Gold Coinage*, edited by Wolfgang Hahn and William E. Metcalf, 135–142. New York: American Numismatic Society, 1988.
——. "The Gold Contents of Fatimid Coins Reconsidered." *Metallurgy in Numismatics* 1 (1980): 99–118, plates 116–111.
Oldfield, Paul. *City and Community in Norman Italy*. Cambridge: Cambridge University Press, 2009.
——. "The Medieval Cult of St Agatha of Catania and the Consolidation of Christian Sicily." *Journal of Ecclesiastical History* 62, no. 3 (2011): 439–456.
——. "Rural Settlement and Economic Development in Southern Italy: Troia and Its Contado, c.1020–c.1230." *Journal of Medieval History* 31 (2005): 327–345.
——. *Sanctity and Pilgrimage in Medieval Southern Italy, 1000–1200*. Cambridge: Cambridge University Press, 2014.
Oman, G. "Notizie bibliographiche sul geografo arabo al-Idrīsī (XII secolo) e sulle opera." *Annali, Istituto Universitario Orientale di Napoli* 11 (1961): 25–61.
Ostrogorsky, George. "The Byzantine Empire in the World of the Seventh Century." *Dumbarton Oaks Papers* 13 (1959): 1–21.
——. *History of the Byzantine State*. Translated by Joan Hussey. Rev. ed. New Brunswick, NJ: Rutgers University Press, 1969.
Ould Bah, Mohamed El Mokhtar. *La littérature juridique et l'évolution du Malikisme en Mauritanie*. Tunis: Université de Tunis, 1981.
The Oxford Dictionary of Byzantium. Edited by Alexander P. Kazhdan et al. 3 vols. New York: Oxford University Press, 1991.
Palmieri, S. "Un esempio di mobilita etnica altomedievale: I saraceni in Campania." In *Montecassino dalla prima alla seconda distruzione. Momenti e aspetti di storia cassinese (secc. VI–IX)*, edited by F. Avagliano, 602–609. Miscellanea Cassinese 55. Montecassino: Pubblicazioni Cassinesi, 1987.
Papaconstantinou, Arietta. "Confrontation, Interaction, and the Formation of the Early Islamic *Oikoumene*." *Revue des études byzantines* 63, no. 1 (2005): 167–181.
Peacock, David P. S., and D. F. Williams. *Amphorae and the Roman Economy: An Introductory Guide*. London: Longman, 1986.
Pellat, Charles. "Ibn Djubayr." *EI*², 3: 755. Leiden: E. J. Brill, 1971.
Pellitteri, Antonio. "The Historical-Ideological Framework of Islamic Famitid Sicily (Fourth/Tenth Century) with Reference to the Works of the Qadi l-Nu'man." *al-Masāq* 7 (1994): 111–163.

Perry, Charles. "Sicilian Cheese in Medieval Arab Recipes." *Gastronomica* 1 (2001): 76–77.
Pesez, Jean-Marie. "Brucato et la civilisation materielle du village en Sicilie médiévale." *Mélanges de l'École Française de Rome, Moyen Âge* 86 (1974): 7–23.
——. "Problèmes d'archéologie médiévale en Sicile." In *Atti del congresso internazionale di studi sulla sicilia normanna*, 225–240. Palermo: Università di Palermo 1973.
Peyronnet, Georges. "Coexistence islamo-chrétienne en Sicile et au moyen-orient." *Islamochristiana* 19 (1993): 55–73.
Pinna, Margherita. *Il Mediterraneo e la Sardegna nella cartografia musulmana (dall'VIII al XVI secolo)*. Nuoro: Istituto superiore regionale etnografico, 1996.
Pinto, Karen C. *Medieval Islamic Maps: An Exploration*. Chicago: University of Chicago Press, 2016.
——. "'Surat Baḥr al-Rum' (Picture of the Sea of Byzantium): Possible Meanings Underlying the Forms." *Eastern Mediterranean Cartographies* 25 / 26 (2004): 223–241.
——. "Ways of Seeing: Scenarios of the World in the Medieval Islamic Cartographic Imagination." PhD thesis, Columbia University, 2002.
Pirenne, Henri. *Mohammed and Charlemagne*. London: G. Allen & Unwin, 1939.
Powell, James M. "Economy and Society in the Kingdom of Sicily under Frederick II: Recent Perspectives." In *Intellectual Life at the Court of Frederick II Hohenstaufen*, edited by William Tronzo, 263–271.Washington, DC: National Gallery of Art, 1994.
——. "Frederick II and the Muslims: The Making of an Historiographical Tradition." In *Iberia and the Mediterranean World of the Middle Ages*, vol. 1, edited by Larry J. Simon, 261–269. Leiden: E. J. Brill, 1995.
——. "La carriere du tourmarque Euphemios, basileus des Romains." In *Histoire et culture dans l'Italie byzantine: Acquis et nouvelles recherches*, edited by Andre Jacob, Jean-Marie Martin, and Ghislaine Noye, 279–317. Rome: École Française de Rome, 2006.
——, ed. *Muslims under Latin Rule, 1100–1300*. Princeton, NJ: Princeton University Press, 1990.
Prigent, Vivien. "Les empereurs isauriens et la confiscation des patrimoines pontificaux d'Italie du sud." *Mélanges de l'École Française de Rome, Moyen Âge* 116, no. 2 (2004): 557–594.
Pringle, Denys. *The Defence of Byzantine Africa from Justinian to the Arab Conquest: An Account of the Military History and Archaeology of the African Provinces in the Sixth and Seventh Century*. Oxford: British Archaeological Reports, 1981.
Pryor, John H. *Geography, Technology and War: Studies in the Maritime History of the Mediterranean, 649–1571*. Cambridge: Cambridge University Press, 1988.
——. "The Naval Architecture of Crusader Transport Ships and Horse Transports Revisited." *The Mariner's Mirror* 76 (1990): 255–273.
——. "Winds, Waves, and Rocks: The Routes and the Perils along Them." In *Maritime Aspects of Migration*, edited by K. Friedland, 71–85. Cologne: Böhlau, 1989.
Purcell, Nicholas. "The Boundless Sea of Unlikeness? On Defining the Mediterranean." *Mediterranean Historical Review* 18, no. 2 (2003): 9–29.

——. "Wine and Wealth in Ancient Italy." *Journal of Roman Studies* 75 (1985): 1–19.

Purpura, Gianfranco. "Il relitto bizantino di Cefalù." *Sicilia Archeologica* 51 (1983): 93–105.

Ramseyer, Valerie. *The Transformation of a Religious Landscape: Medieval Southern Italy, 850–1150*. Ithaca, NY: Cornell University Press, 2006.

Re, Mario. "From Greek Southern Italy to Jerusalem: Monks, Saints and Pilgrims." In *Routes of Faith in the Medieval Mediterranean: History, Monuments, People, Pilgrimage Perspectives. Proceedings of the International Symposium (Thessalonike, 7–10 November 2007)*, edited by Evangelia Hadjitryphonos, 171–176. Thessaloniki, 2008.

——. "Italo-Greek Hagiography." In *The Ashgate Research Companion to Byzantine Hagiography*, vol. 1, edited by Stephanos Efthymiadis, 227–258. Farnham: Ashgate, 2011.

Reif, Stefan C., and Paul Fenton. *Published Material from the Cambridge Genizah Collections: A Bibliography, 1896–1980*. Cambridge: Cambridge University Press, 1988.

Riall, Lucy. *Sicily and the Unification of Italy: Liberal Policy and Local Power, 1859–1866*. Oxford: Clarendon Press, 1998.

——. "Which Road to the South? Revisionists Revisit the Mezzogiorno." *Journal of Modern Italian Studies* 51, no. 1 (2000): 89–100.

Ricotti Prina, D. "La monetazaione Siciliana nell'epoca Bizantina." *Numismatica* 16 (1950): 26–60.

Rizzitano, Umberto. *Storia e cultura nella Sicilia saracena*. Palermo: S. F. Flaccovio, 1975.

——. "Un compendio dell'Antologia di Poeti Arabo-Siciliani." *Atti della Accademia Nazionale dei Lincei* 8, no. 5 (1958): 335–379.

Rodinson, Maxime, A. J. Arberry, and Charles Perry. *Medieval Arab Cookery*. Devon: Prospect Books, 2001.

Rotman, Youval. *Byzantine Slavery and the Mediterranean* World. Cambridge, MA: Harvard University Press, 2009.

Royal, Jeffrey G., and Sebastiano Tusa. "The Levanzo I Wreck, Sicily: A 4th-century AD Merchantman in the Service of the Annona?" *International Journal of Nautical Archaeology* 41, no. 1 (2012): 26–55.

Runciman, Steven. *The Sicilian Vespers: A History of the Mediterranean World in the Later Thirteenth Century*. Cambridge: Cambridge University Press, 1958.

Savage, Elizabeth. "Berbers and Blacks: Ibadi Slave Traffic in Eighth-Century North Africa." *The Journal of African History* 33 (1992): 351–368.

——. *A Gateway to Hell, a Gateway to Paradise: The North African Response to the Arab Conquest*. Princeton, NJ: Darwin Press, 1997.

Savage-Smith, Emilie. "Cartography." In *A Companion to Mediterranean History*, edited by Peregrine Horden and Sharon Kinoshita, 184–199. Oxford: Wiley-Blackwell, 2014.

——. "Maps and Trade." In *Byzantine Trade, 4th–12th Centuries: The Archaeology of Local, Regional and International Exchange, Papers of the Thirty-Eighth Spring Symposium of Byzantine Studies, St John's College, University of Oxford, March 2004*, edited by Marlia Mundell Mango, 15–29. Farnham: Ashgate, 2009.

Savage-Smith, Emilie, and Yossef Rapoport, eds. *The Book of Curiosities: A Critical Edition*. March 2007. www.bodley.ox.ac.uk/bookofcuriosities.
———. *An Eleventh-Century Egyptian Guide to the Universe: The Book of Curiosities*. Leiden: E. J. Brill, 2013.
Seipel, Wilfried, ed. *Nobiles Officinae: Die königlichen Hofwerkstätten zu Palermo zur Zeit der Normannen und Staufer im 12. und 13. Jahrhundert*. Milano: Skira, 2004.
Semple, Ellen Churchill. *The Geography of the Mediterranean Region: Its Relation to Ancient History*. New York: Ams, 1931.
Serjeant, R. B. *Islamic Textiles: Material for a History up to the Mongol Conquest*. Beirut: Librairie du Liban, 1972.
Serrati, John. "Garrisons and Grain: Sicily between the Punic Wars." In *Sicily from Aeneas to Augustus: New Approaches in Archaeology and History*, edited by Christopher Smith and John Serrati, 115–133. Edinburgh: Edinburgh University Press, 2000.
Shavit, Yaacov. "Mediterranean History and the History of the Mediterranean." *Journal of Mediterranean Studies* 4, no. 2 (1994): 313–329.
Shaw, Brent D. "Climate, Environment, and History: The Case of Roman North Africa." In *Climate and History: Studies in Past Climates and Their Impact on Man*, edited by T. M. L. Wigley, M. J. Ingram, and G. Farmer, 379–403. Cambridge: Cambridge University Press, 1981.
———. "A Peculiar Island: Maghrib and Mediterranean." *Mediterranean Historical Review* 18, no. 2 (2003): 93–125.
Shepard, Jonathan. "Byzantium's Last Sicilian Expedition: Scylitzes' Testimony." *Rivista di studi bizantini e neoellenici*, n.s., 14–16 (1977–1979): 145–159.
———. "When Greek Meets Greek: Alexius Comnenus and Bohemond in 1097–98." *Byzantine and Modern Greek Studies* 12, no. 1 (1988): 185–278.
Silverstein, Adam J. *Postal Systems in the Pre-modern Islamic World*. Cambridge: Cambridge University Press, 2007.
Simonsohn, Shlomo. *Between Scylla and Charybdis: The Jews in Sicily*. Leiden: E. J. Brill, 2011.
———. "Sicily: A Millennium of *Convivenza* (or Almost)." In *The Jews of Europe in the Middle Ages (Tenth to Fifteenth Centuries): Proceedings of the International Symposium Held at Speyer, 20–25 October 2002*, edited by Christoph Cluse, 105–121. Turnhout: Brepols, 2004.
Siragusta, G. "Michele Amari." In *Centenario della nascita di Michele Amari*, ix–xliv. Palermo: Stabilimento Tipigrafico Virzi, 1910.
Sizgorich, Thomas. *Violence and Belief in Late Antiquity: Militant Devotion in Christianity and Islam*. Philadelphia: University of Pennsylvania Press, 2009.
Skinner, Patricia. "Amalfitans in the Caliphate of Cordoba—Or Not?" *al-Masāq* 24:2 (2012): 125–138.
———. *Family Power in Southern Italy: The Duchy of Gaeta and Its Neighbours, 850–1139*. Cambridge: Cambridge University Press, 1995.
———. "Gender, Memory and Jewish identity: Reading a Family History from Medieval Southern Italy." *Early Medieval Europe* 13 (2005): 277–296.
———. "'Halt! Be Men!': Sikelgaita of Salerno, Gender and the Norman Conquest of Southern Italy." *Gender and History* 12, no. 3 (2000): 622–641.

——. "Politics and Piracy: The Duchy of Gaeta in the Twelfth Century." *Journal of Medieval History* 21 (1995): 307–319.

Smit, Timothy James. "Commerce and Coexistence: Muslims in the Economy and Society of Norman Sicily." PhD thesis, University of Minnesota, 2009.

Smith, Christopher, and John Serrati, eds. *Sicily from Aeneas to Augustus: New Approaches in Archaeology and History*. Edinburgh: Edinburgh University Press, 2000.

Smith, R. Upsher, Jr. "*Nobilissimus* and Warleader: The Opportunity and the Necessity behind Robert Guiscard's Balkan Expeditions." *Byzantion: Revue internationale des études byzantines* 70, no. 2 (2000): 507–526.

Smith, Romney David. "Calamity and Transition: Re-imagining Italian Trade in the Eleventh-Century Mediterranean." *Past and Present* 228 (2015): 15–56.

Sorbello, Maria. "Multiculturalism in the Mediterranean Basin: An Overview of Recent Immigration to Sicily." In *Sicily and the Mediterranean: Migration, Exchange, Reinvention*, edited by Claudia Karagoz and Giovanna Summerfield, 179–194. New York: Palgrave Macmillan, 2015.

Starr, Joshua. "The Mass Conversion of Jews in Southern Italy (1290–1293)." *Speculum* 21 (1946): 203–211.

Stasolla, Maria G. "Frederic II et le monde musulman." *Islamochristiana* 25 (1999): 67–86.

Stephenson, Paul. *Byzantium's Balkan Frontier: A Political Study of the Northern Balkans, 900–1204*. Cambridge: Cambridge University Press, 2000.

Stern, S. M. "An Embassy of the Byzantine Emperor to the Fatimid Caliph al-Mu'izz." *Byzantion* 20 (1950): 239–258.

——. "Tari: The Quarter-Dinar." *Studi Medievali*, 3rd ser., 11, no. 1 (1970): 177–207.

——. "A Twelfth-Century Circle of Hebrew Poets in Sicily." Pts. 1 and 2. *Journal of Jewish Studies* 1 (1954): 60–79; 2 (1954): 110–113.

Stillman, Norman A. "East-West Relations in the Islamic Mediterranean in the Early Eleventh Century—a Study in the Geniza Correspondence of the House of Ibn 'Awkal." PhD dissertation, University of Pennsylvania, 1970.

——. "The Eleventh Century Merchant House of Ibn ʿAwkal (A Geniza Study)." *Journal of the Economic and Social History of the Orient* 16, no. 1 (1973): 15–88.

Stillman, Yedida K. *Arab Dress: A Short History from the Dawn of Islam to Modern Times*. Leiden: E. J. Brill, 2000.

——. "Costume as Cultural Statement: The Esthetics, Economics, and Politics of Islamic Dress." In *The Jews of Medieval Islam: Community, Society and Identity*, edited by Daniel Frank, 127–144. Leiden: E. J. Brill, 1992.

——. "The Importance of the Cairo Geniza for the History of Medieval Female Attire." *International Journal of Middle East Studies* 7 (1976): 579–589.

Stratos, Andreas N. "The Exarch Olympius and the Supposed Arab Invasion of Sicily in A.D. 652." *Jahrbuch des österreichischen Byzantinistik* 25 (1976): 63–73.

Taddei, Alessandro. "Some Topographical Remarks on Pope Constantine's Journey to Constantinople (AD 710–711)." *Eurasian Studies* 11 (2013): 53–78.

Takayama, Hiroshi. *The Administration of the Norman Kingdom of Sicily*. Leiden: E. J. Brill, 1993.

——. "The Aghlabid Governors in Sicily: 827–909 (Islamic Sicily I)." *Annals of Japan Association for Middle East Studies* 7 (1992): 427–443.

——. "The Fatimid and Kalbite Governors in Sicily: 909–1044 (Islamic Sicily II)." *Mediterranean World* 13 (1992): 21–30.

Talbi, Mohamed. *L'Émirat Aghlabide (184–296/800–909)*. Paris: Librairie d'Amerique et d'Orient, 1966.

Talbot, Alice-Mary. "Byzantine Pilgrimages to the Holy Land from the Eighth to the Fifteenth Century." In *The Sabaite Heritage in the Orthodox Church from the Fifth Century to the Present*, edited by Joseph Patrich, 97–110. Leuven: Peeters, 2001.

——. "Pilgrimage to Healing Shrines: The Evidence of Miracle Accounts." *Dumbarton Oaks Papers* 56 (2002): 153–173.

Tangheroni, Marco. "La Sicilia e il mercato Mediterraneo dalla fine del duecento alla meta del trecento." *Archivio Storico Siciliano*, 4th ser., 23 (1997): 151–165.

Taviani-Carozzi, Huguette. "Léon IX et les Normands d'Italie du Sud." In *Léon IX et son temps*, edited by Georges Bischoff and Benoît-Michel Tock, 299–329. Turnhout: Brepols, 2006.

Taylor, Julie. *Muslims in Medieval Italy*. Lanham, MD: Lexington Books, 2003.

Teall, John L. "The Grain Supply of the Byzantine Empire, 330–1025." *Dumbarton Oaks Papers* 13 (1959): 87–139.

Theotokis, Georgios. *The Norman Campaigns in the Balkans, 1081–1108 AD*. Woodbridge, UK: Boydell & Brewer, 2014.

Throckmorton, Peter, and Gerhard Kapitän. "An Ancient Shipwreck at Pantano Longarini." *Archaeology* 21, no. 3 (1968): 182–187.

Tibbetts, Gerald R. "The Balkhi School of Geographers." In *Cartography in the Traditional Islamic and South Asian Societies*, edited by J. B. Harley and David Woodward, vol. 2, bk. 1, 108–136. Chicago: University of Chicago Press, 1992.

Tibi, Amin. "Byzantine-Fatimid Relations in the Reign of Al-Mu'izz Li-Din Allah (r. 953–975 A.D.) as Reflected in Primary Arabic Sources." *Graeco-Arabica* 4 (1991): 91–107.

Tlili, Abderrahman. "La Sicilia descrita della penna de un autore del X secolo: Ibn Hawqal." *Sharq al-Andalus* 6 (1989): 23–32.

Tolan, John. "The Infidel before the Judge: Navigating Justice Systems in Multiconfessional Medieval Europe." In *Religiöse Vielfalt und der Umgang mit Minderheiten. Vergangene und gegenwärtige Erfahrungen*, edited by Dorothea Weltecke, 57–79. Konstanz: UVK, 2014.

Tonghini, Cristina. "Fatimid Ceramics from Italy: The Archaeological Evidence." In *L'Egypte fatimide: Son art et son histoire. Actes du colloque organisé à Paris les 28, 29 et 30 mai 1998*, edited by Marianne Barrucand, 285–297. Paris: Presses de l'université de Paris-Sorbonne, 1999.

Touati, Houari. *Islam and Travel in the Middle Ages*. Translated by Lydia G. Cochrane. Chicago: University of Chicago Press, 2010.

Toubert, Pierre. "Byzantium and the Mediterranean Agrarian Civilization." In *The Economic History of Byzantium: From the Seventh through the Fifteenth Century*, edited by Angeliki E. Laiou, 377–391. Washington, DC: Dumbarton Oaks, 2002.

Tounta, Eleni. "Saints, Rulers and Communities in Southern Italy: The Vitae of the Italo-Greek Saints (Tenth to Eleventh Centuries) and their Audiences." *Journal of Medieval History* 42, no. 4 (2016): 429–455.

Tramontana, Salvatore. "Ruggero I e la Sicilia musulmana." In *Il mezzogiorno normanno-svevo e le crociate: Atti delle quattordicesime giornate normanno-sveve, Bari, 17–20 Ottobre 2000*, edited by Giosuè Musca, 49–64. Bari: Edizioni Dedalo, 2002.

Travaini, Lucia. "La riforma monetaria di Ruggero II e la circolazione minuta in Italia meridionale tra X e XII secolo." *Rivista Italiana di Numismatica e Scienza Affini* 83 (1981): 133–153.

——. "Le monete in Italia meridionale e in Sicilia dal X al XII secolo." In *Il Mediterraneo I Luoghi e la Memoria*, 2: 55–64. Taranto: Taranto-Castello Aragonese, 1989.

——. "The Normans between Byzantium and the Islamic World." *Dumbarton Oaks Papers* 55 (2001): 179–196.

Treadgold, Warren T. *A History of the Byzantine State and Society*. Palo Alto, CA: Stanford University Press, 1997.

Tronzo, William. *The Cultures of His Kingdom: Roger II and the Cappella Palatina in Palermo*. Princeton, NJ: Princeton University Press, 1997.

——, ed. *Intellectual Life at the Court of Frederick II Hohenstaufen*. Washington, DC: National Gallery of Art, 1994.

Tusa, A. Cutroni. "La circolazione monetaria nella Sicilia Bizantina ed il ripostiglio da Castellana (Palermo)." In *Byzantino-Sicula*, edited by Giuseppe Agnello, 104–110. Palermo: Istituto Siciliano di Studi Bizantini e Neoellenici, 1966.

——. "Monetazione e circolazaione monetaria nella Sicilia bizantina." In *Byzantino-Sicula IV: Atti del I Congresso Internazionale di Archeologica della Sicilia Bizantina (Corleone, 1998)*, edited by Rosa Maria Carra Bonacasa, 413–438. Palermo: Istituto Siciliano di Studi Bizantini e Neoellenici, 2002.

Udovitch, Abraham L. "At the Origins of the Western Commenda: Islam, Israel, Byzantium?" *Speculum* 37, no. 2 (1962): 198–207.

——. "Crossroads of World Trade—from Spain to India." In *L'Egypte fatimide: Son art et son histoire. Actes du colloque organisé à Paris les 28, 29 et 30 mai 1998*, edited by Marianne Barrucand, 681–691. Paris: Presses de l'université de Paris-Sorbonne, 1999.

——. "Formalism and Informalism in the Social and Economic Institutions of the Medieval Islamic World." In *Individualism and Conformity in Classical Islam*, edited by Speros Vryonis and Amin Banani, 42–56. Wiesbaden: Harrassowitz, 1977.

——. "International Trade and the Medieval Egyptian Countryside." In *Agriculture in Egypt: From Pharaonic to Modern Times*, edited by Alan K. Bowman and Eugene Rogan, 267–285. Vol. 96, *Proceedings of the British Academy*. Oxford: Published for the British Academy by Oxford University Press, 1999.

——. "New Materials for the History of Islamic Sicily." In *Del Nuovo sulla Sicilia Musulmana*, edited by Biancamaria Scarcia Amoretti, 183–210. Rome: Accademia Nazionale de Lincei, 1993.

——. "A Tale of Two Cities: Commercial Relations between Cairo and Alexandria during the Second Half of the Eleventh Century." In *The Medieval City*, edited by Harry A. Miskimin, David Herlihy, and Abraham L. Udovitch, 143–162. New Haven, CT: Yale University Press, 1977.

——. "Time, the Sea, and Society: Duration of Commercial Voyages on the Southern Shores of the Mediterranean during the High Middle Ages." In *La navigazione mediterranea nell'alto Medioevo*, 503–546. Spoleto: Presso la sede del Centro, 1978.

Unger, Richard. *The Ship in the Medieval Economy, 600–1600*. London: Croom Helm, 1989.

Unwin, Tim. *Wine and the Vine: An Historical Geography of Viticulture and the Wine Trade*. London: Routledge, 1991.

al-ʿUsh, Muhammad Abū-l-Faraj. *Monnaies Aglabides*. Damascus: Institut Français de Damas, 1982.

Valerian, Dominique. "Ifrīqiyan Muslim Merchants in the Mediterranean at the End of the Middle Ages." *Mediterranean Historical Review* 14, no. 2 (1999): 47–66.

Valero, C. Delgado. "El arte de Ifriqiya y sus relaciones con distintos ambitos del Mediterraneo: al-Andalus, Egipto y Sicilia." *al-Qanṭara* 17, no. 2 (1996): 291–319.

Vasiliev, A. "The 'Life' of St. Peter of Argos and Its Historical Significance." *Traditio* 5 (1947): 163–191.

Verlinden, Charles. "Medieval 'Slavers.'" In *Economy, Society, and Government in Medieval Italy*, edited by David Herlihy, Robert S. Lopez, and Vsevolod Slessarev, 1–14. Kent, OH: Kent State University Press, 1969.

Waley, D. P. "'Combined Operations' in Sicily, A.D. 1060–78." *Papers of the British School at Rome* 22 (1954): 118–125.

Wansbrough, John. "A Judeo-Arabic Document from Sicily." *Bulletin of the School of Oriental and African Studies* 30 (1967): 305–313.

Wasserstein, David. "Byzantium and Al-Andalus." *Mediterranean Historical Review* 2, no. 1 (1987): 76–101.

Watson, Andrew M. *Agricultural Innovation in the Early Islamic World: The Diffusion of Crops and Farming Techniques, 700–1100*. Cambridge: Cambridge University Press, 1983.

West, G. V. B. "Charlemagne's Involvement in Central and Southern Italy: Power and the Limits of Authority." *Early Medieval Europe* 8 (1999): 341–367.

Whalen, Brett E. "God's Will or Not? Bohemond's Campaign against the Byzantine Empire (1105–1108)." In *Crusades: Medieval Worlds in Conflict*, edited by Thomas Madden, James L. Naus, and Vincent Ryan, 111–125. Farnham: Ashgate, 2009.

White, Lynn, Jr. "The Byzantinization of Sicily." *The American Historical Review* 42, no. 1 (1936): 1–21.

——. *Latin Monasticism in Norman Sicily*. Cambridge, MA: Harvard University Press, 1938.

Whittaker, C. R. *Frontiers of the Roman Empire: A Social and Economic Study*. Baltimore, MD: Johns Hopkins University Press, 1994.

Wickham, Chris. *Early Medieval Italy: Central Power and Local Society, 400–1000.* London: Macmillan, 1981.
——. *Framing the Early Middle Ages: Europe and the Mediterranean, 400–800*. Oxford: Oxford University Press, 2005.
Wilkinson, John. *Jerusalem Pilgrims before the Crusades*. 2nd ed. Warminster, England: Aris & Phillips, 2002.
Wolf, Kenneth Baxter. *Making History: The Normans and Their Historians in Eleventh-Century Italy*. Philadelphia: University of Pennsylvania Press, 1995.
Woodward, David. "Medieval *mappaemundi*." In *The History of Cartography*, vol. 1, *Cartography in Prehistoric, Ancient, and Medieval Europe and the Mediterranean*, edited by J. B. Harley and David Woodward, 286–370. Chicago: The University of Chicago Press, 1987.
Yarrison, James Lee. "Force as an Instrument of Policy: European Military Incursions and Trade in the Maghrib, 1000–1355." PhD dissertation, Princeton University, 1982.
Zeitler, Barbara. "'Urbs Felix Dotata Populo Trilingui': Some Thoughts about a Twelfth-Century Funerary Memorial from Palermo." *Medieval Encounters* 2, no. 2 (1996): 114–139.
Zeldes, Nadia. "Aspects of Married Life of Jewish Women Converts in Italy." In *Donne nella storia degli ebrei d'Italia*, edited by M. Luzzati and C. Galasso, 97–108. Florence, 2007.
——. *The Former Jews of This Kingdom: Sicilian Converts after the Expulsion 1492–1516.* Leiden: E. J. Brill, 2003.
——. "The Last Multi-cultural Encounter in Medieval Sicily: A Dominican Scholar, an Arabic Inscription, and a Jewish Legend." *Mediterranean Historical Review* 21 (2006): 159–191.
——. "Palermo and Sicily." In the *Encyclopedia of Jews in the Islamic World*, vol. 4, edited by Norman A. Stillman and Phillip Isaac Ackerman-Lieberman, 1–5. Leiden: E. J. Brill, 2010.
Zuckerman, Constantin. "Learning from the Enemy and More: Studies in 'Dark Centuries' Byzantium." *Millennium: Jahrbuch zu Kultur und Geschichte des ersten Jahrtausends n.Chr. / Yearbook on the Culture and History of the First Millennium C.E.* 2 (2005): 79–135.
Zuretti, Carlo O. "La espugnazione di Siracusa nell'880." In *Centenario della nascita di Michele Amari*, 165–184. Palermo: Stabilimento Tipigrafico Virzi, 1910.

INDEX

Page numbers in *italics* indicate maps and illustrations. Specific works will be found under the author's name, unless anonymous.

hagiographies: Byzantine Sicily in, *53–63*; on Muslim raids on Sicily, 32, 54, 56, 59, 60–63, 79–80; on population movements due to Muslim incursions, 63–64, 79–80, 107–9; on slave trade, 103, 104–5
hajj and *hajji*, 167, 168n172
Hamāt, 229
Harūn al-Rashīd, 88
al-Ḥasan b. ʿAlī, 218
Ḥasan ibn Ali al-Kalbī, 119
Hauteville family: Bohemond of Taranto (son of Robert Guiscard), 217, 235; Drogo de Hauteville, 183; Robert Guiscard (Robert de Hauteville), 174, 175, 176–77, 182, 183, 216–17; Roger, first count of Sicily (Roger de Hauteville), 175, 177, 182–86, 188; Roger II (Norman king of Sicily), 125–26, 175, 214, 218, 219n18, 230, 231; Tancred (nephew of Bohemond of Taranto), 235; Tancred de Hauteville, 175n3, 181, 182; William de Hauteville, 100, 182, 183; William II (Norman king of Sicily), 215, 219, 224, 225–26, 228, 231–32, 235, 239
Heliodorus, in *Vita* of Leo of Catania, 56–59
Hereford Mappa Mundi, 244–45, *244*
Hieron (king of Syracuse), 13n28
Hilālian invasion, 185n28, 186, 210
Hohenstaufens, 16, 215, 230, 242. *See also* Frederick II
Horden, Peregrine, 4n11, 11, 21, 23n56
hot springs, 19
Ḥudūd al-ʿĀlam, 130
Huneberc of Heidenheim, 64–65

Ibn Aʿtham al-Kūfi, 82n10
Ibn al-Athīr, 85n20, 86–87, 92, 94n39, 97–98, 121, 183n20
Ibn al-Birr, 148, 206
Ibn Ḥamdīs, 139–40, 205–6
Ibn Ḥawqal, 19, 111, 120–21, 123, 127, 131–39, 138n62, 142, 152, 155n126, 160n147, 230, 231, 246
Ibn al-Ḥawwās (Belcamet), 184
Ibn Ḥayyān, 168
Ibn ʿIdhārī, 83–85
Ibn Jubayr, 19, 23n56, 127, 129n39, 152, 153–54n116, 168n172, 198n59, 213, 221, 223–28, 231, 232, 233n56, 235, 237–40
Ibn Khallikān, 140, 141, 148, 205, 206n80, 218, 232n53
Ibn Qalāqis, 219, 231–32
Ibn al-Qaṭṭāʿ, 138, 140, 206
Ibn Rushd, 223n28
Ibn Rustah, 128
Ibn Siblūn, 146–47, 166–67
Ibn al-Thumna (Betumen), 152n106, 164–65, 183–84
Ibn Zurʿa, 233n56
Ibrāhīm II (Aghlabid *emīr*), 119–20
Ibrahīm b. Faraḥ, 162
iconoclasm, 49
al-Idrīsī, Abū ʿAbd Allāh Muḥammad, 19n45, 125–27, 153n113, 230–31, *232*, *237*
Ifrīqiya. *See* North Africa
indigo, 151, 153–55, 156n131, 159, 162, 192, 195
intellectual and religious connections: of Norman Sicily, 228–35, *232*, *234*; "toleration," 179, 225, 228n42; travel and communication patterns, 32
intellectual and religious connections of Sicily under dār al-Islām, 122–41; cartographical and geographical descriptions, 123–38, *126*, *129*; of Egypt and Muslim Sicily, 139, 140; negative view of Ibn Ḥawqal, 132–37; North Africa and Muslim Sicily, 139, 140, 141; scholars and poets living and working in Sicily, 135–36, 137–41; *ʿulamāʾ* (Muslim scholars), 137, 139, 141, 229
Irene (Byzantine empress), 40, 41, 42, 50
Ischia, 105
Islamicate world. *See* dār al-Islām
Ismāʿīl b. Faraḥ, 208–9
Ismāʿīl b. Faraḥ al-Qābisī, 210–11
al-Iṣṭakhrī, 130–31
Italy: Byzantine territories in, 42–43; coins from Muslim Sicily in, 163, 170–72, *171*; dār al-Islām, contact with Sicily under, 115, 121–22; Jews in, 169n177; Muslim raids and Sicilian flight to, 63–64; Norman Sicily, trade routes through, 239–40; Normans in, 176–77, 180–83, 216–17; political unity of Sicily with, 16. *See also specific Italian cities*

Jacob b. Ismaʿīl al-Andalusī, 153
Jerusalem and Sicily, *243*, *244*; Crusades and Crusaders, 214, 217, 219, 226, 234–35, 247; in hagiographies, 53, 54, 60, 63, 69; Jews in, 169, 207; Latin pilgrims to, 64–66, 180, 233; Norman Sicily's intellectual and religious connections

Ingram Content Group UK Ltd.
Milton Keynes UK
UKHW040314240323
419035UK00019B/406

9 781501 752162